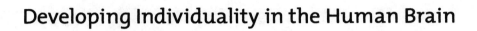

Developing Individuality in the Human Brain

Developing Individuality in the Human Brain

A TRIBUTE TO MICHAEL I. POSNER

EDITED BY

Ulrich Mayr, Edward Awh, and Steven W. Keele

DECADE
of BEHAVIOR
2000-2010

AMERICAN PSYCHOLOGICAL ASSOCIATION
WASHINGTON, DC

MT

Published by
American Psychological Association
750 First Street, NE
Washington, DC 20002
www.apa.org

To order
APA Order Department
P.O. Box 92984
Washington, DC 20090-2984

Tel: (800) 374-2721; Direct: (202) 336-5510
Fax: (202) 336-5502; TDD/TTY: (202) 336-6123
Online: www.apa.org/books/
E-mail: order@apa.org

In the U.K., Europe, Africa, and the Middle East, copies may be ordered from
American Psychological Association
3 Henrietta Street
Covent Garden, London
WC2E 8LU England

Typeset in Century Schoolbook by World Composition Services, Inc., Sterling, VA

Printer: Sheridan Books, Inc., Ann Arbor, MI
Cover Designer: Berg Design, Albany, NY
Project Manager: Debbie Hardin, Carlsbad, CA

The opinions and statements published are the responsibility of the authors, and such opinions and statements do not necessarily represent the policies of the American Psychological Association.

Library of Congress Cataloging-in-Publication Data

Developing individuality in the human brain : a tribute to Michael I. Posner / edited by Ulrich Mayr, Edward Awh, and Steven W. Keele.—1st ed.
    p. cm.—(Decade of behavior)
  Includes bibliographical references and index.
  ISBN 1-59147-210-5
  1. Cognitive neuroscience.   2. Developmental neurobiology.   3. Posner, Michael I.
I. Posner, Michael I.   II. Mayr, Ulrich.   III. Awh, Edward.   IV. Keele, Steven W.
V. Series.

  QP360.5.D485 2005
  612.8′233—dc22
                                                           2004023178

British Library Cataloguing-in-Publication Data
A CIP record is available from the British Library.

Printed in the United States of America
First Edition

4/3/06

APA Science Volumes

Attribution and Social Interaction: The Legacy of Edward E. Jones

Best Methods for the Analysis of Change: Recent Advances, Unanswered Questions, Future Directions

Cardiovascular Reactivity to Psychological Stress and Disease

The Challenge in Mathematics and Science Education: Psychology's Response

Changing Employment Relations: Behavioral and Social Perspectives

Children Exposed to Marital Violence: Theory, Research, and Applied Issues

Cognition: Conceptual and Methodological Issues

Cognitive Bases of Musical Communication

Cognitive Dissonance: Progress on a Pivotal Theory in Social Psychology

Conceptualization and Measurement of Organism–Environment Interaction

Converging Operations in the Study of Visual Selective Attention

Creative Thought: An Investigation of Conceptual Structures and Processes

Developmental Psychoacoustics

Diversity in Work Teams: Research Paradigms for a Changing Workplace

Emotion and Culture: Empirical Studies of Mutual Influence

Emotion, Disclosure, and Health

Evolving Explanations of Development: Ecological Approaches to Organism–Environment Systems

Examining Lives in Context: Perspectives on the Ecology of Human Development

Global Prospects for Education: Development, Culture, and Schooling

Hostility, Coping, and Health

Measuring Patient Changes in Mood, Anxiety, and Personality Disorders: Toward a Core Battery

Occasion Setting: Associative Learning and Cognition in Animals

Organ Donation and Transplantation: Psychological and Behavioral Factors

Origins and Development of Schizophrenia: Advances in Experimental Psychopathology

The Perception of Structure

Perspectives on Socially Shared Cognition

Psychological Testing of Hispanics

Psychology of Women's Health: Progress and Challenges in Research and Application

Researching Community Psychology: Issues of Theory and Methods

The Rising Curve: Long-Term Gains in IQ and Related Measures

Sexism and Stereotypes in Modern Society: The Gender Science of Janet Taylor Spence

APA Decade of Behavior Volumes

Contents

Contributors

Thomas H. Carr, Michigan State University, East Lansing

B. J. Casey, Weill Medical College of Cornell University, New York

Martha J. Farah, University of Pennsylvania, Philadelphia

Stanislas Dehaene, Service Hospitalier Frederic Joliot, Orsay Cedex, France

John Duncan, MRC Cognition and Brain Sciences Unit, Cambridge, England

Mark H. Johnson, Birkbeck College, London, England

Raymond M. Klein, Dalhousie University, Halifax, Nova Scotia, Canada

Steven W. Keele, University of Oregon, Eugene

Ulrich Mayr, University of Oregon, Eugene

Helen J. Neville, University of Oregon, Eugene

Kimberly G. Noble, University of Pennsylvania, Philadelphia

Michael I. Posner, University of Oregon, Eugene

Marcus E. Raichle, Washington University School of Medicine, St. Louis, Missouri

Mary K. Rothbart, University of Oregon, Eugene

M. Rosario Rueda, Universidad de Granada, Granada, Spain

Foreword

In early 1988, the American Psychological Association (APA) Science Directorate began its sponsorship of what would become an exceptionally successful
activity in support of psychological science—the APA Scientific Conferences
program. This program has showcased some of the most important topics in
psychological science and has provided a forum for collaboration among many
leading figures in the field.

The program has inspired a series of books that have presented cutting-
edge work in all areas of psychology. At the turn of the millennium, the series
was renamed the Decade of Behavior Series to help advance the goals of this
important initiative. The Decade of Behavior is a major interdisciplinary cam-
paign designed to promote the contributions of the behavioral and social sciences to our most important societal challenges in the decade leading up to
2010. Although an important goal has been to inform the public about these
scientific contributions, other activities have been designed to encourage and
further collaboration among scientists. Hence, the series that was the "APA
Science Series" has continued as the "Decade of Behavior Series." This represents one element in APA's efforts to promote the Decade of Behavior initiative
as one of its endorsing organizations. For additional information about the
Decade of Behavior, please visit http://www.decadeofbehavior.org

Over the course of the past years, the Science Conference and Decade of
Behavior Series has allowed psychological scientists to share and explore the
most recent findings in psychology. The APA Science Directorate looks forward
to continuing this successful program and to sponsoring other conferences and
books in the years ahead. This series has been so successful that we have
chosen to extend it to include books that, although they do not arise from
conferences, report with the same high quality of scholarship on the latest
research.

We are pleased that this important contribution to the literature was
supported in part by the Decade of Behavior program. Congratulations to the
editors and contributors of this volume on their sterling effort.

Steven J. Breckler, PhD   Virginia E. Holt
Executive Director for Science   *Assistant Executive Director for Science*

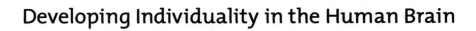

Developing Individuality in the Human Brain

1

A Tribute to Michael I. Posner

Steven W. Keele and Ulrich Mayr

In May 2003, 10 speakers and a large audience gathered at the University of Oregon in Eugene to pay tribute to the enormously influential contributions Michael Posner has made to the disciplines of psychology and cognitive neuroscience. They gathered, moreover, to express appreciation for his profound influence, both personal and professional, on their careers at times when they were students—undergraduate or graduate—postdoctoral fellows, or collaborative scientists. Attendees converged from throughout the United States and around the world.

Posner is not a person who wishes to bask in tributes. Although he might (and did) tolerate tributes during two spring days of celebration, his longstanding goals have always been about science and not about him as a person. He would wish a conference not to focus on the past but rather to push the advance of cognitive science to new depths and into new directions. With this in mind, he himself requested a hand in setting the theme of the conference, a theme reflected in these resulting proceedings and titled Developing Individuality of the Human Brain: A Tribute to Mike Posner.

The theme of these chapters grew from a line of investigation, a rather straight line in retrospect, that stretches from the mid-1960s up to the present. In chapter 12 that Posner himself has prepared for this volume, he elegantly describes this trajectory from his perspective. He began by using simple reaction-time indicators to differentiate among elementary components of reading and of attention. These simple measurement techniques not only allowed isolation of the different components but also allowed investigation of the properties of each. Later Posner proposed that elementary components might constitute an appropriate grain of analysis for mapping mental function into brain structure. He initiated a systematic examination of this idea, first toward elucidating the fundamental cognitive deficit suffered by people with injuries to various brain

We gratefully acknowledge the enthusiasm and financial resources of the University of Oregon's College of Arts and Sciences, Department of Psychology, and Center of Cognitive and Decision Sciences. We give special thanks for the financial and publishing resources of the Science Directorate of the American Psychological Association in making the conference and book possible.

regions. Subsequently he showed the community of researchers in the nascent field of cognitive neuroscience how neuroimaging techniques, starting with positron emission tomography (PET) scan but progressing to other techniques such as functional magnetic resonance imaging (fMRI), could be used to even more precisely map elementary function to specific brain area. Next he merged his interests in mind and brain with developmental psychology to understand the temporal development of component processes of attention. This line of investigation also yielded mapping of cognition to the brain by a correlation of developing mental components with developing brain substructures. The developmental thrust provided a basis for understanding how differences among humans—both normal variation and variation because of disorders—could be understood. The logical next step in this progression, linking specific components to specific genes and to specific environmental input, has already begun, and again we see Posner and some of his close colleagues (e.g., Rothbart & Rueda, chap. 9; Neville, chap. 11, both this volume) as pioneers in this emerging field.

Early Academic Career

In his junior high school years, Posner moved with his family to Seattle, where he subsequently attended the University of Washington, attaining in 1957 a bachelor of science degree—not in psychology but in physics. As a freshly minted physicist, he took a position at Boeing Aircraft as associate research engineer, while simultaneously pursuing a master's degree. Mixed in with studies and work, Posner and Sharon Blanck were married in 1958. Both received their degrees in 1959, this time Posner's was in psychology. The exposure to the Pacific Northwest environment may well explain much of the Posner's lasting love affair with Oregon.

At first, Posner tried to meld physics and psychology, studying psychophysics and auditory processing. Reflecting his enduring interest in scientific application, he suggested to Boeing how alteration of the noise frequency spectrum, as opposed to simply reducing intensity, might not only make jet engines less loud but also affect annoyance, reducing it or increasing it, depending on the nature of spectral change. His academic interests took a sharp turn, however, when he left Washington for additional graduate study in the psychology department at the University of Michigan.

Michigan—with such notable faculty as Paul Fitts, Arthur Melton, and Ward Edwards—was in the forefront of a cognitive psychology vigorously reemerging from the shadow of behaviorism. Posner took Fitts as his mentor. Fitts was a pioneer in the area of human factors, and that practical orientation likely attracted Posner. More important for the directions Posner was to take, however, Fitts was intent on developing a stronger theoretical basis for application. He used the tool of reaction time and Shannon's newly developed theory of information to explore limitations of human information processing, themes that played central roles in Posner's career (see Fitts & Posner, 1967).

In those early years at Michigan and shortly thereafter as a young professor at the University of Wisconsin, Posner applied the new, formal metric of information theory to problems such as concept learning and similarity judgment. Along a different line, he developed an "acid-bath" theory of short-term memory (Posner & Konick, 1966). The acid, rather than etching memories into the brain's slate, ate away at already etched memory, the acid concentration depending on similarity. He also explored memory for movements, stimulating a line of investigation on different codes of movement.

After three daunting winters in Wisconsin, the jewels of sea, mountain, forest, and, of course, an outstanding psychology department, attracted Posner and his wife in 1965 to the University of Oregon. The psychology department had a long and storied history. It is the oldest psychology department in the United States west of the Mississippi River. The department's founding in 1895 predated by a year even the famed Würzburg school so prominent in the history of cognitive psychology. The department's founder, Benjamin Hawthorne, declared at initiation that the proper focus of psychological study was the mind, and indeed it initially was called the department of mental science. At Oregon, Posner joined Ray Hyman and Fred Attneave, two others who were playing prominent, pioneering roles in the application of information theory to cognition. The three received a large program grant from the Advanced Research Projects Agency of the Department of Defense, and with it they bought a "battleship"—a huge PDP-9 computer, which filled a room even though it was miniscule in capacity by modern standards. With the aid of Gil Osgood and some enterprising graduate students, Oregon soon had the most outstanding computer-based psychology lab in the country. From that moment Oregon, and Posner, became a Mecca for cognitive psychologists from around the country and from around the world.

One of us joined Posner the next year as a postdoctoral fellow, the first in a long string of fellows. One of our papers (Posner & Keele, 1968) gained some attention. Following Posner's earlier dissertation work, dot patterns were constructed to serve as examples of different concepts—dogs versus cats so to speak (Posner, 1963). Research participants learned to sort patterns into two categories and then were tested for discrimination accuracy. Surprisingly, the prototypes from which concept examples were constructed were categorized as well as or better than the experienced examples themselves—this despite the fact that the prototypes were not previously experienced. Posner thought the dominance of concept prototype settled an argument between the British philosophers Bishop Berkeley and John Locke about the nature of concepts. He chose the title of the paper: "On the Genesis of Abstract Ideas."

Posner's early research included work on human factors, thinking, memory, motor control, and concept representation. He continued over succeeding years to investigate a wide array of problems. At this point, however, after two years at Oregon, he set down the cornerstones for his most enduring contributions to cognitive psychology and its ultimate merger with neuroscience. He began to work out elementary components of reading and to differentiate processes of attention.

Elementary Components

In 1967, 2 years after arriving at Oregon, Posner and several graduate students began publishing studies on letter matching (e.g., Posner, Boies, Eichelman, & Taylor, 1969; Posner & Mitchell, 1967). Deciding that two letters of different shape had the same name (e.g., upper case "A" and lower case "a") took longer than when they had the same visual shape as well as name (e.g., as two lower case "a"s). Letter matching itself has little intrinsic importance. Nonetheless, the technique provided a simple tool for gaining insight into the central properties of the human cognitive system. One and the same external stimulus—letters in this case—gave rise to distinctly different internal representations or codes—visual codes, phonetic codes, and semantic codes. The codes arose in parallel, contrary to a view dominant at that time of human as serial computer. Other investigators, such as Oregon's Gerry Reicher, discoverer of the famous "word superiority effect," (Reicher, 1969) and even Posner, together with postdoctoral fellow Tom Carr (see chap. 2), visiting professor Sandy Pollatsek, and graduate student Charles Snyder, made similar points regarding the multiple codes of words (Carr, Posner, Pollatsek, & Snyder, 1979)

In addition to implications for reading per se, the letter-matching studies that began in the late 1960s provided an exceptional meta-theoretical point. They illustrated the power of extremely simple reaction time procedures, dubbed chronometric techniques by Posner, for untangling fundamental components of important, complex tasks, not only of reading but also in domains such as motor control. The studies marked the beginning of a central theme in Posner's work: elementary codes and processes.

Tom Carr (chap. 2, this volume) begins by describing this idea inherited from Posner during Tom's postdoctoral years in the late 1970s—that skills are assembled from elementary processes. Using reading as a case example, Carr details the graphemic/orthographic codes that are abstracted from printed word input and translated into phonetic codes. He describes how differences among individual people in their code efficiencies can be deduced using simple measures such as reaction time. He reviews evidence that phonetic mastery correlates with reading success and indeed that phonetic-based schooling programs produce better readers than programs with little phonetic emphasis.

Another outstanding example of the power of componential analysis is provided by Stanislas Dehaene (chap. 4, this volume). Previously Dehaene conducted magnificent studies using reaction time methods to decompose and examine different codes of numeric representation. In this chapter, however, he uses the chronometric method to analyze the activation of semantic codes of words (and numbers), such activation sometimes rising to consciousness and sometimes not. Together Carr and Dehaene provide powerful illustrations of Posner's idea that decomposition of skill into elementary components yields insight and powerful application to important human endeavors.

The letter-matching studies also revealed another aspect of the human information-processing system (Posner & Boies, 1972). A single stimulus, a letter, not only activated internal codes of various types. It also served as a general alerting signal—telling the brain when it is time to pay attention.

Alerting was shown to operate independently of attention drawn to the information content of the stimulus.

This point regarding separable and independent components of attention became the center of focus in subsequent research. Posner worked with a string of illustrious students and postdoctoral fellows, including Ray Klein, Brian Davidson, Charles Snyder, Mary Jo Nissen, Yoav Cohen, Roger Remington, John McLean, Gordon Shulman, Peter McLeod, John Duncan, and others. One paradigm rose to the top. Research participants were cued in which of two boxes on a screen a signal might occur, the task being to press a key whenever a spot appeared in a box, regardless of which box. This exceedingly simple task was to yield clues about the nature not only of alertness but also of selective attention (e.g., Posner, Davidson, & Snyder, 1980).

A cue at a place where a signal might occur very often pulls eye movement to it. Indeed, later in this chapter we will describe how Posner and Rothbart made use of this pulling tendency to study attention in infants who were so young that verbal instruction could not be given. In the case of infants, eye movement gives an indication of where attention is located. Posner and colleagues were able to show at this earlier research period, however, that even when adult participants inhibit eye movement, an internal process of attention shifts to the place where the signal is expected to occur. The attention shift was indexed by temporary improvements in reaction time whenever the signal occurred at the cued location.

One finding about attention to a location is that it could be dissociated into two forms. The occurrence of a cue automatically and rapidly summons attention to its location regardless of eye movement and regardless of intent. In addition, a symbolic cue such as an arrow at fixation could direct attention to a place different from the cue location, again without eye movement. This less automatic form of endogenous orienting is slightly delayed over the automatic exogenous form. Later work by Posner and colleagues, especially the prominent neurologist Robert Rafal, were to place these two forms of orienting in different brain systems. This dissociation also led to a second discovery. If participants were instructed not only to maintain fixation at a central point but also to keep attention there, a noninformative signal occurring elsewhere unavoidably summoned attention to itself, although attention quickly returned to fixation. If an obligatory signal requiring response subsequently occurred at the previously summoned place, response to it was delayed compared to a case in which attention was not previously summoned. It appeared that attention to a previously attended location was "inhibited" (Posner & Cohen, 1984).

Inhibition of return is thought to be a marker of an important control process in attention. The real world is exceedingly complex. Extracting information relevant to a current endeavor requires not only scanning with eye movement but also scanning with attention throughout the visual field. Whatever is in the field pulls attention hither and thither. Inhibition is thought to prevent repeated rescanning of an area already deemed irrelevant. Indeed during a postdoctoral mid-1990s stint with Posner, one of us (Mayr) was inspired to explore a similar mechanism that inhibits previous task sets thereby relinquishing their control over action once they no longer are relevant (Mayr & Keele, 2000).

Despite its apparent simplicity, the search for a full understanding of how exactly inhibition of return operates has been a surprisingly difficult endeavor. Ray Klein has been intricately involved in this attempt, ever since his graduate-student years with Posner in the mid-1970s. He gives a comprehensive account (chap. 4) of a line of research that serves as a model case of how the componential method can be used to characterize attention to locations. He shows us how inhibition-of-return arises from the interaction between endogenous and reflexive systems and how with this framework in mind, we can begin to reexamine individual and developmental differences in basic attentional functioning.

Much of Posner's midperiod work, ranging from the mid-1960s up to the late 1970s, is covered in his influential book, *Chronometric Explorations of Mind* (Posner, 1978). The book laid down a conceptual framework for his work on mapping cognition to brain that was to follow.

Mapping Cognition to Brain

In the early 1980s, Posner put forth a new idea, one that proved to be enormously influential in the merger of cognitive analysis with neuroscience. Elementary components, he suggested, might be the correct grain for mapping mental function to the brain. At first, one might not appreciate the boldness of this proposition. The phrenologists more than a century ago divided the brain into regions responsible for arithmetic, language, motor control, emotions, personality and social traits, and so on. We now find their divisions humorous. But have more "modern" views progressed greatly beyond the phrenologists' view? Many still argue that Broca's and Wernicke's brain areas are for language, cerebellum, and basal ganglia are for motor control, and the like—large brain areas for specific, complex-task domains. Posner raised the possibility that brain regions instead were specialized for elementary processes. Although in some cases, particular, localized processes might be devoted primarily to particular task domains, Posner's analysis opened a search for localized elementary processes accessible by a variety of different kinds of tasks.

The arrival of world-renowned Oscar Marin as chief neurologist at Good Samaritan Hospital in nearby Portland, Oregon, provided the opportunity to test Posner's notion of localization. From the University of Oregon, Posner soon was commuting more than 100 miles to Portland, where he and Marin formed a research and training program. The program attracted talented young neurologists and cognitive psychologists—Fran Friedrich, Avishi Henik, John Walker, Rich Ivry, Alan Wing, David Margolin, Bob Rafal, and others, each of whom have since left their deep marks on what was then an embryonic cognitive neuroscience.

Posner and his colleagues used the same reaction-time techniques they had used for isolating components of attention—techniques such as brightening a box or cueing with an arrow to pull or to drive attention. By examining how damage in one part of the brain affected reaction time, they were able to localize different components of attention to different brain regions (e.g., Posner, Cohen,

& Rafal, 1982; Posner, Walker, Friedrich, & Rafal, 1984). Not only were exogenous and endogenous forms of orienting of attention found to emanate from different regions of the brain, even more elementary components such as disengaging from previous focus, moving to and reengaging a new focus were associated with different brain regions and assembled into a network.

Posner's point about using neurological patients to localize fundamental cognitive components to specific brain regions was firmly established, and he moved to a new approach. He left behind a powerful idea and a cadre of colleagues who continue to this day to make important discoveries about the elementary cognitive functions of cortical and subcortical brain regions.

In 1985, Posner, bringing Gordon Shulman with him, joined Marc Raichle at Washington University in St. Louis. Their goal was to use PET scan neuroimaging to map elementary process to brain. In 1987 to 1989, Posner, Raichle, and Shulman—with Petersen, Fox, Mintun, Sandson, and Dhawan—published a series of landmark studies in *Nature, Science,* and the *Journal of Cognitive Neuroscience* (Petersen, Fox, Posner, Mintun, & Raichle, 1987, 1989; Posner, Petersen, Fox, & Raichle, 1988). Much of Posner's direct contributions and influence regarding the use of neuroimaging in mapping cognitive component to brain is presented in Posner and Raichle's book *Images of Mind* (Posner & Raichle, 1994).

These landmarks were based on much the same logic as Posner's seminal studies of letter matching. Whereas Posner's earlier studies examined change in reaction time as a result of change in elementary process, these neuroimaging studies looked at change in blood flow. While the brain was being scanned for amount of blood flow in different brain regions, participants (a) viewed fixation points, (b) viewed words, (c) named words, or (d) made a semantic translation (e.g., shovel to dig), naming the translated word. Each change in elementary operation altered blood flow in different brain regions, thereby allowing identification of mental component with the brain region. In later studies, the team further clarified the nature of internal codes supported by each targeted brain region. Although simply viewing words activated one region in the posterior cortex, it was not clear whether this region provided a visual word code or whether it merely responded to strings of complex shapes. Additional analysis found that nonwords—that is, letter strings without semantic content whose constituent letters nonetheless fit the spelling rules of English—activated the same posterior region of visual cortex as did real words. Letter-string nonwords without orthographic regularity failed, however, to produce activation, supporting the contention that this decidedly visual area of the human brain had learned the visual properties of English words. In essence, the function of an area of the human visual cortex was altered in response to instruction in reading. Among other things, this seminal study provided groundwork for exploring plasticity of function in the human brain.

These studies of the St. Louis group set a gold standard for research on cognitive to brain mapping, showing as they did how one elementary code or process could be isolated from others and providing the correct grain for understanding brain function. Nowadays extensions of the method frequent all aspects of cognitive neuroscience.

The enormous influence of neuroimaging technology for mapping cognitive function to brain structure is represented in this volume in already mentioned chapters by Carr (chap. 2) and Dehaene (chap. 4). Carr's chapter, describing elementary reading codes and instructional strategies for teaching reading, closes by laying out neuroimaging evidence for two distinct routes from visual graphemic representation to pronunciation. Dehaene, in his chapter, presents among other things a series of neuroimaging experiments that uncover the emergence of word-level understanding in terms of an increasingly abstract cascade of functions along a posterior–frontal axis within the word-form area originally discovered by Posner. Dehaene also shows how researchers can use clever combinations of behavioral, imaging, and computational work to make progress in one of the toughest problems in the neurosciences—namely how, when, and why information processed in the brain enters consciousness.

An important theoretical advance in 1990 by Posner and Steve Petersen was triggered through the integration of results from patient studies on spatial orienting with results from brain imaging studies. The theory proposed distinct attentional networks with each having distinct functional and neuroanatomical properties. A posterior network within the parietal cortex was associated with change of attention from one place to another—disengagement from a former location, movement, and reengagement at another location. An anterior network, specifically associated with the anterior cingulate and related prefrontal cortical areas, becomes active whenever conflict between goal-directed actions and interfering response tendencies need to be resolved. Important elaboration and advance of these early propositions can be found in the chapters of B. J. Casey (chap. 8, this volume) and John Duncan (chap. 5, this volume). Casey presents a detailed analysis about how frontal cortical regions and subcortical regions (basal ganglia) cooperate in regulating different kinds of conflicts, and how different developmental disorders can be characterized in terms of alteration in each of these subfunctions. Duncan provides a somewhat more general claim about prefrontal cortex as the site that represents the currently relevant task model. He proposes that the degree to which this task model contains only relevant aspects while suppressing irrelevant aspects may be at the core of what in psychometric research is associated with general intelligence (g). In this regard, he travels a long way on Posner's journey from characterizing a simple processing component to understanding a fundamentally important, real-world phenomenon.

Mapping cognitive components to brain regions by no means indicates how a brain region accomplishes its computation. Nonetheless, establishing a function of a brain region is a necessary precursor to understanding the mechanism of function. Posner's early behavioral paradigms for decomposing processes of attention have been influential not only in mapping but also in understanding their neurochemical underpinnings. Single-neuron recording using behavioral tasks similar to those Posner had developed for humans already had indicated regions of the monkey brain involved in spatial cueing. Oregon colleagues of Posner, Rich Marrocco, and associated graduate students, were able to register neurochemical responses in local regions around small complexes of neurons receptive to attentional cueing. In addition, they were able to manipulate the time course of the deployment and shifting of attention in response to manipulation of neurotransmitter agonists and antagonists (e.g., Davidson, Cutrell, & Marrocco, 1999; Davidson & Marrocco, 2000). Such studies provide a critical step in understanding physiological mechanisms whereby localized brain regions instantiate their elementary computations.

As mentioned earlier, the neuroimaging revolution in cognitive neuroscience began to a large degree in the influential program initiated by Posner and Raichle. The idea was to relate changes in cognitive activity to changes in regional blood flow. Raichle's chapter 6 in this volume points out a puzzle, however, and in so doing it establishes a new agenda in the search for basic mechanisms that relate brain to function. Most elementary functions, such as activation of word codes or switching the focus of attention from one location to another, take at most a few hundred milliseconds. The spiking of principle neurons that accompany such a function is not only short in duration but also narrowly localized. The overall energy cost of such operation is small compared to the energy reflected in blood flow changes, such changes lasting longer and involving broader areas. This discrepancy in energy costs presents a serious disconnection between concepts. Do blood flow changes reflect specific internal processes such as code activation or attention switching, or do they in some manner reflect a larger, more energy intensive context in which the processes are embedded? Raichle's chapter alerts us to an exciting new challenge regarding our understanding of the link between brain function and cognitive function.

The successes of Posner and his many colleagues, as well as those of numerous others who have now applied his ideas in other task domains, provides a strong case: The elucidation of elementary functions that make up tasks appears not only to provide an appropriate grain for understanding the functional architecture of the human brain but it also provides a beginning foundation to understanding the mechanisms themselves.

Development and Individual Differences

Although few would doubt that genetics, development, and experience contribute to human variation in intelligence and temperament, progress in forging strong links has been limited by their complexity. The analysis of association between brain regions and the elementary functions they support might offer an entry point, providing also an appropriate grain of analysis for understanding the developmental time course of cognitive function, its variation across individuals, and genetic versus experiential contributions. In more recent years, Posner has focused on these themes.

Studies along this line had their origin at the University of Oregon in a series of collaborative studies beginning in 1990 by Posner, long-time faculty colleague Mary Rothbart, then-postdoctoral fellow Mark Johnson, and notable students including Anne Boylan Clohessy, Shaun Vecera, Johannes Rothlind, Cathy Harman, and Lisa Thomas-Thrapp. Some of their initial efforts were reported in a special issue of the *Journal of Cognitive Neuroscience* in fall 1991. About this time, Posner also established the first of a series of collaborations with Jim Swanson, ultimately leading to a revised understanding of attention deficit disorders of children (Swanson et al., 1991).

By examining eye movements as modulated by stimuli and training, Posner and his colleagues were able to map out development of attention and control in infants (e.g., Johnson, Posner, & Rothbart, 1991). An infant of only a few months of age naturally fixated on an interesting, moving shape. Following fixation, two shapes were added, one on each side of the fixated shape. Infants of 2 and 3 months of age had great difficulty in disengaging from initial fixation as long as the initial object remained in view. By 4 months of age, however, the young child could disengage from a persisting object to look at another, suggesting that a critical component of attention had matured. This point in time was consistent with maturational changes in parts of the brain thought from neurological studies to serve disengagement. Moreover, infants for whom the disengagement was first achieved preceded other infants in achieving temperamental aspects of self-control, such as the ability to be soothed by a distracting stimulus.

At about the same 4-month time point, other aspects of attention came into play. If shape of the central stimulus predicted where the next stimulus would occur, infants began to make anticipatory eye movement toward the forthcoming stimulus. Although each of these three indicators of attention—disengagement, anticipation, and correct choice—developed on average at about the same time, their onsets were not correlated, different infants achieving them in different order. It appeared that, as in adults where components such as disengaging, moving, and selecting depend on different brain regions, the infant regions mature independently as well. These features of attention that depended on external cues developed much earlier than ability to spontaneously alternate attention between places in space, a type of internal control. The latter did not develop until sometime between 6 and 18 months of age (Vecera, Rothbart, & Posner, 1991). These differences were thought to depend on differential maturation periods of posterior and anterior cortical components of Posner and Petersen's (1990) attentional network.

This type of work raises fundamental questions about what makes brain systems develop. Johnson (chap. 7, this volume) describes a framework (interactive specialization approach) of how to think about these issues, and he applies it to the case of the emergence of a network of cortical regions that he refers to as the social brain. For example, by providing a detailed analysis of what serves as face cues during different developmental periods, he can show how rather general brain networks through experience can become selectively tuned to prefer certain types of information. In general, by this view, neurocognitive development should be seen not so much as the maturation of specific brain areas but as the experience-driven emergence of functionally adequate interactions between several brain areas.

Following these initial investigations of development and individual difference, Posner was asked to found a new center at Cornell Medical School, the Sackler Institute for Developmental Psychobiology. The institute's intent is reflected closely in the theme of this volume. The center is to study the emergence of fundamental components of cognition in the context of brain development and educational environment. One theme, pursued by Bruce McCandliss—a former graduate student of Posner's—and other colleagues, examines the development of processes of reading, the role of educational variation on normal and impaired reading, and the influence of reading instruction on brain function. This important societal theme clearly extends the earlier research themes pioneered by Posner and thoroughly reported in this volume by Carr (chap. 2).

Another theme of the Sackler Institute derives from Posner's analysis of anterior and posterior attention networks and associated methods for disentangling elementary components. This theme has moved in two remarkable, interrelated directions. Posner, Swanson, Casey, and others at the Sackler Institute have made a case that childhood disorders—attention deficit disorder, Tourette's syndrome, childhood schizophrenia, obsessive–compulsive disorder—can be related to deficiencies in conflict resolution (or executive control) components of the anterior attention network. Recent evidence suggests that some of these disorders depend on alteration in one or a few specific genes. The linkage of disorder to elementary component in turn allows linkage of genetic variation to variation in attentional components (see, e.g., Fan, McCandliss, Sommer, Raz, & Posner, 2002; Fan, Wu, Fossella, & Posner, 2001; Fossella et al., 2002). Thus, the idea of elementary components as conceptualized by Posner some decades ago is providing fundamental insight in yet another domain. Details about these ideas are provided both in Posner's chapter 12 (this volume) and in chapter 8 by B. J. Casey, who is Posner's successor as director of the Sackler Institute.

Three additional chapters in this volume by Rothbart and Rueda, Farah, and Neville relate to the developmental themes that form part of Posner's most current interests, including an emphasis on training in the light of understanding elementary components. Rothbart and Rueda (chap. 9) examine individual differences in effortful control in children, showing how it can be measured with laboratory conflict tasks and related to the frontal cortical components of the Posner-Peterson anterior network of attention that support executive function. They present preliminary results indicating that deficiencies in effortful control may be remediable by concentrated cognitive training targeted specifically at executive function.

Prospects for training-based improvement in executive function could have considerable importance for some segments of society. Martha Farah, in chapter 10, shows that children of low socioeconomic status perform more poorly than children of higher status on executive function measures (e.g., performance on a go–no-go conflict task) also known to depend on the anterior attentional system. The low socioeconomic status children also exhibit impairment on language–verbal measures but not at all or to a lesser degree on memory, spatial, and perceptual measures. Given the differential pattern of Farah's results, given the Rothbart-Rueda preliminary evidence for training effects on executive function, and given the likelihood that differences in language and verbal abilities are highly dependent on experiential differences, one might hope that early educational intervention tailored from knowledge of cognitive process might successfully intervene with low socioeconomic status children.

These hopes that education based on knowledge of cognitive components would pay off in improved intellectual performance rests on a premise that representational function of rather broad regions of cortex are modifiable by experience. In this regard, chapter 11 by Helen Neville, a leading investigator of brain plasticity, provides some critical hints. Her main theme is that different functional brain systems display markedly different degrees of plasticity. For example, deafness and blindness per se have highly specific effects on some but not other subsystems within the remaining modalities. Knowing the neural systems and related plasticity profiles relevant for specific cognitive subsystems puts us in a good position to target interventions for particular functions and particular time periods. Neville describes intervention programs that are underway to facilitate language development in both typically developing and language-impaired individuals. In the long run, linking the interaction between environmental input and genetic predisposition will contribute to one of Posner's current foci: working to optimize human development.

Conclusion

When we examine Posner's work over a period now exceeding 30 years, it provides inspiration for students and young researchers. For the layperson, it provides an avenue of understanding into the workings of the human mind. The simple procedures, such as reaction time tasks, that researchers use to decompose the mind into its constituents often seem exceedingly abstract and far removed from the real world. To find that small regions of the brain are dedicated to particular elementary functions; to find that variation in such function underlies disorders of executive function; to find genes that influence the function—finding these kinds of things provides a powerful validation of basic psychological research. Posner's examination of elementary processes has truly moved researchers toward a fundamental level of understanding human cognition. All indications are that such basic understanding will have enormous influence in dealing with problems of cognitive development that derive either from deficiency of experience or from genetic differences.

This introduction makes abundantly clear the unbounded respect the contributors of this book have for Posner's contributions to cognitive psychology and its merger with neuroscience. We hope it also is abundantly clear the great affection we hold for Posner for his impact on our individual careers and our personal lives. The respect and honor are not, however, from this group alone. Dozens and dozens of people, of whom we have mentioned only a sample in this introduction, have felt Posner's touch. An extraordinarily large number of honors have been bestowed on him, from the beginnings of his career through to the present. These honors emanated from local (University of Oregon), to regional, to national, and to international organizations. We list a smattering of honors that correspond with the evolution of Posner's research themes in Exhibit 1.1.

Exhibit 1.1. Honors

American Institute for Research, Dissertation award in the area of learning, perception and motivation, 1962

Editor, *Journal of Experimental Psychology: Human Perception and Performance*, 1974–1979

Ersted Award for Distinguished Teaching, University of Oregon, 1975

APA Distinguished Scientific Contribution Award, 1980

Elected to U.S. National Academy of Sciences, 1981

Fellow, American Academy of Arts and Sciences, 1986

Howard Crosby Warren Medal of the Society of Experimental Psychologists, 1988

Distinguished Scientific Lecture, American Psychological Association, 1992

Invited Presidential Address, Society for Neuroscience, Washington, DC, 1993

Scientist of the Year Award, Oregon Academy of Sciences, 1995

Dana Foundation Award for Pioneering Research in Medicine (Neuroscience), 1996

John T. McGovern Medal and Lecture, American Association for the Advancement of Science, 1998

Honorary Doctoral Degree, University of Padova, Italy, 1998

Karl Lashley Award, American Philosophical Society (joint with M. E. Raichle), 1998

Honorary Doctoral Degree, University of Granada, Spain, 1999

Pasarow Foundation Award in Medical Research (Neuropsychiatry; joint with M. E. Raichle), June 2000

Grawemeyer Award for Psychology Contribution (joint with M. E. Raichle and S. E. Petersen)

Honorary Degree, University of Nottingham, 2002

Honorary Degree, University of Paris, 2002

International Science Prize, Fyssen Foundation (France), 2003

References

Carr, T. H., Posner, M. I., Pollatsek, A., & Snyder, C. R. R. (1979). Orthography and familiarity effects in words processing. *Journal of Experimental Psychology: General, 108,* 389–414.

Davidson, M. C., Cutrell, E. B., & Marrocco, R. T. (1999). Scopolamine slows the covert orienting of attention in primates to cued visual stimuli. *Psychopharmacology, 142,* 1–8.

Davidson, M. C., & Marrocco, R. T. (2000). Local infusion of scopolamine into lateral intraparietal cortex alters covert orienting in rhesus monkeys. *Journal of Neurophysiology, 83,* 1536–1549.

Fan, J., McCandliss, B. D., Sommer, T., Raz, M., & Posner, M. I. (2002). Testing the efficiency and independence of attentional networks. *Journal of Cognitive Neuroscience, 3,* 340–347.

Fan, J., Wu, Y., Fossella, J., & Posner, M. I. (2001). Assessing the heritability of attentional networks. *BioMed Central Neuroscience, 2,* 14.

Fitts, P. M., & Posner, M. I. (1967). *Human performance.* Belmont, CA: Brooks/Cole.

Fossella, J., Sommer, T., Fan, J., Wu, Y., Swanson, J. M., Pfaff, D. W., et al. (2002). Assessing the molecular genetics of attention networks. *BioMed Central Neuroscience, 3,* 14.

Johnson, M. H., Posner, M. I., & Rothbart, M. K. (1991). Components of visual orienting in early infancy: Contingency learning, anticipatory looking and disengaging. *Journal of Cognitive Neuroscience, 3,* 335–344.

Mayr, U., & Keele, S. (2000). Changing internal constraints on action: The role of backward inhibition. *Journal of Experimental Psychology: General, 129,* 4–26.

Petersen, S. E., Fox, P. T., Posner, M. I., Mintun, M., & Raichle, M. E. (1987). Positron emission tomographic studies of the cortical anatomy of single word processing. *Nature, 331,* 585–589.

Petersen, S. E., Fox, P. T., Posner, M. I., Mintun, M., & Raichle, M. E. (1989). Positron emission tomographic studies of the processing of single words. *Journal of Cognitive Neuroscience, 1,* 153–170.

Posner, M. I. (1963). An information approach to thinking. *Air Force Office of Scientific Research Report 2635* (ASTIA Document 276136). Washington, DC: U.S. Air Force Office of Scientific Research.

Posner, M. I. (1978). *Chronometric explorations of mind.* Hillsdale, NJ: Erlbaum.

Posner, M. I., & Boies, S. J. (1972). Components of attention. *Psychological Review, 78,* 391–408.

Posner, M. I., Boies, S. J., Eichelman, W., & Taylor, R. (1969). Retention of visual and name codes of single letters. *Journal of Experimental Psychology Monography, 79,* 1–16.

Posner, M. I., & Cohen, Y. (1984). Components of attention. In H. Bouma & D. Bowhuis (Eds.), *Attention and performance X* (pp. 531–556). Hillsdale, NJ: Erlbaum.

Posner, M. I., Cohen, Y., & Rafal, R. D. (1982). Neural systems control of spatial orienting. *Proceedings of the Royal Society of London, 298,* 187–198.

Posner, M. I., Davidson, B. J., & Snyder, C. R. R. (1980). Attention and the detection of signals. *Journal of Experimental Psychology: General, 109,* 160–174.

Posner, M. I., & Keele, S. W. (1968). On the genesis of abstract ideas. *Journal of Experimental Psychology, 77,* 353–363.

Posner, M. I., & Konick, A. F. (1966). On the role of interference in short-term retention. *Journal of Experimental Psychology, 72,* 221–231.

Posner, M. I., & Mitchell, R. F. (1967). Chronometric analysis of classification. *Psychological Review, 74,* 392–409.

Posner, M. I., & Petersen, S. E. (1990). The attention system of the human brain. *Annual Review of Neuroscience, 13,* 25–42.

Posner, M. I., Petersen, S. E., Fox, P. T., & Raichle, M. E. (1988). Localization of cognitive functions in the human brain. *Science, 240,* 1627–1631.

Posner, M. I., & Raichle, M. E. (1994). *Images of mind.* New York: Scientific American Library.

Posner, M. I., Walker, J. A., Friedrich, F. J., & Rafal, R. D. (1984). Effects of parietal lobe injury on covert orienting of visual attention. *Journal of Neuroscience, 4,* 1863–1874.

Reicher, G. M. (1969). Perceptual recognition as a function of meaningfulness of stimulus material. *Journal of Experimental Psychology, 81,* 275–280.

Swanson, J. M., Posner, M. I., Potkin, S., Bonforte, S., Youpa, D., Cantwell, D., et al. (1991). Activating tasks for the study of visual–spatial attention in ADHD children: A cognitive anatomical approach. *Journal of Child Neurology, 6,* S119–S127.

Vecera, S. P., Rothbart, M. K., & Posner, M. I. (1991). Development of spontaneous alternation in infancy. *Journal of Cognitive Neuroscience, 3,* 351–354.

2

On the Functional Architecture of Language and Reading: Trade-Offs Between Biological Preparation and Cultural Engineering

Thomas H. Carr

The enduring legacy of Michael Posner's research derives from a set of ideas that have come to occupy center stage in understanding the human mind, its intellectual capacities, and how those capacities are supported by the brain. Posner was instrumental in developing these ideas into their modern form, and he has applied them with a power and energy matched by few other investigators of human cognition. I begin by describing these ideas. Then I review and try to integrate a wide range of studies of language and reading using these ideas as a guiding framework.

Mental Operations

The first idea is that perceiving, thinking, and acting can be understood as organized sequences of mental operations (Carr, 1984, 1986; Carr & Pollatsek, 1985; Carr, Pollatsek, & Posner, 1981; Posner, 1973, 1985). A mental operation takes input of a particular type and transforms it into output of a particular type, communicating the output to other mental operations that can use it as input.

Inputs and outputs are internal representations of information—sensory information from the outside world, retrieved memories of past experience, thoughts, and commands that move the muscles to produce actions. Each mental operation relies on a specialized knowledge base that defines and enables it to implement the mapping between inputs and outputs that is the operation's speciality. Different mental operations perform different information-processing jobs. To perform a task, one must pick and choose from the available repertoire of mental operations, treating them as building blocks from which to compose an organized sequence of operations that, if executed correctly, will get the task done. If a task requires a transformation of input to output that is not part of the currently available repertoire, then a new mental operation must be learned. As I show later, adding new mental operations to the capabilities of the visual and language systems is absolutely crucial to learning to read.

Formal models have simulated mental operations in a variety of ways. Some modelers have instantiated mental operations as algebraic interactions between feature vectors (Hintzman, 1988; Metcalfe, 1991, 1997), some as production systems (Anderson, 1983; Newell, 1990), and some as connectionist networks of varying grain size, ranging from localist networks in which each output node corresponds in one-to-one fashion with one of the representations that the operation is capable of activating (Besner, 1999; Collins & Loftus, 1975; Morton, 1969) to fully distributed parallel processing in which outputs are patterns of activation across large numbers of small feature-like components (Masson, 1999; O'Reilly & Munakata, 2000; Plaut, 1999). A few models—including some that are successful in modeling language and reading—are hybrid systems with multiple grain sizes or multiple types of representation and computation (Coltheart, Rastle, Perry, Landon, & Ziegler, 2001; Dell, Burger, & Svec, 1997; Dell & O'Seaghdha, 1994; Zorzi, Houghton, & Butterworth, 1998).

These variations in modeling format elicit intense debate among their devotees (for an interesting analysis of the relative success of these various formats, see Simon & Kaplan, 1989; for one kind of discussion of the partisan debate, see Carr, 1999). The goal at present, however, is not to decide among concrete formalisms, but to focus on what is common across them. In all cases, inputs that have already been activated are systematically transformed into outputs that constitute newly activated information in the mind. This alchemist's trick of creating new information from old is the key to achieving goal-directed task performance. To reiterate, people perform tasks by piecing together and implementing a sequence of mental operations that takes them from the initial stimulus situation or starting information to the end state that is the goal of the task. This end state may be a retrieved memory, a thought, or an action. The first idea, then, is that tasks are performed via an organized sequence of mental operations.

Attention

The second idea is that there are control processes to oversee the assembly and execution of an organized sequence of mental operations, thereby adding the notion of attention to the analysis and understanding of cognitive processes (Posner, 1973, 1985; Posner & Petersen, 1990; Posner & Raichle, 1994). Sequences of mental operations are governed by attentional processes that moderate overall arousal, selection, and maintenance of goals to be pursued; selection of perceptual inputs for detailed processing; short-term maintenance of activated representations that are needed as intermediate products; computation of decisions; and selection and execution of actions. These attentional processes moderate the flow of information among the information-transforming mental operations needed for a goal-directed task, and they work to coordinate the pursuit of multiple goals (and hence multiple streams of information-transforming operations) that might compete with one another in complex task environments.

Empirically, these various functions of attention have been pursued somewhat independently (e.g., see Yantis, 2000, for a review of selection of inputs for further processing, and Pashler, 2000, for a review of coordination of multiple tasks). Theoretically, however, they have been treated as interrelated and interacting components of an attention system (Baddeley, 2001; Carr, 1979, 1992; Carr & Bacharach, 1976; Meyer & Kieras, 1997; Pashler, 1997; Posner & Petersen, 1990; Posner & Raichle, 1994; Shallice, 1988). Thus the mechanisms of attention stand separate from the sequence of mental operations that they control. Interactions between the mechanisms of attention and the assembled sequence of component mental operations produce execution of task performance in real time.

Practice Makes Perfect: Expertise, Automaticity, and the Acquisition of Skill

The two ideas described so far are that cognition is achieved by organized sequences of mental operations assembled and governed by mechanisms of attention. A third idea stimulated by Posner is that the level of involvement of the various mechanisms of attention in task performance is not a constant. The need for attentional governance varies with instruction, practice, and the resulting level of task-relevant knowledge, expertise, and automaticity. The more one knows about a task, the more likely the task is to be performed correctly via an effective and efficient sequence of mental operations. The more a sequence of mental operations has been performed, (a) the more likely it is to be stored in memory as a directly activatable program or procedure (Anderson, 1993; Fitts & Posner, 1967; Keele & Summers, 1976; Posner & Snyder, 1975); (b) the larger is the collection of episodic memories or instances of its past performance that can be retrieved to help guide its current performance (Logan, 1988); and (c) the more likely are some or all of the required representations and component mental operations to be primed (that is, already partially activated) by recent experience (Bock, 1995; Carr, McCauley, Sperber, & Parmelee, 1982; Dagenbach, Carr, & Wilhelmsen, 1989; Neely, 1991; Posner & Snyder, 1975; Sudevan & Taylor, 1987). Knowledge and practice turn a novice's initial rough attempts at a task into the fluently executable skill of the expert.

How does this happen? Fluent execution is supported by a shift away from close attentional control. Via the three processes named above—proceduralization, amassing of episodic instances, and priming—practice makes performance of a task more automatic and reduces its burden on the mechanisms of attention. Sequences of mental operations actively constructed for the first time and held together to support a novel task draw the most heavily on the mechanisms of attention and are the most difficult to perform accurately and fluently. The difficulty posed by a novel task is especially great when instruction is minimal (so that the performer is not sure what mental operations to try), and when attention is distracted by irrelevant stimuli or spread thin by multiple task demands (so that the performer's ability to oversee the novel sequence of operations is at risk).

Thus instruction and practice are important factors in the relation between attention and mental operations and in the level of expertise a person exhibits at a particular task. Instruction facilitates learning an effective and efficient sequence of mental operations for the task's performance (Carr, 1984; Crossman, 1959; Fitts & Posner, 1967; Proctor & Dutta, 1995). Practice gradually frees performance of that sequence from the need for constant step-by-step monitoring by the attention system (Beilock, Carr, MacMahon, & Starkes, 2002; Beilock, Weirenga, & Carr, 2002; Brown & Carr, 1989; Carr, 1992; Fitts & Posner, 1967; Logan, 1988; Schneider & Shiffrin, 1977; Sieroff & Posner, 1988). Together, instruction and practice produce learning, and learning results in more fluent and less attention-demanding performance—that is, greater automaticity.

Enter Biology Versus Culture

At this point, with the focus on learning and automaticity, the underlying genetic substrate of the human being as a biological organism becomes critically important to understanding differences among tasks in how easy they are to learn and how frequently people who try to learn them end up failing. To a first approximation, there are two major support systems for skill acquisition: biological preparation and cultural engineering. Biology prepares people to gravitate toward, attempt, and become skilled at some task performances quite readily, giving those tasks a head start on learning and automatization. It is as if those tasks, or at least their rudiments in the form of a plan or blueprint on which to build, already exist in a dormant form in the nervous system and are just waiting to be triggered. But people are creative creatures, constantly inventing new tasks for themselves, turning these novel tasks into fluent skills through practice, and spreading these new skills to others through social interaction and various acts of instruction. Instruction can be formal, as in the school classroom, or it can happen less formally during interactions between parent and child, tutor and tutee, friend and friend.

People have been learning skills such as walking and running; or recognizing, reaching for, grasping, and throwing objects; or speaking and listening, for a long time—more than enough time for the foundations of these skills to get built into our biology. Other skills, however, such as reading and writing, have only been around for a few thousand years—not much time for biological adaptation to provide a lot of help. Nevertheless reading and writing have become central to living an informed, rewarding, and successful life in most cultures. Still other skills, such as chess, calculus, golf, basketball, automobile repair, commodity futures trading, and computer programming are even newer and are even less likely to enjoy the benefits of a heavily prepared biological foundation specific to that skill.

The invention of new tasks, the social transmission that spreads them, and the societal adoption that makes some of them necessary to life success force people to go far beyond biological preparation, gaining access to and control over biologically provided resources and harnessing them to the needs of the new task (Rozin, 1976). People must work hard to master complicated sequences of difficult mental operations that nature never imagined and hence did not build into the biological repertoire of prepared task performances. Culturally engineered tasks place greater burdens on attentional resources; require more direct, systematic, and intensive instructional support; and show greater individual variation in achieved skill level compared to biologically prepared tasks. In the theoretical world of cognitive psychology and cognitive neuroscience, the difference between biologically prepared and culturally engineered tasks is extremely interesting. It opens a unique window into the particular properties, strengths, and weaknesses of the human information processing machinery and how biology and experience combine to propel its development. In the practical world of people's everyday lives, the difference is important—we must take it into account and learn to manage it so that societally valued culturally engineered tasks can be mastered as closely as possible to the level of expertise that is more easily and universally achieved with biologically prepared tasks.

Reading as a Test Case

Reading is a prime example of a culturally engineered skill—a "skill of the artificial," as Simon (1981) might have called it. Because reading bears a close structural and functional relationship to a parent skill that is heavily biologically prepared—spoken language—it can serve extremely well as a model system for comparing and constrasting cultural engineering and biological preparation as foundations of skill acquisition. Furthermore, the answers gained by the study of reading clearly *matter*. Reading is at the top of the list of biologically unprepared but practically useful skills to be acquired if one wants to function well in modern societies. Most societies around the world value reading, most jobs require it in one way or another, and most governments spend large amounts of money trying to teach it to as many citizens as possible.

Despite the money and effort expended, individual variation in learning to read is high, even in a native language whose spoken form has already been mastered, and a substantial number of people fare so poorly at learning to read that they get labeled dyslexic, meaning that they tried hard to learn to read but they could not. These properties contrast strongly with learning the native spoken language on which reading is built, where individual variation in achieved competence is smaller and far fewer people fail to reach reasonably proficient standards of performance (Caplan, Carr, Gould, & Martin, 1999; Gleitman & Rozin, 1977; Liberman, 1995; Rozin & Gleitman, 1977). It would be good to know how these properties of reading should be understood theoretically, and how they can be dealt with instructionally.

Determining the Brain's Problem in Learning to Read

What specific modifications must be made to the natural information processing capacities of the human brain to create a reader out of a normally developing child who is equipped with the usual complement of biologically prepared cognitive and linguistic capacities?

The Cognitive and Linguistic Status of the Prereading Child

Around the world, children commonly enter school-based reading instruction somewhere between ages 5 and 8. By this time, they are already accomplished visual and linguistic information processors. Before they know how to read, almost all children know how to perceive, understand, and act on the visually-perceptible world, and how to listen, speak, and engage in conversation. Although 5- to 8-year-old children may not be at adult levels in the speed, accuracy, and complexity of these skills, or in their freedom from distractibility and attentional limitations when trying to exercise them, they are nevertheless quite impressive in absolute terms. They have come a long way since infancy.

Despite their visual, motor, and linguistic accomplishments, however, prereading children do not know how to read. Reading requires that a new set of skills be developed—treating visual stimuli as words comprising texts that refer to and describe objects, scenes, and events in symbolic form, rather than presenting visual evidence of objects, scenes, and events directly to the machinery of visual perception. Prereading children possess a well-established language system that is biologically prepared to listen to linguistic input collected by the ears—but it does not know how to look at linguistic input collected by the eyes. Furthermore, prereading children possess a well-established visual system that is biologically prepared to construct object representations and piece them together into scenes and track them over time to construct events—but it does not know how to construct word representations and string them together into sentences and texts. The language system is not a visual system, and the visual system is not a language system.

Thus the primary problem to be solved in turning a prereader into a beginning reader is to establish an effective interface between vision and language. Considerable evidence from a wide variety of sources indicates that this interface is established at the level of the word, and that learning to analyze and recognize visually presented words *as* linguistic entities rather than as visual objects is the difficult but indispensable task facing the prereader.

Recognizing Words as Linguistic Entities Is the Foundation of Reading Skill

To learn to read, the brain must make a choice. Is a printed word just another visual object with parts? Are these objects laid out in space like visual scenes? Do the objects move around as causal events unfold? If so, the job is simple—the visual system can create structural descriptions of the parts and how they fit together and pass these structural descriptions on to inferotemporal and parahippocampal cortex, where they are identified as members of object categories and placed relative to one another in environmental space, just like always. These structural descriptions will make contact with visual associative memory. Particular structural descriptions will retrieve object-specific, scene-specific, and event-specific knowledge about identity, category memberships, functions, affordances, and past experiences.

Alternatively, maybe a word is not just another object. Maybe it needs to be treated as an instance of language (whatever that is—keep in mind that in the prereading child, the visual system is not a language system). If a word is an instance of language instead of an object, then the visual system needs to learn some new skills (for reviews, see Adams, 1990; Carr & Posner, 1995; Rieben & Perfetti, 1991; Rozin & Gleitman, 1977).

These skills still involve visual shapes, but they are no longer three-dimensional parts connected together in three-dimensional space to form objects, or even two-dimensional pictures representing such three-dimensional configurations. They are two-dimensional shapes organized into two-dimensional spatial arrays, with linear order crucial in both dimensions. In alphabetic writing systems such as English, Welsh, Spanish, Italian, Finnish, Russian, Serbo-Croatian, Hebrew, or Arabic, the shapes are letters and clusters of letters called *graphemes,* which are strung together in systematic, highly structured sequences to spell words.

Some sequences of graphemes are common, others are rarer but perfectly acceptable, and others are illegal—they simply do not occur in the spelling system of the written language. These constraints on graphemic order and combination are referred to as the orthographic structure of the writing system. Every skilled reader is sensitive to orthographic structure. If I ask you, as a skilled reader of English, to say which of the following sequences of letters—bluck, cbptklm, pasp, ckik—follows the acceptable patterns of English spelling and hence could conceivably be the spelling of a word, you would have no trouble deciding that the correct answer is the first string "bluck" and the third string "pasp." These so-called pseudowords possess all the right properties to be part of the English lexicon—they just do not happen to have been chosen to be words, at least so far in the development of the language. The second string "cbptklm" and the fourth "ckik" are not acceptable as English spellings. Such a decision can be reached intuitively, relying on knowledge that is basically implicit (those strings just do not look right) or explicitly, relying on knowledge of varying degrees of precision and certainty that can be formulated for report (there are no vowels in "cbptklm," and all English spellings have vowels in them; and "ck" corresponds to a sound that can occur at the beginning of a word, but the spelling "ck" itself can only occur at the end of a word, so "ckik" cannot be an English spelling). One might even rely on rules of spelling learned in a formal way ("i before e except after c" being one that many people can recite, although it does not help with this set of examples).

Note that some of the knowledge needed to make these orthographic judgments is specifically visual (in English, "ck" never appears as the first grapheme of a word, although it is perfectably acceptable and, in fact, quite common in the middle as in "pickle" or at the end as in "kick"). Much of our orthographic knowledge, however, seems to correspond to or even depend on knowledge of patterns of pronunciation ("bluck" and "pasp" are acceptable because they can be pronounced in a way that sounds like English). This realization points to the most profound fact about the problem that reading poses for the brain: the new skills that the visual system must learn are not just visual. They also involve phonemes and how phonemes are strung together and integrated to make a spoken word. This is because the graphemes are symbols that refer to and map onto the pronunciations of the spoken language. The ultimate goal of the new skills that the visual system must learn involves phonological recoding—the set of mental operations that transform visual representations coded in terms of sequences of graphemes into phonological representations coded in terms of sequences of phonemes. Given that phonological recoding relies on new mental operations not already in the prereader's repertoire, we can expect that learning them will be attention demanding, and hence that both the conditions of instruction and the conditions under which the skills must be deployed will prove to be crucial. Simpler conditions, less cluttered conditions will be better, and conditions crafted specifically to focus on and highlight just what needs to be learned will be better.

Is this argument correct? One might wonder at the outset just what is the evidence that underlies the claim that learning to recognize visual words as linguistic entities is the foundation of the reading process, and that phonological recoding is a crucial part of this foundation?

Evidence From Eye Movements While Reading Text

For approximately 100 years, perceptual and cognitive scientists have been developing more and more accurate methods of measuring the pattern of eye movements that takes place during reading. This pattern consists of a sequence of fixations, each bringing foveal vision to bear on a few letters of text—six to eight or so at a time can actually be resolved to the point of explicit identification in normally sized text at normally chosen reading distances, and perhaps twice that number might influence processing in some fashion, taking into account implicit effects from letters that have been partially processed but not explicitly recognized. Fixations last for 150 to 400 ms or thereabouts, with the average fixation lasting 200 to 250 ms. Each fixation is followed by a ballistic saccade that moves the direction of gaze to the next point of fixation. Most of these saccades move forward in the text, averaging about eight letters or so, but 10% to 15% are regressions that take the eyes back to a region of text that has been fixated before.

Measuring eye movements has amassed a large body of knowledge about the spatial pattern and time course of gathering information from text (for reviews, see Carr, 1986; Just & Carpenter, 1987; Rayner, 1999; Rayner & Pollatsek, 1989). Judging from where and when the eyes are aimed, children read text word by word. On average, elementary-school-aged readers look at every content word, usually more than once. Highly literate college-aged adults do much the same, still looking at almost every content word, and spending two or more fixations on longer words. Highly literate adults skip most function words and may skip some familiar high-frequency words that are predictable from context, with skipping more likely for shorter words than for longer ones. But most content words—nouns, verbs, modifiers—receive at least one fixation. Thus words are important units of information acquisition, even for readers who are skilled and experienced.

Furthermore, both the overall length and the internal orthographic structure of a word influence where within that word the eye is most likely to fixate. The preferred landing position for the initial fixation on a word of fewer than about seven or eight letters is just to the left of the word's center. The initial landing position shifts further into the word if the initial graphemes of the word are a high-frequency combination that appears frequently in the written language and hence has been encountered many times in the past. The initial landing position shifts closer to the beginning of the word if the initial graphemes are a rarer combination with which the reader is not as experienced. These shifts happen as a function of graphemic frequency per se, with the overall frequency of the words controlled. Such sensitivity to orthographic structure makes it clear that words are not encoded as visual wholes, or at least not solely in such terms, but instead are encoded in terms of sequences of graphemes. Why should this be? The hypothesized answer is that such a coding strategy facilitates contact with the phonological representations of the language system and hence facilitates establishing the vision–language interface that supports phonological recoding.

Evidence From Word-Processing Tasks

Measuring eye movements tells researchers where information is being gathered from text, and how long it takes to get it. Measuring the speed and accuracy of making specific judgments about letter strings with particular properties can tell us about the details of how a letter string is encoded and evaluated. Gibson, Osser, and Pick (1963) asked first and third graders to report what they could see from brief tachistoscopic presentations of three different kinds of letter strings: real words, pseudowords, and random strings. The difference between words and pseudowords indexes the impact of familiarity and meaning over and above the impact of orthographic structure and pronounceability. The difference between pseudowords and random strings indexes the impact of orthographic structure and pronounceability per se. To a rough first approximation, one might think of the word–pseudoword difference as pointing toward recognizing words as familiar objects, whereas the pseudoword–random string difference points toward recognizing words as linguistic entities. First graders showed an advantage for three- and five-letter words over both pseudowords and random strings, demonstrating sensitivity to familiarity and meaning. They showed a smaller advantage of three-letter pseudowords over random strings, but no advantage of five-letter pseudowords. Thus in this demanding task, first graders showed an ability to treat words as objects and the beginnings of a possibly emerging ability to treat words as linguistic entities. By third grade, the advantage for pseudowords over random strings was there for the longer stimuli as well, although with the five-letter stimuli, words were still recognized better than pseudowords. One might conclude that mastery of orthographic and phonological structure is a lagging consequence of reading instruction and experience—beginning readers first treat letter strings as individual objects, gradually acquiring the structural knowledge needed to treat them as linguistic entities.

Similar developmental trends were observed by McCandliss, Posner, and Givon (1997) in studies of young adults learning an artificial writing system with an alphabetic orthography, and by Givon, Yang, and Gernsbacher (1990) in a study of young adults learning to read Spanish as a second language. Haynes and Carr (1990) found that the pseudoword advantage over random strings in visual same–different matching—a task especially sensitive to visual encoding (Carr, Pollatsek, & Posner, 1981)—predicted not only reading comprehension but the ability to learn new word meanings from context among Taiwanese young adults learning to read English as a second language. These results indicate that the gradual education of the visual system about orthographic structure and how to map orthography onto phonology and meaning discovered by Gibson and colleagues is in fact an accompaniment to learning to read a new writing system regardless of age and past experience with other writing systems, not a developmentally driven phenomenon limited to young children learning to read for the first time. For an expanded version of this argument, see Posner and McCandliss (1999).

Evidence From Individual Differences in Semantic Priming of Oral Reading

I now turn more specifically to evidence involving the activation of word meaning and its relation to comprehension, but still in the context of recognizing individual words. Perfetti, Goldman, and Hogaboam (1979) compared good and poor fifth-grade readers in two tasks. One was a cloze task in which content words were deleted from sentences and children were asked to fill in the blanks—to guess the words that had been deleted. Each deleted word was semantically consistent with the sentence and moderately predictable from it, as determined by preacquired norms. The cloze task provided a measure of how well each child understood the sentence and could use that understanding to predict an upcoming word. The other task was timed oral reading of intact versions of the same sentences. Some of the sentences were completed with the semantically consistent, predictable content word that had been deleted in the cloze task, whereas other sentences were completed with a semantically inconsistent and unpredictable word. Pronunciation latencies for these two kinds of target words were compared to provide a measure of semantic priming—how much did each child make use of and rely on or benefit from semantic consistency and predictability during online reading of intact text?

As one might expect, good readers more often filled in the blanks in the cloze task with words that were semantically and syntactically appropriate, completing the sentence in a sensible and grammatically correct manner. More of the good readers' completions were, in fact, just the word that had been deleted—and hence would be the semantically consistent target word if that sentence were read in its intact form. Thus good readers understood the sentences better and were more capable of using their understanding to predict upcoming words. These results were not surprising.

One might also expect that the greater comprehension and predictive prowess of good readers would translate into greater semantic priming effects.

However, this did not happen. Good readers showed smaller semantic priming effects, in both absolute and percentage terms. In particular, good readers slowed down much less and made many fewer errors on the inconsistent, unpredictable words than did the poor readers. The poor readers were significantly hampered by inconsistent context. Their errors were often words that were semantically consistent with the context, showing a reliance on context to help infer upcoming words that good readers did not show.

Perfetti and colleagues (1979) argued from these results that although good readers can use context to make guesses about upcoming words, as indicated by their superior cloze performance, they do not need to do so during online, real-time reading. Their stimulus-driven word recognition skills are fast and accurate enough to take priority. It is the poor readers, whose word recognition skills are weaker, who rely on context for help. Even though the poor readers' grasp of the context is not always very good, they try to apply what grasp they have in an attempt to compensate for word recognition skills that are not up to the job on their own—and, as demonstrated by their errors, this reliance on context can backfire.

Thus in a task that specifically involves phonological recoding—the oral reading or "naming" task—better readers are better at recognizing words based only on the visual stimulus information from the individual word itself, independently of cues from context. Biemiller (1970) observed from the nature of errors in oral reading that normally developing readers pass through a stage of relying on context but pass out of it as their stimulus-driven word recognition skills consolidate and solidify. Beyond the first few years of reading instruction and practice, it is the mark of the poor reader, not the good reader, to rely on contextual cues rather than stimulus-driven word recognition. Stanovich (1980) has extended the argument for compensatory use of context by poor readers to a much wider domain of reading tasks.

Evidence From Individual Differences in Comprehension and What Predicts Them

Oral reading is an important real-life skill—ask any parent who reads *Good Night, Moon* to a 3-year-old, or any president who reads from the teleprompter to give a speech about a war. Nevertheless, one might prefer evidence from comprehension measured directly rather than inferred from semantic priming in oral reading, on grounds that if one must choose one or the other, understanding what one reads is more useful than being able to read it aloud fluently.

There is now a large body of evidence demonstrating a developmentally extended hierarchy of prediction among measures of reading and reading-related abilities. Preschoolers' letter knowledge (being able to name the letters of the alphabet) and phonological awareness (being able to judge whether two spoken words rhyme, to break syllables apart and exchange their initial sounds, to play word games involving phoneme deletion and substitution such as "pig latin," and so on) predict their later success in school phonics activities, including learning the acceptable spelling patterns that constitute orthographic structure and learning to work out the correct pronunciations of printed pseudowords—a behavioral manifestation of phonological recoding. Success in phonics activities and pronouncing printed pseudowords predict correct recognition of printed real words. Finally, pronunciation of pseudowords and recognition of real words predict reading comprehension. For reviews of this evidence, see Adams (1990); Manis, Szeszulski, Holt, and Graves (1990); Rieben and Perfetti (1991); and Goswami (1999). Furthermore, pronunciation of pseudowords and recognition of real words remain independent predictors of reading comprehension even among highly literate college students, and even after controlling for a wide variety of other potentially important predictors of reading comprehension, such as IQ, world knowledge, and spoken language comprehension (Cunningham, Stanovich, & Wilson, 1990). Thus the predictive power of mastering orthographic structure, phonological structure, and the mental operations of phonological recoding extends beyond oral reading per se. Learning to recognize words as linguistic entities does appear to be the foundation of the reading process.

Evidence From the Impact of Instruction

It is by now extremely well established empirically that beginning reading curricula should include a regimen of phonics activities—specific instruction and practice aimed at becoming acquainted with orthographic structure, phonological structure, and phonological recoding. Such curricula produce greater achievement on average during the first two to four years of formal reading instruction than do curricula that deemphasize or exclude phonics activities (Adams, 1990; Chall, 1967, 1983; Evans & Carr, 1985; National Reading Panel, 2000; Rayner, Foorman, Perfetti, Pesetsky, & Seidenberg, 2002). Furthermore, as I have just shown, the skills of word recognition acquired through such activities predict subsequent reading success, including reading comprehension.

School instruction does not begin from nothing. There is a growing body of evidence on the nature and impact of parent-child book-reading activities, focusing on the preschool years. These activities provide various kinds of reading experience and informal reading instruction, laying the groundwork for the more formal instruction that lies ahead in school. Evans and colleagues (Evans, Bell, Mansell, & Shaw, 2001; Evans, Moretti, Shaw, & Fox, 2003) videotaped parents reading books with their preschool children, applying an observational coding scheme to assign the observed activities to categories. The focus was on situations in which the children were trying to do at least some of the reading.

They have found that parents differ substantially along three dimensions: (a) their emphasis on overall comprehension, making sure that their children understood the message the narrative was trying to convey; (b) their emphasis on using context to guess words, encouraging their children to pay attention to pictures and other cues to overall meaning to figure out what a particular unknown word might be; and (c) their emphasis on having fun, using book-reading as a tool to create positive social interaction. Where parents stand along these dimensions can be predicted from their beliefs about what reading is for and how it is done, which Evans and colleagues measured in separate questionnaires.

More interesting were two things parents do that are not predicted by their beliefs. First, parents tend not to let mistakes pass. If a child gets a word wrong, the parent is likely to correct the mistake, either supplying the correct word or leading the child through another attempt at its identification. This is quite consistent with the literature on skill acquisition—learning proceeds more rapidly with feedback about success (for a review, see Proctor & Dutta, 1995).

Second, all parents engage to some degree or another in phonics instruction, again regardless of expressed beliefs about the nature of reading. They call attention to letters and how those letters might be translated into pronunciations, make suggestions based on similarity of spelling or sound, and in other ways focus on how the writing system encodes phonology and maps onto spoken words. This is quite consistent with the literature on reading instruction as already discussed—reading progress is facilitated by a regimen of phonics activities. Furthermore, the amount of phonics-like instruction during pre-school parent–child book-reading correlates positively with reading progress once school instruction begins. Thus it would appear that the parents studied by Evans and colleagues were to greater or lesser degree intuitive scientists, seeming naturally to grasp the truths that have been so hard-won in the literature on reading instruction and implementing them in varying amounts in their interactions with their children. The amounts predicted how much good is done. A regimen of phonics instruction, combined with feedback on success at recognizing words and understanding the sentences they make up, facilitates reading development.

Third, there is the issue of how a child's own relative skill at spoken language influences his or her progress at learning to read. Although variation in spoken language skill is less than that observed in reading, there is some. Does it make a difference in learning to read?

One way to address this question is to specifically seek out children with exceptionally strong spoken language skills. Crain-Thoreson and Dale (1992) selected children for verbal precocity at age 20 months and followed them longitudinally. Although they remained verbally advanced relative to other children, they did not show more rapid reading development by virtue of their greater language skills. What did predict emerging literacy was degree of exposure to letter names and sounds, and other kinds of phonics-related activities, in the home. This study suggests in yet another way that strong spoken language skills are not enough to become literate. Specific instruction in what I have been calling the new set of skills that the brain needs to learn is a required ingredient.

A second way to address the question of how spoken language skill relates to reading progress is to investigate the impact of different kinds of formal reading instruction. Suppose that the relation between spoken language skill and reading progress is indeed dependent on and mediated by instructional support for educating the visual system about orthography and establishing a visual–phonological interface with the language system. If so, then beginning-reading curricula that emphasize such phonics-related activities should be more conducive to helping children bring to bear their existing spoken language skills in making reading progress.

To find out, Evans and Carr (1985) compared two curricula in a naturalistic study of classroom activities in a large urban school system. One was a curriculum whose reading instruction consisted of phonics, guided instruction at learning word meanings from context, and guided instruction at writing and spelling—activities aimed at treating words as linguistic entities and providing feedback about success. The other was a radical version of the so-called whole language curriculum. Children made up stories and told them to the teacher, who wrote the stories down. These stories became the children's reading texts, and the words in the stories were put on flash cards to teach whole-word visual recognition—an activity that treats words as visual objects.

In the phonics and guided instruction curriculum, measures of spoken language competence including sentence complexity and mean length of utterance correlated positively with reading achievement measured at the end of the school year. However, in the whole language curriculum, despite its well-intentioned attempts to help children use their own preexisting language and personal interests as the basis for learning to read, the correlations were significantly negative. That is, children with stronger spoken language skills actually achieved less in learning to read than children with weaker spoken language skills. Evans and Carr concluded from this striking result that spoken language skills can mesh with and facilitate reading development—but only if explicit instruction is aimed at giving children the tools they need to take advantage of their spoken language. These tools involve educating the visual system about writing, and establishing an interface between visual knowledge of writing and linguistic knowledge of word forms and their internal structure—that is, the tools that allow a child to treat written words as linguistic entities rather than visual objects.

The Reading Wars

Although the scientific evidence is considerable (and in my view overwhelming in its breadth, consistency, and weight), the idea that learning to recognize printed words as linguistic entities is the foundation of reading skill is nevertheless a hotly debated proposition. Not everyone believes it, especially in educational circles, in which ideological and sociopolitical commitments about reading are strong. Such a valuable societal commodity as reading should engage people's commitments, and it should inspire passion in the public arena. However, commitment and passion should not displace the scientific evidence.

This debate as it plays out in the public arena is illustrated in a column by Norman Lockman (2003) of the *Wilmington News Journal,* which I came across in my local newspaper one morning while working on this chapter. The title was "Reading Is Too Vital for Games: Educators' Efforts to Ease Conflicts Hurt Neediest Kids." I quote Lockman because I believe he has gotten the instructional implications of the scientific evidence just right, and the more this happens the better it will be for the prospects of children learning to read.

Lockman begins with the premise that schools do children no favors if they adopt teaching methods that promote enjoyment and personal interest but do not establish the skill that is supposed to be taught. How can one argue with that? He goes on to say,

> I've always thought reading meant being able to pick up a piece of unfamiliar written material and decipher its contents in order to understand the thoughts (or instructions) of someone other than myself. It's the key to learning everything else.
>
> So what is the point of teaching a child to understand his own scribblings as means of learning to read? The educational progressives say it avoids "drill and kill," by which they mean avoiding the drudgery of learning the basics of written language by boring repetition.
>
> I think it comes down to hedging bets by teachers who do not want to be held responsible for the absolutes of achieving full literacy among children with no personal or parental understanding of its value and no motivation to acquire it. It's a pedagogical dodge.
>
> Learning to read is not easy. I can remember struggling with reading material that was frustrating to comprehend and resenting teachers who insisted that I do so. But I also remember feeling triumphant when it began to make sense.

Summing Up the Brain's Problem in Learning to Read

Several enhancements of brain functional organization must be achieved to get a nascent reading system up and operating. The visual system needs to be educated about writing—learning component symbols and the orthographic structure that characterizes how the symbols are combined into patterns of spelling. Word and pseudoword superiority effects in visually sensitive tasks such as same–different matching, search for target letters, and tachistoscopic report index the development of this capability. Word superiority effects indicate the initial lexical basis of this knowledge—the reader is learning the visual configuration of specific words as a start. Pseudoword superiority indicates broader learning and the consolidation and generalization of lexical knowledge into patterns of orthography. In addition, the phonological system must be made accessible at the level of syllabic structure—onsets and rimes—and, ideally, at the even more analytic level of the phoneme. Engagement in phonological awareness activities forges this level of accessibility, and successful performance of such activities provides behavioral evidence that it is being achieved. An interface needs to be established between the visual system and the phonological system, so that visual representations of orthography can map onto the language system's phonological representations of pronunciation and vice versa. Phonics activities and guided practice at sounding out pronounceable strings of letters—whether words or pseudowords—creates this interface, and success at pronouncing pseudowords provides behavioral evidence that it is being established. The more consistent the generalizable patterns and the fewer the exceptions to those patterns, the faster skills at treating printed words as rule-governed linguistic entities are established (Ellis &

Hooper, 2001). English, however, requires mastery of many exceptions, and progress is slower. These skills, in turn, predict success at higher levels of processing, including text comprehension, both in the short term among elementary school students and in the long term—even among college students.

The Neural Substrate of the Solution: What Does the Reading System Look Like Once the Vision–Language Interface Is Established?

Two major bodies of evidence address this question. One is evidence from trauma-induced brain damage; the other is evidence from neuroimaging.

Traumatic Dyslexia: Evidence From Lesion Damage

Three major types of trauma-induced dyslexia can be found consequent to specific brain damage (Banich, 1997; McCarthy & Warrington, 1990). Pure alexia harms the recognition of all types of words and pseudowords, essentially knocking out the reading system in all respects. Pure alexia most often results from damage to left extrastriate and anterior occipital visual cortex.

Surface dyslexia differentially harms the recognition and proper pronunciation of words with exceptional spelling-to-pronunciation mappings—words that violate the generalizable patterns that occur most frequently in the written language. Such exceptions include words such as "blood," "pint," "sword," "then," and "know." The errors produced in surface dyslexia tend to regularize these exception words, as if the ability has been lost to retrieve and apply word-specific lexical knowledge to override the central tendencies of the body of known patterns of phonological recoding. One way of thinking about surface dyslexia is that it constitutes relative loss of the ability to treat words as visual objects accompanied by the relative sparing of the ability to treat words as linguistic entities. Consistent with this way of thinking, surface dyslexia results from damage to inferior occipitotemporal cortex, anterior to the regions most often involved in pure alexia and further along in the ventral visual stream involved in object recognition and associative memory.

Finally, phonological dyslexia involves a complementary pattern to surface dyslexia. There is relative preservation of the ability to recognize and properly pronounce familiar words, whether consistent with the general patterns of spelling-to-pronunciation mapping or exceptional. What is differentially harmed is recognition and pronunciation of less frequent words, especially regular-consistent ones, and in particular, applying the generalizable patterns of spelling-to-pronunciation mapping to generate a reasonable pronunciation for a pseudoword or a real but unknown word. Phonological dyslexia looks like relative loss of the ability to treat words as linguistic entities accompanied by the relative sparing of the ability to treat words as visual objects. It most often results from damage in regions of occipitotemporal and occipitoparietal cortex anterior and superior to the regions involved in pure alexia.

This tripartite anatomy of trauma-induced dyslexia suggests that in learning to read, the brain does not make an all-or-none choice between treating words as objects or as linguistic entities. Opting for redundancy (as is often the case in biological systems), the brain pursues both possibilities. Visual word processing begins in extrastriate visual cortex, then diverges, with lexically-specific, associative-memory-based processing differentially supported by a ventral pathway into inferior temporal cortex and linguistic analysis of orthography and its mapping onto phonology differentially supported by a more dorsal pathway into superior temporal and inferior parietal cortex.

Evidence From Neuroimaging of the Normal Brain

The perils of drawing conclusions about normal functional organization from the consequences of brain damage are well known. However, the advent of neuroimaging—particularly positron emission tomography (PET) and functional magnetic resonance imaging (fMRI)—has enabled such conclusions to be treated as hypotheses that can be explored in the undamaged brains of normal readers.

OCCIPITAL ORTHOGRAPHIC PROCESSING: THE VISUAL WORD FORM SYSTEM. Warrington and Shallice (1980) were the first to hypothesize that pure alexia represents damage to an area of brain tissue specifically devoted to creating a visual representation of a printed word. At the same time, a large body of behavioral evidence had been accumulated from tasks known to emphasize visual rather than lexical-semantic, phonological, or articulatory processing, with the most diagnostic results coming from same–different matching of simultaneously-presented letter strings (Carr, Pollatsek, & Posner, 1981). This evidence converged on the hypothesis that the visual system "knows" the orthographic structure of the written language and uses that knowledge in constructing representations of words and word-like letter strings (Carr, Pollatsek, & Posner, 1981; Carr, Posner, Pollatsek, & Snyder, 1979; for additional reviews of the evidence, see Carr, 1986; Carr & Pollatsek, 1985; Henderson, 1982).

These two hypotheses—one anatomical, one computational—were brought together in the seminal PET imaging work of Petersen, Fox, Posner, Mintun, and Raichle (1989). These investigators found that blood flow in a region of left medial extrastriate cortex increased relative to a baseline fixation condition in a variety of tasks with visually presented words but not in tasks with auditorily presented words. Another crucial test of this region's properties was performed by Petersen, Fox, Snyder, and Raichle (1990). They found that not just words but also pseudowords activated left medial extrastriate cortex relative to a fixation baseline, but looking at random strings of letters did not.

Based on this evidence, Posner and Carr (1992) suggested that the occipital region, called the visual word form area by Warrington and Shallice (1980), is an orthographic encoding mechanism—a region of tissue that performs the mental operation of preparing a representation of letter identities and their order for letter strings with sufficient orthographic structure to be word candidates. These representations are shipped forward to inferotemporal, temporoparietal, and prefrontal cortex for lexical-semantic, phonological, and articulatory processing. Carr and Posner (1995) went further, arguing that the visual word form area constitutes a primary gateway from the visual system to the language system—the visual-system front end of the vision–language interface that must be established to ensure that a listener–speaker can become a competent reader.

Subsequent neuroimaging investigations have shifted the most likely anatomical locus for the visual word form area slightly in the anterior direction from the early results of Petersen and colleagues. The weight of evidence now suggests that orthographic encoding is most likely to be found in occipitotemporal fusiform gyrus, rather than extrastriate cortex, although there is some variability from person to person in how posterior in the visual system the region begins (see Cohen et al., 2000 and Polk & Farah, 2002, for reviews). Such individual variability is to be expected in neural systems, highlighting the need to examine the functional-anatomical data of each person rather than focusing only on averaged group data. Based on such analyses, it is now quite clear that this region of tissue can be found in most mature readers. It responds to visual but not auditory words (Dehaene, Le Clec'H, Poline, Le Bihan, & Cohen, 2002). It cares about the order in which letters occur and not just which letters are present (McCandliss, Bolger, & Schneider, 2000). It responds to pseudowords just about as vigorously (Dehaene, Naccache, et al., 2001; Polk & Farah, 2002) and on just about the same time-course (Ziegler, Besson, Jacobs, Nazir, & Carr, 1997) as it responds to words. Finally, it operates on what the cognitive literature on word recognition has called "abstract letter identities"— representations of letter identity that are independent of purely visual variation such as letter case or typefont (Besner, Coltheart, & Davelaar, 1984; Carr, Brown, & Charalambous, 1989)—rather than to visual familiarity per se. For example, Dehaene, Naccache, and colleagues (2001) and Polk and Farah (2002) both report that the left occipitotemporal region that responds approximately equivalently to words and pseudowords does so as strongly for aLtErNaTiNg-CaSe stimuli as for the visually much more familiar pure case stimuli standardly encountered in reading. From this finding Polk and Farah suggested that this brain region ought to be called the "abstract word form area" rather than the "visual word form area." This proposal is quite consistent with Carr and Posner's argument that this region of the visual system is an orthographic encoding mechanism capable of serving the "abstractionist" needs of spelling-to-pronunciation translation in particular and communication with the linguistic system more in general.

TEMPORAL AND TEMPOROPARIETAL PHONOLOGICAL PROCESSING IDENTIFIES DYSLEXIC INDIVIDUALS. From anatomical and functional imaging data, Cohen and colleagues (2000) argue that the visual word form area is the first completely abstract, position-invariant encoding region in the ventral-stream sequence involved in word processing, and the last purely visual region. They argue also that its connectivity is both to further ventral-stream regions and more dorsally, to posterior temporal and temporoparietal regions, both left and right hemispheric.

This posterior temporal and temporoparietal connectivity, combined with the lesion evidence regarding phonological dyslexia already described, suggests that the rest of the vision–language interface crucial for phonological recoding lies in posterior temporal and temporoparietal cortex. To document a role for these regions in phonological processing related to reading ability, Temple and colleagues (2001) used fMRI to assess activation during a task that required rhyming judgments about pairs of letters. Relative to a baseline task that required visual same–different matching, Temple and colleagues found increased activation in left posterior superior temporal gyrus—the vicinity of Wernicke's area—in 10-year-old normal readers. This activation was absent in 10-year-old dyslexic readers. Shaywitz et al. (1998), using a task that required rhyme judgments about pseudowords as the phonological task and judgments of letter case as the visual baseline, found the same difference in left posterior superior temporal activation in a comparison of normal and dyslexic adults. Given the large body of evidence that Wernicke's area and adjacent tissue is heavily involved in a wide variety of language tasks involving phonology (for a review, see Binder & Price, 2001), the absence of activation in this area during phonological judgments is a clear indicator of a deficit in the preferred pathway for phonological processing among these dyslexic readers.

When a preferred pathway fails to develop, the brain often tries to find a compensatory strategy for getting the required processing accomplished. An fMRI investigation of the development of reading-related functional anatomy in normal and dyslexic children adds to the evidence for deficient occipital-temporoparietal development and also points toward a possible compensatory strategy. Shaywitz and colleagues (2002) found that poorer readers showed less activation overall both in occipital regions (the visual word form area) and in posterior superior temporal gyrus, supramarginal gyrus, and angular gyrus (Wernicke's area and adjacent tissue). Furthermore, poorer readers showed smaller correlations between the patterns of activation that did occur in the visual word form area and those in superior temporal and temporoparietal cortex. This evidence of reduced functional connectivity suggests specifically that communication between regions of the type that appears to be required for an effective vision–language interface was not being established.

Instead, poorer readers showed relatively greater activation in prefrontal cortex, especially inferior frontal gyrus in and around Broca's area as well as the right-hemisphere homologues of these areas. As Shaywitz and colleagues speculated, this increased activity in frontal speech-production-oriented regions may be in compensation for the poor connections from the visual system to posterior phonological regions—perhaps an attempt on the brain's part to substitute direct articulatory coding of printed words for the linguistically analytic aspects of phonological recoding that are the speciality of posterior temporal and temporoparietal structures.

As I demonstrate in the final section of the chapter, normal adult readers also show evidence that suggests direct articulatory coding in frontal motor regions, but they do so preferentially for high-frequency words that are likely to be familiar. Less familiar low-frequency words show evidence of greater reliance on posterior analysis in selecting an appropriate pronunciation, and all words produce activation in the temporoparietal regions that the above studies found to be silent in dyslexic individuals.

TEMPOROPARIETAL PHONOLOGICAL PROCESSING IN NORMAL ADULT READERS: COORDINATING LINGUISTIC ANALYSIS AND MEMORY RETRIEVAL. If the brain is relying on two kinds of knowledge about words—object-like word-specific retrieval from a lexical associative memory system and more abstract linguistic mappings from strings of graphemes to strings of phonemes—then a coordination problem arises. How are these two kinds of knowledge combined so that the right answer is obtained for any given word?

By definition, the two kinds of knowledge produce different answers for exception words, and hence compete. They produce the same answer for "regular" words consistent with the generalizable patterns and hence might help each other out. Behavioral studies of speeded pronunciation of single words produce evidence of exactly such cooperation and competition in the mature, well-established reading systems of young adults (for reviews, see Bernstein & Carr, 1996; Bernstein, DeShon, & Carr, 1998; Coltheart et al., 2001; Plaut, McClelland, Seidenberg, & Patterson, 1996). Pronunciation latencies are fast and errors are few for familiar, high-frequency words, and compliance with the generalizable patterns of spelling-to-pronunciation mapping makes only a small difference or no difference at all. Here, lexically specific associative knowledge, established and strengthened through many past encounters with each high frequency word, is sufficiently easy to access to override any conflict that might arise between the pronunciation suggested by the common patterns and the specific mapping required for that particular word. For low-frequency words, however, different results are observed. Lexically-specific associative knowledge is weaker for such words, because they have been processed many fewer times in the past, making consistency with the generalizable patterns a potentially stronger influence on the selection of a pronunciation. Low-frequency consistent words show evidence of cooperation between the two sources of knowledge—despite their lower familiarity, they are pronounced almost as rapidly and accurately as high-frequency words. Low-frequency exception words, in contrast, are pronounced 10% to 25% slower, and with higher error rates, than low-frequency regular-consistent words. Errors, though of course much less frequent than in surface dyslexia, follow the same tendency toward regularizations in which the exception word is pronounced as if it were a pseudoword. As word-specific associative knowledge about a particular word's pronunciation gets weaker and less accessible, the impact of the weight of evidence from generalizable patterns increases.

How to model the computations by which these two kinds of knowledge are taken into account and adjudicated is a contentious issue in cognitive psychology. There are divergent views concerning whether the two kinds of knowledge are represented together in a common format within a well-integrated and interactive "single mechanism"—the parallel-distributed-processing connectionist network approach (see Harm, McCandliss, & Seidenberg, 2003; Plaut, 1999; Plaut, McClelland, Seidenberg, & Patterson, 1996)—or in different formats with memory retrieval and application of generalizable patterns operating relatively independently of one another—the dual or multiple route approach (see Besner, 1999; Coltheart et al., 2001; Zorzi et al., 1998).

Behavioral data—reaction times and accuracies in word recognition experiments—have so far been unable to provide a definitive resolution. Perhaps one can gain a different kind of leverage on understanding this problem by trying to trace the functional anatomy that underlies the overall behavioral performances. Neuroimaging can be applied to this problem. To do so, however, requires diagnostic manipulations capable of identifying particular brain regions that might be involved in phonological recoding, and determining which if any of these regions are sensitive to the generalizable patterns alone and which rely on or interact with word-specific associative memory in carrying out their processing.

A straightforward approach to such diagnosis is to choose manipulations that make the sought-for processing harder or easier. An obvious choice for phonological recoding is regularity or consistency. Phonological recoding is easier for regular words that are consistent with the generalizable patterns. Phonological recoding is harder and more complicated for exception words— the sequences of graphemes contained in exception words activate a wider range of possibilities for how those graphemes should be pronounced. Whenever a decision must be made among a wider range of choices, that decision becomes more difficult. Hence regions of tissue that vary systematically in activation with a manipulation of consistency are candidates to be involved in phonological recoding.

How might one diagnose the involvement of word-specific associative memory? Whereas the generalizable patterns are just that—applicable to any orthographically well-structured letter string, even pseudowords that have never been encountered before, word-specific knowledge depends on having stored a representation in memory for a particular word, and being able to activate and retrieve that representation in an accurate and timely manner. Word-specific knowledge varies in strength as a function of the frequency with which it has been processed in the past, and stronger representations are easier to activate and retrieve. Hence word frequency is a candidate manipulation for diagnosing the involvement of word-specific associative memory. An interaction between consistency and frequency would suggest that a region of tissue involved in phonological recoding (as indicated by its sensitivity to consistency) relies on or interacts with word-specific associative memory in doing its job (as indicated by the fact that the consistency effect is modulated by the frequency of the particular word being recoded). Fiez, Balota, Raichle, and Petersen (1999) have used consistency and frequency in this way using PET.

A second possibility, and one that seems especially potent, is to use repetition priming as the diagnostic for word-specific retrieval. A recently activated word representation is more accessible regardless of frequency (Scarborough, Cortese, & Scarborough, 1977), and this increased accessibility can persist for minutes to hours—enough time to cover the duration of a neuroimaging experiment (Brown & Carr, 1993). Thus it can be determined whether a region identified as relevant to phonological recoding by virtue of its sensitivity to consistency is also sensitive to repetition priming by looking for an interaction between consistency and repetition in this region's activation. Such an influence of repetition priming would show that the recent activation of a specific word's memorial representation matters to the phonologically relevant processing responsibilities of this particular region.

Huang, Colombo, Carr, and Cao (2002, 2003) have applied such logic in an fMRI investigation that combined consistency of spelling-to-pronunciation mapping with repetition priming in a block design—four runs of trials, with each of these imaging runs consisting of periods of rest alternating with periods of reading words silently to oneself. Activation during the periods of reading was assessed against a baseline defined by activation during the rest periods immediately preceding and following each period of reading.

The repetition priming manipulation was implemented by having participants read a list of words outside the scanner at the beginning of the experiment, half with regular-consistent spelling-to-pronunciation mappings and half with exceptional mappings. These words appeared again in the scanner, the regular-consistent words during one of the four imaging runs and exception words during another. The other two imaging runs consisted of words that had not been seen before in the experiment, again with regular-consistent words in one run and exception words in another.

Huang and colleagues conducted two experiments following this design, one with high-frequency words and one with low-frequency words. In both experiments, two regions of inferior parietal cortex adjacent to Wernicke's area—supramarginal gyrus and angular gyrus—responded to consistency, with activation greater for exception words than for regular-consistent words, and showed no sensitivity at all to repetition priming. This activation tended to be bilateral. Treating the two regions as a single region of interest and testing for effects of hemisphere revealed equivalent left and right activation for high-frequency words, but a larger consistency effect in the left hemisphere than in the right for low-frequency words. In no case, however, was there an impact of repetition priming. Thus supramarginal and angular gyri taken together behaved as if they were involved in implementing the generalizable patterns of spelling-to-pronunciation mapping but without much regard for word-specific memory retrieval—their activity differed little as a function of frequency and not at all as a function of having just processed the same word a few minutes earlier.

While the supramarginal and angular gyri did not respond to repetition priming, sensitivity to recency of encounter with particular words was shown by other regions of tissue—in particular, Wernicke's area and its right-hemisphere homologue for low-frequency words, and frontal motor areas for high-frequency words. I now explore these effects. For low-frequency words, Wernicke's area and its right-hemisphere homologue produced a complex consistency by repetition interaction. For unprimed words, activation was greater for exception words than for regular-consistent words. But for primed words, this pattern reversed—activation was greater for regular-consistent words than for exception words, as if making the word's specific representation in lexical memory more accessible actually increased the difficulty of deciding between specific lexical information and generalized pattern-driven information, despite the fact that the two sources of information were pointing toward the same ultimate decision.

It is tempting to suggest from this complicated reaction to priming that Wernicke's area must be involved in managing and coordinating pattern-generated output from the supramarginal and angular gyri with word-specific and hence repetition-primable output from lexical memory. Before making such a suggestion, however, it is necessary to take into account the results for high-frequency words, which were different. For high-frequency words, Wernicke's area behaved similarly to the supramarginal and angular gyri, showing only an effect of consistency. But the consistency by repetition interaction was not lost—instead it moved. With high-frequency words, primary motor cortex and supplementary motor area were sensitive to repetition in this way, showing approximately the same pattern of activation that Wernicke's area showed for low-frequency words. Here, it is tempting to suggest that with the increased practice at turning written words into pronunciations, frontal motor areas can "go it alone," so to speak, in managing and coordinating the requisite knowledge and selecting an appropriate pronunciation, perhaps by direct reference to stored articulatory programs. Thus repetition priming as a diagnostic for reliance on lexically specific memory retrieval exposes a possible trade-off between anterior and posterior regions, in which the pronunciation of less familiar words is overseen by Wernicke's area, with its well-documented phonological sophistication, but pronunciation for more familiar words is taken up directly by the motor apparatus.

Conclusion

In this chapter I have described a preliminary study. Replication of these imaging results and further investigation of what kinds of codes are being generated or operated on by posterior versus anterior brain structures is needed before these suggestions about division of computational labor in the neural machinery of spelling-to-pronunciation translation can be regarded as more than speculation. Regardless of how the results obtained so far are ultimately interpreted, however, they do demonstrate that sensitivity to factors that influence selecting and producing a pronunciation are widely distributed through the brain. Consistency moderates neural activity in posterior and anterior regions in both hemispheres, and repetition priming moderates the sensitivity to consistency that is shown by some of these regions but not all of them. Much work remains to be done to map out the functional anatomy and processing characteristics of this network of regions—understanding the phonological and articulatory aspects of phonological recoding lags far behind the exquisite knowledge that has been gained of orthographic encoding in the visual word form area. This work will proceed using the tools of cognitive neuroscience that Posner has been so instrumental in helping to develop.

References

Adams, M. J. (1990). *Beginning to read: Thinking and learning about print.* Cambridge, MA: MIT Press.

Anderson, J. R. (1983). *The architecture of cognition.* Cambridge, MA: Harvard University Press.

Anderson, J. R. (1993). *Rules of mind.* Hillsdale, NJ: Erlbaum.

Baddeley, A. D. (2001). Is working memory still working? *American Psychologist, 56,* 849–864.

Banich, M. T. (1997). *Neuropsychology: The neural bases of mental function.* Boston: Houghton-Mifflin.

Beilock, S. L., Carr, T. H., MacMahon, C., & Starkes, J. L. (2002). When attention becomes counterproductive: Divided versus skill-focused attention in performance of sensorimotor skills by novices and experts. *Journal of Experimental Psychology: Applied, 8,* 6–16.

Beilock, S. L., Weirenga, S., & Carr, T. H. (2002). Expertise, attention, and memory in sensorimotor skill execution: Impact of novel task constraints on dual-task performance and episodic memory. *Quarterly Journal of Experimental Psychology, 55A,* 1211–1240.

Bernstein, S., & Carr, T. H. (1996). Dual route theories of print to sound: What can be learned from concurrent task performance? *Journal of Experimental Psychology: Learning, Memory, and Cognition, 22,* 86–116.

Bernstein, S. E., DeShon, R. P., & Carr, T. H. (1998). Concurrent task demands and individual differences in reading: Discriminating artifacts from real McCoys. *Journal of Experimental Psychology: Learning, Memory, and Cognition, 24,* 822–844.

Besner, D. (1999). Basic processes in reading: Multiple routines in localist and connectionist models. In R. M. Klein & P. A. McMullen (Eds.), *Converging methods for understanding reading and dyslexia* (pp. 413–458). Cambridge, MA: MIT Press.

Besner, D., Coltheart, M., & Davelaar, E. (1984). Basic processes in reading: Computation of abstract letter identities. *Canadian Journal of Psychology, 38,* 126–134.

Biemiller, A. J. (1970). The development of the use of graphic and contextual information as children learn to read. *Reading Research Quarterly, 6,* 75–96.

Binder, J., & Price, C. J. (2001). Functional neuroimaging of language. In R. Cabeza & A. Kingstone (Eds.), *Handbook of functional neuroimaging of cognition* (pp. 187–252). Cambridge, MA: MIT Press.

Bock, J. K. (1995). Sentence production: From mind to mouth. In J. L. Miller & P. D. Eimas (Eds.), *Speech, language, and communication: Handbook of perception and cognition* (2nd ed., Vol. II, pp. 181–216). San Diego, CA: Academic Press.

Brown, J. S., & Carr, T. H. (1993). Limits on perceptual abstraction in reading: Asymmetric transfer between surface forms differing in typicality. *Journal of Experimental Psychology: Learning, Memory, and Cognition, 19,* 1277–1296.

Brown, T. L., & Carr, T. H. (1989). Automaticity in skill acquisition: Mechanisms for reducing interference in concurrent performance. *Journal of Experimental Psychology: Human Perception and Performance, 15,* 686–700.

Caplan, D., Carr, T. H., Gould, J., & Martin, R. (1999). Language and communication. In M. J. Zigmond, F. E. Bloom, S. C. Landis, J. L. Roberts, & L. R. Squire (Eds.), *Fundamental neuroscience* (pp. 1487–1519). San Diego, CA: Academic Press.

Carr, T. H. (1979). Consciousness in models of information processing: Primary memory, executive control, and input regulation. In G. Underwood & R. Stevens (Eds.), *Aspects of consciousness* (Vol. 1, pp. 127–253). London: Academic Press.

Carr, T. H. (1981). Building theories of reading ability: On the relation between individual differences in cognitive skills and reading comprehension. *Cognition, 9,* 73–113.

Carr, T. H. (1984). Attention, skill, and intelligence: Some speculations on extreme individual differences in human performance. In P. Brooks, C. McCauley, & R. D. Sperber (Eds.), *Learning, cognition, and mental retardation* (pp. 189–215). Hillsdale, NJ: Erlbaum.

Carr, T. H. (1986). Perceiving visual language. In K. Boff, L. Kaufman, & J. Thomas (Eds.), *Handbook of perception and human performance* (pp. 29-1–29-92). New York: Wiley.

Carr, T. H. (1992). Automaticity and cognitive anatomy: Is word recognition automatic? *American Journal of Psychology* (Special Issue on varieties of automaticity), *105,* 201–237.

Carr, T. H. (1999). Trying to understand reading and dyslexia: Mental chronometry, individual differences, cognitive neuroscience, and the impact of instruction as converging sources of evidence. In R. Klein & P. McMullen (Eds.), *Converging methods for understanding reading and dyslexia* (pp. 459–491). Cambridge, MA: MIT Press.

Carr, T. H., & Bacharach, V. R. (1976). Perceptual tuning and conscious attention: Mechanisms of input regulation in visual information processing. *Cognition, 4,* 281–302.

Carr, T. H., Brown, J. S., & Charalambous, A. (1989). Repetition and reading: Perceptual encoding mechanisms are very abstract but not very interactive. *Journal of Experimental Psychology: Learning, Memory, and Cognition, 15,* 763–778.

Carr, T. H., Brown, T. L., Vavrus, L. G., & Evans, M. A. (1990). Cognitive skill maps and cognitive skill profiles: Componential analysis of individual differences in children's reading efficiency. In T. H. Carr & B. A. Levy (Eds.), *Reading and its development: Component skills approaches* (pp. 1–55). New York: Academic Press.

Carr, T. H., McCauley, C., Sperber, R. D., & Parmelee, C. M. (1982). Words, pictures, and priming: On semantic activation, conscious identification, and the automaticity of information processing. *Journal of Experimental Psychology: Human Perception and Performance, 8,* 757–777.

Carr, T. H., & Pollatsek, A. (1985). Recognizing printed words: A look at current theories. In D. Besner, T. G. Waller, & G. E. MacKinnon (Eds.), *Reading research: Advances in theory and practice* (pp. 1–82). Orlando, FL: Academic Press.

Carr, T. H., Pollatsek, A., & Posner, M. I. (1981). What does the visual system know about words? *Perception and Psychophysics, 29,* 183–190.

Carr, T. H., & Posner, M. I. (1995). The impact of becoming literate on the functional anatomy of language processing. In B. de Gelder & J. Morais (Eds.), *Speech and reading: A comparative approach* (pp. 267–301). Hove, England: Erlbaum.

Carr, T. H., Posner, M. I., Pollatsek, A., & Snyder, C. R. R. (1979). Orthography and familiarity effects in word processing. *Journal of Experimental Psychology: General, 108,* 389–414.

Chall, J. (1967). *Learning to read: The great debate.* New York: McGraw-Hill.

Chall, J. (1983). *Stages of reading development.* New York: McGraw-Hill.

Cohen, L., Dehaene, S., Naccache, L., Lehericy, S., Dehaene-Lambertz, G., Henaff, M.-A., et al. (2000). The visual word form area: Spatial and temporal characterization of an initial state of reading in normal and posterior split-brain patients. *Brain, 123,* 291–307.

Collins, A. M., & Loftus, E. F. (1975). A spreading-activation theory of semantic processing. *Psychological Review, 82,* 407–428.

Coltheart, M., Rastle, K., Perry, C., Landon, R., & Ziegler, H. (2001). A dual-route cascaded model of visual word recognition and reading aloud. *Psychological Review, 108,* 204–256.

Crain-Thoreson, C., & Dale, P. S. (1992). Do early talkers become early readers? Linguistic precocity, preschool language, and emergent literacy. *Developmental Psychology, 28,* 421–429.

Crossman, E. R. (1959). A theory of the acquisition of speed-skill. *Ergonomics, 2,* 153–166.

Cunningham, A. E., Stanovich, K. E., & Wilson, M. R. (1990). Cognitive variation in adult college students differing in reading ability. In T. H. Carr & B. A. Levy (Eds.), *Reading and its development: Component skills approaches* (pp. 129–159). San Diego, CA: Academic Press.

Dagenbach, D., Carr, T. H., & Wilhelmsen, A. (1989). Task-induced strategies and near-threshold priming: Conscious influences on unconscious perception. *Journal of Memory and Language, 28,* 412–443.

Dehaene, S., Le Clech'H, G., Poline, J.-B., Le Bihan, D., & Cohen, L. (2002). The visual word form area: A prelexical representation of visual words in the fusiform gyrus. *NeuroReport, 13,* 321–325.

Dehaene, S., Naccache, L., Cohen, L., Le Bihan, D., Mangin, J.-F., Poline, J.-B., et al. (2001). Cerebral mechanisms of word masking and unconscious repetition priming. *Nature Neuroscience, 4,* 752–758.

Dell, G. S., Burger, L. K., & Svec, W. R. (1997). Language production and serial order: A functional analysis and a model. *Psychological Review, 104,* 123–147.

Dell, G. S., & O'Seaghdha, P. G. (1994). Inhibition in interactive activation models of linguistic selection and sequencing. In D. Dagenbach & T. H. Carr (Eds.), *Inhibitory processes in attention, memory, and language* (pp. 409–453). San Diego, CA: Academic Press.

Ellis, N. C., & Hooper, A. M. (2001). Why learning to read is easier in Welsh than in English: Orthographic transparency effects evinced with frequency-matched tests. *Applied Psycholinguistics, 22,* 571–599.

Evans, M. A., Bell, M., Mansell, J., & Shaw, D. (2001, April). *Parental coaching in child-to-parent book reading: Associations with parent values and child reading skill.* Paper presented at the Biennial Meeting of the Society for Research in Child Development, Minneapolis, MN.

Evans, M. A., & Carr, T. H. (1985). Cognitive abilities, conditions of learning, and the early development of reading skill. *Reading Research Quarterly, 20,* 327–350.

Evans, M. A., Moretti, S., Shaw, D., & Fox, M. (2003). Parent scaffolding in children's oral reading. *Early Education and Development* (Special Issue on Vygotskyian perspective in early childhood education), *14,* 363–388.

Evans, M. A., Shaw, D., & Bell, M. (2000). Home literacy activities and their influence on early literacy skills. *Canadian Journal of Experimental Psychology, 2,* 65–75.

Fiez, J. A., Balota, D. A., Raichle, M. E., & Petersen, S. E. (1999). Effects of lexicality, frequency, and spelling-to-sound consistency on the functional anatomy of reading. *Neuron, 24,* 205–218.

Fitts, P. M., & Posner, M. I. (1967). *Human performance.* Monterey, CA: Brooks/Cole.

Gibson, E. J., Osser, H., & Pick, A. (1963). A study in the development of grapheme–phoneme correspondences. *Journal of Verbal Learning and Verbal Behavior, 2,* 142–146.

Givon, T., Yang, L., & Gernsbacher, M. A. (1990). *The processing of second language vocabulary: From attended to automated word recognition.* Eugene: Institute for Cognitive and Decision Sciences and Center for Cognitive Neuroscience of Attention, University of Oregon.

Gleitman, L., & Rozin, P. (1977). The structure and acquisition of reading I: Orthographics and the structure of language. In A. S. Reber & D. Scarborough (Eds.), *Toward a psychology of reading* (pp. 1–53). Hillsdale, NJ: Erlbaum.

Goswami, U. (1999). Integrating orthographic and phonological knowledge as reading develops: Onsets, rimes, and analogies in children's reading. In R. M. Klein & P. A. McMullen (Eds.), *Converging methods for understanding reading and dyslexia* (pp. 57–76). Cambridge, MA: MIT Press.

Harm, M. W., McCandliss, B. D., & Seidenberg, M. S. (2003). Modeling the successes and failures of interventions for disabled readers. *Scientific Studies of Reading, 7,* 155–182.

Henderson, L. (1982). *Orthography and word recognition in reading.* New York: Academic Press.

Haynes, M., & Carr, T. H. (1990). Writing system background and second-language reading: A component skills analysis of English reading by native speaker–readers of Chinese. In T. H. Carr & B. A. Levy (Eds.), *Reading and its development: Component skills approaches* (pp. 375–421). New York: Academic Press.

Hintzman, D. L. (1988). Judgments of frequency and recognition memory in a multiple-trace memory model. *Psychological Review, 95,* 528–551.

Huang, J., Colombo, L., Carr, T. H., & Cao, Y. (2002, June). *Computational roles of temporo-parietal cortex in reading words.* Sendai, Japan: Human Brain Mapping.

Huang, J., Colombo, L., Carr, T. H., & Cao, Y. (2003, July). *Computational roles of temporo-parietal cortex in reading low frequency words.* Toronto, Quebec, Canada: International Society for Magnetic Resonance in Medicine.

Just, M. A., & Carpenter, P. A. (1987). *The psychology of reading and language comprehension.* Newton, MA: Allyn & Bacon.

Keele, S. W., & Summers, J. J. (1976). The structure of motor programs. In G. E. Stelmach (Ed.), *Motor control: Issues and trends* (pp. 109–142). New York: Academic Press.

Liberman, A. (1995). The relation of speech to reading and writing. In B. de Gelder & J. Morais (Ed.), *Speech and reading: A comparative approach* (pp. 15–32). Hove, England: Erlbaum.

Lockman, N. A. (2003, September 1). Reading is too vital for games: Educators' efforts to ease conflicts hurts neediest kids. *Lansing State Journal,* 6A.

Logan, G. D. (1988). Toward an instance theory of automatization. *Psychological Review, 95,* 583–598.

Manis, F. R., Szeszulski, P. A., Holt, L. K., & Graves, K. (1990). Variation in component word recognition and spelling skills among dyslexic children and normal readers. In T. H. Carr & B. A. Levy (Eds.), *Reading and its development: Component skills approaches* (pp. 207–259). San Diego, CA: Academic Press.

Masson, M. E. J. (1999). Interactive processes in word identification: Modeling context effects in a distributed memory system. In R. M. Klein & P. A. McMullen (Eds.), *Converging methods for understanding reading and dyslexia* (pp. 373–412). Cambridge, MA: MIT Press.

McCandliss, B. D., Bolger, D. J., & Schneider, W. (2000, November). *Habituating visual features versus cognitive codes: An event-related fMRI study of abstract word representation in extrastriate cortex.* Paper presented at the meeting of the Society for Neuroscience, San Francisco.

McCandliss, B. D., Posner, M. I., & Givon, T. (1997). Brain plasticity in learning visual words. *Cognitive Psychology, 33,* 88–110.

McCarthy, R., & Warrington, E. (1990). *Cognitive neuropsychology.* San Diego, CA: Academic Press.

Metcalfe, J. (1991). Recognition failure and the composite memory traced in CHARM. *Psychological Review, 98,* 529–553.

Metcalfe, J. (1997). Predicting syndromes of amnesia from a composite holographic associative recall/recognition model (CHARM). *Memory, 5,* 233–253.

Meyer, D. E., & Kieras, D. E. (1997). EPIC—A computational theory of executive cognitive processes and multiple-task performance: Part 1. Basic mechanisms. *Psychological Review, 104,* 3–65.

Morton, J. (1969). Interaction of information in word recognition. *Psychological Review, 76,* 165–178.

Neely, J. H. (1991). Semantic priming effects in visual word recognition: A selective review of current findings and theories. In D. Besner & G. W. Humphreys (Eds.), *Basic processes in reading: Visual word recognition* (pp. 264–336). Hillsdale, NJ: Erlbaum.

Newell, A. (1990). *Unified theories of cognition.* Cambridge, MA: Harvard University Press.

National Reading Panel. (2000). *Teaching children to read: An evidence-based assessment of the scientific research literature on reading and its implications for reading instruction.* Bethesda, MD: National Institute of Child Health and Human Development.

O'Reilly, R. C., & Munakata, Y. (2000). *Computational explorations in cognitive neuroscience.* Cambridge, MA: MIT Press.

Pashler, H. (1997). *The psychology of attention.* Cambridge, MA: MIT Press.

Pashler, H. (2000). Task switching and multitask performance. In S. Monsell & J. Driver (Eds.), *Control of cognitive processes: Attention and performance XVIII* (pp. 277–308). Cambridge, MA: MIT Press.

Perfetti, C. A., Goldman, S., & Hogaboam, T. (1979). Reading skill and the identification of words in discourse context. *Memory and Cognition, 7,* 273–282.

Petersen, S. E., Fox, P. T., Posner, M. I., Mintun, M., & Raichle, M. E. (1989). Positron emission tomographic studies of the processing of single words. *Journal of Cognitive Neuroscience, 1,* 153–170.

Petersen, S. E., Fox, P. T., Snyder, A. Z., & Raichle, M. E. (1990). Activation of extrastriate and frontal cortical areas by visual words and word-like stimuli. *Science, 249,* 1041–1044.

Plaut, D. C. (1999). Computational modeling of word reading, acquired dyslexia, and remediation. In R. M. Klein & P. A. McMullen (Eds.), *Converging methods for understanding reading and dyslexia* (pp. 339–372). Cambridge, MA: MIT Press.

Plaut, D. C., McClelland, J. L., Seidenberg, M. S., & Patterson, K. (1996). Understanding normal and impaired word reading: Computational principles in quasi-regular domains. *Psychological Review, 103,* 56–115.

Polk, T. A., & Farah, M. J. (2002). Functional MRI evidence for an abstract, not perceptual, word-form area. *Journal of Experimental Psychology: General, 131,* 65–72.

Posner, M. I. (1973). *Cognition.* San Francisco: Freeman.

Posner, M. I. (1985). *Chronometric explorations of mind* (2nd ed.). Hillsdale, NJ: Erlbaum.

Posner, M. I., & Carr, T. H. (1992). Lexical access and the brain: Anatomical constraints on models of word recognition. *American Journal of Psychology, 105,* 1–26.

Posner, M. I., & McCandliss, B. D. (1999). Brain circuitry during reading. In R. M. Klein & P. A. McMullen (Eds.), *Converging methods for understanding reading and dyslexia* (pp. 305–338). Cambridge, MA: MIT Press.

Posner, M. I., & Petersen, S. (1990). The attention system of the human brain. *Annual Reviews of Neuroscience, 13,* 25–42.

Posner, M. I., & Raichle, M. E. (1994). *Images of mind.* New York: Scientific American Books.

Posner, M. I., & Snyder, C. R. R. (1975). Attention and cognitive control. In R. L. Solso (Ed.), *Information processing and cognition: The Loyola Symposium* (pp. 55–82). Hillsdale, NJ: Erlbaum.

Proctor, R., & Dutta, A. (1995). *Skill acquisition and human performance.* Thousand Oaks, CA: Sage.

Rayner, K. (1999). What have we learned about eye movements during reading? In R. M. Klein & P. A. McMullen (Eds.), *Converging methods for understanding reading and dyslexia* (pp. 23–56). Cambridge, MA: MIT Press.

Rayner, K., Foorman, B. R., Perfetti, C. A., Pesetsky, D., & Seidenberg, M. S. (2002, March). How should reading be taught? *Scientific American,* 85–91.

Rayner, K., & Pollatsek, A. (1989). *The psychology of reading.* Englewood Cliffs, NJ: Prentice-Hall.

Rieben, L., & Perfetti, C. A. (1991). *Learning to read.* Hillsdale, NJ: Erlbaum.

Rozin, P. (1976). The evolution of intelligence and access to the cognitive unconscious. In J. M. Sprague & A. N. Epstein (Eds.), *Progess in psychobiology and physiological psychology.* New York: Academic Press.

Rozin, P., & Gleitman, L. R. (1977). The structure and acquisition of reading II: The reading process and acquisition of the alphabetic principle. In A. S. Reber & D. L. Scarborough (Eds.), *Toward a psychology of reading* (pp. 55–141). Hillsdale, NJ: Erlbaum.

Scarborough, D. L., Cortese, C., & Scarborough, H. S. (1977). Frequency and repetition effects in lexical memory. *Journal of Experimental Psychology: Human Perception and Performance, 3,* 1–17.

Schneider, W., & Shiffrin, R. M. (1977). Controlled and automatic human information processing: I. Detection, search, and attention. *Psychological Review, 84,* 1–66.

Shallice, T. (1988). *From neuropsychology to mental structure.* Cambridge, England: Cambridge University Press.

Shaywitz, B. A., Shaywitz, S. E., Pugh, K. R., Mencl, W. E., Fulbright, R. K., Skudlarski, P., et al. (2002). Disruption of posterior brain systems for reading in children with developmental dyslexia. *Biological Psychiatry, 52,* 101–110.

Shaywitz, S. E., Shaywitz, B. A., Pugh, K. R., Fulbright, R. K., Constable, R. T., Mencl, W. E., et al. (1998). Functional disruption in the organization of the brain for reading in dyslexia. *Proceedings of the National Academy of Sciences of the United States of America, 95,* 2636–2641. Cambridge, MA: MIT Press.

Sieroff, E., & Posner, M. I. (1988). Cueing spatial attention during processing of words and letter strings in normals. *Cognitive Neuropsychology, 5,* 451–472.

Simon, H. A. (1981). *The sciences of the artificial.* Cambridge, MA: MIT Press.

Simon, H. A., & Kaplan, C. A. (1989). Foundations of cognitive science. In M. I. Posner (Ed.), *Foundations of cognitive science* (pp. 1–47). Cambridge, MA: MIT Press.

Stanovich, K. E. (1980). Toward an interactive-compensatory model of individual differences in reading fluency. *Reading Research Quarterly, 16,* 32–71.

Sudevan, P., & Taylor, D. A. (1987). The cueing and priming of cognitive operations. *Journal of Experimental Psychology: Human Perception and Performance, 13,* 89–103.

Temple, E., Poldrack, R. A., Salidis, J., Deutsch, G. K., Tallal, P., Merzenich, M., et al. (2001). Disrupted neural responses to phonological and orthographic processing in dyslexic children: An fMRI study. *NeuroReport, 12,* 1–9.

Tinker, M. A. (1958). Recent studies of eye movements in reading. *Psychological Bulletin, 55,* 215–231.

Warrington, E. K., & Shallice, T. (1980). Word-form dyslexia. *Brain, 103,* 99–112.

Yantis, S. (2000). Goal-directed and stimulus-driven determinants of attentional control. In S. Monsell & J. Driver (Eds.), *Control of cognitive processes: Attention and performance XVIII* (pp. 73–104). Cambridge, MA: MIT Press.

Ziegler, J., Besson, M., Jacobs, A., Nazir, T. A., & Carr, T. H. (1997). Neural correlates of orthographic and semantic processing: A multitask comparison using event-related potentials. *Journal of Cognitive Neuroscience, 9,* 758–775.

Zorzi, M., Houghton, G., & Butterworth, B. (1998). Two routes or one in reading aloud? A connectionist dual process model. *Journal of Experimental Psychology: Human Perception and Performance, 24,* 1131–1161.

3

On the Role of Endogenous Orienting in the Inhibitory Aftermath of Exogenous Orienting

Raymond M. Klein

The concept of attention had a central role in the early days of psychological science, a role that was reflected in William James's metaphorical spotlight. The central region of the spotlight's beam illuminates well-defined contents, while its immediately surrounding region has only blurry potential for awareness and the remainder is, unless the beam is reoriented, entirely outside of awareness. Among the first scientific explorations of attention, Helmholtz demonstrated that without moving one's eyes, one could give priority to items in one quadrant of the visual field over those in the other quadrants. In spite of the objective methods such as those of Helmholtz, Donders, Ebbinghaus, and others, an overreliance on the introspective method pioneered by Wundt opened the door to a behaviorist reaction to what Watson labeled "subjective psychology" and, in the zeal to describe behavior in terms of observable stimuli and responses, concepts such as attention fell into disfavor and relative disuse.

By the late 1940s, chinks were appearing in the behaviorist armamentarium. In 1949, Hebb would say "We all know that attention and set exist, so we had better get the skeleton out of the closet and see what can be done with it." Cybernetics, human factors, and psycholinguistics (Lachman, Lachman, & Butterfield, 1979) helped fuel the cognitive revolution and clever experiments and integrative theories, such as those of Sperling (1960) and Broadbent (1958), helped return the concept of attention to the center stage of experimental psychology.

Model Task for Studying Spatial Orienting

It is one thing to acknowledge that a hypothetical construct, such as attention, might be important and worth studying objectively, it is quite another to develop a set of experimental tools for exploring such a concept in a fruitful and scientifically respectable way. In this regard, Michael Posner's paradigmatic contributions to contemporary psychology are legion. I believe there are several reasons for the huge following that some of his methods have garnered. No doubt their intuitive face validity is one important contributor. These paradigms hone into the core of a concept and the key questions that puzzle scholars about it. Indeed, the relatively tight connection between a paradigm and an elegant conceptual framework is a related attractive feature. This is nowhere clearer than with Posner's spatial cuing paradigm and his proposal of a beam of attention that is disengaged, moved, and engaged (Posner, Cohen, & Rafal, 1982) under voluntary control by the observer or reflexive control by an external event (Posner, 1980).

Another source of the popularity of Posner's paradigms is their basic simplicity. The letter-matching, dual-task probe and cuing paradigms, to mention a few, are easy to administer, and the data patterns tend to be robust and easy to understand. Indeed, Posner (1996) discusses the appeal of simplicity via analogy with the concept of a model system in neurobiology. A model system might be the simplest neural architecture that exhibits the target property. In psychology a model task is the simplest one that can define the operations of a particular cognitive system. When a scholar is interested in linking what we know about the mind based on behavioral data with the neural substrate that controls the behavior and implements the mind, it is the simple task or model system that holds the most promise. Some of the most fruitful neuro-scientific methods (single-unit recording; localizable reversible lesions; microdialysis) are too invasive to be used routinely with humans. Less invasive techniques such as functional magnetic resonance imaging (fMRI) and transcranial magnetic stimulation may, as their spatial resolution improves, begin to live up to their potential. Hence, simple tasks that can be performed by rats or monkeys have the obvious advantage over the more complex tasks that seem to showcase human cognitive abilities. Two powerful methods in cognitive neuroscience are to explore how it develops and how it breaks down when damaged. To be able to explore a construct, such as the orienting of attention, in the developing (infants, toddlers, children) or the damaged (individuals following strokes or cognitive loss because of disease) brain, it is essential to use tasks simple enough for these individuals with these brains to perform.

This chapter is about the orienting of attention, and in particular a consequence of orienting that appears to inhibit subsequent orienting. At the foundation of what we know and how we think about the orienting of attention and inhibition of return (IOR) are the contributions of Posner and his collaborators: the model task he pioneered, the empirical patterns produced with it, and the conceptual framework developed to explain these patterns.

These developments were rooted in work done in the 1970s, work that was originally presented at meetings of the Psychonomic Society and in a book chapter (Posner, Nissen, & Ogden, 1978). A broad audience was reached in 1980 when Posner published two seminal papers in the area of the orienting of attention: Posner (1980) and Posner, Davidson, and Snyder (1980).[1] Each of these papers presented experiments in which variants of the simple cueing

---

[1] A quick check using the Web of Science (October 2003) reveals that between them these two papers (Posner, 1980; Posner et al., 1980) had been cited more than 2000 times since 1989.

paradigm illustrated in Figure 3.1 were used to reveal the nature and under-lying mechanism of shifts of attention in space. Two enduring ideas ensued from these papers. One is the spotlight metaphor alluded to above that was vigorously readvanced by Posner, Snyder, and Davidson (1980). The other is the 2 × 2 classification scheme (Figure 3.2; see Klein, Kingstone, & Pontefract, 1992 for what I believe is the first use of such a figure) wherein we can distin-guish what is being oriented, the eyes or attention, which Posner (1980) called overt and covert orienting, respectively and whether orienting is controlled by the stimulus or by the observer, which Posner referred to as exogenous and endogenous control, respectively. Although not having precisely the same meanings as exogenous and endogenous, the terms, bottom-up and top-down are often used interchangeably with them.

Following a central stimulus (e.g., an arrow) that signals the likely location of the upcoming target and immediately following an uninformative peripheral event (e.g., luminance increase), performance at the cued location is enhanced relative to an otherwise equivalent uncued location. Interestingly, performance at the cued location is often better than if there had been a neutral cue, and performance at the uncued location is often worse than if there had been a neutral cue. When the terminology introduced by Posner and Snyder (1975) is applied to these differences, they are referred to as the benefits and costs (respectively) of orienting (see middle of Figure 3.1).

Discovery of Inhibition of Return

It was in Cohen's dissertation that an inhibitory aftermath of exogenous covert orienting was uncovered and thoroughly explored. These findings became widely known after they were presented by Posner at Attention and Perfor-mance X, and later appeared in a chapter in the conference proceedings volume (Posner & Cohen, 1984).[2] The key finding is obtained when the model task is combined with uninformative peripheral cues and the cue-target stimulus onset asynchrony (SOA) is parametrically manipulated.

At the short SOAs, there is facilitation of target processing in the vicinity of the cue. This early benefit is nearly universally attributed to the reflexive capture of attention by the cue. In Posner and Cohen's study (1984) two different methods were used to ensure that, once so captured, attention would not remain at the cued location: either targets were more likely to be presented at fixation than at the peripheral locations, or following the peripheral cue, a second cue was presented at fixation. Essentially, the first method relies on endogenous control by the observer, while the second relies on exogenous control by the stimulus, to return attention to fixation. In both cases, the early facilitation reversed and at longer SOAs the time to detect stimuli was delayed at the originally cued location. At longer intervals, the initial pattern reverses and the time to detect signals becomes slower at the originally cued location. This

---

[2]A quick check using the Web of Science (October 2003) reveals that this seminal paper (Posner & Cohen, 1984) had been cited more than 600 times since 1989.

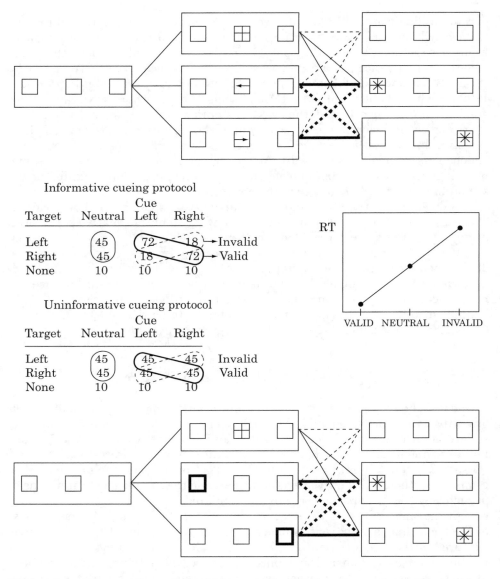

Figure 3.1. Two paradigms for exploring orienting. Endogenous cueing is illustrated in the upper flowchart where the events on a trial are presented from left to right. The lines connecting the boxes illustrate the possible state transitions. The probabilities of the different transitions are shown below in the table labeled "Informative Cueing Protocol." Exogenous cueing is illustrated in the lower flowchart, and the probabilities of transitions for purely exogenous cueing are shown in the table labeled "Uninformative Cueing Protocol." In both protocols a fixation display is followed by a cue display and sometime later by the presentation of a target (asterisk, in this example). In some studies, peripheral cues that elicit orienting exogenously are combined with the informative cueing probabilities in a hybrid protocol. The typical pattern of results is illustrated in the inset in the middle of the figure. When the target calls for a simple or choice manual or verbal response, and no eye movements are executed, the cue elicits covert orienting. When the target calls for a target-directed saccade, the cue activates or prepares overt orienting. In both procedures trials with neutral cues are indicated by thin solid lines between the cue and target arra; trials with valid cues are indicated by thick solid lines; trials with invalid cues are indicated by thick dotted lines; and catch trials are indicated by thin dashed lines. Copyright by Raymond M. Klein.

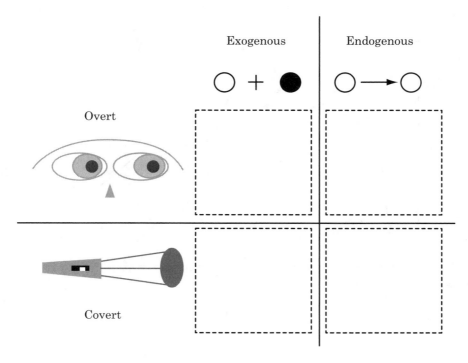

Figure 3.2. A 2 × 2 matrix is used to illustrate the distinction between overt and covert orienting and their control by exogenous and endogenous mechanisms. Data from Klein, Kingston, and Pontefract (1992).

inferior performance at the originally attended location was subsequently called IOR (Posner et al., 1985). IOR was not merely a name for the empirical pattern, but a shorthand for its explanation: After leaving a peripherally cued location, the beam of attention was inhibited from returning there.

Characteristics of Inhibition of Return

Much has been learned about the properties of IOR since its discovery in 1984.

Time Course

The data from more than 20 IOR studies in which the cue-target SOA was varied was summarized by Samuel and Kat (2003). Superimposed on their meta-analysis, shown in Figure 3.3, is the data from Posner and Cohen's time course study. This figure reveals how well Posner and Cohen's pattern has stood up to the test of time and methodological variation that characterizes the studies included in Samuel and Kat's review. It is worth noting that in many subsequent studies of IOR in adult participants, IOR was observed without either of the methods, referred to above, that Posner and Cohen (1984)

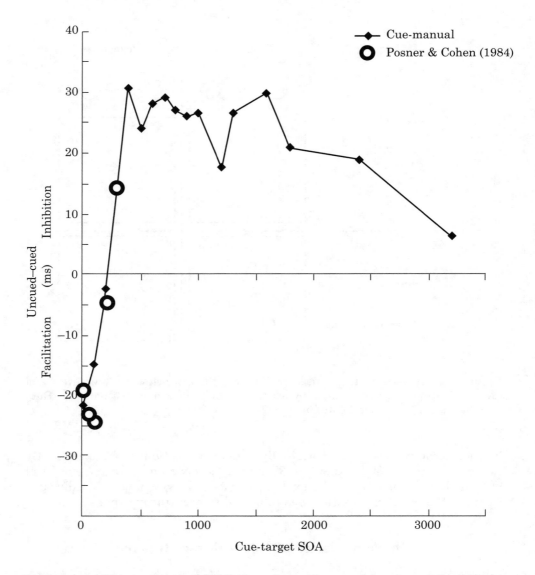

Figure 3.3. The time course of IOR in studies using a peripheral cue followed by a simple manual detection task (solid line). The time course data of Posner and Cohen (1984) is shown as circles. SOA = stimulus onset asynchrony. Copyright by Raymond M. Klein.

used to ensure that attention did not remain at the cued location. Apparently, in normal adults, the equal likelihood of targets appearing at the two peripheral locations is sufficient to motivate disengagement from the peripheral cue and the return of attention to fixation or to some other neutral state. Quite importantly, IOR is relatively long lasting and in some studies has been seen at cue-target SOAs as long as 3 seconds.

There is variability, however, in the time course of the appearance of IOR; variability that is associated with task as well as individual differences. This variability, which is the subject of later sections of this chapter, will be explained using concepts advanced by Posner and others to help understand the orienting of attention.

Spatial Coding

By interposing an eye movement between the cue and target, Posner and Cohen (1984; see also Maylor & Hockey, 1985) demonstrated that IOR was not retinotopic, but rather coded in environmental coordinates. Tipper, Driver, and Weaver (1991) later demonstrated, by moving the displayed objects after one of them had been cued, that IOR could be tagged to objects. The degree to which IOR may be tagged to objects or locations seems to depend on the degree to which the objects in a scene are integrated (Tipper, Jordan, & Weaver, 1999). When it is elicited, object-based IOR is quite robust, as it has been shown to survive occlusion of a cued object when it moves behind a visual barrier (Yi, Kim, & Chun, 2003).

Whatever the frame of reference in which IOR is primarily coded, the effect itself appears to be graded: reaction times are slowest at the cued location and they decrease monotonically with increasing distance from the cued location (Bennett & Pratt, 2001; Maylor & Hockey, 1985; Snyder, Schmidt, & Kingstone, 2001).

Recent findings from my laboratory (Klein, Christie, & Morris, in press) illustrate this gradient effect. We presented cues simultaneously at from one to four out of eight possible equicentric locations. After a 200 ms SOA, the center was brightened and then after an additional 200 ms, a target, requiring a simple detection response, was presented while we monitored eye position to ensure that covert rather than overt orienting was engaged. The results from trials with a single cue are shown in Figure 3.4 (left panel). This gradient is similar to that reported previously by other investigators (Dorris, Taylor, Klein, & Munoz, 1999; Maylor & Hockey, 1985; Pratt, Spalek, & Bradshaw, 1999). We obtained a striking finding on trials when more than one location was cued and the center of gravity of the cue was substantially removed from the fixation (or the net vector of the cue was substantially greater than zero, see Figure 3.4, right panel). Whether or not the target fell on a cued or uncued location had only a small impact on performance. As with a single cue, the vector difference between the target and the cue's net vector gave rise to a 40 ms gradient. The two gradients (following a single cue or simultaneous multiple cues) have nearly identical slopes. On the assumption that the oculomotor system is activated, via population coding, to shift gaze in the net direction of the cue, this finding supports oculomotor activation as the critical causal factor in generating IOR (see next section).

After IOR has been generated at one location or tagged to one object, is the inhibition maintained or lost when subsequent events generate tags at additional locations? Tipper, Weaver, and Watson (1996) demonstrated that whereas IOR at previously cued locations declines as subsequent locations are

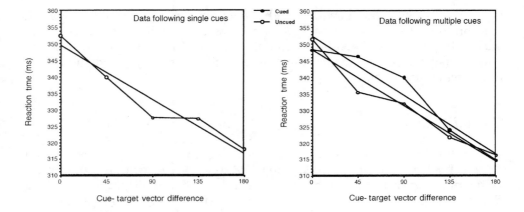

Figure 3.4.   Reaction time to detect targets presented in eight equally spaced locations around fixation as a function of the angular difference between the net vector of the target and a cue composed of one to four simultaneously presented elements at possible target locations. Data following a single cue are shown in the left panel. Data following multiple-simultaneous cues (with two, three, or four elements) are shown in the right panel. Data from cues with a net vector of zero (e.g., a cue with elements at 90° and 270°) or close to zero have been excluded. From Klein, Christie, and Morris (in press). Copyright by Raymond M. Klein.

cued, IOR can nevertheless be maintained at multiple locations. Snyder and Kingstone (2000; see also Dodd, Castel, & Pratt; 2003) found significant IOR at cued locations after up to four subsequent locations had been cued; and Paul and Tipper (2003) demonstrated a greater capacity for the storage of inhibitory tags when objects, rather than locations in empty space, had been cued.

Cause and Effect

Taylor and Klein's (1998) review of IOR points to the importance of distinguishing the conditions necessary and sufficient for causing IOR from the effects on processing that are engaged once IOR has been generated. Evidence strongly converges on oculomotor activation as the cause of IOR. Stimuli that directly activate the oculomotor system generate IOR whether or not they are the target of an eye movement. Alone, this finding is ambiguous: Either the stimulus, the oculomotor activation or the exogenous orienting of attention might be the causal agent. However, Rafal, Calabresi, Brennan, and Sciolto (1989) demonstrated that endogenous oculomotor preparation, once canceled, also led to IOR. In this condition there was no asymmetrical peripheral stimulation. Some scholars might assert, in light of the intimate linkage between eye movements and attention, that this finding is consistent with the orienting of attention being the cause of IOR. It must be kept in mind, however, that IOR is not found after an endogenous shift of attention has been canceled. Therefore, to be viable this view requires a caveat based on the distinction between endogenous and exogenous control of attention: exogenous, but not endogenous, orienting of attention may be the cause of IOR.

Various effects of IOR have been proposed, including inhibition of perception, attention (Reuter-Lorenz, Jha, & Rosenquist, 1996), and action. Researchers have also proposed that IOR disconnects stimuli from their dominant actions (Fuentes, Vivas, & Humphreys, 1999) and that IOR is a bias against responding toward the originally cued location (Ivanoff & Klein, 2001; Klein & Taylor, 1994). If IOR delayed sensory/perceptual processing, then it would be expected to shift the point of subjective simultaneity (PSS) in a temporal order judgment task or to generate illusory line motion (ILM) toward the inhibited location. Studies that have explicitly tested for these effects failed to find any evidence that IOR delays sensory/perceptual processing (Klein, Schmidt, & Müller, 1998). Even if there is no delay in arrival times, there is, nevertheless, good evidence that IOR does have deleterious effects on perceptual processing. This has been observed using a measure of perceptual sensitivity (d') in a signal detection paradigm (Handy, Jha, & Mangun, 1999), and using a dual-stream rapid serial visual presentation (RSVP) task (Klein & Dick, 2002). On the other hand, Ivanoff and Klein (2001) recently provided strong support for Klein and Taylor's suggestion that IOR was characterized by a bias against responding to stimuli at the originally cued location. This was seen in the relatively low false alarm rate when no-go stimuli were presented at the originally cued location. If the orienting of attention is construed as a response, then it seems quite reasonable to assume that the bias carries over to attentional orienting and therefore that the effects on perception may be mediated by delayed shifts of attention to targets at the originally cued location. That said, the degree to which IOR is primarily attentional or primarily action-based may depend on the degree to which eye movements are activated or suppressed during the experiment (Taylor & Klein, 2000; see also Kingstone & Pratt, 1999).

Function of Inhibition of Return:
Encourage Attention to the New

From the rich empirical foundation they established, Posner and Cohen (1984) hypothesized that the function of IOR is to bias orienting toward novel and away from previously inspected object and locations. During search for targets that do not pop out there would be an advantage to keep track of which objects and locations have already been inspected. Considering Posner and Cohen's functional interpretation, I suggested that IOR might be an inhibitory tagging system that facilitated search and other foraging behaviors (Klein, 1988). To test this proposal I presented simple detection probes immediately after observers had performed either a popout or a difficult (serial) search and in locations that had been empty in the search array (off-probes) or in the locations of displayed items (on-probes). If IOR were generated whenever attention is removed from one distractor in order to inspect another one, then on-probe reaction time (RT) should be greater than off-probe RT following serial but not popout search. This is the pattern reported by Klein (1988) and later replicated and extended by Müller and von Mühlenen (2000) and Takeda and Yagi (2000), whose studies demonstrated the importance of probing for IOR with the search array still present. Using oculomotor search for a camouflaged target (Waldo from the *Where's Waldo* series of books by Martin Hanford), Klein and MacInnes (1999) confirmed the importance of retaining the scene while measuring IOR with saccadic reaction time during a search episode and MacInnes and Klein (2003) extended this finding to probes presented after a search episode. Using a paradigm in which a sequence of inspections (accomplished with shifts in gaze) is controlled by the experimenter, McCarley, Wang, Kramer, Irwin, and Peterson (2003) demonstrated that IOR is not parasitic upon endogenous preparatory behavior, but rather that previous orienting itself biases subsequent orienting (see also MacInnes & Klein, 2003).

It is worth noting that several of the characteristics described in the previous section are necessary for IOR to serve the function of a foraging facilitator as envisioned by Klein (1988):

1. The inhibitory tags must be local and graded.
2. They must be coded in environmental coordinates, so they can be preserved when people move their eyes.
3. They must be coded in object coordinates, so they can be preserved when the objects people inspect move.
4. They must last long enough (several seconds) to operate during typical search episodes.
5. It must be possible to tag or inhibit several objects/locations at the same time.

Neural Implementation

A variety of evidence converges on an important role for the superior colliculus (SC) in generating IOR. IOR is reduced in individuals with damage to the SC (Posner, Rafal, Choate, & Vaughan, 1985; Sapir, Soroker, Berger, & Henik, 1999); it is larger for temporal hemi-field stimuli (e.g., Rafal, Calabresi, Brennan, & Sciolto, 1989) which has a stronger SC representation; it occurs in infants for whom SC, but not the cortex is developed (Valenza, Simion, & Umilta, 1994; see next section); it occurs in blindsight patients, who have lesions to V1 but intact subcortical pathways (Danziger, Fendrich, & Rafal, 1997); and it interacts with the gap effect (Hunt & Kingstone, 2003), which is mediated by disinhibition of oculomotor programming in the SC (Munoz & Wurtz, 1993). These lines of evidence led me to encourage Muñoz and his colleagues to determine whether the monkey showed IOR at a behavioral level (Dorris et al., 1999), so that we could record from SC neurons while IOR was being generated (Dorris, Klein, Everling, & Muñoz, 2002). On the one hand, we found that the sensory responses of sensorimotor neurons in the intermediate layer of the SC were reduced for targets presented at a previously cued location. On the other, when we produced a saccade by stimulating the SC through the recording electrode, saccades elicited by stimulating the cued region were initiated faster than those elicited by stimulating the opposite, uncued region. Together these results suggest that the SC itself is not inhibited, but rather inputs reaching the SC are already reduced in amplitude.

This implication converges with other findings pointing to cortical mechanisms as involved in preserving the inhibition over time and coding it in representational frames (environmental and object) that is beyond the capability of the SC. For example, object-based IOR is not preserved when a cued object moves between the left and right visual fields in a patient whose corpus callosum has been severed (Tipper et al., 1997) and damage to the right parietal lobe interferes with the environmental (but not with the location) coding of IOR (Sapir, Hayes, Henik, Danziger, & Rafal, 2004).

Development: Infant Studies of Inhibition of Return

Some of the most interesting evidence about the neural circuitry that may implement IOR comes from studies of infants. Working with Posner and his colleague, Rothbart, Johnson generated the first studies on the early development of IOR (Johnson, 1994; Johnson, Posner, & Rothbart, 1994; Johnson & Tucker, 1996). This work was designed to test hypotheses about the development of orienting in infancy based on the relative rates of development of neural systems (Johnson, 1990) known to mediate orienting in the adult (see Figure 3.5).

Subsequent studies of orienting in infants have, for the most part, confirmed Johnson's predictions. To elicit the orienting that might generate IOR in infants, two methods have been used. In the covert method, a peripheral stimulus is presented so briefly that a saccade is not initiated to foveate it. In the overt method, a peripheral stimulus onset is accompanied by offset of fixation, and the subsequent saccade to the peripheral stimulus is followed by a central event to return gaze to fixation. All studies of orienting in infants have used overt orienting, or saccadic eye movements, to measure the effects of prior covert or overt orienting. Rather remarkably, following overt orienting, newborns show IOR in the form of slower saccades in the direction of the immediately preceding saccade (Simion, Valenza, Umilta, & Dalla, 1995; Valenza, Simion, & Umilta, 1994). Because the SC is relatively fully operational in newborns, this observation is consistent with evidence suggesting that the SC is implicated in causing IOR (Rafal et al., 1989). SC activity is regulated by inhibitory projections through the basal ganglia and substantia nigra. According to Johnson (1990) this pathway, which comes into play at around one month of age, encourages obligatory attention and response repetition or perseveration (Johnson, Posner, & Rothbart, 1994). A tendency to repeat the previous response or previously activated response will work against IOR, hence the IOR that is seen in newborns is absent in 1- to 2-month olds (Butcher, Kalverboer, & Geuze, 1999; Johnson, 1994; Johnson & Tucker, 1996). With the subsequent development of frontocortical systems, control over the inhibitory subcortical projections to the SC from the basal ganglia/substantia nigra is achieved, and overt IOR reappears (Clohessy, Posner, Rothbart, & Vecera, 1991; Harman, Posner, Rothbart, & Thomas-Thropp, 1994; Johnson & Tucker,

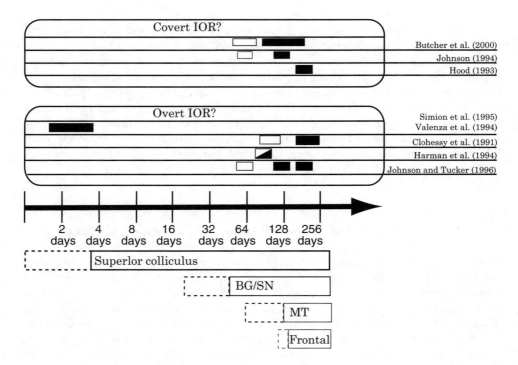

Figure 3.5. The relative time course of maturation of different systems involved in orienting as discussed by Johnson (1990) is shown by the rectangles below the time line. Studies finding IOR (black rectangles) and failing to find IOR (open rectangles) in infants of different ages and using covert (no eye movement to the cue) and overt (eye movements to the cue) orienting as the causal event are shown above the time line. The split rectangle of Harman and colleagues reflects that IOR was obtained when target eccentricities were 10° but not when they were 30°. IOR = inhibition of return. Copyright by Raymond M. Klein.

1996) and covert IOR begins to emerge (Butcher et al., 1999; Hood, 1993; Johnson, 1994).

Variability in the Time Course of Inhibition of Return: Task Differences

In 1997, Lupianez and colleagues varied, in an exceptionally thorough and well-designed study, whether the observer was required to merely detect a target or make a two-choice discrimination about a nonspatial attribute (color) of a target. This was the first study to clearly demonstrate that the time course of IOR's appearance might depend on task factors: IOR emerged between 100 and 400 ms when the task was detection, and between 400 and 700 ms when the task was a two-choice color discrimination. In a recent review of IOR (Klein, 2000), I proposed an attentional control setting theory for this variation. According to this theory,

1. The observer sets the level of attention to be allocated to a target to perform the task (e.g., low intensity for a simple detection task; high intensity for a difficult discrimination).
2. Attentional control settings (ACSs) cannot be changed rapidly; therefore, the ACS put in place to process the target will apply to the cue.
3. The more intensely attention is allocated to the cue, the longer attention will dwell on it and therefore, the later inhibition will be observed.

As noted in Klein (2000), IOR may begin with the cue but may not be seen in performance because the facilitation due to attention is greater than the inhibition that are present simultaneously (for behavioral evidence supporting this possibility, see Berlucchi, Chelazzi, & Tassinari, 2000). Alternatively, IOR may not begin until attention is withdrawn from the cued location. Either way, IOR may not be seen in a behavioral measure until attention is withdrawn from the cued location. Thus, the finding of early IOR when a manipulation is used that encourages the rapid withdrawal of attention from a peripherally cued location (see Danziger & Kingstone, 1999) cannot distinguish between these two alternative construals of when IOR actually begins. The aforementioned theory is about variation in the appearance of IOR because of the timing of attentional disengagement from the cue. It is mute on the issue whether IOR actually begins when the cue is presented or when attention is removed from it. Neuroscientific evidence shows that some levels of processing are inhibited even while attention remains at the cued location to facilitate target processing (see Klein, 2004; Klein, Muñoz, Dorris, & Taylor, 2001) thus supporting the view that IOR, at least at some levels of processing, begins with the cue.

The idea, implicit in Posner and Cohen's methodological choices (1984, see p. 4), that IOR will not appear until attention is voluntarily removed from the cue was tested recently (Klein, Castel, & Pratt, 2004) by loading up verbal working memory.[3] Loading up working memory should interfere with the endogenous control of attention (see Jonides, 1981; Bleckley, Durso, Crutchfield, Engle, & Khanna, 2004) and consequently, if the ACS theory is correct, should delay removal of attention from the cued location and delay the appearance of IOR. This is precisely what we found.

Extension From Task Differences to Individual Differences

If the ACS theory of the time course of the appearance of IOR were correct, then time course differences linked to task differences might also generalize to individual differences. In particular, individuals with underdeveloped or degraded voluntary control over attention should be less likely to, or slower to, disengage attention from an uninformative peripheral cue—unless disengagement is accomplished exogenously via a second cue at fixation.

---

[3] We chose verbal working memory because previous research (Castel, Pratt, & Craik, 2003) had demonstrated that once caused, a spatial working memory task interfered with IOR while a verbal memory load did not.

Examination of the literature reveals apparently puzzling data that support this proposal.

A good starting point this discussion was a lifespan study of IOR by Brodeur and Enns (1997). Although infants and young adults show IOR, Brodeur and Enns's 6- to 10-year-olds did not. MacPherson, Moore, and myself (MacPherson, Klein, & Moore, 2003) thought that this apparent paradox might be because of a failure of the children to disengage their attention from the uninformative peripheral cue. Therefore, we tested young (5- to 10-year-old) and older (11- to 17-year-old) children on a simple detection task with SOAs ranging from 120 ms to 780 ms. We used two different cuing procedures: single peripheral cue and a double cue procedure in which there is a fixation cue after the peripheral cue and before the target. As Figure 3.6a illustrates, our findings with the single cue procedure replicate those of Brodeur and Enns. Children between the ages of 5 and 11 do not seem to show IOR in this paradigm. The puzzling aspect of this finding is that the infant data (Figure 3.5) suggests that by 6 months infants are showing both covert and overt IOR much like adults. It seems unlikely, then, that 5- to 11-year-olds would not show IOR. With the double cue procedure, we found equal if not greater IOR in the young than in the older children (though its appearance was delayed). Thus it is not the case that 5- to 10-year-olds have an IOR deficiency. Quite the contrary, if there is a deficiency it is a failure to endogenously disengage attention from an uninformative cue.

Brodeur and Enns (1997) found a similar result when they compared elderly participants with younger controls: the older participants did not seem to show IOR at any SOA. In a similar study with an increased range of SOAs, Castel, Chasteen, Scialfa, and Pratt (2003) did find significant IOR in the elderly but, consistent with Brodeur and Enns, the appearance of IOR was substantially delayed in this group (see Figure 3.6b). In much the same way that we did (MacPherson et al., 2003) with children, Faust and Balota (1997) demonstrated that any group differences in the magnitude of IOR that might exist between normal participants and the elderly could be normalized by using a double cue procedure.

There is at least one patient group that is thought to have deficient endogenous control mechanisms: people suffering from schizophrenia. The data from two studies comparing IOR in individuals with schizophrenia with control participants are presented in Figure 3.6c. This figure also shows a dramatic delay, among individuals with schizophrenia, in the time at which IOR becomes apparent after an uninformative peripheral cue. When individuals with schizophrenia and controls are compared using both the single and double cue procedures the time course difference apparent in Figure 3.6c is reduced but not eliminated.

Implications

In a typical search episode, the target is already present in an array whose items are inspected, sometimes one-by-one, until the target is found. In such a situation the target is not a new stimulus whose appearance might cause

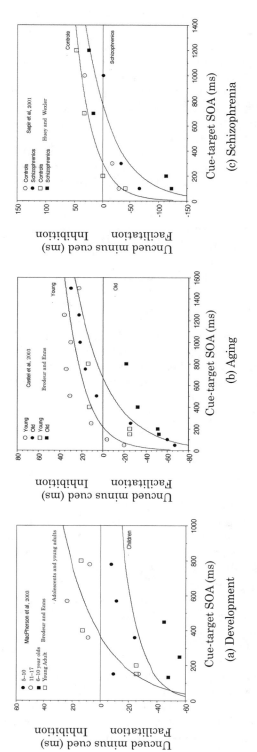

Figure 3.6. Cueing effects (facilitation is negative; inhibition positive) for three special populations (unfilled symbols) and comparison groups (filled symbols) are plotted as a function of cue-target SOA. For each, panel studies were selected if uninformative peripheral cues, more than two cue-target SOAs, and a single cue (with no cue back to fixation) had been used. (a) Data from two studies (Brodeur & Enns, 1997; MacPherson et al., 2003) comparing children between the ages of 5 and 11 and either adolescents (MacPherson et al., 2003) or college students (Brodeur & Enns, 1997); (b) data from two studies (Brodeur & Enns, 1997; Castel et al., 2003) comparing elderly with young normal controls; (c) data from two studies (Huey & Wexler, 1994; Sapir, Henik, Dobrusin, & Hochman, 2001) comparing individuals with schizophrenia and normal controls. Note that Castel and colleagues tested at longer SOAs than are shown in panel (b), but to maintain consistency with the other panels, data from these longer SOAs are not shown here. SOA = stimulus onset asynchrony. Copyright by Raymond M. Klein.

attention to reflexively disengage from the last attended (e.g., invalidly cued) location. Hence—if IOR plays the foraging facilitator role I have attributed to it, individual differences in the ability or tendency to disengage from an array element that is being attended, such as those illustrated in Figure 3.6, ought to be associated with slower search rates. It is therefore suggestive that visual search in the elderly shows a steeper slope than in younger participants. As suggested by D'Aloisio and Klein (1990) and others, the elderly may suffer from a difficulty disengaging attention. In that case, there would be an increased delay or dwell time following the inspection of each array item. Of course, because the elderly show RT delays in almost all tasks, it is possible to explain their slow search without making this assumption; nevertheless, this possibility does not rule out a mediating role for slower disengagement by the elderly.

It, nevertheless, remains to be shown that there is a causal relationship between the time course of IOR's appearance and search rate. One suggestive piece of evidence comes from separate studies of the magnitude of IOR and search efficiency in individuals suffering from autism. If greater IOR meant more accurate storage of the inhibitory tags that might discourage reinspections during search, then greater IOR would be associated with shallower serial search slopes. O'Riorden, Plaisted, Driver, and Baron-Cohen (2001) demonstrated that autistic children are more efficient at serial search (that is they show shallower slopes) than normal children. In her PhD dissertation, Brian (2000), demonstrated that high functioning autistic adults showed greater IOR than control participants. What is needed to test this causal linkage with confidence is the collection of evidence about the time course and magnitude of IOR and search efficiency in the same groups of individuals.

Conclusion

I began this chapter by highlighting the model task Posner developed for studying the orienting of attention. Discovered and well-characterized by Posner and Cohen (1984), IOR is both an empirical pattern observed with this model task and a theoretical description (Posner et al., 1985) that has stood the test of time. Even though it is generally accepted that subcortical circuitry involving the SC is necessary for the generation of the inhibitory tags that Posner and Cohen (1984) speculated might serve as a novelty-seeking mechanism, individual differences (whether associated with differences in development, aging, disease or brain damage) in the appearance (or time course of the appearance) of IOR may not be rooted in this subcortical circuitry. As Posner and Cohen (1984) astutely realized, IOR may not be observed unless attention is withdrawn from the location or object toward which it had originally been attracted. It is a testament to the power of Posner's paradigm and the ideas that it spawned that by the end this chapter, these ideas have been used to help explain individual variability in the manifestation of IOR in terms of individual differences in the likelihood and speed of voluntary control of attentional disengagement (Posner, Cohen, & Rafal, 1982) from an exogenously attended location.

References

Bennett, P. J., & Pratt, J. (2001). The spatial distribution of inhibition of return. *Psychological Science, 12,* 76–80.

Berlucchi, G., Chelazzi, L., & Tassinari, G. (2000). Volitional covert orienting to a peripheral cue does not suppress cue-induced inhibition of return. *Journal of Cognitive Neuroscience, 12,* 648–663.

Bleckley, M. K., Durso, F. T., Crutchfield, J. M., Engle, R. W., & Khanna, M. M. (2004). Individual differences in working memory capacity predict visual attention allocation. *Psychological Bulletin and Review, 10,* 884–889.

Brian, J. (2000). *Inhibition in autism: Evidence of excessive inhibition-of-return.* Unpublished doctoral dissertation, York University, Toronto, Quebec, Canada.

Broadbent, D. E. (1958). *Perception and communication.* Oxford, England: Pergamon Press.

Brodeur, D. A., & Enns, J. T. (1997). Covert visual orienting across the lifespan. *Canadian Journal of Experimental Psychology, 51,* 20–35.

Butcher, P. R., Kalverboer, A. F., & Geuze, R. H. (1999). Inhibition of return in very young infants: A longitudinal study. *Infant Behavior and Development, 22,* 303–319.

Castel, A. D., Chasteen, A. L., Scialfa, C. T., & Pratt, J. (2003). Adult age differences in the time course of inhibition of return. *Journal of Gerontology, 58,* 256–259.

Castel, A. D., Pratt, J., & Craik, F. I. M. (2003). The role of spatial working memory in inhibition of return: Evidence from divided attention tasks. *Perception and Psychophysics, 65,* 970–981.

Clohessy, A. B., Posner, M. I., Rothbart, M. K., & Vecera, S. P. (1991). The development of inhibition of return in early infancy. *Journal of Cognitive Neuroscience, 3,* 345–350.

D'Aloisio, A., & Klein, R. M. (1990). Aging and the deployment of visual attention. In J. Enns (Ed.), *The development of attention: Research and theory* (pp. 447–466). North Holland: Amsterdam.

Danziger, S., Fendrich, R., & Rafal, R. (1997). Inhibitory tagging of locations in the blind field of hemianopic patients. *Consciousness and Cognition, 6,* 291–307.

Danziger, S., & Kingstone, A. (1999). Unmasking the inhibition of return phenomenon. *Perception and Psychophysics, 61,* 1024–1037.

Dodd, M. D., Castel, A. D., & Pratt, J. (2003). Inhibition of return with rapid serial shifts of attention: Implications for memory and visual search. *Perception and Psychophysics, 65,* 1126–1135.

Dorris, M. C., Klein, R. M., Everling, S., & Muñoz, D. P. (2002). Contribution of the primate superior colliculus to inhibition of return. *Journal of Cognitive Neuroscience, 14,* 1256–1263.

Dorris, M. C., Taylor, T., Klein, R. M., & Muñoz, D. P. (1999). Influence of previous visual stimulus or saccade on saccadic reaction times in monkey. *Journal of Neurophysiology, 81,* 2429–2436.

Faust, M. E., & Balota, D. A. (1997). Inhibition of return and visuospatial attention in healthy older adults and individuals with dementia of the Alzheimer type. *Neuropsychology, 11,* 13–29.

Fuentes, L. J., Vivas, A. B., & Humphreys, G. W. (1999). Inhibitory tagging of stimulus properties in inhibition of return: Effects on semantic priming and flanker interference. *Quarterly Journal of Experimental Psychology, 52A,* 149–164.

Handy, T. C., Jha, A. P., & Mangun, G. R. (1999). Promoting novelty in vision: Inhibition of return modulates perceptual-level processing. *Psychological Science, 10,* 157–161.

Harman, C., Posner, M. I., Rothbart, M. K., & Thomas-Thropp, L. (1994). Development of orienting to locations and objects in human infants. *Canadian Journal of Experimental Psychology, 48,* 301–318.

Hood, B. (1993). Inhibition of return produced by covert shifts of visual attention in 6-month-old infants. *Infant Behavior and Development, 16,* 245–254.

Huey, E. D., & Wexler, B. E. (1994). Abnormalities in rapid, automatic aspects of attention in schizophrenia: blunted inhibition of return. *Schizophrenia Research, 14,* 57–63.

Hunt, A. R., & Kingstone, A. (2003). Inhibition of return: Dissociating attentional and oculomotor components. *Journal of Experimental Psychology: Human Perception and Performance, 29,* 1068–1074.

Ivanoff, J., & Klein, R. M. (2001). The presence of a nonresponding effector increases inhibition of return. *Psychonomic Bulletin and Review, 8,* 307–314.

Johnson, M. H. (1990). Cortical maturation and the development of visual attention in early infancy. *Journal of Cognitive Neuroscience, 2,* 81–95.

Johnson, M. H. (1994). Visual attention and the control of eye movements in early infancy. In C. Umiltà & M. Moscovitch (Eds.), *Attention and performance XV: Conscious and unconscious processing* (pp. 291–310). Cambridge, MA: MIT Press.

Johnson, M. H., Posner, M. I., & Rothbart, M. K. (1994). Facilitation of saccades toward a covertly attended location in early infancy. *Psychological Science, 5,* 90–93.

Johnson, M. H., & Tucker, L. A. (1996). The development and temporal dynamics of spatial orienting in infants. *Journal of Experimental Child Psychology, 63,* 171–188.

Jonides, J. (1981). Voluntary versus automatic control over the mind's eye's movements. In J. B. Long & A. D. Baddeley (Eds.), *Attention and performance* (Vol. 9, pp. 187–203). Hillsdale, NJ: Erlbaum.

Kingstone, A., & Pratt, J. (1999). Inhibition of return is composed of attentional and oculomotor processes. *Perception and Psychophysics, 61,* 1046–1054.

Klein, R. M. (1988). Inhibitory tagging system facilitates visual search. *Nature, 334,* 430–431.

Klein, R. M. (2000). Inhibition of return. *Trends in Cognitive Sciences, 4,* 138–147.

Klein, R. M. (2004). Orienting and inhibition of return. In M. S. Gazzaniga (Ed.), *The newest cognitive neurosciences* (3rd ed.). Cambridge, MA: MIT Press.

Klein, R. M., Castel, A., & Pratt, J. (2004). *The effects of memory load on the timecourse of inhibition of return.* Manuscript in preparation.

Klein, R. M., Christie, J. J., & Morris, E. (in press). Vector averaging of inhibition of return. *Psychonomic Bulletin and Review.*

Klein, R. M., & Dick, B. (2002). Temporal dynamics of reflexive attention shifts: A dual-stream rapid serial visual presentation exploration. *Psychological Science, 13,* 176–179.

Klein, R. M., Kingstone, A., & Pontefract, A. (1992). Orienting of visual attention. In K. Rayner (Ed.), *Eye movements and visual cognition: Scene perception and reading* (pp. 46–67). New York: Springer-Verlag.

Klein, R. M., & MacInnes, W. J. (1999). Inhibition of return is a foraging facilitator in visual search. *Psychological Science, 10,* 346–352.

Klein, R. M., Muñoz, D. P., Dorris, M. C., & Taylor, T. L. (2001). Inhibition of return in monkey and man. In C. Folk & B. Gibson (Eds.), *Attraction, distraction, and action: Multiple perspectives on attention capture* (pp. 27–47). Amsterdam: Elsevier.

Klein, R. M., Schmidt, W. C., & Müller, H. K. (1998). Disinhibition of return: Unnecessary and unlikely. *Perception and Psychophysics, 60,* 862–872.

Klein, R. M., & Taylor, T. L. (1994). Categories of cognitive inhibition with reference to attention. In D. Dagenbach & T. Carr (Eds.), *Inhibitory processes in attention, memory and language* (pp. 113–150). San Diego, CA: Academic Press.

Lachman, R., Lachman, J. L., & Butterfield, E. C. (1979). *Cognitive psychology and information processing.* Hillsdale, NJ: Erlbaum.

Lupianez, J., Milan, E. G., Tornay, F. J., Madrid, E., & Tudela, P. (1997). Does IOR occur in discrimination tasks? Yes, it does, but later. *Perception and Psychophysics, 59,* 1241–1254.

MacInnes, W. J., & Klein, R. M. (2003). Inhibition of return biases orienting during the search of complex scenes. *Scientific World Journal, 3,* 75–86.

MacPherson, A. C., Klein, R. M., & Moore, C. M. (2003). Inhibition of return in children and adolescents. *Journal of Experimental Child Psychology, 85,* 337–351.

Maylor, E. A., & Hockey, R. (1985). Inhibitory component of externally controlled covert orienting in visual space. *Journal of Experimental Psychology: Human Perception and Performance, 11,* 777–787.

McCarley, J. S., Wang, R. F., Kramer, A. F., Irwin, D. E., & Peterson, M. S. (2003). How much memory does oculomotor search have? *Psychological Science, 14,* 422–426.

Müller, H., & von Mühlenen, A. (2000). Probing distractor inhibition in visual search. *Journal of Experimental Psychology: Human Perception and Performance, 26,* 1591–1605.

Muñoz, D. P., & Wurtz, R. H. (1993). Fixation cells in monkey superior colliculus. II. Reversible activation and deactivation. *Journal of Neurophysiology, 70,* 576–589.

O'Riordan, M. A., Plaisted, K. C., Driver, J., & Baron-Cohen, S. (2001). Superior visual search in autism. *Journal of Experimental Psychology: Human Perception and Performance, 27,* 719–730.

Paul, M. A., & Tipper, S. P. (2003). Object-based representations facilitate memory for inhibitory processes. *Experimental Brain Research, 148,* 283–289.

Posner, M. I. (1980). Orienting of attention. *Quarterly Journal of Experimental Psychology, 32,* 3–25.

Posner, M. I. (1996). Interaction of arousal and selection in the posterior attention network. In A. Baddeley & L. Weiskrantz (Eds.), *Attention: Selection, awareness, and control* (pp. 390–405). Oxford, England: Clarendon Press.

Posner, M. I., & Cohen, Y. (1984). Components of visual orienting. In H. Bouma & D. G. Bouwhuis (Eds.), *Attention and performance* (Vol. 10, pp. 531–556). Hillsdale, NJ: Erlbaum.

Posner, M. I., Cohen, A., & Rafal, R. D. (1982). Neural systems control of spatial orienting. *Proceedings of the Royal Society of London, B 298,* 187–198.

Posner, M. I., Davidson, B. J., & Snyder, J. J. (1980). Attention and the detection of signals. *Journal of Experimental Psychology: General, 109,* 160–174.

Posner, M. I., Nissen, M. J., & Ogden, W. C. (1978). Attended and unattended processing modes: The role of set for spatial location. In H. L. Pick & E. Saltzman (Eds.), *Modes of perceiving and processing information* (pp. 137–158). Hillsdale, NJ: Erlbaum.

Posner, M. I., Rafal, R. D., Choate, L. S., & Vaughan, J. (1985). Inhibition of return: Neural basis and function. *Cognitive Neuropsychology, 2,* 211–228.

Posner, M. I., & Snyder, C. R. R. (1975). Attention and cognitive control. In R. L. Solso (Ed.), *Information processing and cognition: The Loyola Symposium* (pp. 55–85). Hillsdale, NJ: Erlbaum.

Pratt, J., Spalek, T. M., & Bradshaw, F. (1999). The time to detect targets at inhibited and non-inhibited locations: Preliminary evidence for attentional momentum. *Journal of Experimental Psychology: Human Perception and Performance, 25,* 730–746.

Rafal, R. D., Calabresi, P. A., Brennan, C. W., & Sciolto, T. K. (1989). Saccade preparation inhibits reorienting to recently attended locations. *Journal of Experimental Psychology: Human Perception and Performance, 15,* 673–685.

Reuter-Lorenz, P. A., Jha, A. P., & Rosenquist, J. N. (1996). What is inhibited in inhibition of return? *Journal of Experimental Psychology: Human Perception and Performance, 22,* 367–378.

Samuel, A. G., & Kat, D. (2003). Inhibition of return: A graphical meta-analysis of its timecourse, and an empirical test of its temporal and spatial properties. *Psychonomic Bulletin and Review, 10,* 897–906.

Sapir, A., Hayes, A., Henik, A., Danziger, S., & Rafal, R. (2004). Parietal lobe lesions disrupt saccadic remapping of inhibitory location tagging. *Journal of Cognitive Neuroscience, 16,* 503–509.

Sapir, A., Henik, A., Dobrusin, M., & Hochman, E. Y. (2001). Attentional asymmetry in schizophrenia: Disengagement and inhibition of return deficits. *Neuropsychology, 5,* 361–370.

Sapir, A., Soroker, N., Berger, A., & Henik, A. (1999). Inhibition of return in spatial attention: Direct evidence for collicular generation. *Nature Neuroscience, 2,* 1053–1054.

Simion, F., Valenza, E., Umilta, C., & Dalla, B. (1995). Inhibition of return in newborns is temporo-nasal asymmetrical. *Infant Behavior and Development, 8,* 189–194.

Snyder, J. J., & Kingstone, A. (2000). Inhibition of return and visual search: How many separate loci are inhibited. *Perception and Psychophysics, 62,* 452–458.

Snyder, J. J., Schmidt, W. C., & Kingstone, A. (2001). Attentional momentum does not underlie the inhibition of return effect. *Journal of Experimental Psychology: Human Perception and Performance, 27,* 1420–1432.

Sperling, G. (1960). The information available in brief visual presentations. *Psychological Monographs, 74,* 1–29.

Takeda, Y., & Yagi, A. (2000). Inhibitory tagging in visual search can be found if search stimuli remain visible. *Perception and Psychophysics, 62,* 927–934.

Taylor, T. L., & Klein, R. M. (1998). On the causes and effects of inhibition of return. *Psychonomic Bulletin and Review, 5,* 625–643.

Taylor, T. L., & Klein, R. M. (2000). Visual and motor effects in inhibition of return. *Journal of Experimental Psychology: Human Perception and Performance, 26,* 1639–1656.

Tipper, S. P., Driver, J., & Weaver, B. (1991). Object-centred inhibition of return of visual attention. *Quarterly Journal of Experimental Psychology [A], 43,* 289–298.

Tipper, S. P., Jordan, H., & Weaver, B. (1999). Scene-based and object centered inhibition of return: Evidence for dual orienting mechanisms. *Perception and Psychophysics, 61,* 50–60.

Tipper, S. P., Rafal, R., Reuter-Lorenz, P. A., Starrveldt, Y., Ro, T., Egly, R., et al. (1997). Object based facilitation and inhibition from visual orienting in the human split brain. *Journal of Experimental Psychology: Human Perception and Performance, 23,* 1522–1532.

Tipper, S. P., Weaver, B., & Watson, F. L. (1996). Inhibition of return to successively cued spatial locations: commentary on Pratt and Abrams (1995). *Journal of Experimental Psychology: Human Perception and Performance, 22,* 1289–1293.

Valenza, E. L., Simion, F. L., & Umilta, C. L. (1994). Inhibition of return in newborn infants. *Infant Behavioral Development, 17,* 293–302.

Yi, D.-J., Kim, M.-S., & Chun, M. M. (2003). Inhibition of return to occluded objects. *Perception and Psychophysics, 65,* 1222–1230.

4

Imaging Conscious and Subliminal Word Processing

Stanislas Dehaene

You have just begun to read this chapter. Your eyes are currently scanning this sentence at a rate of three or four saccades per second. Almost unfailingly, in a fraction of a second, your visual system manages to transform those black marks on paper into recognized letters, then words, then meanings. Yet you are unaware of the complexity of those mental operations: your consciousness is entirely focused on their end result, the meaning of the text. The long chain of unconscious computations that precedes conscious access is, by definition, inaccessible to introspection and, in the early days of scientific psychology, was thought to be inaccessible to experimentation. If anything, however, the conscious step now seems even more mysterious—it is hard to even imagine what magical wand could turn mechanical brain computations into consciously accessible states of mind.

In the past decades, we have learned a lot about the architecture of the word recognition system. The methods that have permitted a dissection of word recognition processes are attributable, to a large extent, to the work of Michael Posner. In the first half of his career, he and others such as Shepard and Sternberg made seminal contributions to modern mental chronometry (Posner, 1978). Later, Posner went on to explore the cerebral underpinnings of the mental representations that mental chronometry had inferred, using (and helping develop) the new tool of cognitive neuroimaging. He quickly saw the revolutionary potential of this new method: "The microscope and telescope opened vast domains of unexpected scientific discovery. Now that new imaging methods can visualize the brain systems used for normal and pathological thought, a similar opportunity may be available for human cognition" (Posner, 1993; p. 673).

Parts of this article have also been used in chapters by Dehaene and Changeux (2004) and Dehaene (2003). I thank Jean-Pierre Changeux, Lionel Naccache, and Claire Sergent for their essential contributions, Nancy Kanwisher and Ulrich Mayr for their useful feedback, and the Institut National de la Santé et de las Recherche Médicale, Commissariat à l'Energie Médicale, and McDonnell Foundation for their financial support.

Reading the first cognitive neuroimaging paper (Petersen, Fox, Posner, Mintun, & Raichle, 1988) was, for me, a highly memorable moment. Two key advantages of brain imaging were immediately apparent. First, imaging provided a new method of functional dissection of the hierarchy of cognitive operations (Posner, Petersen, Fox, & Raichle, 1988). Second, even the highest stages of processing that often eluded chronometric analysis, such as the complex semantic manipulations inherent in the verb generation task, were analyzable and associated with reproducible activation sites. In my opinion, this possibility of imaging the cerebral underpinnings of any mental activity, without requiring the research participant to perform an overt response or even an actual task, was a powerful factor in the resurgence of interest for higher cognition and consciousness, since it permitted the visualization of the substrates of covert attentive states (Pardo, Fox, & Raichle, 1991; Posner & Petersen, 1990) and revealed the striking contribution of previously neglected areas such as the anterior cingulate (Pardo, Pardo, Janer, & Raichle, 1990).

Both word recognition and consciousness have become huge fields of research that cannot possibly be reviewed in a short chapter. My purpose is more limited: to revisit the organization of the visual word recognition system, focusing on a single issue that my colleagues and I have addressed in several experiments: what patterns of activity characterize nonconscious and conscious words? Using pattern masking, words can be presented on the retina for several tens of milliseconds, and yet fail to be consciously seen by the participant. This raises two obvious questions. First, to what extent are such subliminal words processed in the brain? Second, what cerebral events distinguish subliminal words from words that are consciously reportable? Focusing on those well-defined questions narrows down the problem of consciousness to a more tractable level.

This chapter is divided in three parts. First, I review the empirical data on the neuroimaging of masked words. I then describe a putative integrative theory based on the hypothesis of a "conscious neuronal workspace" (Dehaene & Changeux, 2000; Dehaene, Kerszberg, & Changeux, 1998; Dehaene & Naccache, 2001; Dehaene, Sergent, & Changeux, 2003). This model emphasizes the role of distributed neurons with long-distance connections, particularly dense in prefrontal, cingulate, and parietal regions. These neurons are capable of interconnecting multiple specialized processors and can broadcast signals at the brain scale in a spontaneous and sudden manner, thus creating a global availability that, according to our hypothesis, is experienced as consciousness (see also Baars, 1989). In the third part, I examine recent experiments that tested some predictions of the workspace model.

Neuroimaging of Subliminal Word Processing

How can one experimentally distinguish the substrates of conscious access from the considerable amount of neural activity that occurs nonconsciously? In laboratory tests, our approach has consisted in exploring paradigms in which symbolic information is deliberately presented under subliminal conditions. By studying to what extent such information is processed, and what brain areas it contacts, one can progressively draw a negative picture, as it were, of which aspects of brain activity do not suffice to give rise to consciousness. Subliminal priming has also proven an important tool in decoding the stages of representation of words in various brain areas.

General Logic of Subliminal Priming Studies

In a typical subliminal priming experiment, each trial consists in the consecutive presentation, at the same screen location, of a random configuration of letters or geometrical shapes (premask), a first word (the prime), another random configuration of symbols or shapes (postmask), and a second word (the target). The prime word is presented briefly, typically 10 to 50 ms. The target is presented for a much longer duration, typically 500 ms. Finally, the stimulus onset asynchrony between the prime and target is short (typically 60 to 120 ms). Under those conditions, research participants report seeing only the masks and the target word, but not the prime.

This subjective invisibility can be confirmed by asking participants to perform an explicit task on the primes. In recent experiments, my colleagues and I have used a forced-choice identification task in which participants have to select, among two alternative words, the one that matches the prime. With a 29 ms prime presentation duration, performance typically does not differ from chance (Dehaene et al., 2001). With slightly longer primes, slightly better performance may be observed, but it typically does not correlate with the amount of subliminal priming found (Greenwald, Draine, & Abrams, 1996; Vorberg, Mattler, Heinecke, Schmidt, & Schwarzbach, 2003). Other tasks such as prime presence–absence judgment (Dehaene, Naccache, et al., 1998) or prime categorization (Naccache & Dehaene, 2001b) yield similar results.

In spite of their subjective invisibility, the prime words impact on the processing of target words. This can be demonstrated by varying the relation between the prime and target. The simplest design compares trials in which the same word is presented twice, as both prime and target, with trials in which different words are presented as prime and target. In this condition of repetition priming, response times to the target are consistently shorter on repeated than on nonrepeated trials (e.g., Forster & Davis, 1984). By systematically varying the physical, phonological, or even semantic proximity between the prime and target, it is then possible to probe which levels of word processing underlie this facilitation effect.

To identify the brain systems activated by masked words, functional imaging can be combined with masked priming (Dehaene, Jobert, et al., in press; Dehaene, Naccache, et al., 1998; Dehaene, Naccache, et al., 2001; Naccache & Dehaene, 2001a). Functional magnetic resonance imaging (fMRI) is currently too slow to separate the cerebral activity induced by the prime and by the target. Thus, one necessarily measures the total activity induced by the prime-target pair (relative, say, to a control situation in which only the masks are presented). In spite of this limitation, one can still acquire knowledge of the processing of the prime by varying the type of relation between the prime and target. When the prime and the target are the same word, there is a measurable reduction in brain activation compared to a situation in which the prime and the target are different words. Measuring where this subliminal repetition suppression effect occurs provides an indirect image of the brain areas that have been traversed by the hidden prime word. This can be supplemented by recordings of event-related potentials, which have an appropriate temporal resolution to follow the dynamics of prime- and target-induced activations.

Subliminal Priming in the Visual Word Form System

Dehaene and colleagues (2001) first examined the cerebral bases of subliminal word repetition priming. FMRI data were collected in a fast event-related paradigm while research participants performed a bimanual semantic classification task on visual words. Unbeknownst to them, each target word was preceded by a subliminal prime. My colleagues and I used a 2 × 2 design in which the prime and target could be the same word or different words and could appear in the same or different case, thus defining four types of events. The amount of activation in each of those events was identified relative to a fifth event in which only the masks were presented and no response was required (see Figure 4.1).

The behavioral results showed that response times were faster on repeated trials, whether or not the words shared the same case. In searching for the cerebral bases of this effect, two distinct types of brain regions were identified. The right extrastriate occipital cortex showed repetition suppression only for physically identical primes and targets, suggesting a role for right visual areas in coding the precise visual features of the letters (Marsolek, Kosslyn, & Squire, 1992). The left fusiform gyrus, however, showed repetition suppression whenever the same word was repeated, whether in the same case or not. Thus, this region appears to encode the word string in a case-independent fashion.

This region may provide the cerebral substrate of the visual word form system (Posner & Carr, 1992; Warrington & Shallice, 1980), a structural representation of visual words as an ordered sequence of abstract letter identities or multiletter graphemes, invariant for size, font, and case (Cohen et al., 2002; Dehaene, Le Clec'H, Poline, Le Bihan, & Cohen, 2002; Molko et al., 2002). It is roughly symmetrical to the right-hemispheric fusiform face area, and may play for visual word recognition the same role that similar or neighboring regions of the fusiform and lingual gyri play for other visual objects such as faces, objects, or places. In adults, it has become partially attuned to a specific script, as shown by its greater response to real words than to consonant strings of similar arbitrary shape (Cohen et al., 2002). Indeed, in children this area activates in direct proportion to the child's reading skills, and its response is absent in dyslexic readers who have not developed expertise in word recognition (Paulesu et al., 2001; Shaywitz et al., 2002).

To further specify the exact nature of the word representation attained by subliminal primes in the visual word form area. I recently performed two more repetition priming experiments (Dehaene, Jobert, et al., 2004). The first examined whether visual features alone could explain priming in this region.

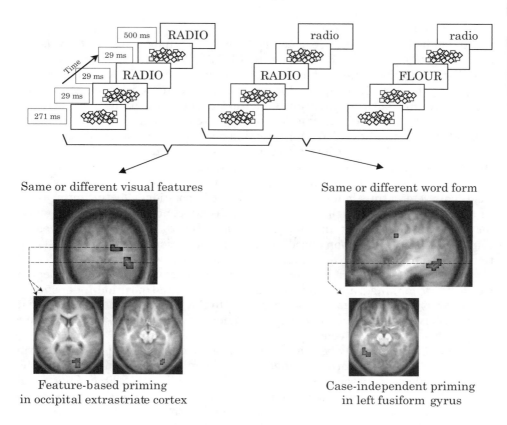

Same or different visual features   Same or different word form

Feature-based priming   Case-independent priming
in occipital extrastriate cortex   in left fusiform gyrus

Figure 4.1. Imaging of subliminal priming in the visual word-recognition system. Repetition suppression is observed in occipital extrastriate cortex, particularly in the right hemisphere, when a word is physically repeated; and in the left fusiform gyrus (visual word form area) when a word is repeated with or without case change. Data from Dehaene et al. (2001).

To this end, the visual similarity of upper and lowercase letters was manipulated. Half of the prime-target pairs were words made of letters that are highly similar in upper and lower case (e.g., Oo, Pp). The other half used only highly dissimilar letters (e.g., Aa, Gg) for which the uppercase–lowercase association is essentially arbitrary. The same strip of left fusiform cortex as in Experiment 1 showed replicable subliminal repetition suppression that was present even when the letters were visually dissimilar (the same effect was also observed in response times, replicating earlier results, e.g., Bowers, Vigliocco, & Haan, 1998). This confirmed that this region is not solely concerned with visual shapes but encodes letter strings using a culturally acquired abstract letter code.

A second experiment examined whether single letters or larger units such as graphemes or whole words are encoded in the visual word form area. To repeat letters without repeating words, anagrams were used. For instance, by priming the French target word "REFLET" with the prime "trefle," almost all of the middle letters (r, e, f, l, e) could be repeated. By moving the prime relative to the target (e.g., "trefle" followed by "REFLET"), it was even possible to repeat those letters at the same retinal location without repeating the same word. By comparing this to a word-repeated trial, with or without a shift in letter position, the nature and position invariance of the neural codes underlying priming could be tested. Would priming depend on letter repetition, word repetition, or both? The results revealed an interesting dissociation between posterior and anterior areas. The posterior portion of the visual word form area ($y = -68$ in the Talairach coordinate system) showed repetition suppression only when the same letters were repeated at the same retinal location, regardless of their case. This region thus holds a case-invariant but position-selective letter code. At a more anterior position ($y = -56$), location-independent priming was found for both repeated words and anagrams compared to a control, nonrepeated condition. Thus, this region encodes a case- and position-invariant representation of visual units that are smaller that the whole word. Finally, in a still more anterior fusiform region ($y = -48$), priming became greater for repeated words than for anagrams, thus revealing a case- and position-independent whole-word code, or at least a code sensitive to the larger graphemic units that distinguish a word from its anagram. Behavioral response times were sensitive only to this whole-word code.

Two conclusions may be drawn from those studies at the visual word form level. First, behavioral priming effects provide only a coarse indication of the various levels of representations traversed by a subliminal prime. Functional imaging reveals a much richer variety of priming effects, ranging from feature-based to letter or whole-word based priming. Furthermore, this hierarchical organization is remarkably reproducible across subjects, even for a culturally acquired activity such as reading. I am reminded once again of the words of Posner: "It is a popularly held belief in psychology that the cognitive functions of the brain are widely distributed among different brain areas. Nevertheless, imaging studies reveal a startling degree of region-specific activity. When thought is analyzed in terms of component mental operations, a beautiful localization emerges" (Posner, 1993, p. 673).

A second conclusion is that subliminal primes can be processed quite far along the ventral visual identification pathway. Although several studies have identified a tight correlation between ventral fusiform activity and the contents of visual consciousness (e.g., Bar et al., 2001; Grill-Spector, Kushnir, Hendler, & Malach, 2000), fusiform activity is not sufficient for conscious reportability.

Subliminal Semantic Access: The Case of Numbers

Can subliminal words be processed beyond the visual system? The issue of semantic access from masked words remains controversial in psychology. In laboratory tests, we obtained positive evidence for subliminal semantic access by using a small set of high-frequency words with simple semantics: number words.

Initially, evidence for subliminal semantic access came from the observation of motor priming (Dehaene, Naccache, et al., 1998). We engaged research

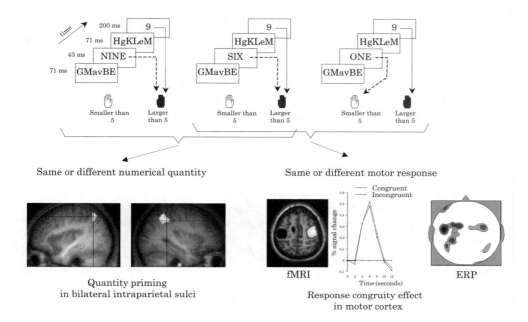

Figure 4.2. Imaging of subliminal semantic and motor priming during number comparison. Repetition suppression is observed in the left and right intraparietal sulci when the same numerical quantity is repeated (regardless of number notation). Motor priming is observed in the left and right motor cortices as a function of the response induced by the subliminal primes. Data from Dehaene, Naccache, et al. (1998); Naccache and Dehaene (2001a). ERP = event related potential; fMRI = functional magnetic resonance imaging.

participants in a number comparison task, where they classified target numbers as larger or smaller than five using their left or right hand. Unbeknowst to them, subliminal numerical primes were presented just before the target, and these primes could also be larger or small than five. Thus, the size of the primes could be congruent or incongruent with the subsequent target. This response congruity factor was found to interfere with participants' response times. Furthermore, it yielded a response conflict in motor cortex that was measurable in both event related potentials (ERPs) and fMRI (see Figure 4.2; Dehaene, Naccache, et al., 1998).

That participants could activate the motor cortex of the hand that would have been appropriate for responding to the prime seemed to imply that participants had unconsciously categorized the prime as larger or smaller than five. Thus, motor priming was initially taken as a clear, though indirect, proof of semantic processing of subliminal numbers (Dehaene, Naccache, et al., 1998). However, there was an alternative interpretation: the observed motor activation could be due to direct motor specification (Neumann & Klotz, 1994). Because a small number of stimuli—the digits 1, 4, 6, and 9 and the corresponding words—were repeatedly used as both primes and targets, participants could have learned to associate each visual stimulus with the corresponding response, thus bypassing semantic access. Indeed, such a shortcut was recently demonstrated by Abrams and Greenwald (2000). In an affective categorization task, new primes that were made of fragments of previous seen targets yielded subliminal motor priming solely based on visual fragments, not on whole-word meaning. For instance the prime word SMILE, created from the targets words SMUT and BILE, ended up paradoxically priming the negative rather than the positive response. Thus, although the task required semantic categorization, and although a priming effect was observed, the primes only received a shallow, nonsemantic analysis of their component letters and the associated responses (see also Damian, 2001).

New experiments and reanalyses have now demonstrated that the number priming results do not easily fall prey to a similar nonsemantic interpretation. First, other analyses (Naccache & Dehaene, 2001b) demonstrated that the motor priming effect was present in the first block of trials and that neither motor priming nor the classical semantic distance effect were affected by practice. Those findings are inconsistent with the idea that the task is increasingly being performed via a nonsemantic route. Second, we replicated our original behavioral experiments with novel numbers that are only presented as primes, never as targets (Naccache & Dehaene, 2001b). Because those numbers are never seen consciously and are never responded to, they cannot be associated with motor responses. Yet in two different experiments, those novel primes were found to cause significant motor priming, indicating that at least part of the motor priming effect arises from a genuinely semantic route. This positive effect of novel numerical primes has now been replicated and extended by others (e.g., Greenwald, Abrams, Naccache, & Dehaene, 2003; Kunde, Kiesel, & Hoffmann, 2003; Reynvoet, Caessens, & Brysbaert, 2002). Importantly, both Greenwald and colleagues (2003) and Kunde and colleagues (2003) have found that it depends partly on the instructions and stimulus content. Research participants may perform using direct stimulus-response associations if the instructions emphasize fast responding to a small number of stimuli (Kunde et al., 2003); or they may learn to respond only to the individual component digit of two-digit numerals, if those digits are entirely predictive of the motor response (Greenwald et al., 2003). If the stimuli and instructions force participants to perform a genuine number comparison, however, subliminal semantic priming that generalizes to novel primes is found.

Finally, we obtained more direct evidence for semantic-level repetition priming. Independently of motor priming, when participants were engaged in the number comparison task, their responses were also accelerated when the prime and the target represented the same quantity, possibly in different notations (e.g., prime NINE, target 9), relative to congruent but nonrepeated trials (e.g., prime SIX, target 9; Dehaene, Naccache, et al., 1998; Koechlin, Naccache, Block, & Dehaene, 1999). Furthermore, this form of priming, which we termed quantity priming, depended on the numerical distance between the prime and target, clearly suggesting semantic mediation (Koechlin et al., 1999; Naccache & Dehaene, 2001b; Reynvoet, Brysbaert, & Fias, 2002; Reynvoet, Caessens, et al., 2002). A neuroimaging version of this paradigm showed that this notation-independent quantity priming in a bilateral intraparietal region was thought to be involved in the semantic representation and manipulation of numerical quantities (Naccache & Dehaene, 2001a).

In summary, priming effects with subliminal numbers have been observed at both the semantic (intraparietal) and motor levels. This provides a clear indication that semantic-level processing of masked primes is possible. It should be noted that digits are some of the most frequent visual symbols and are semantically unambiguous. The ease and speed of visual-to-semantic transduction may explain why it seems easier to obtain semantic priming with numbers than with other types of words (Abrams & Greenwald, 2000; Damian, 2001).

Differences Between Unconscious and Conscious Word Processing

The masking paradigm also provides a way to address the second key issue associated with subliminal processing: What are the changes in brain activity that distinguish subliminal and conscious situations? A simple experiment consists in measuring the fMRI or ERP correlates of brain activity evoked by words in minimally different masked and unmasked situations (Dehaene et al., 2001). In this experiment, participants viewed a constant stream of visual shapes. Occasionally, a readable word would appear. Unbeknownst to the participants, however, there were other moments in which subliminal words were presented. The difference between the visible and invisible conditions was minimal. It merely involved shuffling the order of the mask and blank screen that preceded and followed the word presentation. In the masked condition, the order was blank-mask-word-mask-blank, and the 29-ms word was thus made invisible by the masks; in the visible condition, the order was mask-blank-word-blank-mask, and the word was unmasked. Two types of control trials were also included in which the same temporal context sequences were presented, but a blank appeared instead of the word. Contrasting word-present and word-absent trials subtracted away the effect of the masking context, even with temporally sensitive methods such as ERP recordings, and allowed us to image only the activations induced by a visible or invisible word. Note that, contrary to the above masking experiments, this method looks at the brain activation caused by masked words directly, rather than indirectly through their priming effects on subsequent words.

Using this design, my colleagues and I found that the masked words caused a small transient bottom-up activation in extrastriate cortex, fusiform gyrus, and precentral cortex. In particular, the presence of a subliminal activation in the left visual word form area was replicated. This activation was small, however, and decreased with distance from the primary visual cortex. When the words were unmasked, however, activation greatly increased in the same areas. Furthermore, it also extended to other distant parietal, inferior prefrontal and midline precentral/cingulate areas. Functional correlation studies revealed that unmasking also enhanced the long-distance correlation between the left fusiform gyrus and several of those anterior sites. Finally, ERP recordings in the same paradigm demonstrated that the P1 and N1 waves were present for the masked words, though attenuated and more focal. Conscious processing was associated with a drastic enhancement of those components as well as with the emergence of a N400 and late positive complex (P300), two waves that were absent or greatly reduced in the masked situation.

Interpretation of those findings should be cautious for several reasons. First, masking itself may have a rather peripheral effect, perhaps even at the level of the retina. Hence, some of the differences between visible and invisible words, such as the reduction in early visual activation, may be related to peculiarities of the masking paradigm rather than to consciousness itself. Indeed, data from the inattentional blink suggest that lack of consciousness may occur without any reduction in the P1, N1, and even the N400 components of event-related potentials (Vogel, Luck, & Shapiro, 1998). Second, research participants were engaged in a mental naming task that, of course, could only be done on the visible words. Hence, it is not known which of the observed differences between visible and invisible words related to the task rather than to consciousness per se (if the latter notion is even valid—by definition, consciousness always affords access to a greater variety of processes than does subliminal processing).

With those limitations in mind, this study nevertheless yielded several cerebral correlates of consciousness, all of which have also been observed in several other studies (see, e.g., Rees, Kreiman, & Koch, 2002). Those include amplification of perceptual activity, presence of prefrontal and cingulate activation, long-distance correlations with prefrontal cortex and cingulate, and presence of a P300 waveform.

The Neuronal Workspace Hypothesis

The theory of the global neuronal workspace (Dehaene, Kerszberg, et al., 1998; Dehaene & Naccache, 2001; Dehaene, Sergent, et al., 2003) was proposed to tentatively explain why these various characteristics tend to frequently cohere together as correlates of conscious reportability. This theory is historically rooted in a long neuropsychological tradition, dating back to Hughlings Jackson and perpetuated among others by Baddeley, Shallice, Mesulam, and Posner, which emphasizes the hierarchical organization of the brain and separates lower automatized systems from increasingly higher and more autonomous supervisory executive systems. It also builds on Fodor's distinction between the vertical modular faculties and a distinct isotropic central and horizontal system that is capable of sharing information across modules. Finally, it relates to Baars's cognitive theory of consciousness, which distinguishes a vast array of unconscious specialized processors running in parallel, and a single limited-capacity serial workspace that allows them to exchange information (Baars, 1989).

Baars, however, did not specify how the psychological construct of a conscious workspace could be implemented in terms of neuronal networks. By contrast, Changeux and I have had a long-standing collaboration on the development of computational neural network models that aimed at specifying the contribution of prefrontal cortex to increasingly higher cognitive tasks (Dehaene & Changeux, 1989, 1991, 1997; Dehaene, Kerszberg, et al., 1998).

We successively considered how a network could retain an active memory across a long delay (Dehaene & Changeux, 1989); how it could encode abstract rules that could be selected from external or internal rewards (Dehaene & Changeux, 1991); and finally how networks based on those principles could pass complex planning tasks such as the Tower of London test or the Stroop test (Dehaene & Changeux, 1997; Dehaene, Kerszberg, et al., 1998). The neuronal workspace model is the last development of the neuronal architectures that we proposed to address those specific problems.

Two Computational Spaces in the Brain

The neuronal workspace hypothesis distinguishes two computational spaces in the brain, each characterized by a distinct pattern of connectivity.

1. The network of processors. Subcortical networks and most of the cortex can be viewed as a collection of specialized processors, each attuned to the processing of a particular type of information. Processors vary widely in complexity, from the elementary line segment detectors in area V1 or the motion processors in area MT, to the visual word form processor in the human fusiform gyrus, or the mirror–neuron system in area F5. In spite of this diversity, processors share characteristics of specialization, automaticity, and fast feedforward processing. Their function is made possible by a limited number of local or medium-range connections that bring to each processor the encapsulated inputs necessary to its function.
2. The global neuronal workspace. We postulate the existence of a distinct set of cortical workspace neurons characterized by their ability to send and receive projections to many distant areas through long-range excitatory axons. These neurons therefore no longer obey a principle of local, encapsulated connectivity, but rather break the modularity of the cortex by allowing many different processors to exchange information in a global and flexible manner. Information that is encoded in workspace neurons can be quickly made available to many brain systems, in particular the motor and speech-production processors for overt behavioral report. We hypothesize that the entry of inputs into this global workspace constitutes the neural basis of access to consciousness (see Figure 4.3).

Top-Down Amplification and Dynamic Mobilization

Among the long-distance connections established by workspace neurons, top-down connections play an essential role in the temporary mobilization of a given content into consciousness. Top-down attentional amplification is the mechanism by which modular processors can be temporarily mobilized and made available to the global workspace, and therefore enter into consciousness. According to this view, the same brain processes may, at different times, contribute to the content of consciousness or not. To enter consciousness, it is not

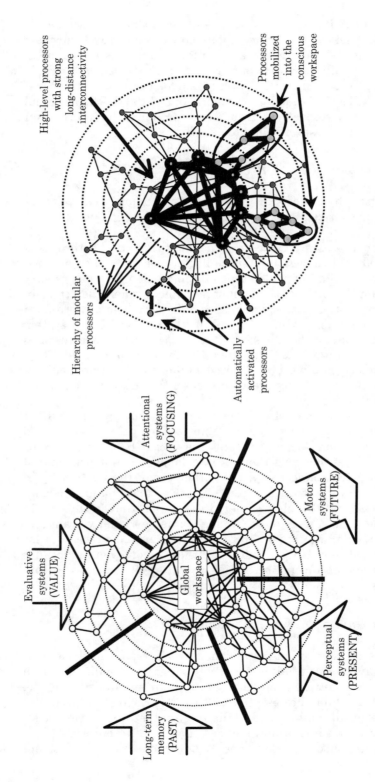

Figure 4.3. Schematic architecture of the workspace model (after Dehaene, Kerszberg, et al., 1998). In this diagram inspired by Mesulam, cerebral processors (circles) and their connections are represented in a hierarchy (primary areas on the outer circle, central associative areas in the center). Areas rich in workspace neurons (center) are tightly interconnected by a divergent set of connections. This long-range connectivity supports brain-scale states of activity (right diagram) in which distant processors are mobilized, amplified, and interconnected through the workspace. From "A Neuronal Model of a Global Workspace in Effortful Cognitive Tasks," by S. Dehaene, M. Kerszberg, and J. P. Changeux, 1998, *Proceedings of the National Academy of Sciences of the United States of America, 95,* p. 14530. Copyright 1998 by the Academy of Sciences of the United States of America. Adapted with permission.

sufficient for a processor to be activated; this activity must also be amplified and maintained over a sufficient duration for it to become accessible to multiple other processes. Without such "dynamic mobilization," a process may still contribute to cognitive performance, but only nonconsciously.

A consequence of this hypothesis is the absence of a sharp anatomical delineation of the workspace representations. In time, the contours of the workspace fluctuate as different brain circuits are temporarily mobilized, then abandoned by a given global representation. Workspace neurons are present in many areas, but at any given time only a particular set of these neurons contribute to the mobilized workspace content. They are part of what may be referred to, in a selectionist framework, as a generator of diversity (Changeux & Dehaene, 1989). As time elapses, the activity of workspace neurons is characterized by a series of discrete episodes of spontaneous metastable coherent activation separated by sharp transitions. This would fit with the introspective feeling of a stream of consciousness, compared by William James to a sequence of flights and perchings of a bird.

Criteria for Conscious Access

To be able to be mobilized in the conscious workspace, a mental object must meet three criteria:

1. Active firing. The object must be represented as a firing pattern of neurons. There is, of course, considerable information that is already stored in the nervous system, in a latent form, for instance, in synaptic connections and weights, neurotransmitter release efficiencies, receptor densities, and so on. The model predicts that such information does not become conscious. It can only be read-out indirectly through its contribution to neural firing.
2. Long-distance connectivity. The active neurons must possess a sufficient number of reciprocal anatomical connections to distributed workspace neurons, particularly in prefrontal, parietal, and cingulate cortices. This criterion implies that the activity of many neurons, for instance in subcortical and brainstem nuclei, is excluded from conscious mobilization (e.g., circuits for respiration or emotion). In many cases, we only become aware of those circuits through their indirect effects on other representations, for example, in somatic cortical areas.
3. Dynamic mobilization. At any given moment, workspace neurons can only sustain a single global representation, the rest of workspace neurons being inhibited. This implies that, out of the multiple active cortical representations that could become conscious, only one will receive the appropriate top-down amplification and be mobilized into consciousness. The other representations are temporarily nonconscious. It would only take a small reorientation of top-down signals to access them, but, according to our views, until this is achieved they do not participate in consciousness.

Workspace Modulation and Selection by Reward

Workspace neurons are assumed to be the targets of two different types of neuromodulatory inputs. First, workspace neurons display a constantly fluctuating spontaneous activity, whose intensity is modulated by ascending activating systems, for instance from cholinergic, noradrenergic, and serotoninergic nuclei in the brain stem, basal forebrain, and hypothalamus. Those systems therefore modify the state of consciousness through different levels of arousal. Second, the stability of workspace activity is modulated by ascending reward inputs arising from the limbic system (via connections to the anterior cingulate, orbitofrontal cortex, and the direct influence of ascending dopaminergic inputs). External or internal goals and rewards may thus stabilize or destabilize particular contents of the conscious workspace. Active representations that fit with the current goal of the organism are selected and maintained over a longer period. Conversely, active representations that lead to error are rejected. This mental selection process has been simulated in former models, which account for classical cognitive tasks such as the Wisconsin card sorting test (Dehaene & Changeux, 1991), the Tower of London (Dehaene & Changeux, 1997), and the Stroop task (Dehaene, Kerszberg, & Changeux, 1998).

Brain Anatomy of the Neuronal Workspace

The neuronal workspace hypothesis posits that, as a whole, the workspace neurons are reciprocally connected via long-distance axons to many if not all of the cortical processors, thus permitting locally available information to be brought into consciousness. Nevertheless, these neurons may be more densely accumulated in some areas than in others. Anatomically, long-range cortico-cortical tangential connections, including callosal connections, originate mostly from the pyramidal cells of layers II and III, which give or receive the so-called "association" efferents and afferents. Those layers are thicker in von Economo's type 2 (dorsolateral prefrontal) and type 3 (inferior parietal) cortical structures. In the monkey, those areas entertain a strong interconnection among themselves as well as with the anterior and posterior cingulate, the association cortex of the superior temporal sulcus, and the parahippocampal region, thalamus, and striatum (Goldman-Rakic, 1988). The high concentration of neurons with long-distance axons in those areas may explain why they frequently appear coactivated in neuroimaging studies of conscious effortful processing.

Although we emphasize cortico-cortical connectivity, it should be noted that cortico-thalamic columns are the processing units in the brain and in our recent simulation (Dehaene, Sergent, et al., 2003). Thus, long-distance connections between thalamic nuclei may also contribute to the establishment of a coherent brain-scale state (Llinas, Ribary, Contreras, & Pedroarena, 1998). Studies of split-brain patients should be particularly helpful in delineating the relative contribution of cortical and subcortical connections to workspace coherence.

Our model leads to the prediction that long-distance connections have been the target of a recent evolutionary pressure in the course of hominization and are particularly developed in the human species. In that respect, it can be noted that the relative anatomical expansion of cortical areas rich in long-axon neurons, such as the prefrontal cortex, may have contributed to important changes in the functional properties of the workspace (see Changeux, 2002). It is also noteworthy that a particular type of spindle cell, which establishes long-distance projections, is found in the anterior cingulate cortex of humans and great apes, but not other primates (Allman, Hakeem, Erwin, Nimchinsky, & Hof, 2001). Detailed anatomical studies of transcortical connectivity in the human brain have also revealed the presence of distant transcortical projections, that for instance link directly the right fusiform gyrus to multiple areas of the left-hemisphere including Broca's and Wernicke's areas (Di Virgilio & Clarke, 1997). It is anticipated that those key components of the verbal reportability system are connected to many cortical areas, given the variety of percepts and concepts that we can name or understand through language.

Some Predictions for Word and Number Processing

The framework of the neuronal workspace model applies readily to the above data on subliminal word processing. One must simply assume that the fusiform visual word form system and, in the case of numbers, the parietal quantity representation and comparison systems are automatized processors that can function in a purely bottom-up or feedforward fashion. The activation of motor cortex by subliminal primes also indicates that even a temporary chain of processors, prepared according to task instructions, can be traversed by subliminal information. This is compatible with the workspace model inasmuch as it is assumed that the prime-induced activation is sufficient for feedforward propagation through a task-prepared circuit but is too brief to be stabilized by descending amplification from workspace neurons. Finally, the differences observed between conscious and unconscious word processing (Dehaene et al., 2001)—amplification of processor activity, correlated activation of distant prefrontal, parietal, and cingulate sites, emission of a broad P300—conform closely to the expectations of the workspace model.

More recently, my colleagues have been inspired by the workspace model to perform additional experiments that tested critical predictions of the model. Three of them are described below: the relation between attention and consciousness; the role of the anterior cingulate; and the all-or-none character of conscious access.

Attention Without Consciousness

Within the framework of the workspace model, top-down attentional selection and amplification is necessary for the access of a representation to consciousness. However, attention and consciousness cannot be equated. Even when attention is present, it may not always be sufficient for a stimulus to gain access to consciousness. Thus, the model predicts that attention may modulate the depth of subliminal processing, while still failing to make the stimuli conscious.

Naccache, Blandin, and I recently tested this prediction using our number priming paradigm. We reasoned that all of the priming experiments described above allowed research participants to deploy attention to the target. Would the prime effect be modulated or even disappear if participants were unable to attend at the time of prime presentation? In three different experiments, we recently showed that when the prime-target pair occurs at an unpredictable moment, thus preventing the deployment of temporal attention, then subliminal priming effects disappear (Naccache, Blandin, & Dehaene, 2002). This indicates that the idea that subliminal priming reflects a purely passive process of spreading activation can be rejected. Rather, subliminal primes benefit from an attentional amplification, although this may not be sufficient for them to enter into the conscious workspace.

Consciousness and the Anterior Cingulate

Following previous proposals (e.g., Posner, 1994), the neuronal workspace model proposes that functions that depend on central executive control, such as inhibition or conflict detection, require consciousness. Recently, my colleagues and I applied this prediction to the anterior cingulate activation. Although the anterior cingulate activates in many conflict tasks (Botvinick, Braver, Barch, Carter, & Cohen, 2001), these tasks typically involve conscious conflicts. We predicted that a subliminal form of conflict should not lead to anterior cingulate activation.

To test this idea, we capitalized on our previous research showing that the number priming paradigm could generate a motor conflict without consciousness (Dehaene, Naccache, et al., 1998). We, therefore, contrasted the motor conflict effects generated by subliminal and supraliminal numerical primes (Dehaene, Artiges, et al., 2003). Both effects generated behavioral response interference, although the effect was smaller for subliminal primes (14 ms) than for supraliminal primes (34 ms). As predicted, however, the anterior cingulate showed a conflict effect only with supraliminal primes, not with subliminal primes. Furthermore, patients with schizophrenia with known anterior cingulate and prefrontal cortex impairments showed normal subliminal priming, but abnormal supraliminal motor interference. Thus, the subliminal motor conflict generated by masked numbers is resolved spontaneously, without requiring the deployment of executive attention resources. Our results support the early insight that anterior cingulate is tightly associated with conscious processing (e.g., Posner, 1994) and suggest that the executive control processes associated with prefrontal and cingulate cortices can only operate on consciously perceived stimuli. At the very least, they indicate that there is more to anterior cingulate activation than a mere mechanical activation whenever discrepant representations are present in motor cortex (Botvinick et al., 2001). There is a nonlinear relation between the amount of response conflict and the amount of cingulate activation, which implies that a threshold level of conflict is necessary for the anterior cingulate to activate. The neuronal workspace theory also predicts that this threshold should coincide with the threshold for conscious perception of the primes.

All-or-None Dynamics of Consciousness

In the neuronal workspace model, the distinct anatomical connectivity of work-space neurons leads to qualitatively distinct patterns of activity. Because of their global recurrent connectivity, workspace neurons have the capacity of igniting suddenly in a self-amplifying manner as soon as a minimum subset of them is activated. At any given moment, the state of activity of workspace is therefore characterized by the intense activation of a subset of workspace neurons, the rest of workspace neurons being actively inhibited (see Figure 4.4). This particular set of active workspace neurons may be viewed as a neuronal correlate of the content of consciousness. For instance, the conscious report of a visual word might be constituted by the simultaneous, coordinated activation of workspace neurons in the fusiform visual word form area and in distributed temporal, parietal, prefrontal, and cingulate sites associated with speech production.

For stimuli close to threshold, this predicts that conscious access should be all-or-none. Neural activity is either sufficient to trigger a reverberating loop of bottom-up and top-down activity that quickly attains a self-sustained level; or it remains below this threshold and only a briefly decaying bottom-up activation is seen. This nonlinear response was explicitly demonstrated in a detailed simulation of realistic thalamo-cortical networks (Dehaene, Sergent, et al., 2003). The simulations showed that a brief thalamic stimulation can lead to the ignition of a large set of distant cortical areas, which remain active through self-sustaining reverberatory loops for tens of milliseconds beyond the initial stimulus duration. Crucially, during this period of workspace occupancy by a first stimulus T1, another T2 can still be processed by peripheral thalamo-cortical processors but often cannot activate workspace neurons until the representation of T1 had vanished. This temporary inability showed many parallels with the attentional blink, a well-known psychological paradigm in which research participants are temporarily unable to report stimuli while they are attending to another task (Chun & Potter, 1995; Vogel et al., 1998).

Further simulations lead to the prediction that the attentional blink is a dynamic all-or-none phenomenon. In my simulation, depending on random fluctuations in spontaneous activity prior to stimulus arrival, ascending activity can be sufficient to trigger self-amplifying recurrent activity, or it can remain below threshold and only transient bottom-up activity was seen. Thus, for a fixed T1-T2 lag, simulated firing rates in higher areas and other indices of global activity (gamma-band power, long-distance cross-correlation) are distributed bimodally across trials—either global and long-lasting, or local and short-lived.

The theory, therefore, predicts that the apparent gradual drop in report-ability observed during the attentional blink may be an artificial consequence of averaging across trials with full access awareness and others with no awareness. Sergent and I tested this prediction experimentally using a modified attentional blink paradigm in which research participants reported to what extent they had seen a word (T2) within a rapid letter stream that contained another target letter string (T1; Dehaene, Sergent, et al., 2003). To obtain a continuous measure of subjective perception, we asked participants to move a

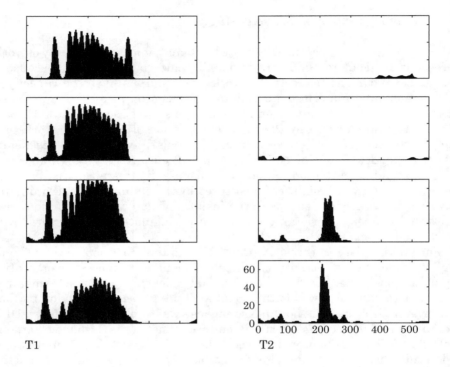

Figure 4.4. Instantaneous firing rate of simulated neurons in four hierarchically organized areas as observed in a recent neuronal implementation of the workspace model (Dehaene, Sergent, et al., 2003). A first stimulus (T1, left), although presented for only 40 ms, yields a short bottom-up activation followed by a long-lasting reverberating global state of activity. The latter is hypothesized to make T2 available for report by multiple satellite systems (not shown). The presentation of a second, competing stimulus (T2, right) during this period of global activity yields only a short-lived, bottom-up propagation of activity; thus, T2 is not reportable. This sequence of activity may provide a preliminary characterization of the neuronal events responsible for the attentional blink, in which processing of a first target T1 yields a temporary lack of consciousness of a subsequent stimulus T2. From "A Neuronal Model Linking Subjective Reports and Objective Physiological Data During Conscious Perception," by S. Dehaene, C. Sergent, and J. P. Changeux, 2003, *Proceedings of the National Academy of Sciences of the United States of America, 100,* p. 8523. Copyright 2003 by the Academy of Sciences of the United States of America. Adapted with permission.

cursor on a continuous scale, from "not seen" on the left to "maximal visibility" on the right. The results indicated that subjective perception during the blink is indeed all-or-none. At the peak of the blink, which occurred ~260 ms after T1, the very same stimulus T2 was either fully perceived (cursor placed on maximal visibility; ~50% of trials), or totally unseen (cursor placed on "not seen"). Participants almost never used intermediate cursor positions, although controls showed that they were able to in other psychophysical situations. This experiment substantiates the hypothesis that conscious states are associated with a fast all-or-none dynamic phase transition in a large-scale neuronal network. More generally, the concept of a sudden ignition, self-amplified by recurrent top-down/bottom-up interaction, may begin to explain the very notion of a threshold or "limen" of consciousness.

Conclusion

It is encouraging that there is increasing empirical and theoretical agreement about the essential ingredients for a theory of consciousness. The proposed neuronal workspace theory, indeed, can be seen as a physiological implementation of the classical concept of a central executive, supervisory attentional, or self-regulation system (e.g., Norman & Shallice, 1980; Posner & Rothbart, 1998) that accesses and modulates lower-level processors. At the neuronal network level, a key role is given to connections with the prefrontal cortex and anterior cingulate, in agreement with Bianchi (1922), Crick and Koch (1995), and Posner and Rothbart (1998). Finally, the concept of reverberatory, recurrent or reentrant projections in perceptual awareness has been abundantly mentioned in the past (Changeux, 1983; Di Lollo, Enns, & Rensink, 2000; Edelman, 1993; Lamme & Roelfsema, 2000).

Not surprisingly, all of these properties have been part and parcel of Posner's views on consciousness for a long period of time. The emphasis on the anterior cingulate as a crucial node in the conscious executive attention system, in particular, is a remarkable discovery that we owe to recent advances in brain imaging, as this region was largely neglected in neuropsychological research prior to the cognitive neuroimaging experiments of Posner, Petersen, Raichle, and colleagues. More broadly, many of the themes in this chapter, such as the idea that there are identifiable architectures of consciousness, that most cerebral processes are nonconscious, and that consciousness is associated with attentional amplification, can be traced back to Michael Posner.

In the précis of their book *Images of Mind,* Posner and Raichle (1995) described some of the criteria that a putative complete theory of cognitive neuroscience should fulfill:

> A theory of cognitive neuroscience would tell us how the brain works. It would be integrated in two senses. It would give an account at all the levels described in our general framework, from a specification of the cognitive systems to an understanding of the cellular mechanisms that support them. It would also describe how these cognitive systems achieve the subjective conscious experience that we call mind.

They ended by modestly stating: "We do not think that such an integrated theory is at hand, at least not in our hands." Clearly, such a theory is not in anyone's hands as yet. However, if we all somehow feel that this remote goal has become a bit closer in the past decades, we owe it in large part to the revolutionary conceptual and methodological tools devised by Posner.

References

Abrams, R. L., & Greenwald, A. G. (2000). Parts outweigh the whole (word) in unconscious analysis of meaning. *Psychological Science, 11,* 118–124.

Allman, J. M., Hakeem, A., Erwin, J. M., Nimchinsky, E., & Hof, P. (2001). The anterior cingulate cortex. The evolution of an interface between emotion and cognition. *Annals of the New York Academy of Sciences, 935,* 107–117.

Baars, B. J. (1989). *A cognitive theory of consciousness.* Cambridge, England: Cambridge University Press.

Bar, M., Tootell, R. B. H., Schacter, D. L., Greve, D. N., Fischl, B., Mendola, J. D., et al. (2001). Cortical mechanisms specific to explicit visual object recognition. *Neuron, 29,* 529–535.

Bianchi, L. (1922). *The mechanism of the brain and the functions of the frontal lobes.* New York: W. Wood.

Botvinick, M. M., Braver, T. S., Barch, D. M., Carter, C. S., & Cohen, J. D. (2001). Conflict monitoring and cognitive control. *Psychological Review, 108,* 624–652.

Bowers, J. S., Vigliocco, G., & Haan, R. (1998). Orthographic, phonological, and articulatory contributions to masked letter and word priming. *Journal of Experimental Psychology: Human Perception and Performance, 24,* 1705–1719.

Changeux, J. P. (1983). *Neuronal man.* Paris: Fayard.

Changeux, J. P. (2002). *The physiology of truth: Neuroscience and human knowledge.* Paris: Odile Jacob.

Changeux, J. P., & Dehaene, S. (1989). Neuronal models of cognitive functions. *Cognition, 33,* 63–109.

Chun, M. M., & Potter, M. C. (1995). A two-stage model for multiple target detection in rapid serial visual presentation. *Journal of Experimental Psychology: Human Perception and Performance, 21,* 109–127.

Cohen, L., Lehericy, S., Chochon, F., Lemer, C., Rivaud, S., & Dehaene, S. (2002). Language-specific tuning of visual cortex? Functional properties of the visual word form area. *Brain, 125*(Pt. 5), 1054–1069.

Crick, F., & Koch, C. (1995). Are we aware of neural activity in primary visual cortex? *Nature, 375,* 121–123.

Damian, M. F. (2001). Congruity effects evoked by subliminally presented primes: Automaticity rather than semantic processing. *Journal of Experimental Psychology: Human Perception and Performance, 27,* 154–165.

Dehaene, S. (2003). The neural bases of subliminal priming. In N. Kanwisher & J. Duncan (Eds.), *Attention and performance: Functional neuroimaging of visual cognition* (Vol. 20, p. 20). New York: Oxford University Press.

Dehaene, S., Artiges, E., Naccache, L., Martelli, C., Viard, A., Schürhoff, F., et al. (2003). Conscious and subliminal conflicts in normal and schizophrenic subjects: The role of the anterior cingulate. *Proceedings of the National Academy of Sciences of the United States of America, 100,* 13722–13727.

Dehaene, S., & Changeux, J. P. (1989). A simple model of prefrontal cortex function in delayed-response tasks. *Journal of Cognitive Neuroscience, 1,* 244–261.

Dehaene, S., & Changeux, J. P. (1991). The Wisconsin Card Sorting Test: Theoretical analysis and modelling in a neuronal network. *Cerebral Cortex, 1,* 62–79.

Dehaene, S., & Changeux, J. P. (1997). A hierarchical neuronal network for planning behavior. *Proceedings of the National Academy of Sciences of the United States of America, 94,* 13293–13298.

Dehaene, S., & Changeux, J. P. (2000). Reward-dependent learning in neuronal networks for planning and decision making. *Progress in Brain Research, 126,* 217–229.

Dehaene, S., & Changeux, J. P. (2004). Neural mechanisms for access to consciousness. In M. Gazzaniga (Ed.), *The cognitive neurosciences* (3rd ed.). New York: Norton.

Dehaene, S., Jobert, A., Naccache, L., Ciuciu, P., Poline, J. B., Le Bihan, D., et al. (in press). Letter binding and invariant recognition of masked words: Behavioral and neuroimaging evidence. *Psychological Science, 15,* 307–313.

Dehaene, S., Kerszberg, M., & Changeux, J. P. (1998). A neuronal model of a global workspace in effortful cognitive tasks. *Proceedings of the National Academy of Sciences of the United States of America, 95,* 14529–14534.

Dehaene, S., Le Clec'H, G., Poline, J. B., Le Bihan, D., & Cohen, L. (2002). The visual word form area: A prelexical representation of visual words in the fusiform gyrus. *NeuroReport, 13,* 321–325.

Dehaene, S., & Naccache, L. (2001). Towards a cognitive neuroscience of consciousness: Basic evidence and a workspace framework. *Cognition, 79,* 1–37.

Dehaene, S., Naccache, L., Cohen, L., Le Bihan, D., Mangin, J. F., Poline, J. B., et al. (2001). Cerebral mechanisms of word masking and unconscious repetition priming. *Nature Neuroscience, 4,* 752–758.

Dehaene, S., Naccache, L., Le Clec'H, G., Koechlin, E., Mueller, M., Dehaene-Lambertz, G., et al. (1998). Imaging unconscious semantic priming. *Nature, 395,* 597–600.

Dehaene, S., Sergent, C., & Changeux, J. P. (2003). A neuronal network model linking subjective reports and objective physiological data during conscious perception. *Proceedings of the National Academy of Sciences of the United States of America, 100,* 8520–8525.

Di Lollo, V., Enns, J. T., & Rensink, R. A. (2000). Competition for consciousness among visual events: The psychophysics of reentrant visual processes. *Journal of Experimental Psychology: General, 129,* 481–507.

Di Virgilio, G., & Clarke, S. (1997). Direct interhemispheric visual input to human speech areas. *Human Brain Mapping, 5,* 347–354.

Edelman, G. M. (1993). Neural Darwinism: Selection and reentrant signaling in higher brain function. *Neuron, 10,* 115–125.

Forster, K. I., & Davis, C. (1984). Repetition priming and frequency attenuation in lexical access. *Journal of Experimental Psychology: Learning, Memory, and Cognition, 10,* 680–698.

Goldman-Rakic, P. S. (1988). Topography of cognition: Parallel distributed networks in primate association cortex. *Annual Review of Neuroscience, 11,* 137–156.

Greenwald, A. G., Abrams, R. L., Naccache, L., & Dehaene, S. (2003). Long-term semantic memory versus contextual memory in unconscious number processing. *Journal of Experimental Psychology: Learning, Memory, and Cognition, 29,* 235–247.

Greenwald, A. G., Draine, S. C., & Abrams, R. L. (1996). Three cognitive markers of unconscious semantic activation. *Science, 273,* 1699–1702.

Grill-Spector, K., Kushnir, T., Hendler, T., & Malach, R. (2000). The dynamics of object-selective activation correlate with recognition performance in humans. *Nature Neuroscience, 3,* 837–843.

Koechlin, E., Naccache, L., Block, E., & Dehaene, S. (1999). Primed numbers: Exploring the modularity of numerical representations with masked and unmasked semantic priming. *Journal of Experimental Psychology: Human Perception and Performance, 25,* 1882–1905.

Kunde, W., Kiesel, A., & Hoffmann, J. (2003). Conscious control over the content of unconscious cognition. *Cognition, 88,* 223–242.

Lamme, V. A., & Roelfsema, P. R. (2000). The distinct modes of vision offered by feedforward and recurrent processing. *Trends in Neuroscience, 23,* 571–579.

Llinas, R., Ribary, U., Contreras, D., & Pedroarena, C. (1998). The neuronal basis for consciousness. *Philosophical Transactions: Biological Sciences, 353,* 1841–1849.

Marsolek, C. J., Kosslyn, S. M., & Squire, L. R. (1992). Form-specific visual priming in the right cerebral hemisphere. *Journal of Experimental Psychology: Learning, Memory, and Cognition, 18,* 492–508.

Molko, N., Cohen, L., Mangin, J. F., Chochon, F., Lehericy, S., Le Bihan, D., et al. (2002). Visualizing the neural bases of a disconnection syndrome with diffusion tensor imaging. *Journal of Cognitive Neuroscience, 14,* 629–636.

Naccache, L., Blandin, E., & Dehaene, S. (2002). Unconscious masked priming depends on temporal attention. *Psychological Science, 13,* 416–424.

Naccache, L., & Dehaene, S. (2001a). The priming method: Imaging unconscious repetition priming reveals an abstract representation of number in the parietal lobes. *Cerebral Cortex, 11,* 966–974.

Naccache, L., & Dehaene, S. (2001b). Unconscious semantic priming extends to novel unseen stimuli. *Cognition, 80,* 215–229.

Neumann, O., & Klotz, W. (1994). Motor responses to non-reportable, masked stimuli: Where is the limit of direct motor specification. In C. Umiltà & M. Moscovitch (Eds.), *Attention and performance XV: Conscious and non-conscious information processing* (pp. 123–150). Cambridge, MA: MIT Press.

Norman, D. A., & Shallice, T. (1980). Attention to action: Willed and automatic control of behavior. In R. J. Davidson, G. E. Schwartz, & D. Shapiro (Eds.), *Consciousness and self-regulation* (Vol. 4, pp. 1–18). New York: Plenum Press.

Pardo, J. V., Fox, P. T., & Raichle, M. E. (1991). Localization of a human system for sustained attention by positron emission tomography. *Nature, 349,* 61–64.

Pardo, J. V., Pardo, P. J., Janer, K. W., & Raichle, M. E. (1990). The anterior cingulate cortex mediates processing selection in the Stroop attentional conflict paradigm. *Proceedings of the National Academy of Sciences of the United States of America, 87,* 256–259.

Paulesu, E., Demonet, J. F., Fazio, F., McCrory, E., Chanoine, V., Brunswick, N., et al. (2001). Dyslexia: cultural diversity and biological unity. *Science, 291,* 2165–2167.

Petersen, S. E., Fox, P. T., Posner, M. I., Mintun, M., & Raichle, M. E. (1988). Positron emission tomographic studies of the cortical anatomy of single-word processing. *Nature, 331,* 585–589.

Posner, M. I. (1978). *Chronometric explorations of the mind.* Hillsdale, NJ: Erlbaum.

Posner, M. I. (1993). Seeing the mind. *Science, 262,* 673–674.

Posner, M. I. (1994). Attention: The mechanisms of consciousness. *Proceedings of the National Academy of Sciences of the United States of America, 91,* 7398–7403.

Posner, M. I., & Carr, T. H. (1992). Lexical access and the brain: Anatomical constraints on cognitive models of word recognition. *American Journal of Psychology, 105,* 1–26.

Posner, M. I., & Petersen, S. E. (1990). The attention system of the human brain. *Annual Review of Neuroscience, 13,* 25–42.

Posner, M. I., Petersen, S. E., Fox, P. T., & Raichle, M. E. (1988). Localization of cognitive operations in the human brain. *Science, 240,* 1627–1631.

Posner, M. I., & Raichle, M. E. (1995). Precis of images of mind. *Behavioral and Brain Sciences, 18,* 327–383.

Posner, M. I., & Rothbart, M. K. (1998). Attention, self-regulation and consciousness. *Philosophical Transactions: Biological Sciences, 353,* 1915–1927.

Rees, G., Kreiman, G., & Koch, C. (2002). Neural correlates of consciousness in humans. *Nature Reviews Neuroscience, 3,* 261–270.

Reynvoet, B., Brysbaert, M., & Fias, W. (2002). Semantic priming in number naming. *Quarterly Journal of Experimental Psychology A, 55,* 1127–1139.

Reynvoet, B., Caessens, B., & Brysbaert, M. (2002). Automatic stimulus–response associations may be semantically mediated. *Psychonomic Bulletin and Review, 9,* 107–112.

Shaywitz, B. A., Shaywitz, S. E., Pugh, K. R., Mencl, W. E., Fulbright, R. K., Skudlarski, P., et al. (2002). Disruption of posterior brain systems for reading in children with developmental dyslexia. *Biological Psychiatry, 52,* 101–110.

Vogel, E. K., Luck, S. J., & Shapiro, K. L. (1998). Electrophysiological evidence for a postperceptual locus of suppression during the attentional blink. *Journal of Experimental Psychology: Human Perception and Performance, 24,* 1656–1674.

Vorberg, D., Mattler, U., Heinecke, A., Schmidt, T., & Schwarzbach, J. (2003). Different time courses for visual perception and action priming. *Proceedings of the National Academy of Sciences of the United States of America, 100,* 6275–6280.

Warrington, E. K., & Shallice, T. (1980). Word-form dyslexia. *Brain, 103,* 99–112.

5

Task Models in Prefrontal Cortex

John Duncan

Towards the end of 1978, I spent a few weeks travelling back to the United Kingdom after 2 years of postdoctoral work with Michael Posner's group at the University of Oregon. For entertainment I was reading my prized, signed copy of *Chronometric Explorations of Mind,* just published. During my 2 years in Eugene, Posner had been struggling through the many complex phases of seeing this volume into print; if I remember correctly, he had promised that once this was through he would never write a book again. (This turned out to be one of his worse predictions.)

Although firmly based in the methods of cognitive psychology, Posner's book laid out a research agenda in which, through the common medium of mental chronometry, there would be convergence of behavioral and neurophysiological levels of explanation. At this time, for example, Posner was enthusiastic about the emerging single-unit studies of superior colliculus, parietal cortex, and frontal eye field, and their potential relevance to the questions we asked in cognitive studies of attention. Ten years later, when Mike published his first experiments with the St. Louis positron emission tomography (PET) group, this idea of a converging research agenda turned out to be one of his all-time best predictions, capturing the imagination of the world. Like thousands of others, I have spent the following 25 years filling out the details.

In that spirit, this chapter is concerned with the physiology and psychology of frontal lobe function. In physiological terms, a core idea in the field is regional specialization of function; given the size and anatomical heterogeneity of prefrontal cortex, it seems certain that there must be some corresponding functional segregation. In psychological terms, a core idea is modular executive function; possibly separate regions of prefrontal cortex may be devoted to abstract control functions such as inhibition of unwanted behavior, or switching of mental set. Although admitting some merit in these ideas, the account I shall suggest has a rather different perspective both on regional specialization and on frontal control functions.

Working memory is often taken to be a central aspect of prefrontal function (Goldman-Rakic, 1988). As Posner himself has expressed it, an appealing idea is that prefrontal cortex might "represent information in some temporary store while the brain provides information on what is known about the item" (Posner,

2004). This is a perspective rather different from that of abstract control functions such as inhibition or switching. Instead, prefrontal control is exerted by holding a salient representation of task-relevant content, allowing other processing systems to deliver additional information about that content and related material (see also Miller, 2000). I begin this chapter with a review of results from single-unit and neuroimaging studies, arguing that, instead of tight functional specialization, frontal neurons adapt to code specific information of relevance to a current task. This representation, I suggest, is similar to the working memory of symbolic artificial intelligence programs such as Newell's (1990) SOAR, building a temporary model of some aspect of the world and the actions planned on it. This model, in turn, controls behavior through providing the conditions for both external action and further information retrieval or model elaboration. Finally, I propose that this task-modelling function is closely related to standard measures of fluid intelligence (Cattell, 1971) and describe some new experiments analyzing an associated cognitive phenomenon—"goal neglect" or apparent disregard for a task's requirements (Duncan, Emslie, Williams, Johnson, & Freer, 1996).

An Illustrative Study

Perhaps the strongest evidence for selective prefrontal coding of task-relevant information comes from single-unit recording in the behaving monkey. An example is a recent study of activity in the lateral prefrontal cortex in a target selection task (Everling, Tinsley, Gaffan, & Duncan, 2002).

The task is illustrated in Figure 5.1. On each trial, the monkey saw a series of pictures, presented to left and/or right of fixation. His task was to hold central fixation until seeing a specific target stimulus (a fish), then to make an immediate saccade onto it. In the unilateral task (Figure 5.1a, left), stimuli appeared only to one side or the other. The trial began with a cue (a white square) showing where the stimulus stream would be, followed by a series of 0 to 3 nontargets (hamburgers and teddy bears) and then the target. This task was used to ask whether object-specific responses would be seen in prefrontal neurons, and, if so, what form they would take. In the bilateral task (Figure 5.1a, right), stimuli were the same except that, accompanying each stimulus on the cued side, there was a simultaneous stimulus on the uncued side, which the animal was to ignore. This task was used to investigate modulation of prefrontal responses by spatially directed attention. Recordings were made in a region spanning the principal sulcus, including parts of both dorsolateral and ventrolateral surfaces (Figure 5.1b).

Consider first the unilateral task. Strikingly, there was almost no information in prefrontal responses concerning the distinction between one nontarget and another. Of 161 cells recorded, only one showed a significantly different response to hamburger and teddy bear ($p < .01$). In contrast, over a quarter of all cells (44/161), broadly distributed throughout the recording area (Figure 5.1b), showed significantly different responses to target versus nontargets.

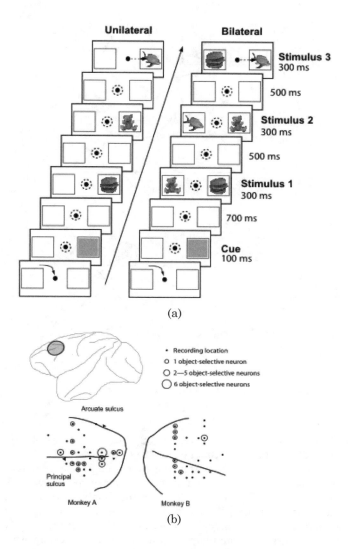

Figure 5.1. Tasks and recording locations from Everling et al. (2002). (a) Example stimulus sequences in unilateral and bilateral tasks. Each trial began when the monkey fixated (curved arrow) a small dot in the center of the screen. A cue (a white square here shaded gray) appeared to left or right, followed by a stream of stimuli in just the cued location (unilateral condition) or in both locations (bilateral condition). Central fixation (dotted circle) was to be maintained until a target (fish) appeared at the cued location, at which point an immediate saccade (dotted arrow) to this target was required. (b) Location of recording sites, with numbers of cells showing significant object (target vs. nontarget) selectivity (excitatory only, $n = 33$). From "Filtering of Neural Signals by Focused Attention in the Monkey Prefrontal Cortex," by S. Everling, C. J. Tinsley, D. Gaffan, and J. Duncan, 2002, *Nature Neuroscience, 5*, p. 672. Copyright 2002 by Nature Publishing Group. Reprinted with permission.

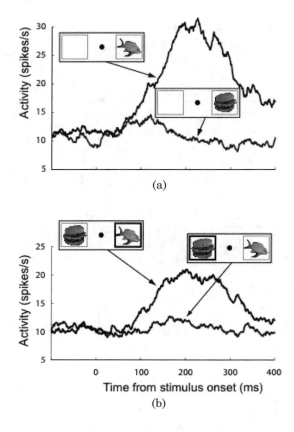

Figure 5.2. Data (mean discharge rates for 33 object-selective cells) from Everling et al. (2002). (a) Unilateral task. Although display icons illustrate stimuli on the right, in fact data for each cell were taken from the preferred location, defined as the side giving stronger responses. Results show strong response to target, with little or no response to nontargets. (b) Bilateral task. Data for displays with one target in the preferred location (here illustrated on right), and one nontarget in the nonpreferred location (illustrated on left). Heavy box (not present in actual display) illustrates attended location. Results show complete suppression of target response when attention is paid to the nontarget location. From "Filtering of Neural Signals by Focused Attention in the Monkey Prefrontal Cortex," by S. Everling, C. J. Tinsley, D. Gaffan, and J. Duncan, 2002, *Nature Neuroscience, 5*, pp. 673–674. Copyright 2002 by Nature Publishing Group. Reprinted with permission.

Mean discharge rates for 33 cells with excitatory responses are shown in Figure 5.2a; they show a strong response to the target, but (on the average) essentially no response to nontargets. A variety of controls (e.g., response on error trials) show that this target response was not related to eye movement, but to the classification of the fish stimulus as a target for this task.

Already this is an interesting result. It is worth emphasizing that, in this study, cells were not selected for response to the task; instead each electrode was advanced until any cell was well isolated, then the task and recording began. Nevertheless, more than a quarter of all recorded cells in this large region of prefrontal cortex appeared to be tuned as approximations to the optimal filter for this task, responding well to the stimulus with some implication for behavior, and ignoring the rest. A current follow-up study shows related results when target identity is not fixed throughout the experiment but varies from trial to trial (Sigala, Kusunoki, Gaffan, & Duncan, 2003).

This principle of selective response to task-relevant input was also strongly supported in the bilateral task. An illustration is shown in Figure 5.2b, showing mean responses of the same 33 target-selective cells for a bilateral display consisting of one target and one nontarget. The example shows data from displays with the target on the cell's preferred side, that is, the side giving stronger responses in the unilateral task, but essentially the same result was seen with the converse arrangement. For the same display, attention could be directed either to the target or to the nontarget, depending on the preceding cue. With attention to the target, there was a strong response, similar to that seen in the unilateral task. When the target occurred on the uncued side—and so was irrelevant to behavior—this prefrontal response was eliminated.

A third example of the same principle is suggested by analysis of neural activity during the delay periods between one stimulus and the next within each trial (Everling, Tinsley, Gaffan, & Duncan, 2004). In the bilateral task, the animal needed to maintain some record of the cued location throughout the trial, indicating which side to attend. In the unilateral task, this was less necessary because stimuli themselves occurred only on one side. Correspondingly, we found that many more cells carried delay-period location information—differential responses for attend-left and attend-right trials—in the bilateral as compared to the unilateral task. Once more, relevance to behavior is a key factor determining response patterns of single prefrontal neurons.

Single-Unit Studies: General Findings

The Everling and colleagues (2002) data illustrate several broad properties of information representation in prefrontal cortex. These same properties have been noted for a wide variety of different tasks, including tests of stimulus categorization and matching, spatial or object working memory, abstract rule following, set switching, and many others. In most cases, recordings have been made on the lateral convexity (Figure 5.1b), although some studies have examined medial and orbital surfaces (e.g., Wallis, Anderson, & Miller, 2001).

First, even when neurons are randomly sampled, many turn out to be related to events in the particular, arbitrary task that the monkey has been set. If the criterion is simply that responses should differ from one task epoch to another, the proportion of task-related neurons can approach 100% (Asaad, Rainer, & Miller, 1998, 2000). Stricter criteria—for example, selective response for a specific object category (Freedman, Riesenhuber, Poggio, & Miller, 2001)—will still be satisfied by substantial proportions of randomly selected neurons.

Second, these task-related responses are of many different kinds. Cells may respond selectively to certain stimuli or stimulus categories, whether in visual, auditory, or tactile modalities (e.g., Fuster, Bodner, & Kroger, 2000; Romo,

Brody, Hernández, & Lemus, 1999). They may discharge in association with particular movements of the hand or eye (e.g., Asaad et al., 1998; Watanabe, 1986b). Many cells show working memory activity, carrying information across brief delays between its presentation and use (e.g., Fuster & Alexander, 1971; Funahashi, Bruce, & Goldman-Rakic, 1989). Many also code abstract task rules (e.g., Wallis et al., 2001), and information about the availability and receipt of rewards (Niki & Watanabe, 1979; Watanabe, 1996).

Third, responses of different kinds will all be found broadly distributed and closely intermingled throughout the recorded area (e.g., Rao, Rainer, & Miller, 1997; Wallis et al., 2001; Watanabe, 1986a). This is not to say that no regional specialization is ever apparent. Object-selective cells, for example, are sometimes most common on the ventrolateral convexity, where information is directly received from inferotemporal cortex (Ó Scalaidhe, Wilson, & Goldman-Rakic, 1999; Wallis et al., 2001). Such specializations, however, are usually statistical rather than absolute, with relatively small differences between regions in proportions of different cell types. The strongest specialization may be seen when only the most highly selective neurons are examined (Ó Scalaidhe et al., 1999).

Fourth, the information coded by prefrontal neurons is strongly constrained by task relevance. As in the Everling and others (2002) study, prefrontal neurons preferentially respond to the relevant objects in a visual display (Rainer, Asaad, & Miller, 1998; Schall, Hanes, Thompson, & King, 1995). They code relevant rather than irrelevant stimulus dimensions (Rao et al., 1997; Sakagami & Niki, 1994). For a fixed stimulus set, prefrontal cells change their properties to reflect currently relevant categorizations (Freedman et al., 2001), discarding within-category stimulus differences.

An Adaptive Coding Account

Together, these results suggest an adaptive coding principle for prefrontal function (Duncan, 2001; see also Duncan & Miller, 2002; Miller & Cohen, 2001). For much of prefrontal cortex, the proposal is that neurons do not have fixed functional properties. Hence, they cannot be segregated into regions with clearly distinct functions. Instead, each neuron potentially has access to many different kinds of information, perhaps through the dense interconnections that exist between one frontal region and another (e.g., Pandya & Yeterian, 1996). For any given task, neurons adapt their function to emphasize information of current relevance—producing a dense, distributed representation of this task's inputs, outputs, rules, rewards, and other related material. This is why so many task-related neurons, coding so many different task features, are so broadly distributed across prefrontal cortex.

These ideas are reminiscent of a central idea in artificial intelligence models addressing complex, organized behavior (e.g., Anderson, 1983; Newell, 1990). For models such as ACT* (Anderson, 1983) and SOAR (Newell, 1990), working memory is far more powerful and complex than a simple buffer preserving stimulus information across a brief delay. The architecture of SOAR, for example, is shown in Figure 5.3. At the heart of the model, working memory

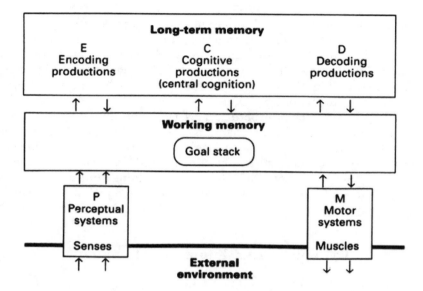

Figure 5.3. Architecture of SOAR. From *Unified Theories of Cognition* by A. Newell, 1990, Cambridge, MA: Harvard University Press, p. 195. Copyright 1990 by Harvard University Press. Reprinted with permission.

builds up a temporary model of some aspect of the world. This can be anything— a chess problem, an environment to be navigated around, a product to be designed. The model includes both the current state of the world, and the goals to be achieved or actions to be taken. In part, it is built up by new perceptual input, and in part, by the program's long-term knowledge of the world and its structure. As reviewed above, the responses of prefrontal neurons suggest exactly this sort of temporary, online model of task-relevant facts and actions.

Crucially, the working memory model in a system such as SOAR controls every aspect of the program's behavior. Actions in SOAR—whether internal, such as adding a new fact to the model, or external, such as moving a particular object—are productions that fire when their enabling conditions are met. It is the working memory model that provides current conditions and hence determines which productions can execute. Although such ideas are consistent with the common view that prefrontal cortex controls cognition, control here is not implemented by abstract functions such as inhibition or set switching. Instead, control is exerted by a representation of task-relevant facts or content (see Kane & Engle, 2003; Kimberg & Farah, 1993).

Of course, neural activity related to working memory is not restricted to prefrontal cortex. In the delay period of a short-term memory task, both single-unit (e.g., Chafee & Goldman-Rakic, 1998) and neuroimaging (e.g., Haxby, Petit, Ungerleider, & Courtney, 2000) experiments show activity in multiple posterior regions, including parietal and temporal cortex. It is correspondingly unlikely that working memory in the sense defined by programs such as SOAR is exclusively based on prefrontal cortex. Modulation of response by task relevance is also found in many brain regions; for example, stronger responses to an attended input throughout much or all of the cortical visual system (Desimone & Duncan, 1995). In many parts of the brain, in other words, cells have the potential to be driven by a range of different inputs—for example, the different stimuli in a visual cell's receptive field—with preference given to those of relevance to current behavior.

Plausibly, the role of prefrontal cortex is to optimize the task model in various ways, for example by increasing its focus on strictly relevant information, or its flexibility as conditions change. In turn, the focus on task-relevant information in prefrontal cortex may support related processing elsewhere in the brain (Miller & Cohen, 2001)—Posner's holding "information in some temporary store while the brain provides information on what is known about the item" (Posner, 2004).

Evidence From Functional Imaging

These ideas suggest that many different task models might be built in much the same regions of prefrontal cortex. From single-unit data we take the message that prefrontal neurons with different task roles are closely intermingled, with at best statistical variations from one region to another. How does this fit with evidence from human neuroimaging?

Limited statistical power means that, inevitably, any one imaging study will show only a part of the true activation associated with its particular cognitive demand. To obtain a more complete picture, one approach is to combine results from a number of similar studies. In one such exercise, Owen and myself assembled data from 20 studies then available in the literature, concerned with a range of cognitive demands including perceptual difficulty, task novelty, suppression of prepotent responses, and two aspects of working memory (Duncan & Owen, 2000). Studies were chosen to represent as pure as possible a manipulation of just one cognitive demand in an otherwise unchanged task. From the 20 selected studies we plotted together all reported activation peaks in prefrontal cortex. The results are shown in colorplate 1, with different shaded squares showing activations associated with different kinds of task demand.

On the one hand, the results show striking clustering of activations within specific prefrontal regions. On the medial surface (middle row), almost all activations lay in and around the dorsal part of the anterior cingulate. On the lateral surface (upper row), there were evident clusters around the posterior part of the inferior frontal sulcus (IFS), and on the frontal operculum/anterior insula (in colorplate 1 projected onto the lateral surface, and showing as a cluster just anterior to the sylvian fissure). Certainly clustering was weaker on the lateral as compared with the medial surface, but still, there were again large regions without activations (see dorsal brain view, bottom left). Activations were also rare on the whole orbital surface (ventral brain view, bottom right).

On the other hand, there was absolutely no clustering by cognitive demand. For all five demands, there was the same joint activation of dorsal anterior cingulate, posterior IFS, and frontal operculum/insula. Although the results show clear regional specialization within prefrontal cortex, this is not specialization based on task content. Instead, much the same prefrontal regions are recruited by diverse cognitive demands.

In fact, a picture of frontal lobe activation roughly such as that shown in colorplate 1 is extremely familiar in the imaging literature, in studies of perception, response choice, episodic memory, language, problem-solving, divided attention, and many other cognitive domains (Duncan & Owen, 2000). At the same time, there are certainly variations on this same broad theme. Verbal tasks, for example, will often produce stronger activation in the left hemisphere, though commonly with clear evidence for a homologous activation on the right (e.g., Postle & D'Esposito, 2000; Thompson-Schill, D'Esposito, Aguirre, & Farah, 1997; Wagner, Maril, Bjork, & Schacter, 2001). As compared to physical tasks such as rote rehearsal, semantic tasks will sometimes produce a more anterior spread of left hemisphere activation (e.g., Wagner et al., 2001). Such results are well explained by the idea that, within prefrontal cortex, cells potentially relevant to verbal tasks are distributed in both hemispheres, but with somewhat different distributions for different verbal operations, and stronger concentration on the left. More generally, variations on the same general theme of prefrontal activation suggest overlapping, but not identical distributions of cells supporting different cognitive operations.

What then should we say of the large regions of prefrontal cortex apparently silent in colorplate 1? On the orbital surface, for example, many imaging studies show activation associated with a task's emotional or motivational content (e.g., Drevets, 2001; O'Doherty, Kringelbach, Rolls, Hornak, & Andrews, 2001). Much of the silent region in colorplate 1, including cortex around the midline on lateral, medial, and orbital surfaces, may show deactivation in simple tasks as compared to a resting baseline (Shulman et al., 1997), something clearly different from the demand-related activations of dorsal anterior cingulate, IFS, and operculum/insula. Against such seemingly clear parcellation, single-unit studies can show that, in any one task, even lateral and orbital surfaces have many neurons performing apparently similar functions (Wallis et al., 2001). More work is needed to clarify the relationship between imaging and single-unit results. Meanwhile it seems likely that, even for such distinct regions as the lateral and orbital surfaces, a degree of functional segregation is modulated by substantial task-dependent plasticity.

Goal Neglect and Spearman's *g*

In the neuropsychological literature, many tests have been used as measures of frontal lobe or executive function. These include Wisconsin card-sorting (Milner, 1963), verbal fluency (Benton, 1968), the Stroop task (Perret, 1974), and others. Commonly, deficits in such tasks are taken to reflect something quite specific related to particular task content—for example, a deficit in set switching for Wisconsin card-sorting, or in inhibition for the Stroop. I propose something different. For any task, performance in part is organized by the flexible task-modelling function of prefrontal cortex. In many and perhaps

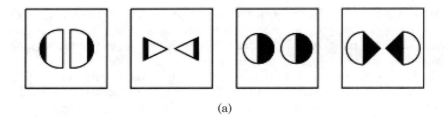

(a)

LHEC   DFIM   TQNK   HJMQ

(b)

Figure 5.4. Typical problem-solving tasks strongly dependent on *g*. The task is to find the picture (a) or letter string (b) that does not belong with the others. From "A Neural Basis for General Intelligence," by J. Duncan, R. J. Seitz, J. Kolodny, D. Bor, H. Herzog, A. Ahmed, et al., 2000, *Science, 289*, p. 479. Copyright 2000 by the National Association for the Advancement of Science. Adapted with permission.

most cases, executive tests are sensitive to frontal lesions not because of their particular content, but because of sensitivity to this general task-modelling function. Indeed, I suggest that any task in principle should be sensitive to impairments in the prefrontal model—though the best tests will be those whose variance is most dependent on this, with least contribution from other factors.

What will the best tests be? For many years (Duncan, 1990, 1993) I have suspected that a clue is given by the psychometric idea of general intelligence or Spearman's *g*. In psychometrics, a key result is ubiquity of positive correlations between one task and another—to some extent at least, the same people tend to do well even in quite different cognitive tests. As Spearman (1904) proposed, one hypothesis is that some general or *g* factor makes a contribution to success in all manner of tasks. The purest tests of *g* will be those whose variance is most dependent on this common factor; these can easily be defined by factor analysis and will be those with the strongest mean correlation with all other tests in a diverse battery. Typically, the best *g* tests turn out to require novel problem-solving with spatial, verbal, or other materials (Figure 5.4). Their broad ability to predict success in other tasks and activities explains their interpretation as measures of general intelligence. My suggestion is that *g* is largely a reflection of the prefrontal task-modelling function; hence the best measures of this function are novel problem-solving tasks of the sort commonly used to measure general intelligence.

Several sorts of evidence bear on this hypothesis. For many years, the conventional wisdom in neuropsychology was that frontal lesions produce little decrement in psychometric intelligence (e.g., Hebb & Penfield, 1940). Even when patients show preserved function on clinical tests such as the Wechsler Adult Intelligence Scale (WAIS; Wechsler, 1955), however, they can be massively impaired on novel problem-solving (Duncan, Burgess, & Emslie, 1995).

Problem-solving or fluid intelligence tests may be especially suitable for neuro-psychological studies, because they assess current function rather than a life-time's previous learning (Cattell, 1971). There is also some evidence from neuroimaging. Certainly, fluid intelligence tests produce strong activations in lateral prefrontal cortex (Duncan et al., 2000; Prabhakaran, Smith, Desmond, Glover, & Gabrieli, 1997). People with high g scores show stronger recruitment of both lateral prefrontal cortex and anterior cingulate when conflict is encountered in an ongoing working memory task (Gray, Chabris, & Braver, 2003). At the same time, these studies also show significant accompanying activations—in particular in parietal and premotor cortex, and sometimes also elsewhere. In this chapter, however, I shall not discuss this evidence in detail. Instead, I shall focus on my original reason for linking frontal lobe function to g—the phenomenon of goal neglect (Duncan, 1990; Duncan et al. 1996), or apparent disregard for known task requirements.

Goal neglect of this sort is an occasional but conspicuous feature of frontal lobe impairment. A patient may know, for example, that he has been asked to squeeze his hand when a light comes on and may repeat this instruction when the stimulus occurs, yet still make no movement (Luria, 1966). In Wisconsin card sorting, a patient will occasionally state that the current sorting rule should be changed yet still continue to use it (Milner, 1963). My interest in this phenomenon stems from an early study of accident proneness among trainee bus drivers (McKenna, Duncan, & Brown, 1986). Occasionally in that study, even people from the normal population showed a form of goal neglect in a complex dichotic listening task; apparently, they were perfectly aware of the task's rules yet still continued to violate them. Importantly, this failure—reminiscent as it was of frontal lobe impairment (Duncan, 1986)—seemed closely related to a standard measure of fluid intelligence. Although goal neglect is sensitive to task details, and often restricted to a small fraction of the normal population, eventually we were able to establish some of its properties in a visual variant of the original dichotic listening task (Duncan et al., 1996).

Stimuli for this visual task are illustrated in Figure 5.5. On each trial, the participant sees 13 pairs of alphanumeric characters, rapidly presented (one pair every 400 ms, 200 ms on with 200 ms interstimulus intervals) in the center of a computer screen. The task is to watch for letters, repeating them aloud as they occur. Importantly, the participant is cued to watch just one side or the other, repeating letters from the attended side and ignoring those on the opposite side. Two cues tell the participant which side to watch. At the beginning of the trial there is a verbal instruction on the screen, saying WATCH LEFT or WATCH RIGHT. Then after the tenth pair there is a second cue, which sometimes instructs a change of sides. Specifically, this cue is a symbol + or −, flashed in the center of the screen at the same speed as the rest of the stimulus sequence (200 ms interstimulus interval following tenth character pair, 200 ms cue, 200 ms interval before next pair). "A +" means that for the remainder of the trial (three more pairs) the participant should watch the right, and "a −" means left. As initial and final side cues are independent, half the trials require a switch when the + or − occurs.

In this task, it is the +/− cue that is sometimes neglected. Typically, a neglecting participant will stay on the same side throughout the trial, as if no

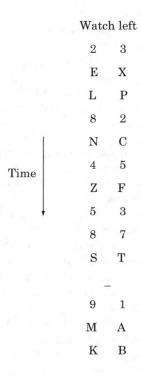

Figure 5.5. Stimuli from Duncan et al. (1996). The task is to repeat just letters from the attended side. For the last part of each trial, side is indicated by a brief central symbol: + for right, – for left. Adapted from Duncan et al. (1996).

+ or – had occurred. Several points are important (Duncan et al., 1996). First, even neglecting participants are always able to repeat back the +/– rule when asked at the end of the experiment. As in the case of frontal goal neglect, there is a mismatch between what is explicitly known of task requirements and what is actually done. Second, there is no absolute inability to follow task instructions. Almost always, neglect disappears if, immediately after each trial, the experimenter points out that the + or – was ignored. Just a few trials of such feedback are usually sufficient to produce correct performance, which then continues to the end of the experiment. Third, the impression that neglecting participants are not even attempting to follow the +/– instruction is confirmed by questions asked at the end of the experiment. A typical comment may be, " I realize now that I haven't been looking out for the plus or minus," or, "I've been letting those go over my head." Subjectively, the requirement was understood but slipped the participant's mind.

Fourth and most important, goal neglect is closely related to fluid intelligence. Typical results (Duncan et al., 1996) are shown in Figure 5.6. Here, 90 participants have been divided into bins based on a standard fluid intelligence test, Cattell's Culture Fair (Institute for Personality and Ability Testing, 1973). Published norms have been used to transform Culture Fair performance to z-scores; a score of 0, for example, means performance at the mean level in the

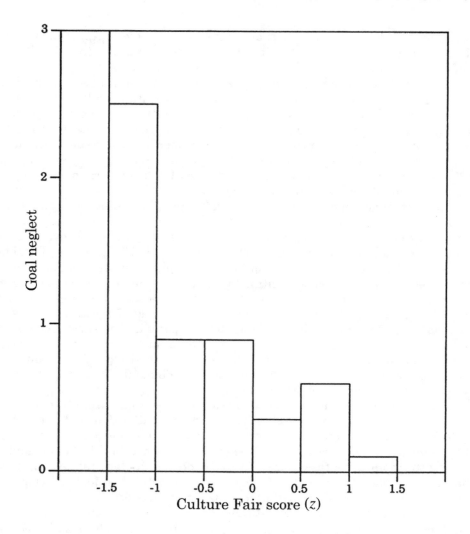

Figure 5.6. Goal neglect score as a function of Culture Fair score in a group of 90 participants from the normal population. Extreme bins include all participants beyond a Culture Fair z-score of plus or minus 1.5. From "Intelligence and the Frontal Lobe: The Organization of Goal-Directed Behavior," by J. Duncan, H. Emslie, P. Williams, R. Johnson, and C. Freer, 1996, *Cognitive Psychology, 30*, p. 271. Copyright 1996 by Blackwell. Adapted with permission.

population, and a score of −1 means performance 1 standard deviation below the mean. The details of the goal neglect score (ordinate) are not important; 3 however is the worst possible score, indicating total neglect of the +/− cue, whereas 0 is the best possible score, indicating essentially perfect cue use. The results show something remarkable. People with Culture Fair scores more than one standard deviation beneath the population mean almost always show complete +/− neglect. People with Culture Fair scores more than 1 standard deviation above the mean essentially never show neglect. Apparently, this simple tendency to forget one task requirement measures something much the same as a conventional problem-solving test of Spearman's *g*.

How might these data be interpreted in terms of a prefrontal task model? The suggestion would be that, as task instructions are received, a model of expected stimuli, actions, and requirements is constructed. Then as performance begins, important stimulus events act as triggers for the appropriate behavior specified in this model. If parts of this model in some sense interfere or compete, then vulnerable parts may lose salience. As a result they may fail to trigger, at least until salience is increased by further environmental input (verbal feedback from the experimenter).

In subsequent experiments (with Alice Parr, Peter Bright, and Sonia Bishop), we have repeatedly confirmed the close association between goal neglect and Spearman's *g*. These experiments have also produced several new findings on the conditions under which neglect occurs. Use of a symbolic side cue (+ or –), for example, is not important—the phenomenon is similar even when cues are arrows (< or >) pointing to the correct side. Neither is the length of the stimulus sequence at the start of each trial important; although it seems possible that a long stimulus sequence would encourage forgetting of the +/– requirement, changing the length from 10 to 25 pairs has no effect. Our main new results, however, concern the idea that different task requirements may compete for salience in the task model. Indeed, competition is important, because neglect does depend on concurrent task demands. This dependence, however, takes a rather intriguing form.

One simple idea would be that competition comes from the online demands of performance itself. Subjectively, the participant's attention could be taken up by monitoring for letters, so that side cues passed unnoticed. In a number of experiments, we have repeatedly failed to find evidence for this. For example, making the monitoring task more difficult by presenting four rather than two characters in each frame certainly decreases the number of letters detected; it has absolutely no effect, however, on neglect of the side cue.

A second idea concerns not real-time task demands, but the complexity of the whole task model. Figure 5.7 shows several kinds of trial from some recent experiments investigating this idea. Again, pairs of characters were presented in the center of a screen, at the same rate as before. This time, each trial was divided into three successive segments, separated by pairs of asterisks. Within each segment, there were either two pairs of letters, or two pairs of numbers. For letters, the task as before was to repeat those on the attended side. For numbers, the task was to add the two on the attended side, and state the result. After the first two segments, and an additional pair of asterisks, there was the second side cue (an arrow in this experiment), then one more segment to complete the trial. Thus for the mixed trial in Figure 5.7c, the correct response would be "H, T . . . 2 . . . 6." Possible trial types were pure letter (Figure 5.7a), pure number (Figure 5.7b), and mixed (Figure 5.7c).

This design allows us to contrast several cases. In one experiment, we compared mixed and pure trial blocks. In both cases, participants were first told about both letter and digit tasks, followed by an explanation of arrow cues. Half the participants then proceeded to a mixed block of 16 trials, within

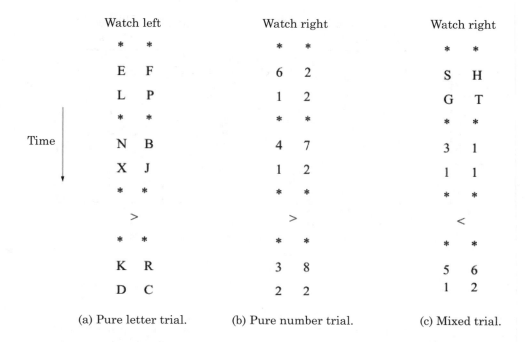

Figure 5.7. Three kinds of trial for goal-neglect experiments using mixed letter and number tasks. Within each trial, asterisk pairs serve as place markers separating one trial segment from the next. For each letter segment, the task is to repeat the two letters from the attended side. For each number segment, the task is to add together the two numbers on the attended side. In mixed blocks, there is a mixture of (a) pure letter trials, (b) pure number trials, and (c) mixed trials. Pure blocks have only letter trials or only number trials. For the last part of each trial, side is indicated by a brief central symbol: > for right, < for left.

which all three trial types were randomly mixed, and half received a different instruction. Before the first eight trials, participants were told that all trials in the first block would be of just one kind, pure letters or pure numbers (counterbalanced across participants). Thus they could temporarily forget about the other task type. Then for the next eight trials, the instruction was reversed—those beginning with letters now had just numbers, and those beginning with numbers now had just letters. The experiment asks whether neglect of the arrows increases when there are more accompanying task requirements to be borne in mind—when participants must be ready for both letters and numbers, as compared to just one or the other.

The results are shown in Figure 5.8a. Again, the details of the neglect score are not important; this time, complete neglect is reflected in a score of 8, whereas 0 again indicates perfect performance. Culture Fair bins are larger than those used in Figure 5.6, because this experiment had fewer participants. The results replicate the close relationship between neglect and Culture Fair. Results are exactly the same, however, for pure- and mixed-block participants. On a block-by-block basis, neglect is insensitive to total task complexity.

Full initial instructions,
pure blocks

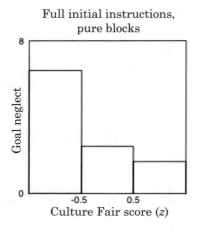

Full initial instructions,
mixed blocks

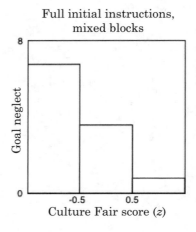

(a)

Full initial instructions,
pure blocks

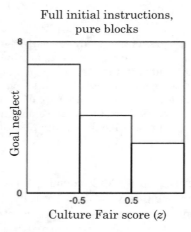

Reduced initial instructions,
pure blocks

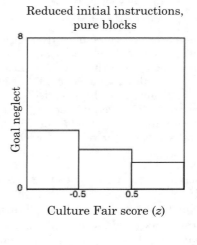

(b)

Figure 5.8. Goal neglect score as a function of Culture Fair score in comparison of (a) pure and mixed blocks with full instructions, and (b) pure blocks with full or reduced instructions. Extreme bins include all participants beyond a Culture Fair z-score of plus or minus 0.5.

Results were quite different, however, in a second experiment manipulating complexity at the level of the whole task model specified in initial instructions. For one group, the procedure exactly copied that of the pure-block participants from the previous experiment. Instructions for the whole task were followed by two pure blocks, one just for letters and one just for numbers. For the second group, there was one simple change. Before the first pure block of eight trials, instructions were given only for the task relevant to this block—just letters or just numbers, counterbalanced across participants. When those eight trials had been completed, instructions were now given for the second task, and the second pure block of this new task was given. For this group with reduced initial instructions, neglect was substantially decreased (Figure 5.8b).

These results make it clear that competition between active task requirements is indeed a key factor in goal neglect. Failure to trigger one task component depends on the demands of others. The most important factor, however, is not online demand over the time interval of a single trial. It is not even complexity over a whole block of trials. The key factor, rather, is complexity of the total task model specified in the original instructions. If this model is relatively simple, there is a strong chance that side cues on each trial will be recognized and appropriately considered. As in all our experiments with these tasks, even one successful trial is sufficient to ensure subsequent good performance; after a first correct trial, therefore, it does not matter if total task complexity is later increased (reduced-instruction participants, second task). What does matter is attempting all trials, even those at the outset, with a more complex total task model. Apparently, competition from the multiple components of this model reduces the salience of the side-cue requirement, producing full goal neglect in a good proportion of the normal participant population.

As we saw earlier, working memory is not exclusively associated with prefrontal cortex. The same may be true of Spearman's g and goal neglect. In our first study of this question (Duncan et al., 1996), deficits in Culture Fair and neglect were specifically associated with frontal lobe lesions. In that study, however, participant groups were rather small; the frontal group, furthermore, consisted largely of participants with closed head injury, resulting in additional diffuse pathology. In subsequent experiments (with Alice Parr, Peter Bright, and Sonia Bishop), we have reexamined the question, and although data are still being collected, already they suggest a more complex picture. As expected, frontal lesions are associated with reductions in g and associated increases in goal neglect. In some participants, especially those with large lesions, this deficit is substantial. Deficits can also be seen, however, in some participants with posterior lesions. More work is needed to clarify these results.

Our account, meanwhile, raises an obvious question. How does task modelling vary from one individual to another, as reflected in the measurement of g? Although it is only a conjecture, one idea is suggested by our prefrontal single-unit data (Everling et al., 2004). In an earlier section of the chapter, I presented data for the most object-selective cells in that study—those responding strongly to targets and much less to nontargets (Figure 5.2). As shown in Figure 5.2b, spatial attention strongly filtered the activity of these cells, with responses to the target fish only when it appeared at an attended location.

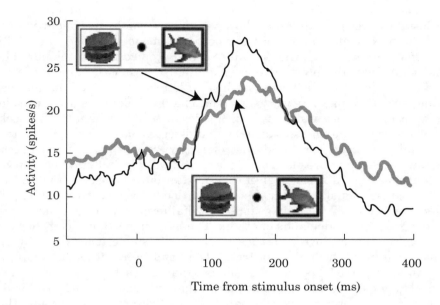

Figure 5.9. Mean discharge rates for 21 location-selective cells from the Everling and others (2000) study. Bilateral task with target in preferred location and nontarget in nonpreferred location: conventions as Figure 2b. For these cells, the target in the preferred location produced some response even when attention was focused away. Data from Everling et al. (2002).

Figure 5.9 shows data for a second set of cells, those with a strong preference not for one object—although as a population they did still respond more strongly to targets—but for one location, left or right. In this case, spatial filtering was less strong—even when attention was focused on a nontarget object in the cell's nonpreferred location, some response was still given to a preferred-location target. Data from the unilateral task confirmed that it was the unat-tended target that drove this response, not the attended nontarget. Although prefrontal cortex may approximate an ideal filter for task-relevant information, obviously this is only an approximation; at least in some cases, even task-irrelevant information retains some prefrontal representation (Lauwereyns et al., 2001). To me it seems appealing that g is largely concerned with a form of mental clarity—with the ability to focus just on that information bearing on a current problem, with all irrelevant details removed (Kane & Engle, 2003; for a related approach to cognitive aging see Hasher, Zacks, & May, 1999). Goal neglect, then, would reflect the cost of poor focus, a weak task component disappearing in the resulting mental noise.

Conclusion

In 1978, when *Chronometric Explorations of Mind* appeared, there was rapidly increasing interest in the use of neuropsychological data to inform cognitive models. But the strong theme was ultra-cognitive; an idea that hardware and software should be distinguished, that psychology concerned software, and that neuropsychological data should therefore be used as strictly behavioral, without reference to actual brain damage.

Among those trained in this tradition, it is still common to hear a similar argument, this time expressed as a criticism of brain imaging. What imaging research tells us, according to this line, is where something happens in the brain. Ultimately, knowledge of where does not bear on questions of how, that is, the functional questions of cognitive models. In fact, I would tend to agree that, in the first 10 years of imaging research, there was strong focus on simple where questions, or human brain mapping. Just as the doubters fear, the result can be curiously static in terms of cognitive theory; indeed knowledge of where does not bear on models of how.

The agenda put forward in *Chronometric Explorations of Mind* saw things differently. On the one hand, a commitment to integration of psychological and neural levels set Posner's approach far away from the ultra-cognitive fashion of the time. On the other hand, the physiological models of interest were just that—physiological rather than anatomical, that is, models of how, not where. As Posner put it, "The experiments described in this book can be viewed as an effort to develop an account at both the information-processing and physiological levels of . . . elementary mental operations" (p. 24). Twenty years later, the field is still catching up with this view, as neuroimaging increasingly turns from human brain mapping to questions of representation, processing, learning, and so on—in short, to questions not of location but of function (Kanwisher & Duncan, 2004). Preliminary as it is, the work in this chapter follows exactly the line Posner prescribed—the attempt to develop functional accounts cast simultaneously at cognitive and neural levels.

References

Anderson, J. R. (1983). *The architecture of cognition.* Cambridge, MA: Harvard University Press.

Asaad, W. F., Rainer, G., & Miller, E. K. (1998). Neural activity in the primate prefrontal cortex during associative learning. *Neuron, 21,* 1399–1407.

Asaad, W. F., Rainer, G., & Miller, E. K. (2000). Task-specific neural activity in the primate prefrontal cortex. *Journal of Neurophysiology, 84,* 451–459.

Benton, A. L. (1968). Differential behavioral effects in frontal lobe disease. *Neuropsychologia, 6,* 53–60.

Cattell, R. B. (1971). *Abilities: Their structure, growth and action.* Boston: Houghton-Mifflin.

Chafee, M. W., & Goldman-Rakic, P. S. (1998). Matching patterns of activity in primate prefrontal area 8a and parietal area 7ip neurons during a spatial working memory task. *Journal of Neurophysiology, 79,* 2919–2940.

Desimone, R., & Duncan, J. (1995). Neural mechanisms of selective visual attention. *Annual Review of Neuroscience, 18,* 193–222.

Drevets, W. C. (2001). Neuroimaging and neuropathological studies of depression: Implications for the cognitive–emotional features of mood disorders. *Current Opinion in Neurobiology, 11,* 240–249.

Duncan, J. (1986). Disorganization of behaviour after frontal lobe damage. *Cognitive Neuropsychology, 3,* 271–290.

Duncan, J. (1990). Goal weighting and the choice of behaviour in a complex world. *Ergonomics, 33,* 1265–1279.

Duncan, J. (1993). Selection of input and goal in the control of behaviour. In A. D. Baddeley & L. Weiskrantz (Eds.), *Attention: Selection, awareness and control. A tribute to Donald Broadbent* (pp. 53–71). Oxford, England: Oxford University Press.

Duncan, J. (2001). An adaptive coding model of neural function in prefrontal cortex. *Nature Reviews Neuroscience, 2,* 820–829.

Duncan, J., Burgess, P., & Emslie, H. (1995). Fluid intelligence after frontal lobe lesions. *Neuropsychologia, 33,* 261–268.

Duncan, J., Emslie, H., Williams, P., Johnson, R., & Freer, C. (1996). Intelligence and the frontal lobe: The organization of goal-directed behavior. *Cognitive Psychology, 30,* 257–303.

Duncan, J., & Miller, E. K. (2002). Cognitive focus through adaptive neural coding in the primate prefrontal cortex. In D. T. Stuss & R. T. Knight (Eds.), *Principles of frontal lobe function* (pp. 278–291). Oxford, England: Oxford University Press.

Duncan, J., & Owen, A. M. (2000). Common regions of the human frontal lobe recruited by diverse cognitive demands. *Trends in Neurosciences, 23,* 475–483.

Duncan, J., Seitz, R. J., Kolodny, J., Bor, D., Herzog, H., Ahmed, A., et al. (2000). A neural basis for general intelligence. *Science, 289,* 457–460.

Everling, S., Tinsley, C. J., Gaffan, D., & Duncan, J. (2002). Filtering of neural signals by focused attention in the monkey prefrontal cortex. *Nature Neuroscience, 5,* 671–676.

Everling, S., Tinsley, C. J., Gaffan, D., & Duncan, J. (2004). *Selective representation of task-relevant objects and locations in the monkey prefrontal cortex.* Manuscript in preparation.

Freedman, D. J., Riesenhuber, M., Poggio, T., & Miller, E. K. (2001). Categorical representation of visual stimuli in the primate prefrontal cortex. *Science, 291,* 312–316.

Funahashi, S., Bruce, C. J., & Goldman-Rakic, P. S. (1989). Mnemonic coding of visual space in the monkey's dorsolateral prefrontal cortex. *Journal of Neurophysiology, 61,* 331–349.

Fuster, J. M., & Alexander, G. E. (1971). Neuron activity related to short-term memory. *Science, 173,* 652–654.

Fuster, J. M., Bodner, M., & Kroger, J. K. (2000). Cross-modal and cross-temporal association in neurons of frontal cortex. *Nature, 405,* 347–351.

Goldman-Rakic, P. (1988). Topography of cognition: Parallel distributed networks in primate association cortex. *Annual Review of Neuroscience, 11,* 137–156.

Gray, J. R., Chabris, C. F., & Braver, T. S. (2003). Neural mechanisms of general fluid intelligence. *Nature Neuroscience, 6,* 316–322.

Hebb, D. O., & Penfield, W. (1940). Human behavior after extensive removal from the frontal lobes. *Archives of Neurology and Psychiatry, 44,* 421–438.

Hasher, L., Zacks, R. T., & May, C. P. (1999). Inhibitory control, circadian arousal, and age. In D. Gopher & A. Koriat (Eds.), *Attention and performance XVII. Cognitive regulation of performance: Interaction of theory and application* (pp. 653–675). Cambridge, MA: MIT Press.

Haxby, J. V., Petit, L., Ungerleider, L. G., & Courtney, S. M. (2000). Distinguishing the functional roles of multiple regions in distributed neural systems for visual working memory. *NeuroImage, 11,* 380–391.

Institute for Personality and Ability Testing. (1973). *Measuring intelligence with the Culture Fair tests.* Champaign, IL: Institute for Personality and Ability Testing.

Kane, M. J., & Engle, R. W. (2003). Working-memory capacity and the control of attention: The contributions of goal neglect, response competition, and task set to Stroop interference. *Journal of Experimental Psychology: General, 132,* 47–70.

Kanwisher, N. G., & Duncan, J. (2004). *Attention and performance XX: Functional brain imaging of visual cognition.* Oxford, England: Oxford University Press.

Kimberg, D. Y., & Farah, M. J. (1993). A unified account of cognitive impairments following frontal lobe damage: The role of working memory in complex, organized behavior. *Journal of Experimental Psychology: General, 122,* 411–428.

Lauwereyns, J., Sakagami, M., Tsutsui, K.-I., Kobayashi, S., Koizumi, M., & Hikosaka, O. (2001). Responses to task-irrelevant visual features by primate prefrontal neurons. *Journal of Neurophysiology, 86,* 2001–2010.

Luria, A. R. (1966). *Higher cortical functions in man.* London: Tavistock.

McKenna, F. P., Duncan, J., & Brown, I. D. (1986). Cognitive abilities and safety on the road: A re-examination of individual differences in dichotic listening and search for embedded figures. *Ergonomics, 29,* 649–663.

Miller, E. K. (2000). The prefrontal cortex and cognitive control. *Nature Reviews Neuroscience, 1,* 59–65.

Miller, E. K., & Cohen, J. D. (2001). An integrative theory of prefrontal function. *Annual Review of Neuroscience, 24,* 167–202.

Milner, B. (1963). Effects of different brain lesions on card sorting. *Archives of Neurology, 9,* 90–100.

Newell, A. (1990). *Unified theories of cognition.* Cambridge, MA: Harvard University Press.

Niki, H., & Watanabe, M. (1979). Prefrontal and cingulate unit activity during timing behavior in the monkey. *Brain Research, 171,* 213–224.

O'Doherty, J., Kringelbach, M. L., Rolls, E. T., Hornak, J., & Andrews, C. (2001). Abstract reward and punishment representations in the human orbitofrontal cortex. *Nature Neuroscience, 4,* 95–102.

Ó Scalaidhe, P., Wilson, F. A. W., & Goldman-Rakic, P. S. (1999). Face-selective neurons during passive viewing and working memory performance of rhesus monkeys: Evidence for intrinsic specialization of neuronal coding. *Cerebral Cortex, 9,* 459–475.

Pandya, D. N., & Yeterian, E. H. (1996). Comparison of prefrontal architecture and connections. *Philosophical Transactions of the Royal Society of London Series B, 351,* 1423–1432.

Perret, E. (1974). The left frontal lobe in man and the suppression of habitual responses in verbal categorical behavior. *Neuropsychologia, 12,* 323–330.

Posner, M. I. (1978). *Chronometric explorations of mind.* Hillsdale, NJ: Erlbaum.

Posner, M. I. (2004). The achievement of brain imaging: Past and future. In N. G. Kanwisher & J. Duncan (Eds.), *Attention and performance XX: Functional brain imaging of visual cognition* (pp. 505–528). Oxford, England: Oxford University Press.

Postle, B. R., & D'Esposito, M. (2000). Evaluating models of the topographical organization of working memory function in frontal cortex with event-related fMRI. *Psychobiology, 28,* 146–155.

Prabhakaran, V., Smith, J. A. L., Desmond, J. E., Glover, G. H., & Gabrieli, J. D. E. (1997). Neural substrates of fluid reasoning: An fMRI study of neocortical activation during performance of the Raven's Progressive Matrices Test. *Cognitive Psychology, 33,* 43–63.

Rainer, G., Asaad, W. F., & Miller, E. K. (1998). Selective representation of relevant information by neurons in the primate prefrontal cortex. *Nature, 393,* 577–579.

Rao, S. C., Rainer, G., & Miller, E. K. (1997). Integration of what and where in the primate prefrontal cortex. *Science, 276,* 821–824.

Romo, R., Brody, C. D., Hernández, A., & Lemus, L. (1999). Neuronal correlates of parametric working memory in the prefrontal cortex. *Nature, 399,* 470–473.

Sakagami, M., & Niki, H. (1994). Encoding of behavioral significance of visual stimuli by primate prefrontal neurons: Relation to relevant task conditions. *Experimental Brain Research, 97,* 423–436.

Schall, J. D., Hanes, D. P., Thompson, K. G., & King, D. J. (1995). Saccade target selection in frontal eye field of macaque: 1. Visual and premovement activation. *Journal of Neuroscience, 15,* 6905–6918.

Shulman, G. L., Fiez, J. A., Corbetta, M., Buckner, R. L., Miezin, F. M., Raichle, M. E., et al. (1997). Common blood flow changes across visual tasks: II. Decreases in cerebral cortex. *Journal of Cognitive Neuroscience, 9,* 648–663.

Sigala, N., Kusunoki, M., Gaffan, D., & Duncan, J. (2003). *Task relevance and cue-target association in the monkey prefrontal cortex* [Abstract]. Program No. 180.8 Abstract Viewer/Itinerary Planner. Washington, DC: Society for Neuroscience Abstracts.

Spearman, C. (1904). General intelligence, objectively determined and measured. *American Journal of Psychology, 15,* 201–293.

Thompson-Schill, S. L., D'Esposito, M. D., Aguirre, G. K., & Farah, M. J. (1997). Role of left inferior prefrontal cortex in retrieval of semantic knowledge: A reevaluation. *Proceedings of the National Academy of Sciences of the United States of America, 94,* 14792–14797.

Wagner, A. D., Maril, A., Bjork, R. A., & Schacter, D. L. (2001). Prefrontal contributions to executive control: fMRI evidence for functional distinctions within lateral prefrontal cortex. *NeuroImage, 14,* 1337–1347.

Wallis, J. D., Anderson, K. C., & Miller, E. K. (2001). Single neurons in prefrontal cortex encode abstract rules. *Nature, 411,* 953–956.

Watanabe, M. (1986a). Prefrontal unit activity during delayed conditional go/no-go discrimination in the monkey. I. Relation to the stimulus. *Brain Research, 382,* 1–14.

Watanabe, M. (1986b). Prefrontal unit activity during delayed conditional go/no-go discrimination in the monkey. II. Relation to go and no-go responses. *Brain Research, 382,* 15–27.

Watanabe, M. (1996). Reward expectancy in primate prefrontal neurons. *Nature, 382,* 629–632.

Wechsler, D. (1955). *Wechsler Adult Intelligence Scale.* New York: Psychological Corporation.

6

Imaging the Human Brain: Reflections on Some Emerging Issues

Marcus E. Raichle

This festschrift for Michael Posner honors the contributions of one of the foremost cognitive scientists of our time. As a scientist, colleague, mentor, and friend, he has influenced the work and careers of virtually all who have had the privilege of working with him and, through his work, has left an indelible imprint. His impact on cognitive neuroscience and, in particular, functional imaging of the human brain, which my colleagues and I experienced first hand, was no exception. Working with our group in St. Louis, he brought the strategies of cognitive psychology (presented in his classic monograph *Chronometric Explorations of Mind,* 1978) to newly emerging functional imaging techniques (e.g., stereotaxic normalization, image averaging, response localization; for a historical review, see Raichle, 2000) that together established the basis of functional imaging strategies that have continued to evolve to the present time (Posner & Raichle, 1994). The evolution of this work has been surprising in terms of the explosive growth of the field of cognitive neuroscience and encouraging with regard to the potential for new insights into the relationship between brain and behavior (e.g., see other articles in this Festschrift as well as a recent *Journal of Neuroscience* miniseries on the subject, Raichle, 2003b).

Probably less evident to those in the social sciences including psychology has been the recent and rapidly accelerating interest in the underlying neurobiology of functional brain imaging signals obtained both with positron emission tomography (PET) and functional magnetic resonance imaging (fMRI; e.g., Ames, 2000; Attwell & Iadecola, 2002; Buckner, 2003; Heeger & Ress, 2002; Lauritzen & Gold, 2003; Logothetis, 2003). This work emerged initially in a climate of skepticism on the part of some in the scientific community about the utility of functional imaging in explaining the relationship between brain function and behavior (e.g., Nichols & Newsome, 1999; Uttal, 2001). Remarkably, this work has led to a thoughtful appraisal of functional imaging signals and also to a reappraisal of the primary signal of the neurophysiologists, the spiking activity of large, principal neurons. Even more interesting is the realization among some that both neurophysiologists and cognitive neuroscientists, because of the narrowness of the focus of their inquiry, have overlooked a major fraction of the functionally relevant activity in the brain (Raichle & Gusnard, 2002).

In this chapter, I review these issues and their possible relevance to the cognitive neuroscience agenda of the future.

Cognitive Neuroscience and Neurophysiology: A Reassessment

It is important to note that although imaging signals (both increases and decreases) are the result of local changes in brain blood flow and metabolism, these changes unequivocally and quite precisely reflect changes in neuronal activity. Although this empirical relationship has been demonstrated with great precision and elegance in recent experiments (e.g., Lauritzen & Gold, 2003; Logothetis, 2003), it is not a new idea (for a historical review see Raichle, 2000). More surprising to many and beautifully demonstrated in these recent experiments is that the neuronal activity responsible for the imaging signals is not the same as that studied routinely by neurophysiologists. How can this be? This difference arises from the fact that neurophysiologists have focused almost exclusively on the output or spiking activity in the cell bodies of large or so-called principal neurons, partly as a practical matter.

Principal neurons are large and when they fire an action potential, the resulting electrical activity is, in a relative sense, large and much more easily recorded than the spiking activity in the small and diverse group of inter-neurons in the same area (Stone, 1973; Towe & Harding, 1970). The activity of these principal neurons may also be more easily interpretable than the so-called local field potentials that arise from axon terminals and their targets, the dendrites (for a recent review of these issues, see Logothetis, 2003).[1] Thus, with these types of sampling biases, most neurophysiologic data would appear to reflect the output of the area of the brain under study as it is manifest in the spiking activity of principal neurons.

Given this neurophysiologic perspective, it is important to point out that brain blood flow and metabolism and, hence, brain imaging are relatively insensitive to spiking activity in the cell bodies of principal neurons because of the low energy demands of spike generation when it occurs in those parts of the cell (i.e., its body) where the cell surface area is low relative to its volume (e.g., see Creutzfeldt, 1975; Schwartz et al., 1979; Sharp, 1976; Sharp, Kauer, & Shepherd, 1977; also summarized in Raichle, 1987). In contrast, imaging informs us about the input to and local information processing within an area of the brain associated with the local field potentials because of the high energy demands and resultant metabolic cost arising from activity in cell processes where surface area is high relative to volume (for recent comprehensive treat-

---

[1] These local field potentials are largely responsible for the electrical signals observed from the scalp with electroencephalography.

ments of this important subject, consult Ames, 2000; Attwell & Laughlin, 2001; Lennie, 2003).

So where does all of this leave the erstwhile cognitive neuroscientist or, for that matter, the neurophysiologist? Certainly, the absence of a correlation between the spiking activity of large neurons reported by neurophysiologists and functional imaging signals reported by cognitive neuroscientists when it occurs does not invalidate the results of either approach. Rather, it should remind us that the two approaches provide different, but highly complementary, information that may at times vary in uncorrelated but, nonetheless, important ways (e.g., note that attentionally mediated increases in primary visual cortex observed with functional imaging are accompanied by minimal changes in spiking activity of principal neurons (Pessoa, Kastner, & Ungerleider, 2003; see also Lauritzen & Gold, 2003). Maintenance of a dialogue between neurophysiology and cognitive neuroscience is essential. The rewards for so doing will almost certainly be a much deeper understanding of how elements of our behavior are actually instantiated in the brain. It is clear at the moment that no discipline has a corner on the truth.

One might end this brief discussion of recent developments at the interface between cognitive neuroscience and neurophysiology and turn to some highlights from the voluminous results pouring forth (for a recent tabulation of the volume of this work, see Illes, Krischen, & Gabrieli, 2003) from a large and rapidly expanding worldwide research imaging infrastructure (Raichle, 2003a) on the neural correlates of almost every imaginable type of behavior and obtained with ever more sophisticated behavioral paradigms and imaging strategies. This would ignore, however, an introduction to what I consider to be one of the most interesting and important issues presently confronting those interested in how the brain instantiates behavior—the fact that the majority of the brain's functional activity remains largely unaccounted for in the context of present cognitive neuroscience research. It is as if we have focused only on the tip of the iceberg. Some perspective taking is in order.

Unaccounted for Functional Brain Activity

The puzzle of the brain's unaccounted for functional activity begins to reveal itself when one considers exactly how the brain's enormous energy budget is actually being spent on the work that it performs.

Appraising the Brain's Energy Budget

In the average adult human, the brain represents about 2% of the total body weight. Remarkably, despite its relatively small size, the brain accounts for about 20% of the oxygen consumed and, hence, calories used by the body (Clark & Sokoloff, 1999), 10 times that predicted by its weight alone. In relation to this high rate of ongoing or basal metabolism (usually measured while resting quietly but awake with eyes closed), regional imaging signals are remarkably small. Thus, regional changes in absolute blood flow are rarely more than 5% to 10% of the resting blood flow of the brain in the areas affected by the task.[2] These are modest modulations in ongoing circulatory activity and often do not appreciably affect the overall rate of brain blood flow during even the most vigorous sensory and motor activity (Fox, Burton, & Raichle, 1987; Fox, Fox, Raichle, & Burde, 1985; Fox, Miezin, Allman, Van Essen, & Raichle, 1987; Sokoloff, Mangold, Wechsler, Kennedy, & Kety, 1955), It is of interest that during the performance of more demanding cognitive tasks (e.g., see Friston, Frith, Liddle, Dolan, Lammertsma, & Frackowiak, 1990; Madsen et al., 1995; Roland, Eriksson, Stone-Elander, & Widen, 1987) even when regions of interest themselves exhibit only moderate changes in activity, overall brain blood flow and metabolism can increase significantly. This suggests the possibility that general processes such as alerting and arousal, explored much earlier by cognitive psychologists (e.g., see chap. on alertness in Posner, 1978, pp. 122–150) and more recently in the work by Cohen, Aston-Jones, and their colleagues (Gilzenrat, Holmes, Rajkowski, Aston-Jones, & Cohen, 2002; Usher, Cohen, Servan-Schreiber, Rajkowski, & Aston-Jones, 1999) may have more widespread effects on cortical activity during the performance of various goal-directed tasks than appreciated. This is a subject that has only recently received attention by the fMRI community in terms of strategies to access its potential importance (Chawla, Rees, & Friston, 1999; Donaldson, Petersen, & Buckner, 2001; Visscher et al., 2003).

The modest nature of these task-induced changes in blood flow is also emphasized when considering the change in energy consumption they represent. Recall that the average resting metabolic activity of the brain is supported by the nearly complete (>90%) oxidation of glucose to carbon dioxide and water, a process known as oxidative phosphorylation in which one molecule of glucose produces energy in the form of 30 adenosine triphosphate (ATP) molecules (Siesjo, 1978). Activations, on the other hand, exhibit an increase in glucose use that is not accompanied by a proportionate increase in oxygen consumption (Fox, Raichle, Mintun, & Dence, 1988), a metabolic process known as glycolysis that produces only 2 ATP per molecule of glucose consumed. From knowledge of these relationships, one can estimate that if blood flow and glucose utilization increase by 10% in a typical area of brain activation, but oxygen consumption does not, the energy consumption of the brain will increase by less than 1%.[3] It should be noted that an important advantage to the glycolytic route is that its rate of ATP production is much faster (twice that of oxidative phosphorylation),

---

[2] Usually, blood flow is used in functional imaging studies with PET because of the ease of measurement and the relatively short measurement time (<1 min) compared with measurements of metabolism which can take as long as 30 to 45 min (Mintun, Raichle, Martin, & Herscovitch, 1984; Reivich et al., 1979).

[3] A similar calculation can be applied to the resting metabolism of the whole brain where 90% to 92% of the glucose consumed is oxidized to carbon dioxide and water and the remainder is converted to lactate (Siesjo, 1978). Thus, about 99% of the energy needs of the brain are met by oxidative phosphorylation and only 1% by glycolysis. However, the latter may be uniquely important in providing for the system an ability to respond to changing neuronal activity even in the resting state (e.g., see Greicius, Krasnow, Reiss, & Menon, 2003; Laufs et al., 2003).

which would be in keeping with the speed required in energy production for activations that occur on a time scale of milliseconds. This rapid change in energy requirements with activation is far faster than the characteristic vascular response time in the normal human brain that takes 1 to 2 seconds to begin following the onset of a change in neuronal activity and does not reach a peak until 6 to 8 seconds after the onset of a change in neuronal activity (Boynton, Engel, Glover, & Heeger, 1996; Buckner et al., 1996). Such a slow response time puts the vasculature well behind changing neuronal events.

Thus, although the brain accounts for 20% of the body's energy consumption, changes in its processes that cognitive neuroscientists and neurophysiologists alike study in an attempt to understand its function are seemingly supported by a tiny fraction of this enormous energy consumption. It seems appropriate to suggest that if one is to understand how the brain works one must account for all of the energy needed to accomplish this work. This view is reinforced when considering the fact that a significant fraction of this metabolic activity is related to functionally significant signaling processes as summarized next.

Measurements of brain energy metabolism using magnetic resonance spectroscopy (Hyder, Rothman, & Shulman, 2002; Shulman, Hyder, & Rothman, 2001; Sibson et al., 1998) in a variety of experimental settings have indicated that up to 80% of the entire energy consumption of the brain is devoted to glutamate cycling and, hence, signaling processes.[4] Complementary analyses using extant anatomic, physiologic, and metabolic data (Attwell & Laughlin, 2001; Lennie, 2003) to assess the cost of different components of excitatory signaling in the gray matter have arrived at essentially the same conclusion. These analyses reveal that approximately 75% of the total energy consumption of the mammalian brain is devoted to various aspects of signaling and information processing carried out by glutamate. Thus, current convergent data would indicate that a majority of the signaling and information processing in the brain, as reflected in the energy it demands, remains unaccounted for and its functional significance unexplained. However, clues as to its nature do exist and should provide interesting avenues for future research.

As one views brain functionality from this energy- or cost-oriented perspective it appears to be represented in two ways. A large fraction, which seems to vary slowly over time (Mintun, Vlassenko, Shulman, & Snyder, 2002), is supported by oxidative phosphorylation. This is the richest source of energy for brain function and the vast majority of the brain's functional activity is supported by it. A second and much smaller fraction in terms of the energy requirements (about 1% overall) is supported by glycolysis. Glycolysis endows those functions it supports with a remarkable ability to respond in temporal synchrony with changes in neuronal activity that occur in the range of milliseconds.[5] One of the important questions such a formulation raises for future

---

[4]Glutamate is the primary excitatory neurotransmitter in the brain and glutamate synapses represent a significant fraction of all synapses.

[5]It is also important to keep in mind that it is variation in this glycolytic fraction brain energy production that is critical to the genesis of the BOLD signal of fMRI (Ogawa, Lee, Kay, & Tank, 1990; Ogawa, Lee, Naycik, & Glynn, 1990).

research is the relationship between those functions supported by oxidative phosphorylation and those supported by glycolysis. Is the difference merely a quantitative one or does it reflect true qualitative differences and, if so, what might these be?

The Nature of the Unaccounted for Neuronal Activity

Neurophysiologists have often noted electrical activity that does not bear an obvious relationship to specific sensory or motor tasks and have usually referred to this as spontaneous activity (Arieli, Sterkin, Grinvald, & Aertsent, 1996; McCormick, 1999; Sanchez-Vives & McCormick, 2000; Shu, Hasenstaub, & McCormick, 2003; Tsodyks, Kenet, Grinvald, & Arieli, 1999).[6] There has been increasing interest in the possibility that in the adult brain this spontaneous activity is not merely "noise" (Ferster, 1996; Harris, Csicvari, Hirase, Dragoi, & Buzsaki, 2003; Kenet, Bibitchkov, Tsodyks, Grinvald, & Arieli, 2003; Leopold, Murayama, & Logothetis, 2003; McCormick, 1999; Sejnowski, 2003).

When recorded in terms of the spiking activity of principal neurons, this spontaneous activity is relatively low in frequency and seemingly random as compared to vigorous bursts of activity seen during task performance. The distributed representation of information in the simultaneous activity of a large number of neurons firing at a low rate is highly energy-efficient (Attwell & Laughlin, 2001). One might posit that for functions of a sustained or tonic nature, there has developed an efficient encoding strategy that is coupled to oxidative phosphorylation as the primary source of energy. This would complement the situation for activations, which represent modest deviations from this more stable baseline activity and where glycolysis assumes an important role as a temporary source of energy needed in support of rapidly varying, time-limited information processing (Fox et al., 1988).[7]

In attempts to relate the large fraction of brain energy consumption devoted to signaling and information processing to specific types of neuronal activity, one must not forget that large, so-called principal neurons are not the only cell types present in the brain. This bias may arise, in part, from the fact that neurophysiological techniques inherently suffer from a significant sampling bias when it comes to monitoring the activity of cells other than the large principal neurons of the cortex (e.g., see Buchwald & Grover, 1970; Grover &

---

[6] Spontaneous activity is also important in the developing nervous system in setting the stage for the introduction of sensory stimuli (Feller, 1999; Weliky, 2000). In considering the role of spontaneous activity in the adult nervous system, future research may benefit from a consideration of a potential overlap between the role of spontaneous activity in the developing and the mature nervous system.
[7] Glycolysis can be not only increased rapidly but also does not require an increase in blood flow (Powers, Hirsch, & Cryer, 1996). Herein lays one of the long-standing puzzles of functional activation: why does the blood flow change? Recent data (Ido, Chang, & Williamson, 2004; Mintun, Vlassenko, Rundle, & Raichle, 2004; Zonta et al., 2003) is beginning to suggest possible links between changes in specific metabolic processes, in this case activity linked glycolysis in the astrocytes, and changes in blood flow. Much more work of this type is needed.

Buchwald, 1970; Stone, 1973; Towe & Harding, 1970; although significant improvements have been made in recent years, see Henze et al., 2000). This bias is especially true in the case of interneurons. Although fewer in number, making up approximately 20% of all neurons in the cortex, interneurons are distinguished by their high tonic firing rates (8- to 10-fold higher than that of principal neurons). Their role is likely critical in determining not only the local representation of information within brain areas (e.g., Csicsvari, Hirase, Czurko, Mamiya, & Buzsaki, 1999; Shelley, McLaughlin, Shapley, & Wielaard, 2002) but communication among areas as well (see below). However, neither the exact details of their role(s) nor cost (e.g., compare Ackerman, Finch, Babb, & Engel, 1984; Chatton, Pellerin, & Magistretti, 2003; McCasland & Hibbard, 1997) have been worked out in detail. As a result, we presently have no clear idea what distinctive effect, if any, changes in their activity have on functional brain imaging signals.

Several interesting ideas have been put forth regarding the functional nature of this spontaneous neuronal activity. One view suggests that it may serve a preparatory or facilitatory role. More specifically, it has been suggested that the response of neuronal circuits is dramatically affected by a continuous and balanced input of both inhibitory and excitatory activity (for review, see Salinas & Sejnowski, 2001). This ongoing balanced activity has been implicated in the generation of spontaneous activity (Shu et al., 2003; Steriade, Timofeev, & Grenier, 2001) and has been demonstrated to facilitate the responsivity of neurons to other incoming signals (Salinas & Sejnowski, 2001; Shadlen & Newsome, 1994; Shu et al., 2003; van Vreeswijk & Sompolinsky, 1996). Such a formulation would be consistent with the suggestion that at least some of the spontaneous activity in the brain is concerned with the dynamics of what might be termed the sculpting of lines of communication (Laughlin & Sejnowski, 2003; Sejnowski, 2003)

From this perspective it could be argued that such facilitatory processes are necessary and expensive components of brain function but not ones that directly involve the representation of information. However, some have suggested that representation of information might, in fact, be a property of such a state (e.g., Harris et al., 2003; Kenet et al., 2003; Shu et al., 2003; Tononi & Edelman, 1998). Here functional brain imaging with both PET and fMRI provide an informative perspective. This emanates directly from the observation of task-independent decreases (TIDs) that are regionally specific and occur during the performance of a wide variety of goal-directed tasks (Binder et al., 1999; Mazoyer et al., 2001; Shulman et al., 1997).

TASK-INDEPENDENT DECREASES. Functional brain imaging has often demonstrated task-dependent decreases (sometimes called deactivations) in brain activity along with the usual task-dependent increases (i.e., so-called activations). The task-dependent activity decreases have been observed in somatosensory cortex (Kawashima, O'Sullivan, & Roland, 1995); during the performance of a visual perception task; in auditory cortex (Ghatan et al., 1998); during a task with auditory distraction; and in portions of the visual cortex not directly engaged in a visual perception task (Shmuel et al., 2002; Smith, Singh, &

Greenlee, 2000). In addition to these task-dependent activity decreases researchers have become increasingly aware of the presence of a unique set of areas that exhibit stereotypical decreases in activity that are largely independent of the nature of the task being performed when the task is compared to a passive resting state condition (Binder et al., 1999; Mazoyer et al., 2001; Shulman et al., 1997). These decreases occur across a wide spectrum of goal-directed tasks and, hence, the designation task-independent decreases or TIDs. They are seen in medial prefrontal and parietal cortices as well as lateral parietal cortex bilaterally and both amygdala (see colorplate 2). The magnitude of some of these decreases can vary with such things as task difficulty (Mc-Kiernan, Kaufman, Kucera-Thompson, & Binder, 2003) and the emotional state of the research participant (Simpson, Snyder, Gusnard, & Raichle, 2001).

From a detailed analysis of the metabolic and circulatory features of the TIDs (Gusnard & Raichle, 2001; Raichle et al., 2001), we have posited that they reveal the presence of functions that are continuously active in the resting state. More specifically, we have suggested that the TIDS do not correspond to activations in the resting state as has been suggested (Mazoyer et al., 2001). Rather, TIDs are areas that, in the resting state, are active rather than activated. From the point of view of their functionality, this would be consistent with functions that are spontaneous and virtually continuous, being attenuated only when we reallocate resources to temporarily engage in goal-directed behaviors, hence our designation of them as default functions (Gusnard & Raichle, 2001; Raichle et al., 2001).

The self-referential nature of the resting state (in the experimental setting this usually means lying or sitting quietly with eyes closed but awake) as experienced by most individuals when contrasted with the usually non–self-referential nature of most tasks studied by cognitive neuroscientists, helps to focus one's thinking when searching for functions that might instantiated in the areas of the brain associated with TIDs. In this vein, Binder and colleagues have suggested that these areas contribute to the thought processing that humans experience during resting consciousness (Binder et al., 1999), while Mazoyer and colleagues have suggested that they represent "the recall and maintenance of multimodal thoughts through free association which characterizes the resting state" in humans (Mazoyer et al., 2001, p. 896). Interestingly, Ingvar articulated similar notions many years ago (Ingvar, 1985).

Evidence also suggests that some of the areas involved in TIDs, particularly posteriorly, are also attenuated in their activity during normal rapid eye movement (REM) and non-REM sleep (for review see Maquet, 2000) and general anesthesia (Fiset et al., 1999). Also recent reports indicate that many of the areas of TIDs exhibit reduced activity during absence seizures (Salek-Haddadi et al., 2003) and during generalized spike and wave discharges in patients with generalized epilepsy (Khani et al., 2003). Such findings raise the possibility that these areas have some relationship to consciousness and states of awareness.

THE RESTING STATE. One of the challenges of determining whether TIDs indicate the presence of default functions is to know how they relate to resting state cognition. In this regard, two recent observations using novel approaches to the study of the resting state provide interesting new information relevant to the relationships among the resting state, TIDs, and a physiologic baseline level of activity in the brain as we have defined it (Raichle et al., 2001).

Using an imaging strategy that has been employed in several laboratories (Biswal, Yetkin, Haughton, & Hyde, 1995; Coren, 1969; Lowe, Mock, & Sorenson, 1998; Xiong, Parsons, Gao, & Fox, 1999), Greicius and colleagues (Greicius, Krasnow, Reiss, & Menon, 2003) explored the interregional temporal correlations of spontaneous fMRI signal fluctuations in the resting state using regions of interest in posterior cingulate and precuneus as well as the ventral anterior cingulate cortex. These regions of interest are among those regularly exhibiting TIDs. What emerged was evidence for significant correlations in the spontaneous activity among a group of areas almost identical with those that have been identified with the TIDs. This paper by Greicius and colleagues (Greicius et al., 2003) is the first to provide direct evidence of coordinated activity in the TIDs areas in the resting state.

The second study by Laufs and colleagues (Laufs et al., 2003) provides additional new data on changes occurring in the resting state by means of a novel combined use of fMRI and electroencephalograms (EEGs). In this study, simultaneous EEG and fMRI were obtained in the resting state (i.e., eyes closed, awake, unconstrained cognition). The EEG was analyzed in terms of activity (power) within the alpha frequency band (8 to 13 Hz) and subsets of the beta frequency band (13 to 16 Hz; 17 to 23 Hz; and 24 to 30 Hz). Changes in the power within these bands over time were correlated with magnitude variations in the regional fMRI signal in the brain. The authors observed that areas in dorsolateral parietal and prefrontal cortices, areas where increases in activity have often been associated with goal-directed attention (e.g., see Corbetta et al., 1998), varied in their activity inversely with alpha power. Thus, as alpha power decreased, activity in these areas increased as measured by the fMRI signal. This result fit nicely with the idea that the presence of alpha activity in the EEG is indicative of a relaxed, nonattentive state. Independently, a significant number of the areas traditionally associated with TIDs varied directly with beta power in the 17 to 23 Hz range.

In the present context, two aspects of this study (Laufs et al., 2003) deserve comment. First, the higher blood oxygen level dependent (BOLD) activity observed in regions that correspond to TID areas, which was associated with increased EEG power in a segment of the beta frequency band (i.e., 17 to 23 Hz), could be interpreted as consistent with an overall role for these areas in spontaneous mental processes in the resting state that have been discussed earlier in this chapter. Second, additional brain areas in parietal and prefrontal cortices, which are traditionally activated in tasks involving goal-directed attention (Corbetta et al., 1998), correlated negatively with alpha power. This suggests that these areas might play some role in the spontaneous mental activity of rest as well. It is important to emphasize that in this study regional brain activity associated with these two EEG frequency bands varied independently. Thus, we are not observing an either/or situation with regard to ongoing introspective mental activities and attentive processing, an idea consistent with the observation that activity modulations (activations and deactivations) are small on top of a large amount of ongoing functional activity in the brain.

To understand how such processes relate to one another and what it really means to change activity within a system are two fascinating challenges facing those interested in how brain instantiates mind.

These studies (Greicius et al., 2003; Laufs et al., 2003) have provided a rich new view of the resting state of the human brain consisting of a fascinating spatially and temporally varying landscape of brain systems. It is information of this type that will help unlock the mystery of the unaccounted for functional activity of the brain. In pursuing this agenda, it is important to know that work at other levels of analysis already provides important complementary information.

Slow spontaneous fluctuations in brain activity (~0.1 Hz) have also been noted by neurophysiologists while recording the activity of single cells and local field potentials with microelectrodes and optical techniques in developing brain (Feller, 1999; Weliky, 2000) and in the adult (Arieli et al., 1996; Leopold et al., 2003; Shu et al., 2003; Tsodyks et al., 1999). Intriguingly, some of this activity appears to reflect dynamically switching cortical states that instantiate default representations of anticipated events (Kenet et al., 2003). This is similar in concept to the interesting theoretical view that the brain develops and maintains a probabilistic model of anticipated events and that ongoing neuronal activity is an internal representation of that model (Olshausen, 2003). It is interesting how close these concepts are to those of the late David Ingvar who posited some time ago the idea of a "memory of the future" in his theory of the temporal organization of conscious awareness (Ingvar, 1985; see also Wheeler, Stuss, & Tulving, 1997).

The exact relationship between the different levels of analysis now before us remains to be firmly established but the rewards for pursuing them are likely to be great.[8] Likewise, understanding the mental correlates of these changing states within the resting brain and their possible relationship to self-focused attention, awareness, and even consciousness represents intriguing challenges for the future. Investigating these and other relationships across many levels of analysis should be a high priority for future research.

Conclusion

Major advances in science often occur when interactions take place between disciplines whose perspectives and tools are mutually complementary. Nowhere is this better exemplified than the interactions that occurred between systems neuroscience and cognitive psychology in the 1980s (Raichle, 2000). Fueled by the new brain imaging tools of PET and MRI, sophisticated behavioral paradigms honed over many decades in cognitive psychology laboratories and prescient early support from the combined resources of the James S. McDonnell Foundation and the Pew Charitable Trusts, the field of cognitive neuroscience

---

[8] For example, it would also be of interest to know whether the so-called up state (Shu et al., 2003) of heightened responsivity in neuronal circuits exhibiting spontaneous activity corresponds to increases in beta or gamma EEG power and, likewise, whether the so-called down state (Shu et al., 2003) of attenuated responsivity is related to increased alpha power in the EEG.

emerged. Work in cognitive neuroscience has become a major force in both cognitive psychology and systems neuroscience as a result. One of the pioneers in forging the important marriage of these two disciplines was Posner (Posner & Raichle, 1994).

As we look to the future of this work it is clear that further integration of levels of analysis will be the key to any major new advances in our understanding of the relationship between brain and behavior. What is particularly exciting presently is that this integration is occurring. It is exemplified by the intense probing of the relationship between brain imaging signals and complex neurophysiologic events of the brain on the one hand and the burgeoning interest in research questions in the social sciences (Cacioppo et al., 2002). This agenda, now expanding in two directions, includes important work from those interested in genetics and cell biology as well as those interested in the most complex and integrative human behaviors studied by social scientists from many disciplines. To work at such complex interfaces will be a challenge for all concerned and require the training of a new generation of researchers capable of doing so. But it will be well worth the effort because the intellectual and societal rewards of so doing will be enormous. Posner will remain a role model for those who accept the challenge.

References

Ackerman, R. F., Finch, D. M., Babb, T. L., & Engel, J. J. (1984). Increased glucose utilization during long-duration recurrent inhibition of hippocampal pyramidal cells. *Journal of Neuroscience, 4,* 251–264.

Ames, A. I. (2000). CNS energy metabolism as related to function. *Brain Research Reviews, 34,* 42–68.

Arieli, A., Sterkin, A., Grinvald, A., & Aertsent, A. (1996). Dynamics of ongoing activity: Explanation of the large variability in evoked cortical responses. *Science, 273,* 1868–1871.

Attwell, D., & Iadecola, C. (2002). The neural basis of functional brain imaging signals. *Trends in Neuroscience, 25,* 621–625.

Attwell, D., & Laughlin, S. B. (2001). An energy budget for signaling in the grey matter of the brain. *Journal of Cerebral Blood Flow and Metabolism, 21,* 1133–1145.

Binder, J. R., Frost, J. A., Hammeke, T. A., Bellgowan, P. S. F., Rao, S. M., & Cox, R. W. (1999). Conceptual processing during the conscious resting state: A functional MRI study. *Journal of Cognitive Neuroscience, 11,* 80–93.

Biswal, B., Yetkin, F., Haughton, V., & Hyde, J. (1995). Functional connectivity in the motor cortex of resting human brain using echo–planar MRI. *Magnetic Resonance in Medicine, 34,* 537–541.

Boynton, G. M., Engel, S. A., Glover, G. H., & Heeger, D. J. (1996). Linear systems analysis of functional magnetic resonance imaging in human V1. *Journal of Neuroscience, 16,* 4207–4221.

Buchwald, J. S., & Grover, F. S. (1970). Amplitudes of background fast activity characteristic of specific brain sites. *Journal of Neurophysiology, 33,* 148–159.

Buckner, R. L. (2003). The hemodynamic inverse problem: Making inferences about neural activity from measured MRI signals. *Proceedings of the National Academy of Sciences of the United States of America, 100,* 2177–2179.

Buckner, R. L., Bandettini, P. A., O'Craven, K. M., Savoy, R. L., Petersen, S. E., Raichle, M. E., et al. (1996). Detection of cortical activation during averaged single trials of a cognitive task using functional magnetic resonance imaging. *Proceedings of the National Academy of Sciences of the United States of America, 93,* 14878–14883.

Cacioppo, J. T., Berntson, G. G., Adolphs, R., Carter, C. S., Davidson, R. J., McClintock, M. K., et al. (Eds.). (2002). *Foundations in social neuroscience.* Cambridge, MA: MIT Press.

Chatton, J.-Y., Pellerin, L., & Magistretti, P. J. (2003). GABA uptake into astrocytes is not associated with significant metabolic cost: Implications for brain imaging of inhibitory transmission. *Proceedings of the National Academy of Sciences of the United States of America, 100,* 12456–12461.

Chawla, D., Rees, G., & Friston, K. J. (1999). The physiological basis of attentional modulation of extrastriate visual areas. *Nature Neuroscience, 2,* 671–676.

Clark, D. D., & Sokoloff, L. (1999). Circulation and energy metabolism of the brain. In G. J. Siegel, B. W. Agranoff, R. W. Albers, S. K. Fisher, & M. D. Uhler (Eds.), *Basic neurochemistry. Molecular, cellular and medical aspects* (6th ed., pp. 637–670). Philadelphia: Lippincott-Raven.

Corbetta, M., Akbudak, E., Conturo, T. E., Snyder, A. Z., Olinger, J. M., Drury, H., et al. (1998). A common network of funtional areas for attention and eye movements. *Neuron, 321,* 761–773.

Coren, S. (1969). Brightness contrast as a function of figure–ground relations. *Journal of Experimental Psychology, 80,* 517–524.

Creutzfeldt, O. D. (1975). Neurophysiological correlates of different functional states of the brain. In D. H. Ingvar & N. A. Lassen (Eds.), *Brain work: The coupling of function, metabolism and blood flow in the brain* (pp. 22–47). Copenhagen, Denmark: Munksgaard.

Csicvari, J., Hirase, H., Czurko, A., Mamiya, A., & Buzsaki, G. (1999). Oscillatory coupling of hippocampal pyramidal cells and interneurons in the behaving rat. *Journal of Neuroscience, 19,* 274–287.

Donaldson, D. I., Petersen, S. E., & Buckner, R. L. (2001). Dissociating memory retrieval processes using fMRI: Evidence that priming does not support recognition memory. *Neuron, 31,* 1047–1059.

Feller, M. (1999). Spontaneous correlated activity in developing visual cortex. *Neuron, 22,* 653–656.

Ferster, D. (1996). Is neural noise just a nuisance? *Science, 273,* 1812.

Fiset, P., Paus, T., Daloze, T., Plourde, G., Meuret, P., Bonhomme, V., et al. (1999). Brain mechanisms of propofol-induced loss of consciousness in humans: A positron emission tomographic study. *Journal of Neuroscience, 19,* 5506–5513.

Fox, P. T., Burton, H., & Raichle, M. E. (1987). Mapping human somatosensory cortex with positron emission tomography. *Journal of Neurosurgery, 67,* 34–43.

Fox, P. T., Fox, J. M., Raichle, M. E., & Burde, R. M. (1985). The role of cerebral cortex in the generation of voluntary saccades: A positron emission tomographic study. *Journal of Neurophysiology, 54,* 348–369.

Fox, P. T., Miezin, F. M., Allman, J. M., Van Essen, D. C., & Raichle, M. E. (1987). Retinotopic organization of human visual cortex mapped with positron emission tomography. *Journal of Neuroscience, 7,* 913–922.

Fox, P. T., Raichle, M. E., Mintun, M. A., & Dence, C. (1988). Nonoxidative glucose consumption during focal physiologic neural activity. *Science, 241,* 462–464.

Friston, K. J., Frith, C. D., Liddle, P. F., Dolan, R. J., Lammertsma, A. A., & Frackowiak, R. S. J. (1990). The relationship between global and local changes in PET scans. *Journal of Cerebral Blood Flow and Metabolism, 10,* 458–466.

Ghatan, P. H., Hsieh, J.-C., Petersson, K. M., Stone-Elander, S., & Ingvar, M. (1998). Coexistence of attention-based facilitation and inhibition in human cortex. *NeuroImage, 7,* 23–29.

Gilzenrat, M. S., Holmes, B. D., Rajkowski, J., Aston-Jones, G., & Cohen, J. D. (2002). Simplified dynamics in a model of noradrenergic modulation of cognitive performance. *Neural Networks, 15,* 647–663.

Greicius, M. D., Krasnow, B., Reiss, A. L., & Menon, V. (2003). Functional connectivity in the resting brain: A network analysis of the default mode hypothesis. *Proceedings of the National Academy of Sciences of the United States of America, 100,* 253–258.

Grover, F. S., & Buchwald, J. S. (1970). Correlation of cell size with amplitude of background fast activity in specific brain nuclei. *Journal of Neurophysiology, 33,* 160–171.

Gusnard, D. A., & Raichle, M. E. (2001). Searching for a baseline: Functional imaging and the resting human brain. *Nature Reviews Neuroscience, 2,* 685–694.

Harris, K. D., Csicvari, J., Hirase, H., Dragoi, G., & Buzsaki, G. (2003). Organization of cell assemblies in the hippocampus. *Nature, 424,* 552–556.

Heeger, D. J., & Ress, D. (2002). What does fMRI tell us about neuronal activity? *Nature Reviews Neuroscience, 3,* 142–151.

Henze, D., Borhegyi, Z., Csicsvari, J., Mamiya, A., Harris, K. D., & Buzsaki, G. (2000). Intracellular features predicted by extracellular recordings in the hippocampus in vivo. *Journal of Neurophysiology, 84,* 390–400.

Hyder, F., Rothman, D. L., & Shulman, R. G. (2002). Total neuroenergetics support localized brain activity: Implications for the interpretation of fMRI. *Proceedings of the National Academy of Sciences of the United States of America, 99,* 10771–10776.

Ido, Y., Chang, K., & Williamson, J. R. (2004). NADH augments blood flow in physiologically activated retina and visual cortex. *Proceedings of the National Academy of Sciences of the United States of America, 101,* 653–658.

Illes, J., Krischen, M. P., & Gabrieli, J. D. E. (2003). From neuroimaging to neuroethics. *Nature Neuroscience, 6,* 205.

Ingvar, D. H. (1985). Memory of the future: An essay on the temporal organization of conscious awareness. *Human Neurobiology, 4,* 127–136.

Kawashima, R., O'Sullivan, B. T., & Roland, P. E. (1995). Positron-emission tomography studies of cross-modality inhibition in selective attentional tasks: Closing the 'mind's eye.' *Proceedings of the National Academy of Sciences of the United States of America, 92,* 5969–5972.

Kenet, T., Bibitchkov, D., Tsodyks, M., Grinvald, A., & Arieli, A. (2003). Spontaneously emerging cortical representations of visual attributes. *Nature, 425,* 954–956.

Khani, Y. A., Dubeau, F., Benar, C.-G., Veilleux, M., Andermann, F., & Gotman, J. (2003, June). *EEG-fMRI findings in patients with idiopathic generalized epilepsy.* Paper presented at the Organization for Human Brain Mapping, New York.

Laufs, H., Krakow, K., Sterzer, P., Egger, E., Beyerle, A., Salek-Haddadi, A., et al. (2003). Electroencephalographic signatures of attentional and cognitive default modes in spontaneous brain activity fluctuations at rest. *Proceedings of the National Academy of Sciences of the United States of America, 100,* 11053–11058.

Laughlin, S. B., & Sejnowski, T. J. (2003). Communication networks in the brain. *Science, 301,* 1870–1874.

Lauritzen, M., & Gold, L. (2003). Brain function and neurophysiological correlates of signals used in functional neuroimaging. *Journal of Neuroscience, 23,* 3972–3980.

Lennie, P. (2003). The cost of cortical computation. *Current Biology, 13,* 493–497.

Leopold, D. A., Murayama, Y., & Logothetis, N. K. (2003). Very slow activity fluctuations in monkey visual cortex: Implications for functional brain imaging. *Cerebral Cortex, 13,* 423–433.

Logothetis, N. K. (2003). The underpinnings of the BOLD functional magnetic resonance imaging signal. *Journal of Neuroscience, 23,* 3963–3971.

Lowe, M. J., Mock, B. J., & Sorenson, J. A. (1998). Functional connectivity in single and multislice echoplanar imaging using resting-state fluctuations. *NeuroImage, 7,* 119–132.

Madsen, P. L., Hasselbalch, S. G., Hagemann, L. P., Olsen, K. S., Bulow, J., Holm, S., et al. (1995). Persistent resetting of the cerebral oxygen/glucose uptake ratio by brain activation: Evidence obtained with the Kety-Schmidt technique. *Journal of Cerebral Blood Flow and Metabolism, 15,* 485–491.

Maquet, P. (2000). Functional neuroimaging of normal human sleep by positron emission tomography. *Journal of Sleep Research, 9,* 207–231.

Mazoyer, B., Zago, L., Mellet, E., Bricogne, S., Etard, O., Houde, O., et al. (2001). Cortical networks for working memory and executive functions sustain the conscious resting state in man. *Brain Research Bulletin, 54,* 287–298.

McCasland, J. S., & Hibbard, L. S. (1997). GABAergic neurons in barrel cortex show strong, whisker-dependent metabolic activation during normal behavior. *Journal of Neuroscience, 17,* 5509–5527.

McCormick, D. A. (1999). Spontaneous activity: Signal or noise? *Science, 285,* 541–543.

McKiernan, K. A., Kaufman, J. N., Kucera-Thompson, J., & Binder, J. R. (2003). A parametric manipulation of factors affecting task-induced deactivation in functional neuroimaging. *Journal of Cognitive Neuroscience, 15,* 394–408.

Mintun, M., Vlassenko, A. G., Rundle, M. M., & Raichle, M. E. (2004). Increased lactate/pyruvate ratio augments blood flow in physiologically activated human brain. *Proceedings of the National Academy of Sciences of the United States of America, 101,* 659–664.

Mintun, M., Vlassenko, A. G., Shulman, G. I., & Snyder, A. Z. (2002). Time-related increase of oxygen utilization in continuously activated human visual cortex. *NeuroImage, 16,* 531–537.

Mintun, M. A., Raichle, M. E., Martin, W. R., & Herscovitch, P. (1984). Brain oxygen utilization measured with O-15 radiotracers and positron emission tomography. *Journal of Nuclear Medicine, 25,* 177–187.

Nichols, M. J., & Newsome, W. T. (1999). The neurobiology of cognition. *Nature, 402,* C35–C38.

Ogawa, S., Lee, T. M., Kay, A. R., & Tank, D. W. (1990). Brain magnetic resonance imaging with contrast dependent on blood oxygenation. *Proceedings of the National Academy of Sciences, 87,* 9868–9872.

Ogawa, S., Lee, T. M., Naycik, A. S., & Glynn, P. (1990). Oxygenation-sensitive contrast in magnetic resonance imaging of rodent brain at high magnetic fields. *Magnetic Resonance in Medicine, 16,* 9–18.

Olshausen, B. A. (2003). Principles of image representation in visual cortex. In L. M. Chalupa & J. S. Werner (Eds.), *The visual neurosciences* (pp. 1603–1615). Cambridge, MA: MIT Press.

Pessoa, L., Kastner, S., & Ungerleider, L. G. (2003). Neuroimaging studies of attention: From modulation of sensory processing to top-down control. *Journal of Neuroscience, 23,* 3990–3998.

Posner, M. I. (1978). *Chronometric explorations of mind.* Englewood Heights, NJ: Erlbaum.

Posner, M. I., & Raichle, M. E. (1994). *Images of mind.* New York: Freeman.

Powers, W. J., Hirsch, I. B., & Cryer, P. E. (1996). Effect of stepped hypoglycemia on regional cerebral blood flow response to physiological brain activation. *American Journal of Physiology, 270,* H554–H559.

Raichle, M. E. (1987). Circulatory and metabolic correlates of brain function in normal humans. In F. Plum (Ed.), *Handbook of physiology: The nervous system V. Higher functions of the brain* (pp. 643–674). Bethesda, MD: American Physiological Society.

Raichle, M. E. (2000). A brief history of human functional brain mapping. In A. W. Toga & J. C. Mazziotta (Eds.), *Brain mapping: The systems* (pp. 33–75). San Diego, CA: Academic Press.

Raichle, M. E. (2003a). Functional brain imaging and human brain function. *Journal of Neuroscience, 23,* 3959–3962.

Raichle, M. E. (2003b). Functional brain imaging and human brain function (miniseries). *Journal of Neuroscience, 23,* 3959–4011.

Raichle, M. E., & Gusnard, D. A. (2002). Appraising the brain's energy budget. *Proceedings of the National Academy of Sciences of the United States of America, 99,* 10237–10239.

Raichle, M. E., MacLeod, A. M., Snyder, A. Z., Powers, W. J., Gusnard, D. A., & Shulman, G. L. (2001). A default mode of brain function. *Proceedings of the National Academy of Sciences of the United States of America, 98,* 676–682.

Reivich, M., Kuhl, D., Wolf, A., Greenberg, J., Phelps, M., Ido, T., et al. (1979). The [18F] fluorodeoxyglucose method for the measurement of local cerebral glucose utilization in man. *Circulation Research, 44,* 127–137.

Roland, P. E., Eriksson, L., Stone-Elander, S., & Widen, L. (1987). Does mental activity change the oxidative metabolism of the brain. *Journal of Neuroscience, 7,* 2373–2389.

Salek-Haddadi, A., Lemieux, L., Merschemke, M., Friston, K. J., Duncan, J. S., & Fish, D. R. (2003). Functional magnetic resonance imaging of human absence seizures. *Annals of Neurology, 53,* 663–667.

Salinas, E., & Sejnowski, T. J. (2001). Correlated neuronal activity and the flow of neural information. *Nature Reviews Neuroscience, 2,* 539–550.

Sanchez-Vives, M. V., & McCormick, D. A. (2000). Cellular and network mechanisms of rhythmic recurrent activity in neocortex. *Nature Neuroscience, 3,* 1027–1034.

Schwartz, W. J., Smith, C. B., Davidsen, L., Savaki, H., Sokoloff, L., Mata, M., et al. (1979). Metabolic mapping of functional activity in the hypothalamo–neurohypophysial system of the rat. *Science, 205,* 723–725.

Sejnowski, T. J. (2003). The computational self. *Annals of the New York Academy of Sciences, 1001,* 262–271.

Shadlen, M. N., & Newsome, W. T. (1994). Noise, neural codes and cortical organization. *Current Opinion in Neurobiology, 4,* 569–579.

Sharp, F. R. (1976). Relative cerebral glucose uptake of neuronal perikarya and neuropil determined with 2-deoxyglucose in resting and swimming rat. *Brain Research, 110,* 127–139.

Sharp, F. R., Kauer, J. S., & Shepherd, G. M. (1977). Laminar analysis of 2-deoxyglucose uptake in olfactory bulb and olfactory cortex of rabbit and rat. *Journal of Neurophysiology, 40,* 800–813.

Shelley, M., McLaughlin, D., Shapley, R., & Wielaard, J. (2002). States of high conductance in a large-scale model of the visual cortex. *Journal of Computational Neuroscience, 13,* 93–109.

Shmuel, A., Yacoub, E., Pfeuffer, J., Van De Moortele, P.-F., Adriany, G., Hu, X., et al. (2002). Sustained negative BOLD, blood flow and oxygen consumption response and its coupling to the positive response in the human brain. *Neuron, 36,* 1195–1210.

Shu, Y., Hasenstaub, A., & McCormick, D. A. (2003). Turning on and off recurrent balanced cortical activity. *Nature, 423,* 288–293.

Shulman, G. L., Fiez, J. A., Corbetta, M., Buckner, R. L., Miezin, F. M., Raichle, M. E., et al. (1997). Common blood flow changes across visual tasks: II. Decreases in cerebral cortex. *Journal of Cognitive Neuroscience, 9,* 648–663.

Shulman, R. G., Hyder, F., & Rothman, D. L. (2001). Cerebral energetics and the glycogen shunt: Neurochemical basis of functional imaging. *Proceedings of the National Academy of Sciences of the United States of America, 98,* 6417–6422.

Sibson, N. R., Dhankhar, A., Mason, G. F., Rothman, D. L., Behar, K. L., & Shulman, R. G. (1998). Stoichiometric coupling of brain glucose metabolism and glutamatergic neuronal activity. *Proceedings of the National Academy of Sciences of the United States of America, 95,* 316–321.

Siesjo, B. K. (1978). *Brain energy metabolism.* New York: Wiley.

Simpson, J. R. J., Snyder, A. Z., Gusnard, D. A., & Raichle, M. E. (2001). Emotion-induced changes in human medial prefrontal cortex: I. During cognitive task performance. *Proceedings of the National Academy of Sciences of the United States of America, 98,* 683–687.

Smith, A. T., Singh, K. D., & Greenlee, M. W. (2000). Attentional suppression of activity in the human visual cortex. *NeuroReport, 11,* 271–277.

Sokoloff, L., Mangold, R., Wechsler, R., Kennedy, C., & Kety, S. S. (1955). The effect of mental arithmetic on cerebral circulation and metabolism. *Journal of Clinical Investigation, 34,* 1101–1108.

Steriade, M., Timofeev, I., & Grenier, F. (2001). Natural waking and sleep states, a view from inside neocortical neurons. *Journal of Neurophysiology, 85,* 1969–1985.

Stone, J. (1973). Sampling properties of microelectrodes assessed in the cat's retina. *Journal of Neurophysiology, 36,* 1071–1079.

Tononi, G., & Edelman, G. M. (1998). Consciousness and the integration of information in the brain. *Advances in Neurology, 77,* 245–250.

Towe, A. L., & Harding, G. W. (1970). Extracellular microelectrode sampling bias. *Journal of Neurophysiology, 29,* 366–381.

Tsodyks, M., Kenet, T., Grinvald, A., & Arieli, A. (1999). Linking spontaneous activity of single cortical neurons and the underlying functional architecture. *Science, 286,* 1943–1946.

Usher, M., Cohen, J. D., Servan-Schreiber, D., Rajkowski, J., & Aston-Jones, G. (1999). The role of locus coeruleus in the regulation of cognitive performance. *Science, 283,* 549–554.

Uttal, W. R. (2001). *The new phrenology.* Cambridge, MA: Bradford Books/MIT Press.

Van Essen, D. C., Harwell, J., Hanlon, D., Dickson, J., Snyder, A. Z., & Cox, R. (2002, June). *Mapping functional activation patterns onto surface-based atlases of cerebral and cerebellar cortex.* Paper presented at the Organization for Human Brain Mapping, Sendai, Japan.

van Vreeswijk, C., & Sompolinsky, H. (1996). Chaos in neuronal networks with balanced excitatory and inhibitory activity. *Science, 274,* 1724–1726.

Visscher, K. M., Miezen, F. M., Kelly, J. E., Buckner, R. L., Donaldson, D. I., McAvoy, M. P., et al. (2003). Mixed blocked/event-related designs separate transient and sustained activity in fMRI. *NeuroImage, 19,* 1694–1708.

Weliky, M. (2000). Correlated neuronal activity and visual cortical development. *Neuron, 27,* 427–430.

Wheeler, M. A., Stuss, D. T., & Tulving, E. (1997). Toward a theory of episodic memory: The frontal lobes and autonoetic consciousness. *Psychological Bulletin, 121,* 331–354.

Xiong, J., Parsons, L. M., Gao, J. H., & Fox, P. T. (1999). Interregional connectivity to primary motor cortex revealed using MRI resting state images. *Human Brain Mapping, 8,* 151–156.

Zonta, M., Angulo, M. C., Gobbo, S., Rosengarten, B., Hossmann, K.-A., Pozzan, T., et al. (2003). Neuron-to-astrocyte signaling is central to the dynamic control of brain microcirculation. *Nature Neuroscience, 6,* 43–50.

7

The Ontogeny of the Social Brain

Mark H. Johnson

One of the most major characteristics of the human brain is its social nature. As adults, we have regions of the brain specialized for processing and integrating sensory information about the appearance, behavior, and intentions of other humans. Sometimes this processing is also extended to other species, such as the family cat, or even to inanimate objects such as our desktop computer. A variety of cortical areas have been implicated in the social brain including the superior temporal sulcus (STS), the fusiform face area (FFA), and orbitofrontal cortex (for recent review, see Adolphs, 2003). One of the major debates in cognitive neuroscience concerns the origins of the social brain in humans, and theoretical arguments abound about the extent to which this is acquired through experience. Mentalistic understanding of other's behavior (theory of mind) has been associated with various neural structures, including the amygdala and the temporal pole, the superior temporal gyrus and the temporo-parietal junction, and parts of the prefrontal cortex (mainly orbitofrontal and medial areas). According to Frith (2001), the neural activity in these regions may reflect different aspects of mental state understanding: the amygdala is involved in understanding emotions through empathy, parts of the temporal lobe represent biological motion and actions, and regions of the frontal cortex play a role in understanding intentional referential mental states, including mental states of the self. The issue I will address in this chapter is how these regions develop their individual functionality and become integrated parts of the adult human social brain network.

Perhaps the most obvious answer to this is that specific genes are expressed in particular parts of cortex and code for patterns of wiring particular for certain computational functions. Although this type of explanation appears to be valid for specialized computations within subcortical structures, a variety of genetic, neurobiological, and cognitive neuroscience evidence indicates that

I acknowledge financial support from the Medical Research Council (United Kingdom; Grant G9715587) and Birkbeck College. I dedicate this chapter to Mike Posner with thanks for so many things. In particular, Mike's generous and thoughtful input was vital during an early sensitive period of my scientific life.

it is, at best, only part of the story for many human cognitive functions dependent on cerebral cortex. As just one example, in human adults experience or practice in certain domains can change the extent of cortical tissue activated during performance of a task. In this chapter I consider the development of the human social brain network from the point of view of three different general perspectives that have been taken on the postnatal development of human brain function.

Three Perspectives on the Functional Development of the Human Brain

Relating evidence on the neuroanatomical development of the brain to the remarkable changes in motor, perceptual, and cognitive abilities during the first decade or so of a human life presents a considerable challenge. I identify three distinct, but not necessarily incompatible, approaches to this issue; (a) a maturational perspective, (b) a skill-learning viewpoint, and (c) interactive specialization (Johnson, 2001). Next, I briefly introduce these three approaches, before examining their assumptions and predictions in a little more detail.

Much of the research to date attempting to relate brain to behavioral development in humans has been from a maturational viewpoint in which the goal is to relate the maturation of particular regions of the brain, usually regions of cerebral cortex, to newly emerging sensory, motor, and cognitive functions. Evidence concerning the differential neuroanatomical development of brain regions can be used to determine an age when a particular region is likely to become functional. Success in a new behavioral task at this age may then be attributed to the maturation of a new brain region. By this view, functional brain development can be viewed as the reverse of adult neuropsychology, with the difference being that specific brain regions (and their corresponding computational modules) are added-in instead of being damaged. In terms of the social brain, one can imagine that although some components are present from birth, other components come online at different postnatal ages.

Despite the intuitive appeal and attractive simplicity of the maturational approach, it does not successfully explain some aspects of human functional brain development. For example, recent evidence suggests that some of the regions that are slowest to develop by neuroanatomical criteria show activity from shortly after birth (Johnson, 2001). Furthermore, where functional activity has been assessed by functional magnetic resonance imaging (fMRI) during a behavioral transition, multiple cortical and subcortical areas appear to change their response pattern (e.g., Luna et al., 2001), rather than one or two previously silent regions becoming active (mature). Finally, associations between neural and cognitive changes based on age of onset are theoretically somewhat unconstrained because of the great variety of neuroanatomical and neurochemical measures that change at different times in different regions of the brain.

In contrast to the above approach, an alternative viewpoint, interactive specialization, assumes that postnatal functional brain development, at least within cerebral cortex, involves a process of organizing patterns of interregional interactions (Johnson, 2001). According to this view, the response properties of a specific region are partly determined by its patterns of connectivity to other regions, and their patterns of activity. During postnatal development changes in the response properties of cortical regions occur as they interact and compete with each other to acquire their role in new computational abilities. From this perspective, some cortical regions may begin with poorly defined functions and consequently are partially activated in a wide range of different contexts and tasks. During development, activity-dependent interactions between regions sharpens up the functions of regions such that their activity becomes restricted to a narrower set of circumstances (e.g., a region originally activated by a wide variety of visual objects, may come to confine its response to upright human faces). The onset of new behavioral competencies during infancy will therefore be associated with changes in activity over several regions, and not just by the onset of activity in one or more additional region(s).

A third perspective on human functional brain development, skill learning, involves the proposal that the changes in neural activity seen during functional brain development in infants and children as they acquire new perceptual or motor abilities are similar to those involved in complex perceptual and motor skill acquisition in adults. With regard to perceptual expertise, Gauthier and colleagues have shown that extensive training of adults with artificial objects (called greebles) eventually results in activation of a cortical region previously associated with face processing, the FFA (Gauthier, Tarr, Anderson, Skudlarski, & Gore, 1999). This suggests that the region is normally activated by faces in adults, not because it is prespecified for faces, but because of our extensive expertise with that class of stimulus. Furthermore, it encourages parallels with the development of face-processing skills in infants (see Gauthier & Nelson, 2001). Although the extent to which parallels can be drawn between adult expertise and infant development still remain unclear, to the extent that the skill-learning hypothesis is correct it presents a possible view of continuity of mechanisms throughout the life span.

Assumptions Underlying the Three Approaches

Gottlieb (1992) distinguished between two approaches to the study of development—deterministic epigenesis in which it is assumed that there is a unidirectional causal path from genes to structural brain changes to psychological function, and probabilistic epigenesis in which interactions between genes, structural brain changes, and psychological function are viewed as bidirectional, dynamic, and emergent. In many ways it is a defining feature of the maturational approach that it assumes deterministic epigenesis; region-specific gene expression is assumed to effect changes in intraregional connectivity that, in turn, allows new functions to emerge. A related assumption commonly made within the maturational approach is that there is a one-to-one mapping between brain and cortical regions and particular cognitive functions, such that specific computations come online following that maturation of circuitry intrinsic to the corresponding cortical region. In some respects, this view parallels mosaic development at the cellular level in which simple organisms (such as C. Elegans) are constructed through cell lineages that are largely independent of each other (Elman et al., 1996). Similarly, different cortical regions are assumed to have different maturational timetables, thus enabling new cognitive functions to emerge at different ages.

Interactive specialization (IS; Johnson, Halit, Grice, & Karmiloff-Smith, 2002) has a number of different underlying assumptions. Specifically, a probabilistic epigenesis assumption is coupled with the view that cognitive functions are the emergent product of interactions between different brain regions, and between the whole brain and its external environment. With regard to the second of these assumptions, IS follows recent trends in adult functional neuroimaging. For example, Friston and Price (2001) point out that it may be an error to assume that particular functions can be localized within a certain cortical region. Rather, they suggest, the response properties of a region are determined by its patterns of connectivity to other regions as well as by their current activity states. By this view, "the cortical infrastructure supporting a single function may involve many specialized areas whose union is mediated by the functional integration among them" (p. 276). Similarly, in discussing the design and interpretation of adult fMRI studies, Carpenter and collaborators have argued that: "In contrast to a localist assumption of a one-to-one mapping between cortical regions and cognitive operations, an alternative view is that cognitive task performance is subserved by large-scale cortical networks that consist of spatially separate computational components, each with its own set of relative specializations, that collaborate extensively to accomplish cognitive functions" (Carpenter et al., 2001, p. 360). Extending these ideas to development, the IS approach emphasizes changes in interregional connectivity, as opposed to the maturation of intraregional connectivity. Although the maturational approach may be analogous to mosaic cellular development, the IS view corresponds to the regulatory development seen in higher organisms in which cell–cell interactions are critical in determining developmental fate. Although mosaic development can be faster than regulatory, the latter has several advantages. Namely, regulatory development is more flexible and better able to respond to damage, and it is more efficient in terms of genetic coding. In regulatory development genes need only orchestrate cellular-level interactions to yield more complex structures (see Elman et al., 1996).

As well as the mapping between structure and function at one age, one can also consider how this mapping might change during development. When discussing functional imaging of developmental disorders, Johnson, Halit, Grice, and Karmiloff-Smith (2002) point out that many laboratories have assumed that the relation between brain structure and cognitive function is unchanging during development. Specifically, in accordance with a maturational view, when new structures come online, the existing (already mature) regions continue to support the same functions they did at earlier developmental stages. The static assumption is partly why it is acceptable to study developmental disorders in adulthood and then extrapolate back in time to early development. Contrary to this view, the IS approach as expounded by Johnson and colleagues (2002) suggests that when a new computation or skill is acquired, there is a reorganization of interactions between brain different structures and regions. This reorganization process could even change how previously acquired cognitive functions are represented in the brain. Thus, the same behavior could be supported by different neural substrates at different ages during development.

Stating that structure–function relations can change with development is all very well, but it lacks the specificity required to make all but the most general predictions. Fortunately, the view that there is competitive specialization of regions during development gives rise to more specific predictions about the types of changes in structure–function relations that should be observed. Specifically, as regions become increasingly selective in their response properties during infancy the overall extent of cortical activation during a given task may therefore decrease. This is because regions that previously responded to a range of different stimuli (e.g., complex animate and inanimate objects), come to confine their activity to a particular class of objects (e.g., upright human faces) and, therefore, do not respond in situations were they used to. Evidence in support of this view will be discussed later.

The basic assumption underlying the skill-learning approach is that there is a continuity of the circuitry underlying skill acquisition from birth through to adulthood. This circuit is likely to involve a network of structures that retains the same basic function across developmental time (a static brain–cognition mapping). However, other brain regions may respond to training with dynamic changes in functionality similar or identical to those hypothesized within the IS framework. Another way in which the skill-learning view differs from the other perspectives is with regard to plasticity.

Plasticity in brain development is a phenomenon that has generated much controversy, with several different conceptions and definitions having been presented. The three perspectives we have discussed provide different viewpoints on plasticity. According to the maturational framework, plasticity is a specialized mechanism that is activated following brain injury. According to the IS approach, plasticity is simply the state of having a region's function not yet fully specialized. That is, there is still remaining scope for developing more finely tuned responses. This definition corresponds well with the view of developmental biologists that development involves the increasing restriction of fate. Finally, according to the skill-learning hypothesis, plasticity is at least the result of specific circuitry that remains in place throughout the life span. Unlike the IS approach, plasticity does not necessarily reduce during development.

Now that I have reviewed the three basic perspectives on human functional brain development, I return to the topic of the social brain and examine which of the perspectives I have outlined best accounts for the existing evidence. I begin with one of the most basic aspects of social cognition—the perception of faces.

Face Perception

One of the best-studied cases of functional specialization in the human cortex is face processing. Several cortical regions within the social brain, including regions of the fusiform gyrus, lateral occipital area, and superior temporal sulcus (Adolphs, 2003; Kanwisher, McDermott, & Chun, 1997) have all been implicated in neuroimaging studies as being face-sensitive regions involved in aspects of encoding and detecting facial information. The stimulus specificity of response has been most extensively studied for the FFA, a region that is more activated by faces than by many other comparison stimuli including houses, textures, and hands (Kanwisher et al., 1997). Although the greater activation of the FFA to faces than other objects has led some to propose it is a face module (Kanwisher et al., 1997); others call this view into question. In particular, investigations demonstrating that (a) the distribution of response across ventral cortex may be more stimulus-specific than the strength of response of a particular region such as FFA (Haxby et al., 2001; Ishai, Ungerleider, Martin, Schouten, & Haxby, 1999; but see Spiridon & Kanwisher, 2002), and (b) that activation of the FFA increases with increasing expertise in discriminating members of nonface categories (Gauthier et al., 2000), together suggest that the region may play a more general role in object processing. However, the observation remains that faces activate the FFA more than any other object, and that the distribution of activity over the ventral cortex for faces differs from other objects in that it is more focal and less influenced by attention (Haxby et al., 2001). How do such specializations arise, and why do face-sensitive regions tend to be located in particular regions of cortex? I will suggest that the three viewpoints outlined above provide different answers to this question.

According to the maturational view, specific genes are expressed within particular cortical regions (such as the FFA) and prewire those areas for face processing. One of several problems with this argument is that differential gene expression within the mammalian cerebral cortex tends to be on a much larger scale than the functional regions identified in imaging studies (e.g., Krubitzer, 2000). According to the skill-learning view, much of the adult social brain network is better characterized as a perceptual skill network, and this coincides with social processing because most human adults are experts in this domain. Finally, according to the IS view, the social brain emerges from other (nonsocial) brain networks as a result of interactions between brain regions, and between the brain and the child's external world.

When considering different accounts of the origins of the social brain, it is useful to begin at birth. A number of studies have shown that newborn infants (in some studies within the first hour of life) preferentially look toward face-like patterns (e.g., Johnson, Dziurawiec, Ellis, & Morton, 1991; Valenza, Simion, Cassia, & Umilta, 1996). There has been considerable debate over the specificity of the mechanisms (or representations) that underlie this behavior. At one extreme is the view that such preferences are simply because of the visual psychophysical properties of faces matching those most ideal for the newborn visual system (consistent with a skill-learning viewpoint). At the other extreme is the view that newborns processing of faces is substantially similar to that in adults, including fully specified representations of individual faces (consistent with one version of the maturational perspective). An intermediate view was advanced by Johnson and Morton (1991), who proposed that newborn face representations could contain the minimum necessary information to elicit adaptive behavior. Specifically, they argued for a mechanism termed Conspec that might contain a representation as simple as three high-contrast blobs in

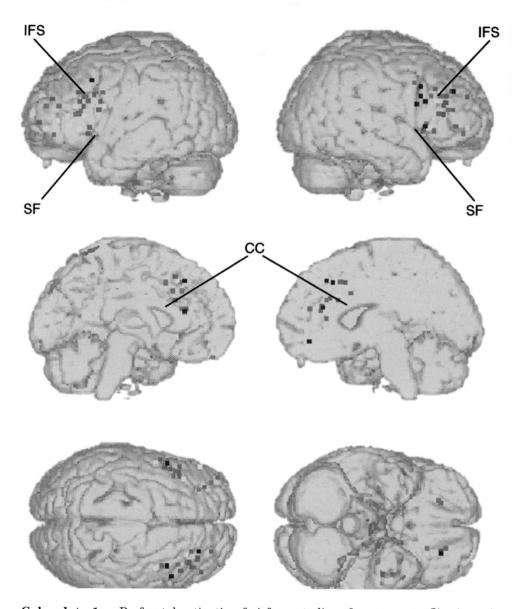

Colorplate 1. Prefrontal activation foci from studies of response conflict (green), task novelty (purple), number of elements in working memory (yellow), working memory delay (red), and perceptual difficulty (blue). Shown are lateral (upper row) and medial (middle row) views of each hemisphere, along with whole brain views from above (bottom left) and below (bottom right). CC = corpus callosum; IFS = inferior frontal sulcus; SF = Sylvian fissure. From "Common Regions of the Human Frontal Lobe Recruited by Diverse Cognitive Demands," by J. Duncan and A. M. Owen, 2000, *Trends in Neurosciences, 23,* pp. 475–483. Copyright 2000 by Elsevier. Reprinted with permission.

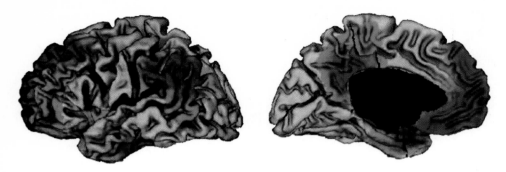

Colorplate 2. Areas of the brain that exhibit task-independent decreases in activity (TIDs) from a resting level of activity during the performance of a wide variety of goal-directed tasks displayed on the cortical surface of a canonical left hemisphere. Data from Van Essen et al. (2002).

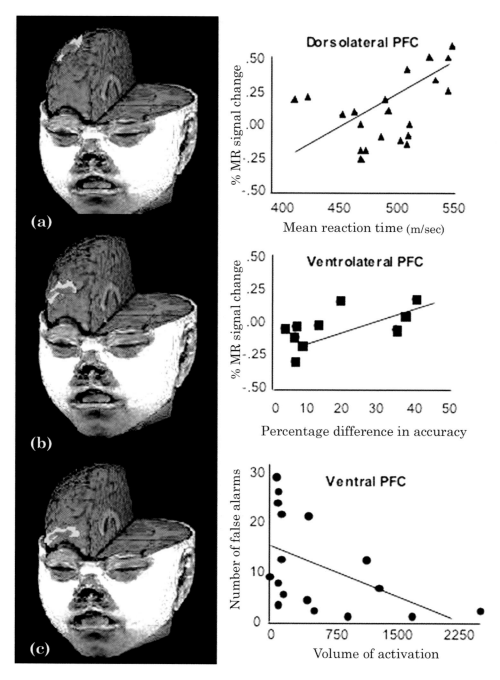

Colorplate 3. Panel A shows regions of brain activity that correlated with behavioral performance on a version of the stimulus selection task. Panel B shows regions of brain activity that correlated with behavioral performance on a version of the response selection task. Panel C shows regions of brain activity that correlated with behavioral performance on a version of the response execution task. MR = magnetic resonance; PFC = prefrontal cortex.

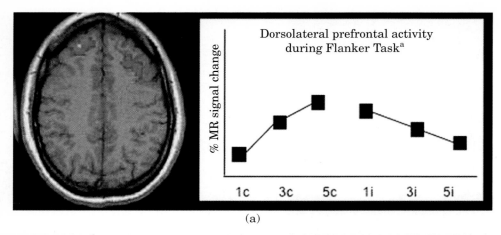

(a)

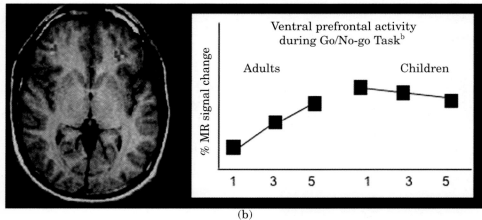

(b)

Colorplate 4. Panel A illustrates prefrontal regions showing a linear increase with increasing conflict and decrease with reduced conflict as a function of the preceding trial types during a flanker task. Preceding trials consisted of one, three, or five compatible flanker trials preceding an incompatible one or one, three, or five incompatible flanker trials preceding an incompatible one. Panel B illustrates prefrontal regions showing a linear increase with increasing conflict as a function of number of go trials preceding a no-go trial. Preceding trials consisted of one, three, or five go trials before a no-go trial. MR = magnetic resonance.
[a]Where 1, 3, and 5 = number of compatible (c) or incompatible (i) trials preceding an incompatible trial.
[b]Where 1, 3, and 5 = number of go trials preceding a no-go trial.

the locations of the eyes and mouth. This skeletal representation may be sufficient to bootstrap other developing systems by providing them with the appropriate input, and in this respect is consistent with the IS approach.

Since these original proposals, several laboratories have focused on determining the representation that underlies the tendency of newborns to orient to faces through empirical investigation and neural network modelling. With regard to the latter, results from neural network simulations suggest that a representation for Conspec as simple as three high-contrast blobs can account for most of the newborn data collected to date, involving a variety of schematic and naturalistic face stimuli (see Bednar & Miikkulainen, 2003). Current debate centers on whether the minimal representation supporting Conspec involves the three high contrast blobs as originally proposed by Johnson and Morton (1991) or whether the representation supports a preference for arrays with a greater number of elements in the upper half of a stimulus (Turati, Simion, Milani, & Umiltà, 2002). However, in both cases the representation is probably close to the minimum sufficient to elicit orienting to faces within the natural environment of the newborn, and given the constraints of the newborn visual system.

Several lines of evidence suggest that this newborn preference is not mediated by the same cortical structures as are involved in face processing in adults, and may be a result of subcortical structures such as the pulvinar. One purpose of this early bias to fixate on faces may be to elicit bonding from adult caregivers. However, I suggest that an equally important purpose is to bias the visual input to plastic cortical circuits. This biased sampling of the visual environment over the first days and weeks of life may ensure the appropriate specialization of later developing cortical circuitry (Morton & Johnson, 1991).

Although the current evidence on newborn face preferences is difficult to reconcile with a strictly skill-learning view of functional brain development, it is not entirely inconsistent with either the maturational or IS approaches. According to at least some versions of the maturational approach primitive abilities in the newborn would be added to by more sophisticated modules maturating at later ages. According to the IS approach, a primitive brain system such as Conspec bootstraps later developing experience-dependent systems by providing the appropriate input for them.

Given that newborn behavior alone cannot help us discriminate between at least two of the perspectives on functional brain development, what about developmental changes over the first few months of life? Specifically, does subsequent development look more like the addition of new components, or the gradual specialization of circuitry for processing of social stimuli?

Although attempts to study changes in brain activity during development are still in their infancy, several labs have examined changes in event-related potentials (ERPs) in face processing (see, for review, de Haan, Johnson, & Halit, 2003). In particular, several labs have focused on an ERP component, termed the N170, which has been strongly associated with face processing in a number of studies on adults (see, for review, de Haan et al., 2003). Specifically, the amplitude and latency of this component vary according to whether or not faces are present in the visual field of the adult volunteer under study. An important aspect of the N170 in adults is that its response is highly selective.

For example, we observed that the N170 showed a different response to human upright faces, than to closely related stimuli such as inverted human faces and upright monkey faces (de Haan, Pascalis, & Johnson, 2002). Although the exact underlying neural generators of the N170 are currently still debated, the specificity of response of the N170 can be taken as an index of the degree of specialization of cortical processing for human upright faces. For this reason we have undertaken a series of studies on the development of the N170 over the first weeks and months of postnatal life.

The first issue we addressed in our developmental studies is when does the face-sensitive N170 emerge? In a series of experiments we have identified a component in the infant ERP that has many of the properties associated with the adult N170, but that is of a slightly longer latency (240 to 290 ms; de Haan et al., 2002; Halit et al., 2003). In studying the response properties of this potential at 3, 6, and 12 months of age we have discovered that (a) the component is present from at least 3 months of age (although its development continues into middle childhood), (b) the component becomes more specifically tuned to human upright faces with increasing age, and (c) there is stronger evidence for adult-like lateralization of the component at older ages. Thus, study of the component is consistent with the idea of increased specialization and localization resulting from development.

More direct evidence for increased localization comes from a recent fMRI study of the neural basis of face processing in children compared to adults (Passarotti et al., 2003). In this study, even when children and adults were matched for behavioral ability (in a face-matching task), children activated a larger extent of cortex around face-sensitive areas than did adults. Similar conclusions can be drawn from a PET study conducted on 2-month-old infants, in which a large network of cortical areas were activated when infants viewed faces compared to a moving dot array (Tzourio-Mazoyer et al., 2002).

Thus, with regard to face perception, the available evidence from newborns allows us to rule out the skill-learning hypothesis, while the evidence on the neurodevelopment of face processing over the first months and years of life is consistent with the kinds of dynamic changes in processing expected from the IS, and not the maturational, approach.

Perceiving and Acting on the Eyes of Another

Moving beyond the relatively simple perception of faces, a more complex attribute of the adult social brain is processing information about the eyes of other humans. There are two important aspects of processing information about the eyes. The first of these is being able to detect the direction of another's gaze to direct your attention to the same object or spatial location. Perception of averted gaze can elicit an automatic shift of attention in the same direction in adults (Driver et al., 1999), allowing the establishment of joint attention (Butterworth & Jarrett, 1991). Joint attention to objects is thought to be crucial for a number of aspects of cognitive and social development, including word learning. The second critical aspect of gaze perception is the detection of direct gaze, enabling mutual gaze with the viewer. Mutual gaze (eye contact) provides the main mode of establishing a communicative context between humans and is believed to be important for normal social development (e.g., Kleinke, 1986; Symons, Hains, & Muir, 1998). It is commonly agreed that eye gaze perception is important for mother—infant interaction, and that it provides a vital foundation for social development (e.g., Jaffe, Stern, & Peery, 1973; Stern, 1974).

With regard to the social brain network, the STS has been identified in several adult imaging studies of eye gaze perception and processing (for review, see Adolphs, 2003). As with cortical face processing above, in adults the response properties of this region are highly tuned (specialized) in that the region does not respond to nonbiological motion (Puce, Allison, Bentin, Gore, & McCarthy, 1998). Although we cannot directly image the functioning of STS in infants, we have conducted a series of behavioral experiments to ascertain the specificity or otherwise of gaze cueing in infants.

Several studies have demonstrated that gaze cues are able to trigger an automatic and rapid shifting of the focus of the adult viewer's visual attention (Driver et al., 1999; Friesen & Kingstone, 1998; Langton & Bruce, 1999). All these studies used variants of Posner's spatial cueing paradigm (e.g., Posner, 1980), where a central or peripheral cue directs the attention to one of the peripheral locations. When the target appears in the same location where the cue was directed (the congruent position), the participant is faster to look at that target compared to another target at an incongruent position relative to the previous cue. Using this paradigm, Schuller and Rossion (2001) presented a face on the screen that was first looking to the research participant and then either to the right or the left. Then a target appeared that could be in the same position where the face was looking, or in the opposite position. The results were that facilitation of visual processing by spatial attention is reflected by enhanced early visual evoked potentials (P1 and N1). Reflexive attention increases visual activity and speeds up the processing of visual attention. Probably, in addition to the areas discussed before, eye gaze tasks activate regions that have been associated with Posner's posterior attention network (Posner, 1980).

When does the ability to use eye gaze direction as an attentional cue start? Previous work with human infants indicates that they start to discriminate and follow adults' direction of attention at the age of 3 or 4 months (Hood, Willen, & Driver, 1998; Vecera & Johnson, 1995). In our studies we examined further the visual properties of the eyes that enable infants to follow the direction of the gaze. We tested 4-month-olds using a cueing paradigm adapted from Hood and colleagues (1998). Each trial begins with the stimulus face eyes blinking (to attract attention), before the pupils shift to either the right or the left for a period of 1500 ms (see Figure 7.1). A target stimulus was then presented either in the same position where the stimulus face eyes were looking (congruent position) or in a location incongruent with the direction of gaze. By measuring the saccadic reaction time of infants to orient to the target we demonstrated that the infants were faster to look at the location congruent with the direction of gaze of the face.

In the second experiment of this series, we manipulated the stimulus face so that the whole face was shifted to one side (right or left) while the pupils remained fixed. In this case the infants were faster to look in the direction in which the whole face was shifted, and not the direction where the pupils were

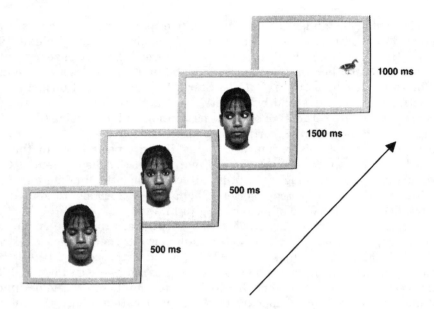

Figure 7.1. Example of the edited video image illustrating the stimulus sequence for Experiment 1 in Farroni et al. (2000). In this trial, the stimulus target (the duck) appears on an incongruent side. From "Infant's Use of Gaze Direction to Cue Attention: The Importance of Perceived Motion," by T. Farroni, M. H. Johnson, M. Brockbank, and F. Simion, 2000, *Visual Cognition, 7*, pp. 705–718. Copyright 2000 by Taylor & Francis. Reprinted with permission.

directed. Therefore, the infants actually followed the biggest object with lateral motion (i.e., the face) and not the eyes. In a third experiment, we used the same paradigm as in the first experiment, but this time when the eyes were opened the pupils were already oriented to the left or right, and the infants were not able to perceive the movement of the pupils. In this case the cueing effect disappeared. Up to this point, the results suggested that the critical feature for eye gaze cue in infants is the movement of the pupils, and not the final direction of the pupils (Farroni, Johnson, Brockbank, & Simion, 2000).

To try to understand this cueing effect better, we did three additional variants of the same procedure (Farroni, Mansfield, Lai, & Johnson, 2003). In the first of these, we examined the effect of inverting the face on cueing. If infants are merely cued by motion, then an inverted face should produce the same cueing as an upright one. To our surprise, the results showed that there was no significant cueing effect, suggesting that the context of an upright face may be important. In the next study we presented infants with a face that was initially presented with averted gaze but that then shifted to the center. If infants are responding just to the motion of elements, they should be cued in the direction opposite to that initially presented. Again, no cueing effect was observed. These results did not support the hypothesis that directed motion of elements is the only determining factor for the cueing effects.

In the last experiment, a more complex gaze shift sequence allowed us to analyze the importance of beginning with a period of mutual gaze: the eyes shifted from center to averted and then back to center. In this experiment, we observed a significant cueing effect. Taken together, these results suggest that it is only following a period of mutual gaze with an upright face that cueing effects are observed. In other words, mutual gaze (eye contact) with an upright face may engage mechanisms of attention such that the viewer is more likely to be cued by subsequent motion. In summary, the critical features for eye gaze cueing in infants are (a) lateral motion of elements and (b) a brief preceding period of eye contact with an upright face.

There is evidence from functional neuroimaging that indicates that a network of cortical and subcortical regions are engaged in eye gaze processing in adults (see Adolphs, 2003). This network of structures overlaps with, but does not completely duplicate, the patterns of activation seen in the perception of motion and the perception of faces in general. Although it may be important to activate the whole network for eye gaze processing, one region in particular, the eye area of the superior temporal sulcus, appears to be critical. The finding that infants are as effectively cued by noneye motion provides preliminary evidence that their STS may be less finely tuned than in adults.

Following the surprising observation that a period of direct gaze is required before cueing can be effective in infants, we determined to investigate the developmental roots of eye contact detection. As discussed earlier, it is already known that human newborns have a visual preference for face-like stimuli (Johnson, Dziurawiec, Bartrip, & Morton, 1992; Valenza et al., 1996), prefer faces with eyes opened (Batki et al., 2000), and tend to imitate certain facial gestures (Meltzoff & Moore, 1977). Preferential attention to faces with direct gaze would provide the most compelling evidence to date that human newborns are born prepared to detect socially relevant information. For this reason we recently investigated eye gaze detection in humans from birth. We (Farroni, Csibra, Simion, & Johnson, 2002) tested healthy human newborn infants by presenting them with a pair of stimuli, one a face with eye gaze directed straight at the newborns, and the other with averted gaze (see Figure 7.2). Videotapes of the baby's eye movements throughout the trial were analyzed by the two recorders. The dependent variables we used were the total fixation time and the number of orienting responses. Results showed that the fixation times were significantly longer for the face with the direct gaze. Furthermore, infants oriented more to the face with direct gaze than that with averted gaze.

In a second experiment, we attempted to gain converging evidence for the differential processing of direct gaze in infants, by recording ERPs from the scalp as infants viewed faces. We studied 4-month-old babies with the same stimuli as those used in the previous experiment with newborns and found a difference between the two gaze directions at the time and scalp location of the previously identified face-sensitive component of the infant ERP (N240/N290; de Haan et al., 2002). As mentioned earlier, this component of the infant ERP is thought to be the equivalent of a well-studied adult face-sensitive component, and in infants is sensitive to changes in the orientation and species of a face, at least by 12 months of age (Halit, de Haan, & Johnson, 2003).

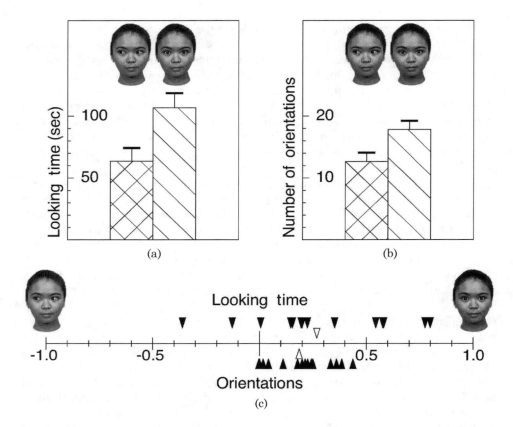

Figure 7.2. Results of the preferential looking study with newborns. (a) Mean looking times (and SE) spent at the two stimulus types. Newborns spent significantly more time looking at the face with mutual gaze than looking at the face with averted gaze. (b) Mean number of orientations toward each type of stimulus. (c) Filled triangles indicate reference scores for the direct gaze over the averted gaze for each individual newborn. Open triangles indicate average preference scores. From "Eye Contact Detection in Humans From Birth," by T. Farroni, G. Csibra, F. Simion, and M. H. Johnson, 2002, *Proceedings of the National Academy of Sciences of the United States of America, 198*, pp. 9602–9605. Copyright 2002 by the Academy of Sciences of the United States of America. Reprinted with permission.

Thus, our conclusion from these studies is that direct eye contact enhances the perceptual processing of faces in 4-month-old infants.

The empirical evidence we and others have gathered on the development and neural basis of eye gaze processing in infants is consistent with the IS perspective on functional brain development (Johnson, 2001). Specifically, we (Farroni et al., 2002) suggest that a primitive representation of high-contrast elements (such as Johnson and Morton's Conspec) would be sufficient to direct orienting in newborns toward faces with eye contact. Therefore, the more frequent orienting to the direct gaze in newborns could be mediated by the same mechanism that underlies newborn's tendency to orient to faces in general.

Specifically, Johnson and Morton (1991) hypothesized that subcortical circuits supported a primitive representation of high-contrast elements relating to the location of the eyes and mouth. A face with direct gaze would better fit the spatial relation of elements in this template than one with gaze averted, suggesting that the functional role of this putative mechanism is more general than previously supposed. This primitive bias ensures a biased input of human faces with direct gaze to the infant over the first days and weeks of life.

According to the IS view, a network as a whole becomes specialized for a particular function. Therefore, we suggest that the eye region of the STS does not develop in isolation, or in a modular fashion, but that its functionality emerges within the context of interacting regions involved in either general face processing or in motion detection. Viewed from this perspective, STS may be a region that integrates motion information with the processing of faces (and other body parts). Although STS may be active in infants, we propose that it is not yet efficiently integrating motion and face information. In other words, while the 4-month-old has good face processing and general motion perception, the infant has not yet integrated these two aspects of perception together into adult eye-gaze perception. By this account, making eye contact with upright face fully engages face processing, which then facilitates the orienting of attention by lateral motion. At older ages, eye gaze perception becomes a fully integrated function where even static presentations of averted eyes are sufficient to facilitate gaze.

Conclusion

In this chapter I considered evidence on the development of the social brain network in relation to three perspectives on human functional brain development. In the relatively well-studied case of face perception, when evidence from several developmental ages is taken into account, I argue that the IS view can best account for the data. In the less well-studied case of eye gaze processing, the evidence obtained so far is also consistent with the IS approach (without ruling out alternatives). We have currently begun to explore two new avenues of research relating to this topic.

One new line of research extends to studying more complex functions associated with the emergence of the social brain. Specifically, we have been interested in the perception and parsing of sequences of human action. In experiments currently underway, infants passively view videos of sequences of human action including biologically impossible actions and accidental versus intentional actions. During this time we record ERP and EEG measures in an attempt to determine when and how infants process human action in the same ways as adults.

In a second line of research we are investigating young children with autism. From the IS perspective autism can be viewed as a failure of the emergence of the typical social brain network. Our ERP experiments to date have demonstrated that while the young autistic child's brain does process the difference between direct and averted gaze, the ERP correlates of this resemble the pattern found in much younger typically developing children. One interpretation of these findings is that although eye gaze processing and face processing evoke different patterns of activation within the typically developing social brain network by early childhood, this is not the case for autistic children because their social brain network is poorly specialized.

There are exiting days ahead for developmental cognitive neuroscience as theoretical advances (such as those described in this chapter), combine with recent technical and methodological advances (such as those associated with brain imaging, genetics, and neural network modelling). It is not surprising that many governmental agencies and leading charities have identified the field as one of the hottest topics in neuroscience. With this in mind, it is startling to think how many of these theoretical and methodological advances can be attributed, at least in part, to Michael Posner. To pick out just a few examples of this influence; his long-standing insistence on talking about brain networks, rather than individual structures, has presaged current theoretical models for understanding brain function and imaging data (Friston & Price, 2001); beginning in the 1980s in his work with Rothbart, he discussed attentional and perceptual development within the context of the child's social environment, as well as the brain systems that might be involved (Posner & Rothbart, 1980); Posner's original idea of adapting adult attentional and cognitive paradigms for use with infants (and making them work) has opened up a whole new vista of infant and toddler and behavioral paradigms beyond the traditional habituation and visual preference procedures. Finally, I recall Posner telling me in 1989 that we had to seriously start to work on the mapping from genes to cognition and that he had been talking to people at a nearby zebra fish development laboratory about it (an idea that in the short term led to the conference "Cognitive Neuroscience of Development: Genes to Behavior" held in Eugene in 1990). Although I agreed with the general spirit of his comment, I was somewhat dubious that I would see a significant start on bridging these fields in my lifetime. But in 2003 Posner and his coauthors published an impressive paper demonstrating that the activation of the anterior cingulate in a attention flanker task correlated highly with the expression of certain genes (Fan, Fossella, Sommer, Wu, & Posner, 2003). Not for the first time, I had underestimated Posner's unique ability to go from a general idea to a specific and convincing experiment.

References

Adolphs, R. (2003). Cognitive neuroscience of human social behaviour. *Nature Reviews Neuroscience, 4,* 165–178.

Batki, A., Baron-Cohen, S., Wheelwright, S., Connellan, J., & Ahluwalia, J. (2000). Is there an innate gaze module? Evidence from human neonates. *Infant Behaviour and Development, 23,* 223–229.

Bednar, J. A., & Miikkulainen, R. (2003). Learning innate face preferences. *Neural Computation, 15,* 1525–1557.

Butterworth, G., & Jarrett, N. (1991). What minds have in common is space: Spatial mechanisms serving joint visual attention in infancy. *British Journal of Developmental Psychology, 9,* 55–72.

Carpenter, P. A., Just, M. A., Keller, T., Cherkassky, V., Roth, J. K., & Minshew, N. (2001). Dynamic cortical systems subserving cognition: fMRI studies with typical and atypical individuals. In J. L. McClelland & R. S. Siegler (Eds.), *Mechanisms of cognitive development: Behavioral and neural perspectives. Carnegie Mellon symposia on cognition* (pp. 353–383). Mahwah, NJ: Erlbaum.

de Haan, M., Johnson, M. H., & Halit, H. (2003). Development of face-sensitive event-related potentials during infancy: A review. *International Journal of Psychophysiology, 51,* 45–58.

de Haan, M., Pascalis, O., & Johnson, M. H. (2002). Specialization of neural mechanisms underlying face recognition in human infants. *Journal of Cognitive Neuroscience, 14,* 199–209.

Driver, J., Davis, G., Ricciardelli, P., Kidd, P., Maxwell, E., & Baron-Cohen, S. (1999). Gaze perception triggers reflexive visuospatial orienting. *Visual Cognition, 6,* 509–540.

Elman, J., Bates, E. A., Johnson, M. H., Karmiloff-Smith, A., Parisi, D., & Plunkett, K. E. (1996). *Rethinking innateness: A connectionist perspective on development.* Cambridge, MA: MIT Press.

Fan, J., Fossella, J., Sommer, T., Wu, Y., & Posner, M. (2003). Mapping the genetic variation of executive attention onto brain activity. *Proceedings of the National Academy of Sciences of the United States of America, 100,* 7406–7411.

Farroni, T., Csibra, G., Simion, F., & Johnson, M. H. (2002). Eye contact detection in humans from birth. *Proceedings of the National Academy of Sciences of the United States of America, 198,* 9602–9605.

Farroni, T., Johnson, M. H., Brockbank, M., & Simion, F. (2000). Infant's use of gaze direction to cue attention: The importance of perceived motion. *Visual Cognition, 7,* 705–718.

Farroni, T., Mansfield, E. M., Lai, C., & Johnson, M. H. (2003). Infants perceiving and acting on the eyes: Tests of an evolutionary hypothesis. *Journal of Experimental Child Psychology, 85,* 199–212.

Friesen, C. K., & Kingstone, A. (1998). The eyes have it! Reflexive orienting is triggered by nonpredictive gaze. *Psychonomic Bulletin and Review, 5,* 490–495.

Friston, K. J., & Price, C. J. (2001). Dynamic representations and generative models of brain function. *Brain Research Bulletin, 54,* 275–285.

Frith, U. (2001). Mind blindness and the brain in autism. *Neuron, 32,* 969–979.

Gauthier, I., & Nelson, C. A. (2001). The development of face expertise. *Current Opinion in Neurobiology, 11,* 219–224.

Gauthier, I., Tarr, M. J., Anderson, A. W., Skudlarski, P., & Gore, J. C. (1999). Activation of the middle fusiform 'face area' increases with expertise in recognizing novel objects. *Nature Neuroscience, 2,* 568–573.

Gauthier, I., Tarr, M. J., Moylan, J., Skudlarski, P., Gore, J. C., & Anderson, A. W. (2000). The fusiform "face area" is part of a network that processes faces at the individual level. *Journal of Cognitive Neuroscience, 12,* 495–504.

Gottlieb, G. (1992). *Individual development and evolution: The genesis of novel behavior.* London: Oxford University Press.

Halit, H., de Haan, M., & Johnson, M. H. (2003). Cortical specialization for face processing: Face-sensitive event-related potential components in 3- and 12-month-old infants. *NeuroImage, 19,* 1180–1193.

Haxby, J. V., Gobbini, M. I., Furey, M. L., Ishai, A., Schouten, J. L., & Pietrini, P. (2001). Distributed and overlapping representations of faces and objects in ventral temporal cortex. *Science, 293,* 2425–2430.

Hood, B. M., Willen, J. D., & Driver, J. (1998). Adult's eyes trigger shifts of visual attention in human infants. *Psychological Science, 9,* 131–134.

Ishai, A., Ungerleider, L. G., Martin, A., Schouten, J. L., & Haxby, J. V. (1999). Distributed representation of objects in the human ventral visual pathway. *Proceedings of the National Academy of Sciences of the United States of America, 96,* 9379–9384.

Jaffe, J., Stern, D. N., & Peery, J. C. (1973). "Conversational" coupling of gaze behavior in prelinguistic human development. *Journal of Psycholinguistic Research, 2,* 321–329.

Johnson, M. H. (2001). Functional brain development in humans. *Nature Reviews Neuroscience, 2,* 475–483.

Johnson, M. H., Dziurawiec, S., Bartrip, J., & Morton, J. (1992). The effects of movement of internal features on infants' preferences for face-like stimuli. *Infant Behavior and Development, 15,* 129–136.

Johnson, M. H., Dziurawiec, S., Ellis, H., & Morton, J. (1991). Newborns' preferential tracking of face-like stimuli and its subsequent decline. *Cognition, 40,* 1–19.

Johnson, M. H., Halit, H., Grice, S. J., & Karmiloff-Smith, A. (2002). Neuroimaging of typical and atypical development: A perspective from multiple levels of analysis. *Development of Psychopathology, 14,* 521–536.

Johnson, M. H., & Morton, J. (1991). *Biology and cognitive development: The case of face recognition.* Oxford, England: Blackwell.

Kanwisher, N., McDermott, J., & Chun, M. M. (1997). The fusiform face area: A module in human extrastriate cortex specialized for face perception. *Journal of Neuroscience, 17,* 4302–4311.

Kleinke, C. L. (1986). Gaze and eye contact: A research review. *Psychological Bulletin, 100,* 78–100.

Krubitzer, L. A. (2000). How does evolution build a complex brain? In G. R. Bock & G. Cardew (Eds.), *Evolutionary developmental biology of the cerebral cortex* (pp. 206–220). Chichester, England: Wiley.

Langton, S. R. H., & Bruce, V. (1999). Reflexive visual orienting in response to the social attention of others. *Visual Cognition, 6,* 541–567.

Luna, B., Thulborn, K. R., Muñoz, D. P., Merriam, E. P., Garver, K. E., Minshew, N. J., et al. (2001). Maturation of widely distributed brain function subserves cognitive development. *NeuroImage, 13,* 786–793.

Meltzoff, A. N., & Moore, M. K. (1977). Imitation of facial and manual gestures by human neonates. *Science, 198,* 74–78.

Morton, J., & Johnson, M. H. (1991). CONSPEC and CONLERN: A two-process theory of infant face recognition. *Psychological Review, 98,* 164–181.

Passarotti, A. M., Paul, B. M., Bussiere, J. R., Buxton, R. B., Wong, E. C., & Stiles, J. (2003). The development of face and location processing: An fMRI study. *Developmental Science, 6,* 100–117.

Posner, M. I. (1980). Orienting of attention. *Quarterly Journal of Experimental Psychology, 32,* 3–25.

Posner, M. I., & Rothbart, M. K. (1980). The development of attentional mechanisms. In J. H. Flower (Ed.), *Nebraska Symposium on Motivation.* Lincoln: University of Nebraska Press.

Puce, A., Allison, T., Bentin, S., Gore, J. C., & McCarthy, G. (1998). Temporal cortex activation in humans viewing eye and mouth movements. *Journal of Neuroscience, 18,* 2188–2199.

Schuller, A. M., & Rossion, B. (2001). Spatial attention triggered by eye gaze increases and speeds up early visual activity. *NeuroReport, 12,* 2381–2386.

Spiridon, M., & Kanwisher, N. (2002). How distributed is visual category information in human occipito-temporal cortex? An fMRI study. *Neuron, 35,* 1157–1165.

Stern, D. N. (1974). Mother and infant at play: The dyadic interaction involving facial, vocal, and gaze behaviors. In Ñ. M. Lewis & L. Rosenblum (Eds.), *The effect of the infant on its caretaker* (pp. 187–213). New York: Wiley.

Symons, L. A., Hains, S. M. J., & Muir, D. W. (1998). Look at me: Five-month-old infants' sensitivity to very small deviations in eye-gaze during social interactions. *Infant Behavior and Development, 21,* 531–536.

Turati, C., Simion, F., Milani, I., & Umiltà, C. (2002). Newborns' preference for faces: What is crucial? *Developmental Psychology, 38,* 875–882.

Tzourio-Mazoyer, N., De Schonen, S., Crivello, F., Reutter, B., Aujard, Y., & Mazoyer, B. (2002). Neural correlates of woman face processing by 2-month-old infants. *NeuroImage, 15,* 454–461.

Valenza, E., Simion, F., Cassia, V. M., & Umiltà, C. (1996). Face preference at birth. *Journal of Experimental Psychology: Human Perception and Performance, 22,* 892–903.

Vecera, S. P., & Johnson, M. H. (1995). Eye gaze detection and the cortical processing of faces: Evidence from infants and adults. *Visual Cognition, 2,* 101–129.

8

Frontostriatal and Frontocerebellar Circuitry Underlying Cognitive Control

B. J. Casey

Cognitive control has been described and referred to over the years by different terminology (e.g., controlled processing, effort, central executive, supervisory attention systems, attentional bias, and conflict resolution). Michael Posner was instrumental in the development of this concept (Posner & Boies, 1972; Posner & Petersen, 1990; Posner & Snyder, 1975) by distinguishing between those processes that require attentional resources or capacity (controlled processes) over those that require little attention or effort (automatic processing). This initial work set the stage for experimental investigations of this psychological construct reflecting top-down control in overriding inappropriate attention and behavior. This ability to override competing actions is a key component of cognitive functioning and cognitive theory today (Allport, 1987; Baddeley, 1986; Braver & Cohen, 2000; Cohen & Servan-Schreiber, 1992; Desimone & Duncan, 1995; Kahneman, 1973; Miller & Cohen, 2001; Posner & Boies, 1971; Posner & Petersen, 1990; Posner & Snyder, 1975; Shallice, 1988; Shiffrin & Schneider, 1977). This construct, its neurobiological basis, development, and disruption in a variety of developmental disabilities, is the central theme of this chapter.

Development of Cognitive Control

Cognitive control matures over childhood and adolescence becoming more efficient across this age range (e.g., Harnishfeger & Bjorkland, 1993). One of the classic examples of the development of cognitive control during the

This work was supported in part by Grants R21 DA15882, R01 MH 066360, R01 MH63255, and P01 MH62196. Special thanks to Matthew C. Davidson, Sarah Durston, John Fossella, Adriana Galvan, David L. Menzer, Kathleen M. Thomas, and Michael Worden for collaborative work reviewed in this chapter.

first year is seen in the progression of an infant's ability to perform the Piagetian A-not-B task (Diamond, 1985; Piaget, 1954; also see Rothbart & Rueda, chap. 9 in this volume). After finding a hidden object in one of two locations (A), the infant then has to override a competing response when the object is then hidden in the second location (B). The ability of the child to perform this task increases gradually from 6 to 12 months. In older children, cognitive control is measured by negative priming or Stroop-like tasks (Tipper, Bourque, Anderson, & Brehaut, 1989); card-sorting tasks (Munakata & Yerys, 2001; Zelazo, Burack, Benedetto, & Frye, 1996); go–no-go tasks (Casey, Trainor, Giedd, et al., 1997; Luria, 1961); incidental learning (Harnishfeger, 1995; Schiff & Knopf, 1985); and flanker tasks (Enns & Akhtar, 1989; Enns, Brodeur, & Trick, 1998; Enns & Cameron, 1987; Eriksen & Eriksen, 1974; Ridderinkhof, van der Molen, & Band, 1997). These studies show a developmental trend in the ability to ignore irrelevant information over the ages of 4 to 12 years (Passler, Isaac, & Hynd, 1985). Across tasks, children have more difficulty ignoring or suppressing competing information or events in favor of more relevant ones. These age-related differences are minimized when no competing information is present (Enns et al., 1998). Thus, one may characterize immature cognition as a vulnerability or greater susceptibility to interference from competing sources (Brainerd & Reyna, 1993; Casey, Forman, et al., 2001; Casey, Thomas, Davidson, Kunz, & Franzen, 2002; Dempster, 1993; Diamond, 1990; Munakata & Yerys, 2001).

Disorders of Cognitive Control

The importance of understanding the neural basis of cognitive control and its development is underscored by its disruption in so many developmental disabilities. A core problem across these disorders is difficulty overriding or suppressing inappropriate thoughts and behaviors. For example, children with attention-deficit/hyperactivity disorder (ADHD) have problems focusing their attention and are described as distractible and impulsive (Barkley, 1997). Children with Tourette's syndrome have difficulty suppressing repetitive movements and vocalizations that are sometimes complex, emotionally provocative and exacerbated by stressful situations (Leckman et al., 1987). Individuals with obsessive–compulsive disorder are characterized by difficulty stopping intrusive thoughts and ritualistic behaviors (Insel, 1988). Patients with childhood-onset schizophrenia appear unable to stop attending to irrelevant thoughts and information (Asarnow, Brown, & Strandburg, 1995). Stereotypes, repeated self-injurious behaviors, and ruminations are all behavioral examples of cognitive control deficits observed in a wide range of disabilities including those with autism, mental retardation, and affective disorders. The prevalence of problems in regulating behavior in so many different developmental disabilities underscores the need for a clearer understanding of the development, individual variability and biological bases of cognitive control.

Neurobiology of Cognitive Control

Clinical Neuroimaging Studies

Striking similarities have been reported in the clinical neuroimaging literature as to the neural circuitry implicated in disorders of cognitive control. This circuitry includes portions of the prefrontal cortex, basal ganglia, and cerebellum. For example, abnormalities in these regions have been reported in ADHD (Castellanos et al., 1994, 1996; Lou, Henriksen, Bruhn, Borner, & Nielsen, 1989), Tourette's syndrome (Peterson et al., 1998; Singer et al., 1993; Wolf et al., 1996) obsessive–compulsive disorder (Baxter et al., 1988; Rosenberg et al., 1997; Swedo et al., 1989) and childhood-onset schizophrenia (Frazier et al., 1996). Abnormalities in size, asymmetry, or glucose metabolism and blood flow are typically reported in studies based typically on either magnetic resonance imaging (MRI) or positron emission tomography (PET). For example, MRI studies of ADHD have revealed abnormalities in the size and symmetry of the basal ganglia (Castellanos et al., 1994, 1996) and recent functional MRI studies show decreased activity in prefrontal cortex and basal ganglia regions (Bush et al., 1999; Durston, Tottenham, et al., 2003; Vaidya et al., 1998). Although fewer studies have examined the function of the cerebellum in these individuals, recent morphometry studies suggest significant reductions in the volume of medial portions of this structure in ADHD (Berquin et al., 1998, Castellanos et al., 2002; Mostofsky, Reiss, Lockhart, & Denckla, 1998). Abnormalities in the basal ganglia, specifically the caudate nucleus, in children with Tourette's syndrome have been reported in PET studies by Wolf and colleagues (1996) and in a functional magnetic resonance imaging (fMRI) study by Peterson and others (1998). PET studies of obsessive–compulsive disorder have revealed hypermetabolic activity in these regions, particularly in the caudate nucleus, anterior cingulate cortex, and orbitofrontal cortex (Baxter et al., 1988; Swedo et al., 1989) that normalize with pharmacological and behavioral treatments. MRI-based decreases in volume of the striatum have been reported also (Rosenberg et al., 1997). MRI-based decreases in size of the basal ganglia and cerebellum have been reported in patients with childhood-onset schizophrenia (Frazier et al., 1996; Giedd et al., 1999) and adults with schizophrenia show hypofrontality when performing "frontal lobe" tasks such as the Wisconsin Card Sorting Task (Berman, Illowsky, & Weinberger, 1988). In autism, frontal and cerebellar abnormalities have been observed reliably (Allen & Courchesne, 2003; Carper, Moses, Tigue, & Courchesne, 2003). So the basal ganglia, cerebellum and prefrontal cortex appear to be significantly involved in a range of disorders that have as a key symptom a problem overriding inappropriate thoughts and actions (i.e., cognitive control).

Single or Multiple Mechanisms

The select review of clinical neuroimaging findings implicate a common cognitive deficit and common neurocircuitry across disorders. As such, a single mechanism may underlie individual differences in cognitive control. Yet, the discrete symptomatology and psychopharmacological treatment of these disorders argue for multiple mechanisms. For example, stimulants are typically prescribed in the treatment of children with ADHD, while neuroleptics and serotonin reuptake inhibitors (SSRI) have been shown to be effective in the treatment of schizophrenia and anxiety disorders, respectively. How then do we constrain our model of whether a single or multiple mechanism(s) underlie cognitive control and its disruption in so many developmental disabilities?

One approach in constraining a model of cognitive control is to turn to what is known about the neuroanatomy and neurophysiology of implicated brain regions (i.e., prefrontal cortex, basal ganglia, and cerebellum). Identification of specific neuroanatomical or neurophysiologic function may ultimately provide valuable information for validating the core features of and distinctions between psychiatric disorders and in turn also constrain our theories of cognitive control.

Frontostriatal and Frontocerebellar Circuitry

The brain regions implicated in developmental disorders of cognitive control include the prefrontal cortex, basal ganglia, and cerebellum. Different prefrontal circuits have been described that involve these brain regions: the frontostriatal and frontocerebellar loops. These circuits are similar in a number of characteristics. For example, both the cerebellum and the basal ganglia project to the prefrontal cortex via the thalamus. The primary neurotransmitter in both the basal ganglia and cerebellum is gamma-aminobutyric acid (GABA), an inhibitory neurotransmitter. Glutamate is found in the prefrontal cortex and thalamus, which is an excitatory neurotransmitter and dopamine is a critical neuromodulator of both circuits (Braver & Cohen, 2002; Cohen & Servan-Schreiber, 1992; Montague, Dayan, & Sejnowski, 1996; Schultz, 1997) that is expressed preferentially in portions of the prefrontal cortex, basal ganglia, and dentate nucleus of the cerebellum, all regions implicated in disorders of cognitive control.

These circuits have been show to support both motor and cognitive behavior with cognitive related actions being driven by projections from the prefrontal cortex and modulated by input from the dentate nucleus of the cerebellum and from the dorsal and ventral striatum of the basal ganglia (caudate and nucleus accumbens). This chapter focuses on prefrontal cognitive loops rather than frontal motor loops.

This circuitry is perhaps most well described within the basal ganglia thalamocortical circuitry for which at least five basal ganglia thalamocortical circuits have been identified (Alexander, DeLong, & Strick, 1986). The basal ganglia thalamocortical circuits include a motor, oculomotor, prefrontal (dorsolateral and lateral orbital), and limbic circuits. These basal ganglia thalamocortical circuits involve the same projection regions (basal ganglia, thalamus, and cortex), but differ in exact projection zone within each region and in the set of thoughts and actions they support (see Figure 8.1).

The general organization of these circuits involves prefrontal projections to different areas of the striatum (i.e., putamen or caudate nuclei depending on whether in motor or cognitive loops, respectively) and then project to either

Basal Ganglia and Cerebellar Thalamocortical Loops

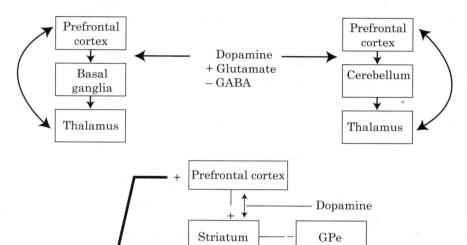

Figure 8.1. Basic circuitry of basal ganglia and cerebellar thalamocortical loops. Specifically, the basal ganglia thalamocortical (frontostriatal) circuitry is also delineated. The frontal cortex projects to different areas of the striatum (i.e., putamen or caudate nuclei) and then projects to either the direct or indirect pathway. The direct pathway involves an inhibitory projection to the internal capsule of the globus pallidus (GPi) and substantia nigra (SNr) resulting in the dampening of an inhibitory projection to the thalamus that results in disinhibition of the thalamus. The indirect pathway consists of an inhibitory projection to the external capsule of the globus pallidus (GPe) that dampens the inhibitory projection to the subthalamic nuclei (STN) resulting in excitation of the internal capsule of the globus pallidus and substantia nigra. GABA = gamma-aminobutyric acid; GPe = globus pallidus; GPi/SNr = globus pallidus/substantia nigra; STN = subthalamic nuclei.

a direct or indirect pathway. The direct pathway involves an inhibitory projection to the internal capsule of the globus pallidus (GPi) and substantia nigra (SNr) resulting in the dampening of an inhibitory projection to the thalamus (i.e., disinhibition). The indirect pathway consists of an inhibitory GABA projection to the external capsule of the globus pallidus (GPe) that dampens the inhibitory projection to the subthalamic nuclei (STN) resulting in excitation of the internal capsule of the globus pallidus and substantia nigra. This in turn leads to inhibition of the thalamus. The direct pathway presumably facilitates cortically mediated behavior while the indirect pathway is thought to inhibit thalamocortically mediated behavior.

As the prefrontal cortex projects directly to the basal ganglia and cerebellum and both project back to the prefrontal cortex via the thalamus, an account of suppression of competing actions may be described here in somewhat more mechanistic terms. That is, the basal ganglia and cerebellum have been implicated in monitoring the frequency and timing of events (Davidson et al., 2003; Hayes, Davidson, Keele, & Rafal, 1998; McClure, Berns, & Montague, 2003; Spencer, Zelaznik, Diedrichsen, & Ivry, 2003; Van Mier & Petersen, 2002). A premise of this chapter is that the ability to predict what and when an event will occur, is an essential component of cognitive control. Knowing when and what to expect is critical for the organism in planning and maintaining appropriate thoughts and actions in different contexts over time. Maintaining representations of such events and information is critical in suppressing competing information. Thus frontocerebellar and frontostriatal circuits may provide neural mechanisms for the maintenance of representations of events over time. In contrast, detecting violations in such predictions (that presumably allows the system to attend to and learn new information) may be linked to intrinsic inhibitory functions of GABA-related functions of the basal ganglia and cerebellum in the absence of frontally driven planned thoughts and actions. According to this view, the basal ganglia and cerebellum do not generate planned or voluntary movements or behaviors per se but rather the prefrontal cortex generates these voluntary actions. They do, however, detect violations in the timing and nature of events, providing the system with a way to shift out of prefrontally driven behavior when highly salient events occur. The basal ganglia and cerebellum then act broadly to inhibit competing thoughts and behaviors that would otherwise interfere with the prefrontally driven goal or behavior (Casey, 2000; Mink, 1996).

This model is consistent with our hypothesis of the way in which prefrontal cortex, basal ganglia, and cerebellum are involved in the inhibition or suppression of inappropriate thoughts and behaviors within the association and limbic circuits. The difference between this model of cognitive control and others (e.g., Diamond, 1990; Iversen & Mishkin, 1970) is the emphasis on the inhibitory function of GABA at the level of the basal ganglia and cerebellum in discussion of inhibitory processes as opposed to others (e.g., Diamond, 1990; Iversen & Mishkin, 1970) emphasizing the role of ventral and orbital prefrontal cortex in inhibitory functions.

How does this circuitry contribute to the symptoms and behaviors observed in the childhood disorders described previously? Assuming that frontostriatal and frontocerebellar pathways are involved in facilitating cortically mediated behaviors, then their disruption may result in constantly interrupted behaviors such as those observed in ADHD or constantly interrupted thoughts such as those observed in schizophrenia. In contrast, if the basal ganglia and cerebellum are involved in shifting out of prefrontally driven thoughts or behaviors (Redgrave, Prescott, & Gurney, 1999) then their disruption may result in irrepressible repetitive behaviors and thoughts similar to those observed in obsessive–compulsive disorder and Tourette's syndrome or in ruminations of hopelessness in depression. Alternatively, neuromodulatory imbalances resulting in hyperfrontal activity could lead to problems in cognitive control resulting in irrepressible repetitive behaviors as seen in Tourettes and hypofrontal activity would lead to constantly interrupted behaviors as seen in ADHD. Consistent with this theory is that different psychiatric and neurologic disorders have been linked to disruptions in specific frontostriatal loops (Alexander et al., 1986, 1991) and more recently to specific frontocerebellar loops (Dum & Strick, 2003; Middleton & Strick, 2002).

Thus our model of cognitive control (Casey, 2000; Casey, Durston & Fossella, 2001) suggests that the basal ganglia and cerebellum are involved in inhibition of competing thoughts and behaviors (Mink, 1996) while the prefrontal cortex is involved in guiding these actions by supporting representations of relevant information against interference from competing sources (Cohen & Servan-Schreiber, 1992; Miller & Cohen, 2001). Information is maintained in an active state over time in prefrontal cortex by means of recurrent excitatory connectivity (Cohen & Servan-Schreiber, 1992). The prefrontal cortex, which consists primarily of excitatory projections (glutamate), is thus involved in maintenance of relevant information for action and disruption of this brain region results in deficits in the ability to carry out the relevant actions as evidenced in ADHD. We hypothesize that the basal ganglia and cerebellum, which consist primarily of inhibitory projections (GABA), are involved in switching or shifting attention elsewhere when there is a lack of sufficient prefrontal input to drive the behavior in an organized way. Disruption to or in the development of these brain regions (basal ganglia and cerebellum) may therefore result in cognitive control deficits related to an inability to shift out of particular behavioral sets (Hayes et al., 1998) as evidenced in Parkinson's disease, obsessive–compulsive disorder, autism, and schizophrenia.

Thus far the evidence cited for the neural basis of cognitive control has been based largely on the clinical neuroimaging literature. However, there is an expansive neuroimaging literature based on studies of healthy adults implicating the frontal lobes in this ability (Cohen et al., 1994; D'Esposito et al., 1995; Duncan & Owen, 2000; Owen, 1997; Smith & Jonides, 1999), particularly when overriding or inhibiting interfering information (D'Esposito, Postle, Jonides, & Smith, 1999). The basal ganglia (Mentzel et al., 1998; Rogers, Andrews, Grasby, Brooks, & Robbins, 2000) and thalamus (Awh, Smith, & Jonides, 1996; Jonides et al., 1997) are also activated in such studies. There is also an expansive literature from studies of patients with frontal lobe lesions supporting the role of related circuitry in overriding interfering information and inhibitory attentional processes (e.g., Fuster, 1985; Leimkuhler & Mesulam, 1985; Metzler & Parkin, 2000; Milner, Petrides, & Smith, 1985; Stuss et al., 1982). More recently computational models have been developed that specifically include aspects of prefrontal cortex, basal ganglia and dopamine function (Braver & Cohen, 2000; Frank, Loughry, & O'Reilly, 2001; Miller & Cohen, 2001) to constrain theories of cognitive control (Munakata & Yerys, 2001).

Converging Evidence for a Mechanistic Model of Cognitive Control

Converging evidence in support of our model of cognitive control is presented below. This work is based largely on a number of behavioral, imaging, lesion, and genetic studies of pediatric and special populations from our laboratory.

Behavioral Studies

One approach to characterizing cognitive control is to probe it during suppression of different types of competing information and during different stages (e.g., Posner & Boies, 1972) of cognitive processing. Accordingly, we have developed a battery of tasks that require the individual to exert control over distracting stimulus information (stimulus selection, Casey, Thomas, Welsh, Livnat, et al., 2000), over competing response alternatives (response selection, Casey et al., 2002), and over execution of a compelling yet inappropriate response (response execution; Casey, Trainor, Orendi, et al., 1997; Durston, Thomas, Worden, Yang, & Casey, 2002). Within each domain, control must be exerted whenever incompatible information poses conflict with the desired action (stimulus selection, response selection, and response execution). Thus cognitive control is engaged in restriction of processing to currently relevant stimulus features (e.g., color) while ignoring other conflicting stimulus features (e.g., shape), restriction of action to appropriate responses (e.g., stimulus response incompatibility) and restriction in executing responses as in a go–no-go paradigm. Both reaction time and accuracy are the dependent variables and the tasks are self-paced for adaptability for younger ages and patient populations with mapping of stimuli to responses, except the response execution task (go–no-go) that is a speeded task with a single response mapping.

The original versions of these three cognitive tasks are described below and in more detail in Casey et al. (2002); Casey, Davidson, et al. (2004); Casey, Thomas, Welsh, Badgaiyan, et al. (2000); Casey, Trainor, Orendi, et al. (1997); Casey, Vauss, and Swedo (1994). The stimulus selection task requires the research participant to select which of three objects presented on a computer screen is unique based on the stimulus attributes of color and shape. The unique attribute changes from trial to trial such that if the relevant attribute was color on the previous trial, shape is the relevant attribute on the subsequent trial. Performance on these trials is compared to performance during a control condition in which trials are blocked by stimulus attribute. This task requires suppression of a previously attended or salient stimulus attribute. The response selection task consists of selecting responses to specific stimuli that are based on compatible (i.e., well-learned) and incompatible mappings. In the compatible mapping condition, a participant is presented with one of the digits 1, 2, 3, or 4 centrally on a computer screen. The participant is instructed to press the corresponding 1st, 2nd, 3rd, or 4th button on a response box. In the incompatible mapping condition, the participant has to reverse these responses so that the numbers 1, 2, 3, and 4 correspond to the 4th, 3rd, 2nd, and 1st buttons, respectively. When a 2 is presented the 3rd button is pressed; when a 1 is presented the 4th button is pressed, and so on. This task requires suppression of a competing overlearned response set (i.e., compatible mappings). The response execution task is a version of the classic go–no-go task. The participant is instructed to respond to any letter but X. Trials are programmed so that 75% of the trials are targets to which the participant should respond. The control condition consists of blocks of trials with only 25% targets. This task requires suppression of a compelling response altogether. Thus the stimulus selection, response selection, and response execution tasks each require suppression of different types of information.

How do these tasks map onto the previously described developmental disorders and their symptoms? Individuals with schizophrenia have been characterized as distractible and as having poor control over intruding thoughts and thus may be most vulnerable in engaging control when there is conflicting salient external or internal input (stimulus selection). Similarly, individuals with ADHD are easily distracted and have difficulty presumably in selectively attending to relevant stimuli too. In contrast, individuals with obsessive–compulsive disorder have intrusive thoughts in the form of obsessions and have difficulty shifting from an obsession or compulsion to an appropriate thought or action. As such they may have more difficulty in engaging control to suppress a conflicting inappropriate response in favor of an alternative appropriate one (response selection). This type of control problem differs from that engaged when suppressing a response altogether as is characteristic of individuals with Tourettes who actually describe a feeling of relief in not suppressing a tic (movement or vocalization). This type of cognitive problem in suppressing movement or talking is not that dissimilar from symptoms of impulsivity in children with ADHD who have difficulty being still and not blurting out answers at inappropriate times. Thus, all four examples of developmental disabilities illustrate different key elements in problems exerting control in the context of conflicting information or timing of actions.

We have collected normative data from more than 100 research participants on our battery of three tasks that are described in detail elsewhere but have summarized the findings below (see Casey, Castellanos, et al., 1997; Casey, Davidson, et al., 2004; Casey, Thomas, Davidson, et al., 2002; Casey, Thomas, Welsh, Badgaiyan, et al., 2000; Casey, Vauss, & Swedo, 1994). As expected from the review of the developmental literature of cognitive control, the pattern of performance on all three cognitive control tasks shows an increase in accuracy and decrease in response latency from early childhood to adolescence that then plateaus as illustrated in Figure 8.2.

Data on these cognitive tasks have been collected on more than 150 typically and atypically developing children including children with Tourette's syndrome, ADHD (Casey, Castellanos, et al., 1997), childhood-onset schizophrenia, and Sydenham chorea (Casey, Vauss, & Swedo, 1994; Casey, Vauss, Chused, & Swedo, 1994; Swedo et al., 1993). Performance of clinical populations relative to age- and sex-matched typically developing children are presented in Figure 8.3. Percent differences were calculated for atypically developing children relative to matched controls in performance on the conflict condition. First, children with childhood-onset schizophrenia show increased response latencies on the stimulus selection task relative to age-matched normal volunteers, but relatively intact performance for the response selection and response execution tasks. In contrast, children with obsessive–compulsive disorder have slower response latencies on the response selection task relative to age-matched normal volunteers, but relatively intact performance for the stimulus selection and response execution tasks. In mean accuracy, children with Tourette's syndrome show deficits on the response execution task while children with ADHD

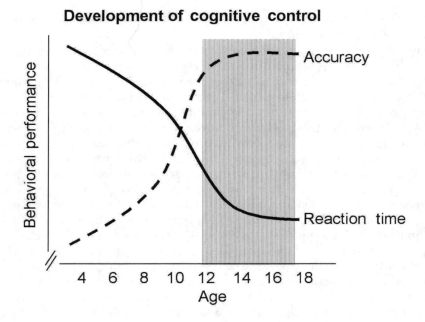

Figure 8.2.   Model of developmental change in cognitive control with age as a function of accuracy and reaction time.

show deficits on both the stimulus selection and response execution tasks. The pattern of performance for the children with ADHD fits with the distractibility and impulsivity observed in this disorder. These data suggest that the aspect of cognitive control affected across these disorders differs according the type of competing information and as such may map onto distinct frontostriatal and frontocerelbellar circuits implicated in representing these different types of information.

MRI-Based Anatomical Evidence

Our clinical behavioral findings fit with the existing literature implicating different parallel frontostriatal circuits supporting different behavioral domains with distinct clinical disorders (Alexander et al., 1991). Therefore, performance on our battery of cognitive tasks may map onto distinct prefrontal circuits. In an effort to examine this structure-function relation more directly, anatomical correlates of cognitive control as measured by our three cognitive tasks were correlated with MRI-based morphometry measures of structures central to the frontal circuits described. Based on a sample of 50 children with and without ADHD, task performance correlated only with MRI-based anatomical measures observed to be abnormal in ADHD (Castellanos et al., 1996). Specifically, size and asymmetry of the right prefrontal cortex, caudate nuclei, and globus pallidum correlated with task performance, but not other areas (e.g., putamen; Casey, Castellanos, et al., 1997). In this particular study,

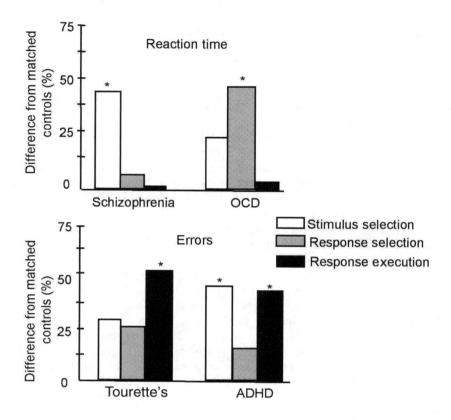

Figure 8.3. Percentage difference in mean reaction times and error rates for the stimulus selection, response selection, and response execution tasks for children with schizophrenia, obsessive–compulsive symptoms, Tourette's syndrome, and ADHD relative to matched controls. Asterisks indicate significant differences between patients and controls in the raw data. ADHD = attention-deficit/hyperactivity disorder; OCD = obsessive–compulsive disorder.

cerebellar volume was not examined. Tests for parallelism in slopes between children with and without ADHD on the structures that correlated with behavioral performance showed differences between the two groups. Specifically, they differed in slope for the stimulus selection and response execution tasks, but not the response selection task, consistent with our behavioral findings (refer back to Figure 8.2). The behavioral and anatomical measures typically correlated for the normal volunteers. In contrast, behavioral data from the children with ADHD typically did not correlate with anatomical measures. In part, these findings may be explained by the large variability so often observed in behavioral performance of children with ADHD in longer reaction times and poorer accuracy overall. Alternatively, abnormalities in the development of basal ganglia and prefrontal related circuitry as reported in the imaging literature (e.g., Castellanos et al., 1996) over this period of development may be a factor. The correlational data for the typical developing children indicate that our cognitive tasks are indirectly related to frontostriatal circuitry and support the hypothesis of the role of these brain regions in cognitive control.

Functional Magnetic Resonance Imaging Evidence

A more direct test of how these cognitive tasks map onto the described circuits is to collect behavior and imaging data simultaneously. We have recently completed functional MRI studies using versions of each of our three cognitive control tasks (Casey, Davidson, Hara, et al., 2004; Casey, Thomas, Davidson, et al., 2002; Casey, Thomas, Welsh, et al., 2000; Casey, Trainor, Orendi, et al., 1997). Our predictions were that activity within projection zones of each of the dorsolateral, ventrolateral, and limbic prefrontal circuits would uniquely correlate with performance during the stimulus selection, response selection and response execution tasks, respectively. Our findings are presented in color-plate 3. First, for the stimulus selection task where the participant has to override or suppress salient stimulus information, we have used two different tasks, the original paradigm (Casey, Vauss, & Swedo, 1994) and a modified version of a flanker task (Eriksen & Eriksen, 1974). Although brain activity was not isolated to the projection zones within the dorsolateral prefrontal circuit for these tasks, only activity in the projection areas for this circuit (i.e., dorsolateral prefrontal cortex and dorsal caudate nucleus) correlated with performance on this task across children (7 years or older) and adults as predicted (Casey, Thomas, Welsh, Badgaiyan, et al., 2000, see colorplate 3, panel A; Casey, Davidson, et al., 2004). For the response selection task, where participants had to override a well-learned behavioral set in favor of a new one, brain regions shown to correlate with accuracy on the task included the ventrolateral prefrontal cortex and ventral caudate nucleus (Casey et al., 2002). Again, our findings show specific task related change in the expected projection zones of the ventrolateral prefrontal circuit. Finally, during performance of the response execution task where the participant had to inhibit a compelling tendency to respond altogether (i.e., go–no-go) the pattern of activity in the orbitofrontal cortex and right anterior cingulate cortex, projection zones for the limbic circuit, correlated with behavioral performance while other activated regions did not (Casey, Trainor, Orendi, et al., 1997). These findings suggest that our battery of cognitive control tasks map rather nicely onto the prefrontal circuits.

Parametric Manipulations of Attentional Conflict. Another approach for testing whether a specific brain region is involved in a particular cognitive process besides performing simple correlations between brain activity in that region and behavioral performance on that specific task is to parametrically manipulate the degree to which this region is recruited. For example, in the case of memory, we could simply vary the items the participant has to hold in memory to test whether brain regions implicated in memory show an increase in activity as the memory load increases. A number of groups have done exactly that manipulation (see Braver et al., 1997; Thomas et al., 1999). Given that we are interested in the neurobiology of cognitive control in the context of maintaining representations against interference from competing sources, we have begun to develop paradigms that parametrically manipulate the salience of competing information in a similar manner.

In this context, we examined the influence of preceding context on attentional conflict using a flanker paradigm (Durston, Davidson, et al., 2003). Nine healthy right-handed adults participated in a rapid mixed trial event-related fMRI study, in which increasing numbers of either compatible or incompatible trials preceded an incompatible trial. In the flanker task, participants are presented with arrows that point to the left (<) or right (>) displayed in the center of a screen. Compatible and incompatible flankers are presented on either side of the target stimulus (e.g., < < < or > < >). Participants are instructed to press the left key if the center stimulus is pointing left (<) and the right key if the center stimulus is pointing right (>). In the flanker task, an incompatible trial is preceded by one, three, or five compatible flanker trials. These task parameter manipulations result in longer reaction times and lower accuracy for the participant as a function of increasing number of preceding targets or compatible trials (Casey, Forman, et al., 2001; Casey, Thomas, Welsh, Badgaiyan, et al., 2000; Durston, Davidson, et al., 2001; Gratton, Coles, & Donchin, 1992).

Behaviorally, mean reaction times for our participants for incompatible trials increased as a function of the number of preceding compatible trials (Durston, Davidson, et al., 2003). As predicted by our model of cognitive control, within the prefrontal cortex, only dorsolateral regions showed monotonic increases in activity with the parametric manipulation (see colorplate 4). This area showed an increase in activity for incompatible trials as the number of preceding *compatible* trials increased and a decrease in activity for incompatible trials as the number of preceding *incompatible* trials increased which paralleled the behavioral findings.

PARAMETRIC MANIPULATIONS OF RESPONSE CONFLICT. In a second study, we developed a parametric version of our response execution task (go–no-go paradigm; Durston, Thomas, Worden, et al., 2002; Durston, Thomas, Yang, et al., 2002). We used event-related fMRI to examine the effect of enhancing interference by increasing the number of go trials preceding a no-go trial (Casey et al., 2001; Durston, Thomas, Worden, et al., 2002). The current versions of our tasks allow for comparisons of no-go trials to one another that differ only in the preceding context (one, three, or five preceding targets). No-go trials were preceded by one, three, or five go trials and then compared to one another. Both children and adults showed an increase in errors with increasing number of go trials preceding a no-go trial.

Analysis of the fMRI data for correct trials showed that successful inhibition of a response to nontargets (no-go trials) was associated with increased ventral prefrontal activity for the adults, but the children who activated prefrontal and parietal regions more than adults showed no increase. Unlike adults, the circuitry appears to be maximally activated in children when suppressing a behavioral response regardless of the number of preceding responses. Similar to our previous study using a go–no-go task, ventral frontostriatal regions correlated with behavioral performance. These findings suggest that immature cognition is more susceptible to interference from competing sources and this is paralleled by maturational differences in underlying frontostriatal circuitry. We therefore show how the maturation of ventral frontostriatal circuitry underlies the development of this ability.

MANIPULATIONS IN TIMING OF RESPONSE CONFLICT. In an effort to clarify the importance of cognitive control in suppressing information and actions in the context of both temporal and stimulus conflict, we performed two subsequent experiments (Davidson et al., 2003, in press). In the first experiment (Davidson et al., in press), we modified the previously described go–no-go task such that either an unexpected stimulus occurred (no-go) or an expected stimulus failed to occur. The striatum was especially sensitive to this manipulation showing a slight increase with the presentation of an unexpected stimulus consistent with previous reports (Durston et al., 2002; Durston, Tottenham, et al., 2003) and a significant decrease in activity to the omission of an expected stimulus. Thus the content of conflicting information appears relevant for the striatal response. In a second study, we presented an expected or unexpected stimulus at an expected or unexpected time. For this manipulation we observed the strongest activity in the cerebellum to the presentation of an expected stimulus at an unexpected time, suggesting sensitivity of this region to the unpredictability of timing of events. These results suggest that the striatum and cerebellum may help engage control systems by detecting violations in the timing and occurrence of events (Davidson et al., 2003, in press).

Lesion Studies

How and when does disruption in the development of frontal circuitry predispose a child to cognitive control deficits? We have completed a number of behavioral and imaging studies examining one population that has a representative disruption in frontostriatal circuitry at the level of the basal ganglia, that of intraventricular hemorrhage (IVH). This population is a relatively large group of children born prematurely with histories of perinatal asphyxia. Perinatal asphyxia during premature births is commonly associated with a hemorrhage in the region of the basal ganglia. The vulnerability of the basal ganglia is because the most metabolically active brain regions are most vulnerable to hemorrhage (see Figure 8.4). In the preterm infant, this region is the germinal matrix, an area within the ventricular wall and adjacent brain regions such as the caudate nuclei (i.e., basal ganglia).

We have recently characterized a sample of 37 such children with structural and functional neuroimaging. Our prediction was if the prefrontal circuits are important in cognitive control then disruption in the circuitry should lead to cognitive control deficits and diagnoses of related developmental disorders (e.g., ADHD). Behavioral and imaging data were collected on seventeen of a cohort of 39 children between the ages of 6 and 9 years with histories of IVH of grade II or higher. We compared their performance to gender and age-matched controls. The patterns of errors made by the children with IVH were

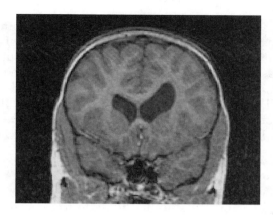

Figure 8.4. Representative MRI coronal slice from a 6-year-old child with a history of IVH of grade III. Note how the ventricles are distended at the expense of the caudate nucleus.

similar to those observed for our sample of children with ADHD and Tourette's syndrome. Specifically, the children with IVH performed worst on the response execution task (78% vs. 90% accuracy, $p < .015$).

It is not surprising that the children with IVH performed similarly to children with ADHD and tic disorders in their behavioral performance given the results of structured clinical interviews. According to structured interviews, 20% of the cohort had a psychiatric diagnosis of ADHD (four times that of the general population). These data are consistent with findings published by Whitaker and colleagues (1997) of children with neonatal insults. According to that study, 22% of children with neonatal insults had at least one psychiatric disorder, the most common being ADHD.

Our structural and functional imaging findings suggest both a reduction in volume and functional activity in the caudate in these children relative to typically developing children (Casey, Thomas, Welsh, et al., 1998). These children activated the anterior cingulate and inferior frontal cortex somewhat less than the normal volunteers, but differences between groups were only significant for the caudate nucleus.

The behavioral and neuroimaging data are consistent with the basal ganglia being involved in cognitive/impulse control. Children with IVH are at greater risk of developing disorders with known inhibitory deficits (e.g., ADHD) and our behavioral findings show that they are impaired on go–no-go task performance relative to healthy children. The imaging results showed little or no activity in the caudate nucleus in children with IVH of grade II or higher, while prefrontal activity was observed more reliably. In sum, disruption of basal ganglia thalamocortical circuits at the level of the basal ganglia appears sufficient to disrupt inhibitory control.

Overall, our behavioral, clinical, and neuroimaging data from our children with IVH are consistent with our hypothesis of disruption in cognitive control at the level of the basal ganglia. First, these children perform poorly on tasks that require them to suppress a compelling response (e.g., response execution tasks). Second, these children are at greater risk of developing disorders with known inhibitory deficits (e.g., ADHD and tic disorders). Third, MRI-based morphometry measures show decreased volume of the basal ganglia, specifically the caudate nucleus, in children with IVH compared to age-matched controls. Fourth, fMRI results showed little to no activity in the caudate nucleus in children with IVH of grade II or higher. In sum, disruption of the basal ganglia thalamocortical circuits at the level of the basal ganglia appears sufficient to disrupt inhibitory control.

Genetic Evidence

Optimal levels of dopamine are needed to perform cognitive tasks requiring the maintenance of internal representations against interference (i.e., cognitive control). Variation in genes known to contribute to the function of dopaminergic signaling may underlie individual variation in this ability. Accordingly, we have begun to examine the relation between variation in dopamine related genes and brain morphometry in populations with cognitive control deficits such as ADHD. This work is based on the assumption that neuroimaging measures may serve as a biological intermediate phenotype to investigate the effect of genes on human behavior, both in normal functioning and neuropsychiatric disorders. ADHD is a prime candidate for such an approach as this is a highly heritable disorder.

SIBLINGS DISCORDANT FOR ATTENTION-DEFICIT/HYPERACTIVITY DISORDER STUDY. Durston and colleagues (2004) examined the influence of increased genetic risk for ADHD on brain morphology in 30 male sibling pairs discordant for ADHD and 30 healthy matched comparison research participants, aged 7 to 19 years. They reported that intracranial volume was reduced in patients with ADHD, while their siblings displayed an intermediate volume between that of patients and controls. Reductions in right prefrontal gray matter were significant for both patients and their unaffected siblings. Only right cerebellar volume was significantly reduced in patients, but not in their unaffected siblings. The finding of reduced intracranial volume in the unaffected siblings of patients with ADHD may suggest an early genetic effect associated with the disorder. The volumetric reductions in cortical areas that have been frequently associated with ADHD are in part present in their unaffected siblings, suggesting that they may be related to genetic susceptibility for the disorder. In contrast, the cerebellum was not affected in the siblings, suggesting that the reduction in cerebellar volume found in patients may be because of processes associated with environmental factors or the disorder per se.

CANDIDATE GENES APPROACH. We examined the influence of candidate genes on gray matter volumes in frontostriatal and frontocerebellar circuitry in individuals with ADHD and their unaffected siblings at increased familial risk for the disorder. We focused on three candidate genes involved in dopamine function, implicated in childhood disorders that involve disruption in cognitive control and that are fairly common in their occurrence in the general population (Durston, Fossella, Casey, et al., 2004).

First, the dopamine D4 receptor gene, DRD4, located on chromosome 11p15 was selected because it has received the most attention in the literature because of its replicated association with ADHD (LaHoste et al., 1996; Smalley et al., 1998; Sunohara et al., 2000; Swanson et al., 1998, 2000). The most well-studied DRD4 polymorphism is a 48 base-pair variable nucleotide tandem repeat (VNTR) in exon III affecting the size of the 3rd intracellular loop of the receptor. This cytoplasmic loop is involved in G-protein coupling and mediation of post-synaptic dopaminergic signal transduction.

In addition to the DRD4, the dopamine transporter (DAT or SLC6A3) gene located on chromosome 5p15.3 was selected as a candidate gene. Methylphenidate, the primary stimulant used in pharmacological treatment of ADHD, blocks this transporter (Volkow et al., 1998) and ADHD patients have been shown to have higher levels of DAT expression in the striatum (Krause, Dresel, Krause, Kung, & Tatsch, 2000). The most well-studied polymorphism is a variable nucleotide tandem repeat (VNTR) in the 3' untranslated region of the DAT gene (Mitchell et al., 2000). As this VNTR is not in the coding region of the DAT gene, it does not affect the protein sequence of the dopamine transporter, but it may affect the translational efficiency and thus the amount of protein expressed (Vandenbergh et al., 2000). Research participants homozygous for the 10-repeat allele show significantly lower dopamine transporter binding than carriers of the 9-repeat allele (Heinz et al., 2000; Jacobson et al., 2000). In a recent meta-analysis a highly significant association between the DAT gene and ADHD was found (Cook, 2000). Methylphenidate, the primary stimulant used in pharmacological treatment of ADHD, blocks this transporter (Volkow et al., 1998) and ADHD patients have been shown to have higher levels of DAT expression in the striatum (Krause et al., 2000).

The third candidate gene we selected was the catechol-O-methyltransferase (COMT) gene located on chromosome 22q11 that catalyzes the transfer of a methyl group from S-adenosylmethionine to catecholamines, including the neurotransmitters dopamine, adrenaline, and noradrenaline. This O-methylation leads to the degradation and clearance of these catecholamines. The most widely used polymorphism in COMT was identified by Lachman and colleagues (1996) who found a G-to-A change at codons 108 and 158 of the COMT gene, resulting in a valine-to-methionine substitution that accounts for a three- to four-fold difference in COMT activity in red blood cells and liver. Recently, Weinberger and colleagues (Egan et al., 2001) found that the COMT genotype was related to performance on the Wisconsin Card Sorting Test and explained 4% of variance ($p = 0.001$) in frequency of perseverative errors. In addition, those with the Met108 alleles showed less prefrontal activity, as measured by fMRI, when performing normally on a working memory task. Interestingly, the Val108 allele was shown to be preferentially transmitted to ADHD probands and was associated with impulsive false alarm errors on a continuous performance task (Eisenberg et al., 1999). Research participants were genotyped for the three candidate genes COMT, DAT, and DRD4. The most widely examined functional polymorphism involves a Valine-to-Methionine substitution, which results in three to fourfold differences in COMT enzyme activity. The Val-allele has been shown to be preferentially transmitted to ADHD probands (Eisenberg et al., 1999). The COMT enzyme is involved in inactivating mono-amines, including dopamine.

We hypothesized that genotype would be associated with reductions in volume in those regions where the genes are preferentially expressed (striatum for the DAT, and prefrontal gray matter for the DRD4 and COMT) and not in others (cerebellum). If reductions in volume are related to increased genetic risk for ADHD, we expect differences in volume related to genotype for both the research participants with ADHD and their unaffected siblings, but not for control participants. However, if reductions in volume are directly related to the pathophysiology of ADHD, individuals with the disorder are expected to display reductions in volume irrespective of their genotype, whereas individuals at increased genetic risk will either not display reductions in volume, or display reductions in volume as a function of their genotype.

Volumetric cerebral measures, derived from whole brain magnetic resonance imaging scans, were compared between groups. Thirty male sibling pairs discordant for ADHD aged 7 to 19 years, and 30 healthy comparison participants matched for age, gender, IQ, socioeconomic status, and hand preference. Volumetric measurements of prefrontal gray matter, caudate nucleus, and cerebellum were performed by a blind rater.

The results suggest no significant effect of COMT genotype on brain morphometry and no significant effect of these genes on cerebellar volume. However, a nice dissociation was shown between DRD4 and DAT in relation to prefrontal and caudate volume measures. For the siblings with ADHD, homozygotes for the common allele of the DAT had smaller caudate volumes than the siblings with a variant allele ($p < 0.05$). For the unaffected siblings, homozygotes for the common allele of the DRD4 had smaller prefrontal gray matter volumes than the siblings with a variant allele ($p < 0.05$). We show an effect of genotype on regional gray matter volume in ADHD that differentiates between individuals with the disorder and those at increased familial risk. These findings demonstrate the utility of combining genotyping with structural neuroimaging and the role of allelic variants on frontostriatal circuitry underlying cognitive control.

In this study we show a reduction in caudate volume as a function of DAT genotype in individuals with ADHD, but not in their unaffected siblings or controls. On average, participants homozygous for the 10-repeat allele have smaller caudate nucleus volumes (see Figure 8.5). The more common 10-repeat allele has been associated with reduced dopamine transport activity (Heinz et al., 2000; Jacobson et al., 2000), suggesting that smaller caudate volumes may be related to reduced local dopaminergic neurotransmission in these individuals. As this effect is not significantly present for either the unaffected siblings or controls, it may reflect an interaction between genes, where the cumulative effect of risk genes allows for a greater impact of DAT genotype on caudate volume.

In contrast, the effect of DRD4 genotype on prefrontal gray matter volume was only present in unaffected siblings. This finding appears to be directly related to the pathophysiology of ADHD, as siblings with ADHD display a

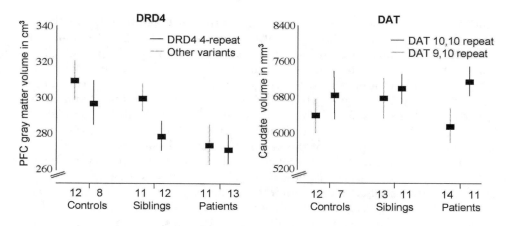

Figure 8.5. Prefrontal gray and caudate volume for individuals with DRD4 4-repeat or variant and DAT1 10-repeat or variant. DAT = dopamine transporter; DRD4 = dopamine D4 receptor gene; PFC = prefrontal cortex.

reduction in prefrontal gray matter volume, irrespective of DRD4 genotype (see Durston, Fossella, Casey, et al., 2004; and Figure 8.2). However, as there is an effect of DRD4 genotype on prefrontal gray matter volume for the unaffected siblings, this suggests that this gene does contribute to the prefrontal finding. Again, as this reduction is present for all participants with ADHD, irrespective of DRD4 genotype, it may be associated with the accumulation of risk genes in addition to environmental factors.

The functional implication of reductions in gray matter volume such as are reported here remains unclear. However, there have been reports of correlations between size of brain structures and functional markers, such as performance on neuropsychological tasks. For instance, Casey and colleagues demonstrated that correlations between measures of cognitive control, such as performance on response inhibition tasks and prefrontal cortex and basal ganglia volumes were not present or reversed in children with ADHD (Casey, Castellanos, et al., 1997). Our report of differential reductions in volume between participants with ADHD and their unaffected siblings who are at increased genetic risk for ADHD may be associated with similar differences in cognitive control between groups. This point will need to be elucidated in future studies, incorporating carefully designed neuropsychological batteries with structural and functional MRI scans for large numbers of participants.

Conclusion

This chapter presents a model of cognitive control whereby the basal ganglia and cerebellum are involved in suppression of actions while the frontal cortex is involved in representing and maintaining relevant information over time and against interference. Developmentally, we propose that the ability to support information against competing sources increases with age thereby facilitating cognitive control and is the result of development within basal ganglia and cerebellar thalamocortical loops. Relevant projections from the prefrontal cortex to the basal ganglia and cerebellum are enhanced while irrelevant projections are eliminated and these connections are reinforced with dopamine related activity. This organization continues throughout childhood and adolescence as evidenced by the prolonged development of prefrontal regions in synapse elimination and myelination, maturation of the dopamine system, and the prolonged development of the cerebellum beyond puberty.

In sum, basal ganglia and cerebellar thalamocortical circuits underlie cognitive control and that cognitive deficits observed across a range of developmental disorders reflect a disruption in the development of these circuits. Five lines of converging evidence for this view were presented including data from clinical, MRI-based morphometry, functional MRI, lesion, and genetic studies. First, we reported that children with developmental disorders involving the prefrontal cortex, basal ganglia, and cerebellum perform poorly on tasks requiring suppression of attention toward a salient stimulus or competing response choice. Furthermore, a dissociation in the pattern of performance on these tasks for each of four disorders was observed implying the involvement of different basal ganglia thalamocortical circuits for each disorder. Second, MRI-based morphometry measures of the frontal cortex and basal ganglia correlated with performance on cognitive tasks indirectly supporting our structure-function hypotheses. Third, a more direct line of evidence for the involvement of the prefrontal cortex in cognitive control was presented based on a functional MRI study. Fourth, behavioral and imaging results from our children with neonatal basal ganglia insults showed deficits in cognitive control and a four-to five-fold increase in developmental disorders with cognitive control problems (ADHD and tic disorders). Fifth, variants in dopamine related genes were shown to be related to individual variation in brain regions implicated in disorders with cognitive control deficits such as ADHD. Evidence provided for the role of the cerebellum in cognitive control is less compelling at this time but provocative. Future studies will no doubt help constrain the role of this structure in cognitive control.

References

Alexander, G. E., Crutcher, M. D., & DeLong, M. R. (1991). Basal ganglia thalamocortical circuits: Parallel substrates for motor, oculomotor, prefrontal and limbic functions. *Progress in Brain Research, 85,* 119–145.

Alexander, G. E., DeLong, M. R., & Strick, P. L. (1986). Parallel organization of functionally segregated circuits linking basal ganglia and cortex. *Annual Review of Neuroscience, 9,* 357–381.

Allen, G., & Courchesne, E. (2003). Differential effects of developmental cerebellar abnormality on cognitive and motor functions in the cerebellum: An fMRI study of autism. *American Journal of Psychiatry, 160,* 262–273.

Allport, A. (1987). Selection for action: Some behavioral and neurophysiological considerations of attention and action. In H. Heuer & A. F. Sanders (Eds.), *Perspectives on perception and action* (pp. 395–419). Hillsdale, NJ: Erlbaum.

Asarnow, R. F., Brown, W., & Strandburg, R. (1995). Children with a schizophrenic disorder: Neurobehavioral studies. *European Archives of Psychiatry and Clinical Neuroscience, 245,* 70–79.

Awh, E., Smith, E., & Jonides, J. (1996). Human rehearsal processes and the frontal lobes: PET evidence. *Annals of the New York Academy of Sciences, 769,* 97–117.

Baddeley, A. D. (1986). *Working memory.* New York: Oxford University Press.

Barkley, R. A. (1997). Behavioral inhibition, sustained attention, and executive functions: Constructing a unifying theory of ADHD. *Psychological Bulletin, 121,* 65–94.

Baxter, L. R., Jr., Schwartz, J. M., Mazziotta, J. C., Phelps, M. E., Pahl, J. J., Guze, B. H., et al. (1988). Cerebral glucosemetabolicrates in nondepressed patients with OCD. *American Journal of Psychiatry, 145,* 1560–1563.

Berman, K. F., Illowsky, B. P., & Weinberger, D. R. (1988). Physiological dysfunction of dorsolateral prefrontal cortex in schizophrenia: IV. Further evidence for regional and behavioral specificity. *Archives of General Psychiatry, 45,* 616–622.

Berquin, P. C., Giedd, J. N., Jacobsen, L. K., Hamburger, S. D., Krain, A. L., Rapoport, J. L., et al. (1998). Cerebellum in attention-deficit hyperactivity disorder: A morphometric MRI study. *Neurology, 50,* 1087–1093.

Brainerd, C. J., & Reyna, V. F. (1993). Domains of fuzzy trace theory. In M. L. Howe & R. Pasnak (Eds.), *Emerging themes in cognitive development: Volume 1. Foundations* (pp. 50–93). New York: Springer-Verlag.

Braver, T. S., & Cohen, J. D. (2000). On the control of control: The role of dopamine regulating prefrontal function and working memory. In S. Monsell & J. Driver (Eds.), *Attention and performance XVIII: Control of cognitive processes* (pp. 713–737). Cambridge, MA: MIT Press.

Braver, T. S., Cohen, J. D., Nystrom, L. E., Jonides, J., Smith, E. E., & Noll, D. C. (1997). A parametric study of prefrontal cortex involvement in human working memory. *Neuro-Image, 5,* 49–62.

Bush, G., Frazier, J. A., Rauch, S. L., Seidman, L. I., Whalen, P. J., Jenike, M. A., et al. (1999). Anterior cingulate cortex dysfunction in ADHD revealed by fMRI and the counting Stroop. *Biological Psychiatry, 45,* 1542–1552.

Carper, R. A., Moses, P., Tigue, Z. D., & Courchesne, E. (2003). Related articles, links cerebral lobes in autism: Early hyperplasia and abnormal age effects. *NeuroImage, 16,* 1038–1051.

Casey, B. J. (2000). Disruption of inhibitory control in developmental disorders: A mechanistic model of implicated frontostriatal circuitry. In R. S. Siegler & J. L. McClelland (Eds.), *Mechanisms of cognitive development: The Carnegie Symposium on Cognition, Vol. 28* (pp. 155–168). Hillsdale, NJ: Erlbaum.

Casey, B. J., Castellanos, F. X., Giedd, J. N., Marsh, W. L., Hamburger, S. D., Schubert, A. B., et al. (1997). Implication of right frontostriatal circuitry in response inhibition and attention-deficit/hyperactivity disorder. *Journal of the American Academy of Child and Adolescent Psychiatry, 36,* 374–383.

Casey, B. J., Davidson, M. C., Hara, Y., Thomas, K. M., Martinez, A., Halperin, J. M., et al. (2004). Role of caudate nucleus in attention switching. *Developmental Science, 7,* 534–542.

Casey, B. J., Durston, S., & Fossella, J. A. (2001). Evidence for a mechanistic model of cognitive control. *Clinical Neuroscience Research, 1,* 267–282.

Casey, B. J., Forman, S. D., Franzen, P., Berkowitz, A., Braver, T. S., Nystrom, L. E., et al. (2001). Sensitivity of prefrontal cortex to changes in target probability: A functional MRI study. *Human Brain Mapping, 13,* 26–33.

Casey, B. J., Thomas, K. M., Davidson, M. C., Kunz, K., & Franzen, P. L. (2002). Dissociating striatal and hippocampal function developmentally with a stimulus–response compatibility task. *Journal of Neuroscience, 22,* 8647–8652.

Casey, B. J., Thomas, K. M., Welsh, T. F., Badgaiyan, R., Eccard, C. H., Jennings, J. R., et al. (2000). Dissociation of response conflict, attentional control, and expectancy with functional magnetic resonance imaging (fMRI). *Proceedings of the National Academy of Sciences of the United States of America, 97,* 8728–8733.

Casey, B. J., Thomas, K. M., Welsh, T. F., Eccard, C. H., Livnat, R., Gagajewski, A., et al. (1998). An fMRI study of response inhibition in children with striatal lesions. *NeuroImage, 7,* S515.

Casey, B. J., Thomas, K. M., Welsh, T. F., Livnat, R., & Eccard, C. H. (2000). Cognitive and behavioral probes of developmental landmarks for use in functional neuroimaging. In J. M.

Rumsey & M. Ernst (Eds.), *The foundation and future of functional neuroimaging in child psychiatry* (pp. 155–168). New York: Cambridge University Press.

Casey, B. J., Trainor, R. J., Giedd, J., Vauss, Y., Vaituzis, C. K., Hamburger, S., et al. (1997). The role of the anterior cingulate in automatic and controlled processes: A developmental neuroanatomical study. *Developmental Psychobiology, 30,* 61–69.

Casey, B. J., Trainor, R. J., Orendi, J. L., Schubert, A. B., Nystrom, L. E., Giedd, J. N., et al. (1997). A developmental functional MRI study of prefrontal activation during performance of a go–no-go task. *Journal of Cognitive Neuroscience, 9,* 835–847.

Casey, B. J., Vauss, Y. C., Chused, A., & Swedo, S. E. (1994). Cognitive functioning in Sydenham's chorea: Part 2. Executive functioning. *Developmental Neuropsychology, 10,* 89–96.

Casey, B. J., Vauss, Y. C., & Swedo, S. E. (1994). Cognitive functioning in Sydenham's chorea: Part 1. Attentional functioning. *Developmental Neuropsychology, 10,* 75–88.

Castellanos, F. X., Giedd, J. N., Eckburg, P., Marsh, W. L., King, A. C., Hamburger, S. D., et al. (1994). Quantitative morphology of the caudate nucleus in attention-deficit hyperactivity disorder. *American Journal of Psychiatry, 151,* 1791–1796.

Castellanos, F. X., Geidd, J. N., Marsh, W. L., Hamburger, S. D., Vaituzis, A. C., Dickstein, D. P., et al. (1996). Quantitative brain magnetic resonance imaging in attention-deficit hyperactivity disorder. *Archives of General Psychiatry, 53,* 607–616.

Castellanos, F. X., Lee, P. P., Sharp, W., Jeffries, N. O., Greenstein D. K., Clasen, L. S., et al. (2002). Developmental trajectories of brain volume abnormalities in children and adolescents with attention-deficit/hyperactivity disorder. *Journal of the American Medical Association, 288,* 1740–1748.

Cohen, J. D., Forman, S. D., Braver, T. S., Casey, B. J., Servan-Schreiber, D., & Noll, D. C. (1994). Activation of prefrontal cortex in a nonspatial working memory task with functional MRI. *Human Brain Mapping, 1,* 293–304.

Cohen, J. D., & Servan-Schreiber, D. (1992). Context, cortex and dopamine: A connectionist approach to behavior and biology in schizophrenia. *Psychological Review, 99,* 45–47.

Cook, E. (2000). *Molecular genetic studies of attention deficit hyperactivity disorder.* Paper presented at Wenner-Gren Foundations International Symposium: Neurobiology of ADHD, Stockholm.

Davidson, M. C., Horvitz, J. C., Tottenham, N., Durston, S. N., Fossella, J. A., & Casey, B. J. (2003). FMRI investigation of circuitry modulated by violations in stimuli and temporal expectations [Abstract]. *Proceedings of the Society for Neuroscience.*

Davidson, M. C., Horvitz, J. C., Tottenham, N., Fossella, J. A., Watts, R., Ulug, A. M., et al. (in press). Dissociation of cingulate and caudate response to unexpected non-rewarding stimuli. *NeuroImage.*

D'Esposito, M., Detre, J. A., Alsop, D. C., Shin, R. K., Atlas, S., & Grossman, M. (1995). The neural basis of the central executive system of working memory. *Nature, 378,* 279–281.

D'Esposito, M., Postle, B. R., Jonides, J., & Smith, E. E. (1999). The neural substrate and temporal dynamics of interference effects in working memory as revealed by event-related functional MRI. *Proceedings of the National Academy of Sciences of the United States of America, 96,* 7514–7519.

Dempster, F. N. (1993). Resistance to interference: Developmental changes in a basic processing mechanism. In M. L. Howe & R. Pasnak (Eds.), *Emerging themes in cognitive development: Vol. 1: Foundations.* New York: Springer-Verlag.

Desimone, R., & Duncan, J. (1995). Neural mechanisms of selective visual attention. *Annual Reviews in Neuroscience, 18,* 193–222.

Diamond, A. (1985). Development of the ability to use recall to guide action, as indicated by infants' performance on AB. *Child Development, 56,* 868–883.

Diamond, A. (1990). Rate of maturation of the hippocampus and the developmental progression of children's performance on the delayed non-matching to sample and visual paired comparison tasks. *Annals of the New York Academy of Sciences, 608,* 394–426.

Dum, R. P., & Strick, P. L. (2003). An unfolded map of the cerebellar dentate nucleus and its projections to the cerebral cortex. *Journal of Neurophysiology, 89,* 634–639.

Duncan, J., & Owen, A. M. (2000). Common regions of the human frontal lobe recruited by diverse cognitive demands. *Trends in Neuroscience, 23,* 475–483.

Durston, S., Davidson, M. C., Thomas, K. M., Worden, M. S., Tottenham, N., Martinez, A., et al. (2003). Parametric manipulation of conflict and response competition using rapid mixed-trial event-related fMRI. *NeuroImage, 20,* 2135–2141.

Durston, S., Fossella, J. A., Casey, B. J., Hulshoff Pol, H. E., Galvan, A., Schnack, H. G., et al. (2004). Differential effects of DRD4 and DAT genotype on fronto-striatal gray matter volumes in boys with ADHD, their unaffected siblings and controls. Manuscript submitted for publication.

Durston, S., Hulshoff Pol, H. E., Schnack, H. G., Buitelaar, J. K., Steenhuis, M. P., Minderaa, R. B., et al. (2004). Magnetic resonance imaging of boys with attention deficit hyperactivity disorder and their unaffected siblings. *American Academy of Child and Adolescent Psychiatry, 43,* 332–340.

Durston, S., Thomas, K. M., Worden, M. S., Yang, Y., & Casey, B. J. (2002). An fMRI study of the effect of preceding context on inhibition. *NeuroImage, 16,* 449–453.

Durston, S., Thomas, K. M., Yang, Y., Ulug, A. M., Zimmerman, R., & Casey, B. J. (2002). A neural basis for development of inhibitory control. *Developmental Science, 5,* 9–16.

Durston, S., Tottenham, N., Thomas, K. M., Davidson, M. C., Eigsti, I.-M., Yang, Y., et al. (2003). Differential patterns of striatal activation in young children with and without ADHD. *Biological Psychiatry, 53,* 871–878.

Egan, M. F., Goldberg, T. E., Kolachana, B. S., Callicott, J. H., Mazzanti, C. M., Struab, R., et al. (2001). Effect of COMT Val 108/158 Met genotype on frontal lobe function and risk for schizophrenia. *Proceedings of the National Academy of Sciences of the United States of America, 98,* 6917–6922.

Eisenberg, J., Mei-Tal, G., Steinberg, A., Tartakovsky, E., Zohar, A., Gritsenko, I., et al. (1999). Haplotype relative risk study of catechol-O-methy-transferase (COMT) and attention deficit hyperactivity disorder (ADHD): Association of the high-enzyme activity Val allele with ADHD impulsive-hyperactive phenotype. *American Journal of American Genetics, 88,* 497–502.

Enns, J. T., & Akhtar, N. (1989). A developmental study of filtering in visual attention. *Child Development, 60,* 1188–1199.

Enns, J. T., Brodeur, P. A., & Trick, L. M. (1998). Selective attention over the life span: Behavioral measures. In J. E. Richards (Ed.), *Cognitive neuroscience of attention: A developmental perspective* (pp. 393–418). Mahway, NJ: Erlbaum.

Enns, J. T., & Cameron, S. (1987). Selective attention in young children: The relations between visual search, filtering and priming. *Journal of Experimental Psychology, 44,* 38–63.

Eriksen, B. A., & Eriksen, C. W. (1974). Effects of noise letters upon the identification of a target letter in a nonsearch task. *Perception and Psychophysics, 16,* 143–149.

Frank, M. J., Loughry, B., & O'Reilly, R. C. (2001). Interactions between frontal cortex and basal ganglia in working memory: A computational model. *Cognitive, Affective, and Behavioral Neuroscience, 1,* 137–160.

Frazier, J. A., Geidd, J. N., Hamburger, S. D., Albus, K. E., Kaysen, D., Vaituzis, A. C., et al. (1996). Brain magnetic resonance imaging in childhood-onset schizophrenia. *Archives of General Psychiatry, 53,* 617–624.

Fuster, J. M. (1985). The prefrontal cortex, mediator of cross-temporal contingencies. *Human Neurobiology, 4,* 169–179.

Giedd, J. N., Jeffries, N. O., Blumenthal, J., Castellanos, F. X., Vaituzis, A. C., Fernandez, T., et al. (1999). Childhood-onset schizophrenia: Progressive brain changes during adolescence. *Biological Psychiatry, 46,* 892–898.

Gratton, G., Coles, M. G. H., & Donchin, E. (1992). Optimizing the use of information: Strategic control of activation and responses. *Journal of Experimental Psychology: General, 4,* 480–506.

Harnishfeger, K. K. (1995). The development of cognitive inhibition: Theories, definitions, and research evidence. In F. N. Dempster & C. J. Brainerd (Eds.), *Interference and inhibition in cognition* (pp. 175–204). New York: Academic Press.

Harnishfeger, K. K., & Bjorkland, F. (1993). The ontogeny of inhibition mechanisms: A renewed approach to cognitive development. In M. L. Howe & R. Pasnek (Eds.), *Emerging themes in cognitive development: Vol. 1. Foundations* (pp. 28–49). New York: Springer-Verlag.

Hayes, A. E., Davidson, M. C., Keele, S. W., & Rafal, R. D. (1998). Toward a functional analysis of the basal ganglia. *Journal of Cognitive Neuroscience, 10,* 178–198.

Heinz, A., Jones, D. W., Raedler, T., Coppola, R., Knable, M. B., & Weinberger, D. R. (2000). Neuropharmacological studies with SPECT in neuropsychiatric disorders. *Nuclear Medicine and Biology, 27,* 677–682.

Insel, T. R. (1988). Obsessive–compulsive disorder: A neuroethological perspective. *Psychopharmacology Bulletin, 24,* 365–369.

Iversen, S. D., & Mishkin, M. (1970). Perseverative interference in monkeys following selective lesions of the inferior prefrontal convexity. *Experimental Brain Resonance, 11,* 376–386.

Jacobsen, L. K., Staley, J. K., Zoghbi, S. S., Seibyl, J. P., Kosten, T. R., Innis, R. B., et al. (2000). Prediction of dopamine transporter binding availability by genotype: A preliminary report. *American Journal of Psychiatry, 157,* 1700–1703.

Jonides, J., Schumacher, E. H., Smith, E. E., Lauber, E. J., Awh, E., Minishima, S., et al. (1997). Verbal working memory load affects regional brain activation as measured by PET. *Journal of Cognitive Neuroscience, 9,* 462–475.

Kahneman, D. (1973). *Attention and effort.* Englewood Cliffs, NJ: Prentice Hall.

Krause, K. H., Dresel, S. H., Krause, J., Kung, H. F., & Tatsch, K. (2000). Increased striatal dopamine transporter in adult patients with attention deficit hyperactivity disorder: Effects of methylphenidate as measured by single photon emission computed tomography. *Neuroscience Letters, 285,* 107–110.

Lachman, H. M., Morrow, B., Shprintzen, R., Veit, S., Parsia, S. S., Faedda, G., et al. (1996). Association of codon 108/1158 catechol-O-methyltransferase gene polymorphism with the psychiatric manifestations of velo-cardio-facial syndrome. *American Journal of Medical Genetics, 67,* 468–472.

LaHoste, G. J., Swanson, J. M., Wigal, S. B., Glave, C., Wigal, T., King, N., et al. (1996). Dopamine D4 receptor gene polymorphism is associated with attention deficit hyperactivity disorder. *Molecular Psychiatry, 1,* 121–124.

Leckman, J. F., Price, R. A., Walkup, J. T., Ort, S., Pauls, D. L., & Cohen, D. J. (1987). Nongenetic factors in Gilles de la Tourette's syndrome. *Archives of General Psychiatry, 44,* 100.

Leimkuhler, M. E., & Mesulam, M. M. (1985). Reversible go-no go deficits in a case of frontal lobe tumor. *Annals of Neurology, 18,* 617–619.

Lou, H. C., Henriksen, L., Bruhn, P., Borner, H., & Nielsen, J. B. (1989). Striatal dysfunction in attention deficit and hyperkinetic disorder. *Archives of Neurology, 46,* 48–52.

Luria, D. M. (1961). *The role of speech in the regulation of normal and abnormal behavior.* New York: Liveright.

McClure, S. M., Berns, G. S., & Montague, P. R. (2003). Temporal prediction errors in a passive learning task activate human striatum. *Neuron, 38,* 1–20.

Mentzle, H. J., Gaser, C., Bolz, H. P., Rzanny, R., Hager, F., Sauer, H., et al. (1998). Cognitive stimulation with the Wisconsin Card Sorting Test: Functional MR imaging at 1.5T. *Radiology, 207,* 399–404.

Metzler, C., & Parkin, A. J. (2000). Reversed negative priming following frontal lobe lesions. *Neuropsychologia, 38,* 363–379.

Middleton, F. A., & Strick, P. L. (2002). Basal-ganglia "projections" to the prefrontal cortex of the primate. *Cerebral Cortex, 12,* 926–935.

Miller, E. K., & Cohen, J. D. (2001), An integrative theory of prefrontal cortex function. *Annual Review of Neuroscience, 24,* 167–202.

Milner, B., Petrides, M., & Smith, M. L. (1985). Frontal lobes and the temporal organization of memory. *Human Neurobiology, 4,* 137–142.

Mink, J. W. (1996). The basal ganglia: Focused selection and inhibition of competing motor programs. *Progress in Neurobiology, 50,* 381–425.

Mitchell, I., Papihs, S. S., Osipova, L., Livshits, G., Leonard, W. R., & Crawford, M. H. (2000). Distribution of the 3' VNTR polymorphismin the human dopamine transporter gene in world populations. *Human Biology, 72,* 295–304.

Montague, P. R., Dayan, P., & Sejnowski, T. J. (1996). A framework for mesencephalic dopamine systems based on predictive Hebbian learning. *Journal of Neuroscience, 16,* 1936–1947.

Mostofsky, S. H., Reiss, A. L., Lockhart, P., & Denckla, M. B. (1998). Evaluation of cerebellar size in attention-deficit hyperactivity disorder. *Journal of Child Neurology, 13,* 434–439.

Munakata, Y., & Yerys, B. E. (2001). All together now when dissociations between knowledge and action disappear. *Psychological Science, 12,* 335–337.

Owen, A. M. (1997). The functional organization of working memory processes within human lateral frontal cortex: The contribution of functional neuroimaging. *European Journal Neuroscience, 9,* 1329–1339.

Passler, M. A., Isaac, W., & Hynd, G. W. (1985). Impulsivity: A multidimensional concept with developmental aspects. *Journal of Abnormal Child Psychology, 8,* 269–277.

Petersen, S. B., Skudlarski, P., Anderson, A. W., Zhang, H., Gatenby, J. C., Lacadie, C., et al. (1998). A functional magnetic resonance imaging study of tic suppression in Tourette's syndrome. *Archives of General Psychiatry, 55,* 326–333.

Piaget, J. (1954). *The construction of reality in the child* (M. Cook, Trans.). New York: Basic Books.

Posner, M. I., & Boies, S. J. (1972). Components of attention. *Psychological Review, 78,* 391–408.

Posner, M. I., & Petersen, S. E. (1990). The attention system of the human brain. *Annual Review of Neuroscience, 13,* 25–42.

Posner, M. I., & Snyder, C. R. R. (1975). Attention and cognitive control. In R. L. Solso (Ed.), *Information processing and cognition: The Loyola Symposium* (pp. 55–82). Hillsdale, NJ: Erlbaum.

Redgrave, P., Prescott, T. J., & Gurney, K. (1999). Is the short-latency dopamine response too short to signal reward error? *Trends in Neuroscience, 22,* 146–151.

Ridderinkhof, K. R., van der Molen, M. W., & Band, G. P. H. (1997). Sources of interference from irrelevant information: A developmental study. *Journal of Experimental Child Psychology, 65,* 315–341.

Rogers, R. D., Andrews, T. C., Grasby, P. M., Brooks, D. J., & Robbins, T. W. (2000). Contrasting cortical and subcortical activations produced by attentional-set shifting and reversal learning in humans. *Journal of Cognitive Neuroscience, 12,* 142–162.

Rosenberg, D. R., Keshevan, M. S., O'Hearn, K. M., Dick, E. L., Bagwell, W. W., Seymour, A. B., et al. (1997). Frontostriatal measurement in treatment-naive children with obsessive–compulsive disorder. *Archives of General Psychiatry, 54,* 824–830.

Schiff, A. R., & Knopf, I. J. (1985). The effect of task demands on attention allocation in children of different ages. *Child Development, 56,* 621–630.

Schultz, W. (1997). Dopamine neurons and their role in reward mechanisms. *Current Opinion in Neurobiology, 7,* 191–197.

Shallice, T. (1988). *From neuropsychology to mental structure.* New York: Cambridge University Press.

Shiffrin, R. M., & Schneider, W. (1977). Controlled and automatic human information processing: II. Perceptual learning, automatic attending and a general theory. *Psychological Review, 84,* 127–190.

Singer, H. S., Reiss, A. L., Brown, J. E., Aylward, E. H., Shih, B., Chee, E., et al. (1993). Volumetric MRI changes in basal ganglia of children with Tourette's syndrome. *Neurology, 43,* 950–956.

Smalley, S. L., Bailey, J. N., Palmer, C. G., Cantwell, D. P., McGough, J. J., Del'Hommme, M. A., et al. (1998). Evidence that the dopamine D4 receptor is a susceptibility gene in attention deficit hyperactivity disorder. *Molecular Psychiatry, 3,* 427–430.

Smith, E. E., & Jonides, J. (1999). Storage and executive processes in the frontal lobes. *Science, 283,* 1657–1661.

Spencer, R. M., Zelaznik, H. N., Diedrichsen, J., & Ivry, R. B. (2003). Disrupted timing of discontinuous but not continuous movements by cerebellar lesions. *Science, 300,* 1437–1439.

Stuss, D. T., Kaplan, E. F., Benson, D. F., Weir, W. S., Chiulli, S., & Sarazin, F. F. (1982). Evidence for the involvement of orbitofrontal cortex in memory functions: An interference effect. *Journal of Comparative Physiology and Psychology, 96,* 913–925.

Sunohara, G. A. K., Roberts, W., Malone, M., Schaxhar, R. J., Tannock, R., Basile, V. S., et al. (2000). Linkage of the dopamine D4 receptor gene. *Journal of the American Academy of Child and Adolescent Psychiatry, 39,* 1537–1542.

Swanson, J., Oosterlaan, J., Murias, M., Schuck, S., Flodman, P., Spence, M. A., et al. (2000). Attention deficit/hyperactivity disorder children with a 7-repeat allele of the dopamine receptor D4 gene have extreme behavior but normal performance on critical neuropsychological tests of attention. *Proceedings of the National Academy of Sciences of the United States of America, 97,* 4754–4759.

Swanson, J. M., Sunohara, G. A., Kennedy, J. L., Regino, R., Fineberg, E., Wigal, T., et al. (1998). Association of the dopamine receptor D4 (DRD4) gene with a refined phenotype of attention deficit hyperactivity disorder (ADHD): A family-based approach. *Molecular Psychiatry, 3,* 38–41.

Swedo, S. E., Leonard, H. L., Schapiro, M. B., Casey, B. J., Mannheim, M. D., & Lenane, M. C., et al. (1993). The psychological sequelae of Sydenham's chorea. *Pediatrics, 91,* 706–713.

Swedo, S. E., Pietrini, P., Leonard, H. L., Schapiro, M. B., Rettew, D. C., Goldberger, E. L., et al. (1989). Cerebral glucose metabolism in childhood-onset obsessive–compulsive disorder. *Archives of General Psychiatry, 49,* 690–694.

Thomas, K. M., King, S. W., Franzen, P. L., Welsh, T. F., Berkowitz, A. L., Noll, D. C., et al. (1999). A developmental functional MRI study of spatial working memory. *NeuroImage, 10,* 327–338.

Tipper, S. P., Bourque, T. A., Anderson, S. H., & Brehaut, J. C. (1989). Mechanisms of attention: A developmental study. *Journal of Experimental Child Psychology, 48,* 353–378.

Vaidya, C. J., Austin, G., Kirkorian, G., Ridlehuber, H. W. Q., Desmond, J. E., Glover, G. H., et al. (1998). Selective effects of methylphenidate in attention deficit hyperactivity disorder: A functional magnetic resonance study. *Proceedings of the National Academy of Sciences of the United States of America, 95,* 14494–14499.

Vandenbergh, D. J., Thompson, M. D., Cook, E. H., Bendahhou, E., Nguyen, T., & Krasowski, M. D., et al. (2000). Human dopamine transporter gene: Coding region conservation among normal, Tourette's disorder, alcohol dependence and attention-deficit hyperactivity disorder populations. *Molecular Psychiatry, 5,* 283–292.

Van Mier, H. I., & Petersen, S. E. (2002). Role of the cerebellum in motor cognition. *Annals of the New York Academy of Sciences, 978,* 334–353.

Volkow, N. D., Wang, G. J., Fowler, J. S., Gatley, S. J., Logan, J., Ding, Y. S., et al. (1998). Dopamine transporter occupancies in the human brain induced by therapeutic doses of oral methylphenidate. *American Journal of Psychiatry, 155,* 1325–1331.

Whitaker, A. H., VanRossem, R., Feldman, J. F., Schonfeld, I. S., Pinto-Martin, J. A., Torre, C., et al. (1997). Psychiatric outcomes on low birth-weight children at age 6 years: Relation to neonatal cranial ultrasound abnormalities. *Archives of General Psychiatry, 54,* 847–856.

Wolf, S. S., Jones, D. W., Knable, M. B., Gorey, J. G., Lee, K. S., Hyde, T. M., et al. (1996). Tourette syndrome: Prediction of phenotypic variation in monozygotic twins by caudate nucleus D2 receptor binding. *Science, 273,* 1225–1227.

Zelazo, P. D., Burack, J. A., Benedetto, E., & Frye, D. (1996). Theory of mind and rule use in individuals with Down's syndrome: A test of the uniqueness and specificity claims. *Journal of Child Psychology and Psychiatry, 37,* 479–484.

9

The Development of Effortful Control

Mary K. Rothbart and M. Rosario Rueda

Michael Posner is one of the most creative and influential psychologists of the past century. He has been a pioneer in cognitive science and is one of the founders of the field of cognitive neuroscience. The experimental paradigms he has developed have provided a major foundation for the imaging of the human brain. It is our great honor and pleasure to work with him as he continues his pioneering efforts, now focusing on attentional development and its relation to education. Our development of marker tasks based on patterns of adult brain activation has allowed us to study infant and child development in neuroscientifically informed, yet nonintrusive ways. Together with Posner, we have been studying temperament in infants and young children in relation to underlying neural networks for self-control.

Our effort began with the study of temperament and proceeded to making links between temperamental dimensions and neural circuitry using marker tasks derived from adult imaging studies. The levels of analysis available for this exploration now range from molecular genetics to the socialization of behavior. We hope that by furthering methodological links between different levels of analysis, a basis will be provided for examining the many exciting questions at their interface. This chapter examines parallel developments of executive attention and self-regulation, as well as the genetic and experience-related factors that influence the functioning of this system.

Defining Temperamental Effortful Control

Temperament refers to individual differences in reactivity and self-regulation assumed to have a constitutional basis (Rothbart & Derryberry, 1981). The term constitutional refers to the relatively enduring biological makeup of the organism, influenced over time by heredity, maturation, and experience. Reactivity refers to the excitability, responsivity, or arousability of the behavioral and physiological systems of the organism, whereas self-regulation refers to neural and behavioral processes functioning to modulate this underlying reactivity (Rothbart & Derryberry, 1981).

Infants come into the world with a set of reactions to their environment that include activity, emotion, and attention. Infants, in turn, differ greatly in their reactions to events. One child is easily frustrated, has only a brief attention span, and cries with even moderate levels of stimulating play; another child enjoys rough play and seeks out exciting events. These reactions to the environment, together with the mechanisms that regulate them, constitute the child's temperament.

Identifying parameters of temperamental reactivity (response latency, rise time, intensity, and recovery time) allows the study of temperament at behavioral, psychophysiological, endocrine, and neural levels (Rothbart & Derryberry, 1981). Although, to date, these parameters have chiefly been used in laboratory studies assessing general dimensions of temperament (e.g., Lemery, Goldsmith, Klinnert, & Mrazek, 1999; Rothbart, Derryberry, & Hershey, 2000), they may in the future allow for more dynamic study of temperament and developmental processes. Distinguishing between reactive and self-regulative characteristics has also been useful in thinking about development generally, in that much of early behavior can be seen as reactive to immediate stimulus events and to endogenous changes in infant state. Later, more self-regulatory systems, particularly the executive attention system, will develop to modulate this reactivity (Derryberry & Rothbart, 1997; Rothbart & Derryberry, 1981).

Temperament arises from our genetic endowment, but it both influences and is influenced by the experience of the individual. Figure 9.1 describes three broad factors of temperament in childhood, with associated lists of lower-level temperament dimensions whose scales load on each factor. Their interrelations within two cultures are also described. Extraversion and negative affect are early developing dimensions of temperament that are present within all cultures studied to date. Effortful control is a later-developing dimension that also appears within all cultures studied.

Our factor analyses of the Children's Behavior Questionnaire (CBQ) identified a general factor of effortful control (attentional shifting, attentional focusing, inhibitory control, and perceptual sensitivity) distinct from factors of surgency (activity level, positive anticipation, high intensity pleasure/sensation seeking, impulsivity, smiling and laughter, and a negative loading from shyness) and negative emotionality (shyness, discomfort, fear, anger/frustration, sadness, and a negative loading from soothability/falling reactivity). We have also found intercorrelations among measures of attentional focusing, attentional shifting, and inhibitory control in adults (Derryberry & Rothbart, 1998).

These factors map conceptually and empirically onto the Extraversion/Positive Emotionality, Neuroticism/Negative Emotionality, and Conscientiousness/Constraint dimensions found in Big Five and Big Three studies of adult personality (Ahadi & Rothbart, 1994; Rothbart, Ahadi, & Evans, 2000). These broad temperament constructs suggest that temperament goes beyond either a set of unrelated traits or generalized characteristics of positive and negative emotionality. Important here are interactions between the child's motivational impulses and his or her efforts to control them.

We used oblique factor rotations allowing us to look at correlations among these broad factors. In U.S. adult as well as child samples, effortful control measures are not related to measures of positive emotionality but are inversely related to negative emotionality. In the People's Republic of China, we found a highly similar factor structure, but different relationships between the reactive

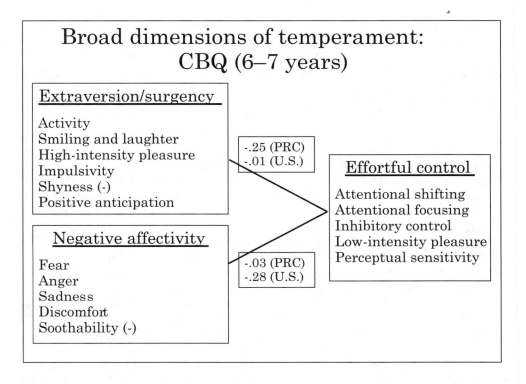

Figure 9.1. Broad dimensions of temperament from the Children's Behavior Questionnaire (Rothbart et al., 2001). CBQ = Children's Behavior Questionnaire; PRC = People's Republic of China.

factors and effortful control (Ahadi, Rothbart, & Ye, 1993; see Figure. 9.1). In the United States, but not China, children higher in effortful control showed lower negative affectivity. In China, but not in the United States, children higher in effortful control were less surgent and extraverted. These findings suggest differences between cultures in the behaviors seen as worthy of control (negative affect in the United States; outgoing behavior in China), and these in turn may be related to cultural values. An important goal of temperament research is to specify processes at the levels of biology and social development that may link the child's early endowment to later expression.

Linking Effortful Control and Executive Attention

Effortful control, defined as the ability to inhibit a dominant response to perform a subdominant response, to detect errors, and to engage in planning, is a major form of self-regulation, and self-regulation has been a central concept in developmental psychology and in the study of psychopathologies. Self-regulation refers to children's ability to control reactions to stress, maintain focused attention, and interpret mental states in themselves and others

(Fonagy & Target, 2002) and is a feature of normal child development (Bronson, 2000).

In two large longitudinal studies (32 to 66 months and 9 to 45 months), Kochanska and her colleagues have assessed five skills involving the capacity to suppress a dominant response to perform a subdominant response (Kochanska, Murray, & Coy, 1997; Kochanska, Murray, & Harlan, 2000; Kochanska, Murray, Jacques, Koenig, & Vandegeest, 1996). These include: delay (e.g., waiting for candy displayed under a transparent cup), slowing motor activity (drawing a line slowly), suppressing and initiating responses to changing signals (go–no-go games), effortful attention (recognizing small shapes hidden within a dominant large shape), and lowering the voice. Laboratory batteries were designed for developmental periods ranging from 22 to 66 months. Beginning at 2.5 years of age, children's performance was highly consistent across tasks, indicating they all appeared to measure a common underlying quality that had developed over time. Measures also showed stability for children across time, with correlations across repeated assessments ranging from .44 for the youngest children (22 to 33 months) to .59 from 32 to 46 months, and to .65 from 46 to 66 months (Kochanska et al., 2000).

What does effortful control mean for temperament and development? It means that unlike early theoretical models of temperament that emphasized how people are moved by the positive and negative emotions or level of arousal, people are not always at the mercy of affect. Using effortful control, people can more flexibly approach situations they fear and inhibit actions they desire. The efficiency of control, however, will depend on the strength of the emotional processes against which effort is exerted (Rothbart, Derryberry, & Hershey, 2000).

Effortful Control and Self-Regulation

Reasons for studying the emergence of executive attention are strengthened because cognitive measures of conflict resolution in laboratory tasks have been linked to aspects of children's effortful self-control in naturalistic settings. Children relatively less affected by spatial conflict also received higher parental ratings of temperamental effortful control and higher scores on laboratory measures of inhibitory control (Gerardi-Caulton, 2000; Rothbart, Ellis, Rueda, & Posner, 2003).

In Oregon, 6- to 7-year-olds high in effortful control have been found to be high in empathy, guilt/shame, and low in aggressiveness (Rothbart, Ahadi, & Hershey, 1994). Eisenberg and her colleagues have also found that 4- to 6-year-old boys with good attentional control tend to deal with anger by using nonhostile verbal methods rather than overt aggressive methods (Eisenberg, Fabes, Nyman, Bernzweig, & Pinulas, 1994). Effortful control may support empathy by allowing attention to the thoughts and feelings of another without becoming overwhelmed by one's distress. To display empathy toward others requires that one interpret their signals of distress or pleasure. Imaging work in normals shows that sad faces activate the amygdala. As sadness increases, this activation is accompanied by activity in the anterior cingulate as part of the attention network (Blair, Morris, Frith, Perrett, & Dolan, 1999). It seems likely that this cingulate activity represents the basis for one's attention to the distress of others.

Similarly, guilt/shame in 6- to 7-year-olds is positively related to effortful control and negative affectivity (Rothbart et al., 1994). Negative affectivity may contribute to guilt by providing strong internal cues of discomfort, increasing the likelihood that the cause of these feelings will be attributed to an internal conscience rather than external reward or coercion (Dienstbier, 1984; Kochanska, 1993). Effortful control may contribute also by providing the attentional flexibility needed to notice these feelings and relate them to feelings of responsibility for one's specific actions and their negative consequences for another person (Derryberry & Reed, 1994, 1996).

Consistent with this analysis, effortful control also appears to play an important role in the development of conscience. The internalization of moral principles appears to be facilitated in fearful preschool-aged children, especially when their mothers use gentle discipline (Kochanska, 1991, 1995; Kochanska et al., 1997). In addition, internalized control is greater in children high in effortful control (Kochanska et al., 1996, 1997, 2000). Thus, two separable control systems appear to regulate the development of conscience. Although fear may provide reactive behavioral inhibition and strong negative affect for association with moral principles, effortful control provides the attentional flexibility required to link negative affect, action, and moral principles. In terms of neural systems, a strongly reactive amygdala would provide the signals of distress that would easily allow empathic feelings toward others, leading to children who might be relatively easy to socialize. In the absence of this form of control, development of the cingulate would allow appropriate attention to other signals.

Individual differences in effortful control are also related to some aspects of metacognitive knowledge, such as theory of mind, that is, knowing that people's behavior is guided by their beliefs, desires, and other mental states (Carlson & Moses, 2001). Moreover, tasks that require the inhibition of a prepotent response are correlated with performance on theory of mind tasks even when other factors, such as age, intelligence, and working memory are factored out (Carlson & Moses, 2001). Inhibitory control and theory of mind share a similar developmental time course, with advances in both areas between the ages of 2 and 5.

Marker Tasks

We have used model tasks related to brain function to assess the executive attention capacities likely to underlie effortful control (Posner & Rothbart, 1998). Monitoring and resolving conflict between incompatible responses requires voluntary and attentive control of action and is considered a function of executive attention. Cognitive tasks involving conflict have been extensively used to measure the efficiency with which control of action is exerted (Botvinick, Braver, Barch, Carter, & Cohen, 2001; Posner & DiGirolamo, 1998).

A basic measure of conflict resolution is provided by the Stroop task. The original form of this task required research participants to report the color of ink a word was written in, when the color word, for example, red, might conflict with the color of ink, for example, blue. We know from adult brain imaging studies that Stroop tasks activate a midline brain structure, the anterior cingulate, which is also associated with other executive attention activities. In a meta-analysis of imaging studies, the dorsal section of the anterior cingulate was found to be activated in cognitive conflict tasks such as variants of the Stroop task (Bush, Luu, & Posner, 2000). An adjacent area of the anterior cingulate was found to be activated by emotional tasks and emotional states. The two divisions also seem to interact in a mutually exclusive way. For instance, when the cognitive division was activated, the affective division tended to be deactivated and vice-versa, suggesting the possibility of reciprocal effortful and emotional controls of attention.

When we know the kind of tasks that activate a given brain region, we can adapt them to children as marker tasks. It is then possible to trace the development of function in the brain areas through children's performances on the tasks. At Oregon, we have used a marker task to assess executive attention (Gerardi-Caulton, 2000; Posner & Rothbart, 1998) in which the child must respond to a spatially conflicting stimulus by inhibiting the dominant response and executing a subdominant response (spatial conflict task). In this task, children sit in front of two response keys, one located to the child's left and one to the right. Each key displays a picture, and on every trial a picture identical to one member of the pair appears on either the left or right side of the screen. Children are rewarded for responding to the identity of the stimulus regardless of its spatial compatibility with the matching response key (Gerardi-Caulton, 2000).

The inhibition of a prompted, but inappropriate response, is also considered basic to action monitoring, and as for conflict resolution, many cognitive tasks have been developed to measure this aspect of executive control. The most common way to measure inhibition is by using a task in which participants respond to one stimulus but are required to inhibit their response when a related stimulus is presented (go–no-go task). Under this instruction, promptness to respond can be manipulated by varying the proportion of go trials, or by presenting a no-go signal at particular time intervals immediately after the go stimulus (stop-signal paradigm). The efficiency of inhibition is measured behaviorally by the number of omissions and false alarms, but it can be also measured using physiological indices, such as muscular preparation or brain activity.

The current chapter stresses recent efforts to develop a neurological basis for self-regulation based on the study of the use of neuroimaging. The tasks described above and others based on them have been used with children to trace the development of executive functions. In turn, the development of neuroimaging techniques has permitted the analysis of neural systems underlying performance on executive tasks with both adults and children. Knowing the neural substrates for effortful control will provide a tool for examining which aspects of this form of self-regulation are subject to genetic influence, as well as investigating how the functioning of this system may be influenced by experience.

Development of Executive Attention

Neural systems related to executive attention make a crucial contribution to temperament. Individuals can voluntarily deploy their attention, allowing them to regulate their more reactive tendencies, and to suppress a dominant response to perform subdominant responses. How can we study the way these networks are created in early childhood?

Developmental studies have stressed the relative lack of executive control in infants (Ruff & Rothbart, 1996). However, a sign of the control of cognitive conflict is found in the first year of life. In A-not-B tasks, children are trained to reach for a hidden object at location A, and then tested on their ability to search for the hidden object at a new location B (Diamond, 1991). Children younger than 12 months tend to look in the previous location A, even though they see the object disappear behind location B. After the first year, children develop the ability to inhibit the prepotent response toward the trained location A, and successfully reach for the new location B (Diamond, 1991). Late in the first year, infants also develop the ability to resolve conflict between their line of sight and their line of reaching when retrieving an object. At 9 months, line of sight dominates completely. If the open side of a transparent box is not in line with the side in view, infants withdraw their hand and reach directly along the line of sight, striking the closed side (Diamond, 1991). In contrast, 12-month-old infants can simultaneously look at a closed side while reaching through the open end to retrieve a toy.

From 2 years of age and older, children are able to perform simple tasks in which their reaction time (RT) can be measured. In one study, toddlers were asked to perform the spatial conflict task described in the previous section (Gerardi-Caulton, 2000). Between 2 and 4 years of age, children progressed from an almost complete inability to carry out the task to relatively good performance. Children 24 months of age tended to perseverate on a single response, while 36-month-old children performed at high accuracy levels. As with adults, the 36-month-olds responded more slowly and with reduced accuracy to incompatible trials. Children who performed well were also described by their parents as more skilled at attentional shifting and focusing, less impulsive, and less prone to frustration reactions. Using a similar task with adults, research participants who performed poorly tended to be high in anxiety and low on self-reported attentional control (Derryberry & Reed, 1998). These findings are consistent with the idea that effortful attention, measured through questionnaire or laboratory methods, may help individuals constrain negative forms of emotion.

At 30 months, when toddlers were first able to successfully perform the spatial conflict task, we found that performance on this task was significantly related to the toddlers' ability to learn ambiguous associations in a visual sequence learning task (Rothbart et al., 2003). In the visual sequence task, a series of cartoons is presented on three different computer monitors in a predict-able sequence. In an unambiguous series, each location is followed by one and only one subsequent location. An ambiguous association refers to a sequence where a location is followed by one of two or more different locations, the particular location depending on its place within the sequence. Any context that helps specify "place" aids in acquiring the sequence representation. Any context that obscures place, such as randomly occurring events of a secondary task, makes the learning of an ambiguous sequence difficult. In essence, moni-toring context is a control mechanism that reduces ambiguity, and such context specification appears dependent on lateral prefrontal cortex (see, for example, Keele, Ivry, Mayr, Hazeltime, & Heuer, 2003). We would then expect that young children would have great difficulty in learning ambiguous sequences until powerful systems of contextual aid become available. In accordance with this prediction, in our studies ambiguous associations within sequences of events were not acquired at above chance levels until about 2 years of age (Clohessy, Posner, & Rothbart, 2001; Rothbart et al., 2003).

Another form of action monitoring is the detection and correction of errors. In the spatial conflict task, RTs following an error were 200 ms longer than those following a correct trial for 30-month-old children, and more than 500 ms longer at 36 months, indicating that children were noticing their errors and correcting them (Rothbart et al., 2003). No evidence of slowing following an error was found at 24 months. A somewhat more difficult conflict is intro-duced when participants must apply information from one verbal command while simultaneously ignoring information from another. One version of the Simple Simon game asks children to execute a response when a command is given by one stuffed animal, while inhibiting responses commanded by a second animal (Jones, Rothbart, & Posner, 2003). Children of 36 to 38 months showed no ability to inhibit their response and no slowing following an error, but at 39 to 41 months, children showed both an ability to inhibit and a slowing of RT following an error. These results suggest that between 30 and 39 months, performance changes in relation to detecting an error response.

Young children have more difficulty than older children and adults in resolving conflict from competing stimulation. We have recently developed a flanker task appropriate for use with children as young as 4 years of age (Rueda et al., 2004; see Figure 9.2). In this task, a row of five fish appear in the center of the screen and the child's job is to help in "feeding" the middle fish by pressing the key corresponding to the direction in which the middle fish is pointing. On half the trials, the flanker fish are pointing in the same direction as the middle fish (congruent trials); on the other half, the flanker fish are pointing in the opposite direction (incongruent trials).

Using this task, we have observed considerable development of conflict resolution up to 7 years of age, but a striking consistency in performance after this age up to adulthood (Rueda et al., 2004). In a pilot study conducted in our lab, we have also attempted to adapt the flanker task to age 3 years, using a touch-screen version. We ran this pilot task with a group of children of 3.5 years of age and found that approximately half of them were unable to under-stand and perform the task. At age 4, however, children did not seem to have trouble understanding the instructions and were able to carry out the task

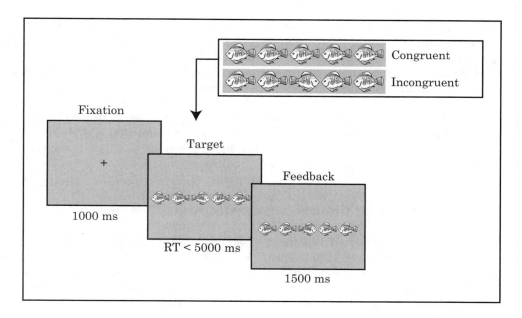

Figure 9.2. Flanker task for children. RT = reaction time.

using response keys, although their RT and conflict effects were considerably longer than those for older children and adults (see Table 9.1).

The greater susceptibility to interference from irrelevant stimulation for young children has been reported using many different tasks, including flanker tasks (Enns, Brodeur, & Trick, 1998; Ridderinkhof & van der Molen, 1995;

Table 9.1. Development of Conflict Resolution as Measured by the Child Version of the Flanker Task

	Age	Overall (RT)	Overall (% of errors)	Conflict (RT)	Conflict (% of errors)
Study 1	4	1,598	12.8	207	5.8
	adults	443	1.4	31	2.3
Study 2	6	931	15.8	115	15.6
	7	833	5.7	63	0.7
	8	806	4.9	71	−0.3
	9	734	2.7	67	1.6
	10	640	2.2	69	2.1
	adults	483	1.2	61	1.6

Note. Conflict is measured by subtracting the data (*RT* or % of errors) for the congruent flanker condition from the data for the incongruent flanker condition. Although the experimental procedures used in Study 1 and 2 were the same, the stimuli in Study 1 were larger than stimuli in Study 2, resulting in slightly smaller conflict scores.

Ridderinkhof, van der Molen, Band, & Bashore, 1997), go–no-go (Casey, Trainor, Giedd, et al., 1997) and stop-signal tasks (Bedard et al., 2002; Ridderinkhof, Band, & Logan, 1999), S-R compatibility tasks (Casey, Thomas, Davidson, Kunz, & Franzen, 2002), Stroop tasks (Gerstadt, Hong, & Diamond, 1994), visual discrimination tasks (Casey, Trainor, Orendi, et al., 1997), and negative priming (Tipper, Bourque, Anderson, & Brehaut, 1989). Depending on the difficulty of the task, developmental differences in the ability to resolve conflict between children and adults can be observed up to middle childhood and early adolescence, suggesting that full maturation of the executive control network does not take place until early adulthood.

Imaging the Executive Attention Network

In the past decade, the development of noninvasive brain imaging methods has permitted the analysis of the anatomy and time course of activations of cognitive functions. A network of brain areas have consistently shown to be active when executive attention is required. This network consists of the anterior cingulate cortex (ACC) and lateral prefrontal areas (Posner & Fan, in press).

Recent studies have been able to dissociate different operations involved in the resolution of conflict and the brain areas within the executive network responsible for these operations. In a functional magnetic resonance imaging (fMRI) study, Botvinick, Nystrom, Fissell, Carter, and Cohen (1999) showed the ACC to be involved in the detection and monitoring of conflict, whereas lateral prefrontal areas have been shown to be mainly related to conflict resolution (Casey, Durston, & Fossella, 2001). Moreover, the detection and resolution of conflict has been anatomically dissociated from selective attention. The selection of relevant information has been associated with a different system that involves areas of the superior parietal cortex and the right sides of the superior frontal gyrus and the cerebellum (Casey et al., 2000). In addition, Fan, Flombaum, McCandliss, Thomas, and Posner (2003) carried out a study in which a group of adults performed three types of conflict tasks (Stroop, spatial conflict, and flanker) while their brain activation was being scanned with fMRI. Although all tasks activated parts of the cingulate gyrus, suggesting an integrated network for conflict processing, some distinct activations were also found for each particular task (see Figure 9.3). This suggests a role for ACC in conflict detection and monitoring but relates conflict resolution to different subregions of the lateral prefrontal cortex, depending on the particular type of information used to induce conflict.

Despite the fact that the special setting for fMRI studies is not easily adapted to children, a number of neuroimaging studies have been conducted with children as young as 6 years of age. In general, children activate the same network of areas as adults when performing similar tasks, although the average volume of activation appears to be remarkably greater in children compared to adults (Casey et al., 2002; Casey, Trainor, Giedd, et al., 1997; Durston et al., 2002). This suggests that the brain circuitry underlying executive functions becomes more focal and refined as it gains in efficiency. In addition to the role

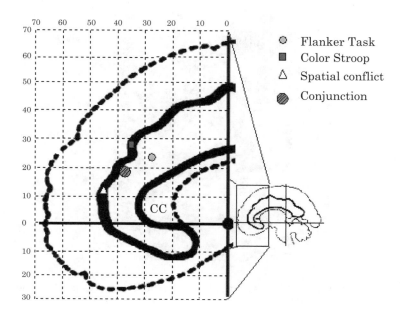

Figure 9.3. Anterior cingulate activations associated with performance in three different conflict tasks. From "Cognitive and Brain Mechanisms of Conflict," by J. Fan, J. I. Flombaum, B. D. McCandliss, K. M. Thomas, and M. I. Posner, 2003, *NeuroImage, 18*, p. 49. Copyright 2003 by Elsevier. Reprinted with permission.

of the ACC in the regulation of cognitive processing, this area appears to be also implicated in the regulation of emotions (Bush, Luu, & Posner, 2000). For instance, in a study by Whalen et al. (1998), a group of research participants showed activation in the dorsal part of the ACC when performing a Stroop-like task, but in ventral areas when the task involved emotional stimuli.

A number of studies have used the temporal resolution of event related potentials (ERPs) to measure the timing of these action-monitoring processes. The N2 and ERN are the two main ERP indexes associated with executive control. The N2 is a preresponse negative deflection in the ERP around 300 ms poststimulus, which appears to be greater (more negative) on trials involving conflict. The N2 is observed over parietal and frontal leads and has been obtained in both flanker (Kopp, Rist, & Mattler, 1996; van Veen & Carter, 2002) and go–no-go tasks (Jackson, Jackson, & Roberts, 1999). In both situations, the N2 has been associated with the withholding of a prepotent but inappropriate response.

The ERN develops around 100 ms following the commission of an error or the display of feedback that an error has been committed, and has a midfrontal topographic distribution. The ERN appears to represent a postresponse index of error detection and monitoring (Dehaene, Posner, & Tucker, 1994; Gehring, Goss, Coles, Meyer, & Donchin, 1993). Recently, van Veen and Carter (2002), using a flanker task, found a common source of activation in the caudal ACC for both N2 and ERN, suggesting that the same conflict detection process

Figure 9.4.   Four-year-old girl wearing the 128-channel geodesic sensor net.

underlies both potentials. The N2 may reflect a preresponse monitoring of the conflict produced by incongruent trials that is resolved in a correct response, while the ERN may relate to a mechanism of adjustment and correction of upcoming responses.

Characteristics of the ERP make this technique amenable to children of all ages. In a recent study conducted in our lab at the University of Oregon, we have used a high-density system of electroencephalography (Tucker, 1993; see Figure 9.4) to register brain activity while 4-years-olds and adults were performing the fish flanker task presented above. This procedure allows for the evaluation of differences between children and adults on the time course for monitoring and resolving conflict. Stimulus-locked ERPs are presented for children and adults in Figure 9.5. Despite dramatically different RTs (1244 ms vs. 443 ms) and conflict resolution times (82 ms vs. 31 ms), the ERP differences between incongruent and congruent trials were strikingly similar. Consistent with other studies (van Veen & Carter, 2002), we found the N2 effect for the adults over the midfrontal leads. The children's data also show a larger negative deflection for the incongruent condition at the midfrontal electrodes. Compared to adults, this effect has a larger size, greater amplitude, and is extended over a longer period of time.

Differences between children and adults in ERP amplitude have been related to brain size and skull thickening. Differences in the latency of components, however, may be more related to observed differences in conflict resolution between children and adults as measured in the flanker task. Although the frontal effect was evident for adults at around 300 ms posttarget, children did not show any difference until approximately 550 ms after the target. In addition, the effect was sustained over a period of 500 ms before the children's responses, in contrast with only 50 ms in the case of adults. This difference observed between children and adults over the frontal channels differed from

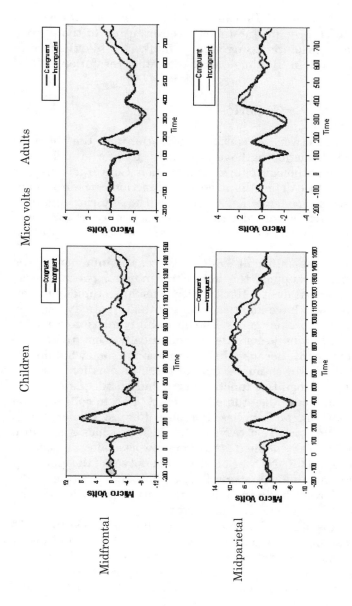

Figure 9.5. ERPs from 4-year-olds and adults on the child version of the flanker task.

other components observed at midparietal channels. For both children and adults, we found a greater positivity for incongruent trials over midparietal leads. For adults, this effect was observed at the time window of the P300, whereas it was more delayed in the case of children (between 800 and 1200 ms posttarget). The P300 is thought to be an index of stimulus evaluation (Coles, Gratton, Bashore, Ericksen, & Donchin, 1985). This parietal effect could reflect developmental differences in the difficulty of orienting to the central target depending on the congruence of surrounding flankers, while the frontal effect could reveal differences in the time course of conflict resolution.

Genetics

Links between the neural network of executive attention and the chemical modulators involved in its functioning have provided a tool for studying the genetic basis of normal and pathological forms of attention. Convergent studies from different fields have helped define the attentional functions in neurochemical and physiological terms (Posner & Fan, in press). The anterior cingulate is only one synapse away from the ventral tegmental area, a source of dopamine neurons. Moreover, the five types of dopamine receptors are all expressed within the cingulate.

To determine if there was sufficient evidence of genetic influence in the efficiency of this network to support the hunt for candidate genes, it was necessary to determine its heritability. Heritability is usually studied by comparing monozygotic twins who have identical genes with dizygotic twins who, like siblings, share about half of their genes. The heritability measure assumes that the mono- and dizygotic twins do not differ systematically in environmental influences on their development. Because this assumption is somewhat doubtful, heritability remains only an estimate. One of the problems for studying the genetic underpinnings of cognitive functions is to find an adequate phenotype for the particular function to be studied. Recently, Fan in collaboration with Posner and others (Fan, McCandliss, Sommer, Raz, & Posner, 2002) developed the Attention Network Test (ANT). This task provides a measure for each of the three anatomically defined attention networks: alerting, orienting, and executive attention. The ANT was used as a phenotype of the efficiency of these three attentional functions in a small scale twin study. In this study, the executive network showed high enough heritability (.89) to justify the search for specific genes (Fan, Wu, Fossella, & Posner, 2001).

DNA from cheek swabs of research participants who performed the ANT could then be used to examine candidate differences in gene polymorphisms related to dopamine. This process demonstrated at least two candidate genes that were related to the executive network to a greater degree than to overall performance as measured by RT and accuracy (Fossella, Posner, Fan, Swanson, & Pfaff, 2002). One of these genes was the dopamine D4 receptor (DRD4) gene, widely reported to be associated with attention deficit hyperactivity disorder (ADHD) and with the personality trait of sensation seeking (Swanson et al., 2000). The other was the MAOA gene, which is related both to dopamine and to norepinepherine.

The DRD4 gene has one area in which a sequence of 48 bases are repeated either two, four, seven, or more times. The presence of the more common four repeat allele appeared to be associated with more difficulty in resolving conflict (Fossella et al., 2002). Interestingly, children with the less common seven repeat allele showed behavioral aspects of ADHD but did not have deficits in overall RT or in conflict as measured by the color-word Stroop task (Swanson et al., 2000).

Evidence from detailed evolutionary studies suggest that the seven repeat allele is under positive selective pressure (Ding et al., 2002), indicating that it might convey some advantages. This might relate to the association of the seven repeat with sensation seeking, a temperament trait that might have conveyed an advantage during human evolution (Ding et al., 2002). This trait might well be a prominent characteristic in individuals with ADHD. These findings are all rather new, and require additional confirmation and extension. However, they do indicate the possible utility in relating genetic differences to specific brain networks and temperamental characteristics.

Neuroimaging can serve as a tool to examine the role of genetic variation in influencing brain networks. The two genes that were associated with differences in conflict RT (DRD4 and MAOA) also produced differences in brain activation within the anterior cingulate gyrus (Fan, Fossella, et al., 2003). The number of participants required to find a significant difference in brain activity were far fewer than those needed to do so when looking at amount of brain activation. A similar result was reported for the BDNF gene (Egan et al., 2003), thought to be related to long-term memory storage. It required several hundred participants with each allele to show a behavioral difference in a memory test, but fewer than 10 participants per group to establish a difference in degree of activation within the hippocampus. These findings indicate that brain imaging may play an important role in examining the influence of genetics on neural networks.

Training of Attention

Rhesus monkeys and chimpanzees have been trained to carry out some of the high-level skills known to produce activation of the anterior cingulate in human adults as a numerical version of the Stroop task (Rumbaugh & Washburn, 1995). After many months of training, rhesus monkeys were able to indicate which of two displays had the larger number of items, even when the larger number of items was in a display made up of the smaller digit (incongruent condition). Although their RTs were similar to humans in showing a difference between incongruent and congruent trials (Washburn, 1998) the trained monkeys made about 25% errors, while humans made only 3% errors in this condition. Additional research showed that cues helping to direct the participant's attention to the target location were more effective with monkeys than with humans. On the other hand, rewards that operated by executive attention are more effective in humans than in monkeys. In general, the monkeys' performance seem more like those of young children whose executive attention is still immature than like human adults.

Informal observations made by Rumbaugh and Washburn indicate that the animals tended to become less aggressive and more sociable after the training. These observations might fit with the central midline control systems and the reciprocal inhibition observed in positron emission tomography (PET) studies between cognitive and emotional tasks. The observations on animals raised the question of whether it might be possible to influence both the cognitive and emotional controls on behavior by systematic training of preschool children in tasks similar to those used with the monkeys. It would clearly not be possible to match the number of trials used with monkeys, but it may be possible to perform some training with young children designed to make subtle improvements on their executive attention during the time that it is undergoing development.

We have created a set of training exercises designed to help preschool children develop their executive attention skills that have been adapted from Rumbaugh and Washburn's (1995) work with primates. Each exercise is presented in the form of a game the child can enjoy. The exercises are designed to teach a set of cumulative skills training the elements of executive attention (Posner & Fan, in press). There are a total of nine exercises structured in three sets depending on the aspect of attention they are targeting: (a) navigating and object-tracking exercises; (b) visual discrimination exercises; and (c) conflict resolution exercises. Using these training programs, a study was run with a group of 4-year-old children. The games were completed in a total of five training sessions, and there was also a pre- and posttraining assessment session. For the pre- and postassessment sessions, the children completed the child version of the ANT (Rueda et al., 2004) and the Kaufman–Brief Intelligence Test (K-BIT; Kaufman & Kaufman, 1990). Parents of the children also completed the CBQ before and two weeks after the training program.

We chose 4-year-olds for the initial test because executive attention as measured by conflict tasks has shown substantial development between 2.5 and 7 years (see previous section on development of executive attention). Thus, we felt that 4-year-olds would be in the process of developing this network and would show a good chance for improvement. For the initial test we ran a small group of 24 four-year-old children (52 months old on average). Half of them were assigned to the experimental group and were run in a total of seven sessions, five training sessions, and pre- and postassessment sessions. The children in the control group participated only in the pre- and postassays.

All but two children completed most of the trials within the 5-day period. The average number of trials performed by the children on the training exercises was 247, 8% of which were incorrect and 4.2% missed. Results on the pre- and postassays for overall RT and the conflict scores are shown in Table 9.2a. A minus sign before the difference score means there was a pre- to posttest improvement. The control group showed as large or larger improvement as the experimental group in overall RT. In conflict scores, the experimental group showed considerable improvement, while the control group showed a small decline, although in none of these cases was the pre–post difference statistically significant, because of high variability across children. In addition, we found that the training produced significant increases in overall IQ and for the visual matrices scale measured by the K-BIT (Table 9.2b).

Table 9.2. Changes in Overall *RT* and Conflict (a) and IQ (b) Scores With Training

| | | (a) Overall | | Conflict | |
		RT	% errors	RT	% errors
Experimental group	Pre	1702	26.3	80.5	14.1
	Post	1453	23.8	51.5	17.4
	Dif	−249	−2.4	−29	+3.4
Control group	Pre	1906	25.0	192.2	12.1
	Post	1456	19.3	210.4	11.3
	Dif	−550	−5.7	+18.2	−0.8

		(b) IQ composite	Vocabulary subtest	Matrices subtest
Experimental group	Pre	111.3	115.3	104.8
	Post	117.4	117.0	113.8
	Dif	+6.1	+1.7	+9.1
Control group	Pre	115.4	116.3	111.4
	Post	115.8	123.1	104.9
	Dif	+0.4	+6.8	−6.4

Note. The conflict effect is measured by subtracting the data (RT or % of errors) for the congruent flanker condition from the data for the incongruent flanker condition.

We also found significant correlations between performance on the training exercises and the degree of improvement experienced by the experimental group on some of the assessment scores. For example, children who needed more trials to advance from one level to the next, and therefore completed more training trials, were the ones improving more in the matrices score ($r = .67$).

For the vocabulary subtest, participants in the control group showed a larger gain than the experimental children, but this was not significant. The vocabulary subtest measures the individual level of language development and verbal conceptualization, which depends greatly on formal schooling and cultural experiences, whereas the matrices subtest measures simultaneous processing, nonverbal reasoning, and fluid thinking (Kaufman & Kaufman, 1990). Matrices scores represent a more abstract and culture-free measure of intelligence, similar to the one provided by Raven's abstract matrices (Raven, Court, & Raven, 1983). Other forms of attention training for children with ADHD have also proven to improve performance on abstract reasoning as measured by Raven's Progressive Matrices (Klingsberg, Forssberg, & Westerberg, 2002). This suggests that training of attention may produce a benefit on a general form of cognitive functioning that extends over a wide range of tasks. Finally, as expected by the short-time period elapsing between the pre- and postassessment sessions, there was little hint of any change in reported temperament scores.

Although the results of this first phase of the study are greatly encouraging, additional investigation involving more extensive controls will be necessary to understand what aspect of the training is important for the fostering of reasoning and attentional skills. During our future training studies, we plan to use high-density electroencephalograms (EEGs) to examine changes in brain networks that might occur as a result of training. Previous studies have shown that we can record ERPs from 4-year-olds and that they show both similarities and differences from adults (see Figure 9.5). The use of ERPs during the pre- and postassessment sessions will allow us to study possible changes in the timing and topography of activations that could be related to the behavioral improvements produced by training.

Conclusion

Effortful control refers to a construct that consistently emerges from factorial analyses of temperament questionnaires. This construct includes the ability to inhibit dominant responses to perform subdominant responses, to detect errors, and to engage in planning. This temperamental dimension appears to be closely related to executive attention. According to cognitive models, executive attention is required in situations that require a careful and attentive control of action. These situations involve overcoming habitual responses (conflict), action planning, novelty, error detection and compensation, and dealing with difficult or dangerous conditions (Norman & Shallice, 1986). The functions associated with executive attention overlap with the more general notion of executive functions in childhood, which includes working memory, planning, switching, and inhibitory control (Welch, 2001). All these capacities, together with the regulatory functions of the attentional systems (Rueda, Posner, & Rothbart, 2004) seem likely to underlie effortful control.

The development of effortful control has been traced using not only temperament questionnaires but also laboratory tasks adopted from adult studies but adapted to children and designed to isolate specific measures of control. On the basis of this research, the system appears to experience considerable development between 2 and 7 years of age. In this chapter, we stressed the crucial role the development of this system has in the internalization of moral principles and socialization as well as the development of the theory of mind.

Making use of appropriate cognitive tasks, neuroimaging studies have provided a valuable understanding of the neural basis for executive attention. Different parts of the anterior cingulate cortex have been shown to be implicated in processing cognitive and emotional information in close connection with other prefrontal areas more related to action-monitoring processes. Developmental studies have suggested that when the system is still immature, a broader area around the same brain circuitry has to be activated during a longer period of time to resolve the same type of conflict situations. Knowing the biological basis of a function opens the door to the possibility of studying its genetic influence. Pioneering studies following this approach have shown the neural network for executive control to be in part determined by the biological background expressed in particular dopamine-related genes. However, the impact of genetic factors on the functioning of the executive control system could wrongly lead the reader to the conclusion that the system cannot be influenced by experience. We reported a cross-cultural study of China and the United States, suggesting that the functioning of this self-regulatory system may be subject to cultural demands.

Finally, we have also presented a recent effort in our laboratory to develop a set of exercises for training attention in younger children. Our training program produced improvement in 4-year-olds' abstract reasoning and conflict resolution abilities. The brain mechanisms responsible for these improvements may be also analyzed in the future using imaging techniques appropriate to young children. Considering effortful control as a central system for the successful development of cognitive and emotional regulation of children's behavior, the training of attentional abilities known to relate to the control of action may be an important complement to preschool and early elementary education.

References

Ahadi, S. A., & Rothbart, M. K. (1994). Temperament, development, and the Big Five. In C. F. Halverson, G. A. Kohnstamm, & R. P. Martin (Eds.), *The developing structure of temperament and personality from infancy to adulthood* (pp. 189–207). Hillsdale, NJ: Erlbaum.

Ahadi, S. A., Rothbart, M. K., & Ye, R. (1993). Children's temperament in the U.S. and China: Similarities and differences. *European Journal of Personality, 7,* 359–378.

Bedard, A. C., Nichols, S., Barbosa, J., Schachar, R., Logan, G. D., & Tannock, R. (2002). The development of selective inhibitory control across the life span. *Developmental Neuropsychology, 21,* 93–111.

Blair, R. J. R., Morris, J. S., Frith, C. D., Perrett, D. I., & Dolan, R. J. (1999). Dissociable neural responses to facial expression of sadness and anger. *Brain, 1222,* 883–893.

Botvinick, M. M., Braver, T. S., Barch, D. M., Carter, C. S., & Cohen, J. D. (2001). Conflict monitoring and cognitive control. *Psychological Review, 108,* 624–652.

Botvinick, M. M., Nystrom, L. E., Fissell, K., Carter, C. S., & Cohen, J. D. (1999). Conflict monitoring versus selection-for-action in anterior cingulate cortex. *Nature, 402,* 179–181.

Bronson M. B. (2000). *Self-regulation in early childhood.* New York: Guilford Press.

Bush, G., Luu, P., & Posner, M. I. (2000). Cognitive and emotional influences in the anterior cingulate cortex. *Trends in Cognitive Science, 4,* 215–222.

Carlson, S. T., & Moses, L. J. (2001). Individual differences in inhibitory control in children's theory of mind. *Child Development, 72,* 1032–1053.

Casey, B. J., Durston, S., & Fossella, J. A. (2001). Evidence for a mechanistic model of cognitive control. *Clinical Neuroscience Research, 1,* 267–282.

Casey, B. J., Thomas, K. M., Davidson, M. C., Kunz, K., & Franzen, P. L. (2002). Dissociating striatal and hippocampal function developmentally with a stimulus–response compatibility task. *Journal of Neuroscience, 22,* 8647–8652.

Casey, B. J., Thomas, K. M., Welsh, T. F., Badgaiyan, R. D., Eccard, C. H., Jennings, J. R., et al. (2000). Dissociation of response conflict, attentional selection, and expectancy with functional magnetic resonance imaging. *Proceedings of the National Academy of Sciences of the United States of America, 97,* 8728–8733.

Casey, B. J., Trainor, R. J., Giedd, J., Vauss, Y., Vaituzis, C. K., Hamburger, S., et al. (1997). The role of the anterior cingulate in automatic and controlled processes: A developmental neuroanatomical study. *Developmental Psychobiology, 3,* 61–69.

Casey, B. J., Trainor, R. J., Orendi, J. L., Schubert, A. B., Nystrom, L. E., Giedd, J. N., et al. (1997). A developmental functional MRI study of prefrontal activation during performance of a go–no-go task. *Journal of Cognitive Neuroscience, 9,* 835–847.

Clohessy, A. B., Posner, M. I., & Rothbart, M. K. (2001). Development of the functional visual field. *Acta Psychologica, 106,* 51–68.

Coles, M. G. H., Gratton, G., Bashore, T. R., Ericksen, C. W., & Donchin, E. (1985). A psychophysiological investigation of the continuous flow model of human information processing. *Journal of Experimental Psychology: Human, Perception and Performance, 11,* 529–553.

Dehaene, S., Posner, M. I., & Tucker, D. M. (1994). Localization of a neural system for error detection and compensation. *Psychological Science, 5,* 303–305.

Derryberry, D., & Reed, M. A. (1994). Temperament and the self-organization of personality. *Development and Psychopathology, 6,* 653–676.

Derryberry, D., & Reed, M. A. (1996). Regulatory processes and the development of cognitive representations. *Development and Psychopathology, 8,* 215–234.

Derryberry, D., & Reed, M. A. (1998). Anxiety and attentional focusing: Trait, state and hemispheric influences. *Personality and Individual Differences, 25,* 745–761.

Derryberry, D., & Rothbart, M. K. (1997). Reactive and effortful processes in the organization of temperament. *Development and Psychopathology, 9,* 633–652.

Diamond, A. (1991). Neuropsychological insights into the meaning of object concept development. In S. Carey & R. Gelman (Eds.), *The epigenesis of mind: Essays on biology and cognition* (pp. 67–110). Hillsdale, NJ: Erlbaum.

Dienstbier, R. A. (1984). The role of emotion in moral socialization. In C. E. Izard, J. Kagan, & R. B. Zajonc (Eds.), *Emotions, cognition, and behavior* (pp. 484–514). New York: Cambridge University Press.

Ding, Y. C., Chi, H. C., Grady, D. L., Morishima, A., Kidd, J. R., Kidd, K. K., et al. (2002). Evidence of positive selection acting at the human dopamine receptor D4 gene locus. *Proceedings of the National Academy of Sciences of the United States of America, 99,* 309–314.

Durston, S., Thomas, K. M., Yang, Y., Ulug, A. M., Zimmerman, R. D., & Casey, B. J. (2002). A neural basis for the development of inhibitory control. *Developmental Science, 5,* F9–F16.

Egan, M. F., Kojima, M., Callicott, J. H., Goldberg, T. E., Kolachana, B. S., Bertolino, A., et al. (2003). The BDNF val66met polymorphism affects activity-dependent secretion of BDNF and human memory and hippocampal function. *Cell, 112,* 257–269.

Eisenberg, N., Fabes, R. A., Nyman, M., Bernzweig, J., & Pinulas, A. (1994). The relations of emotionality and regulation to children's anger-related reactions. *Child Development, 65,* 109–128.

Enns, J. T., Brodeur, D. A., & Trick, L. M. (1998). Selective attention over the life span: Behavioral measures. In J. E. Richards (Ed.), *Cognitive neuroscience of attention: A developmental perspective* (pp. 393–418). Mahwah, NJ: Erlbaum.

Fan, J., Flombaum, J. I., McCandliss, B. D., Thomas, K. M., & Posner, M. I. (2003). Cognitive and brain mechanisms of conflict. *NeuroImage, 18,* 42–57.

Fan, J., Fossella, J. A., Sommer, T., & Posner, M. I. (2003). Mapping the genetic variation of executive attention onto brain activity. *Proceedings of the National Academy of Sciences of the United States of America, 100,* 7406–7411.

Fan, J., McCandliss, B. D., Sommer, T., Raz, M., & Posner, M. I. (2002). Testing the efficiency and independence of attentional networks. *Journal of Cognitive Neuroscience, 3,* 340–347.

Fan, J., Wu, Y., Fossella, J., & Posner, M. I. (2001). Assessing the heritability of attentional networks. *BioMed Central Neuroscience, 2,* 14.

Fonagy, P., & Target, M. (2002). Early intervention and the development of self-regulation. *Psychoanalytic Quarterly, 22,* 307–335.

Fossella, J., Posner, M. I., Fan, J., Swanson, J. M., & Pfaff, D. M. (2002). Attentional phenotypes for the analysis of higher mental function. *Scientific World Journal, 2,* 217–223.

Gehring, W. J., Goss, B., Coles, M. G. H., Meyer, D. E., & Donchin, E. (1993). A neural system for error detection and compensation. *Psychological Science, 4,* 385–390.

Gerardi-Caulton, G. (2000). Sensitivity to spatial conflict and the development of self-regulation in children 24–36 months of age. *Developmental Science, 3,* 397–404.

Gerstadt, C. L., Hong, Y. J., & Diamond, A. (1994). The relationship between cognition and action: Performance of children 3½–7 years old on a Stroop-like day-night test. *Cognition, 53,* 129–153.

Jackson, S. R., Jackson, G. M., & Roberts, M. (1999). The selection and suppression of action: ERP correlates of executive control in humans. *NeuroReport, 10,* 861–865.

Jones, L., Rothbart, M. K., & Posner, M. I. (2003). Development of inhibitory control in preschool children. *Developmental Science, 6,* 498–504.

Kaufman, A. S., & Kaufman, N. L. (1990). *Kaufman Brief Intelligence Test—Manual.* Circle Pines, MN: American Guidance Service.

Keele, S. W., Ivry, R., Mayr, U., Hazeltime, E., & Heuer, H. (2003). The cognitive and neural architecture of sequence representation. *Psychological Review, 110,* 316–339.

Klingsberg, T., Forssberg, H., & Westerberg, H. (2002). Training of working memory in children with ADHD. *Journal of Clinical and Experimental Neuropsychology, 24,* 781–791.

Kochanska, G. (1991). Socialization and temperament in the development of guilt and conscience. *Child Development, 62,* 1379–1392.

Kochanska, G. (1993). Toward a synthesis of parental socialization and child temperament in early development of conscience. *Child Development, 64,* 325–347.

Kochanska, G. (1995). Children's temperament, mothers' discipline, and security of attachment: Multiple pathways to emerging internalization. *Child Development, 66,* 597–615.

Kochanska, G., Murray, K. T., & Coy, K. C. (1997). Inhibitory control as a contributor to conscience in childhood: From toddler to early school age. *Child Development, 68,* 263–277.

Kochanska, G., Murray, K. T., & Harlan, E. T. (2000). Effortful control in early childhood: Continuity and change, antecedents, and implications for social development. *Developmental Psychology, 36,* 220–232.

Kochanska, G., Murray, K. T., Jacques, T. Y., Koenig, A. L., & Vandegeest, K. A. (1996). Inhibitory control in young children and its role in emerging internationalization. *Child Development, 67,* 490–507.

Kopp, B., Rist, F., & Mattler, U. (1996). N200 in the flanker task as a neurobehavioral tool for investigating executive control. *Psychophysiology, 33,* 282–294.

Lemery, K. S., Goldsmith, H. H., Klinnert, M. D., & Mrazek, D. A. (1999). Developmental models of infant and childhood temperament. *Developmental Psychology, 35,* 189–204.

Norman, D. A., & Shallice, T. (1986). Attention to action: Willed and automatic control of behavior. In R. J. Davidson, C. E. Schwartz, & D. Shapiro (Eds.), *Consciousness and self-regulation* (pp. 1–18). New York: Plenum Press.

Posner, M. I., & DiGirolamo, G. J. (1998). Executive attention: Conflict, target detection and cognitive control. In R. Parasuraman (Ed.), *The attentive brain* (pp. 401–424). Cambridge, MA: MIT Press.

Posner, M. I., & Fan, J. (in press). Attention as an organ system. In J. Pomerantz (Ed.), *Neurobiology of perception and communication: From synapse to society. The IVth De Lange Conference.* Cambridge England: Cambridge University Press.

Posner, M. I., & Rothbart, M. K. (1998). Attention, self-regulation, and consciousness. *Philosophical Transactions of the Royal Society of London B, 353,* 1915–1927.

Raven, J. C., Court, J. H., & Raven, J. (1983). *Manual for Raven's progressive matrices and vocabulary scales.* London: H. K. Lewis.

Ridderinkhof, K. R., Band, G. P. H., & Logan, G. D. (1999). A study of adaptive behavior: Effects of age and irrelevant information on the ability to inhibit one's actions. *Acta Psychologica, 101,* 315–337.

Ridderinkhof, K. R., & van der Molen, M. W. (1995). A psychophysiological analysis of developmental differences in the ability to resist interference. *Child Development, 66,* 1040–1056.

Ridderinkhof, K. R., van der Molen, M. W., Band, P. H., & Bashore, T. R. (1997). Sources of interference from irrelevant information: A developmental study. *Journal of Experimental Child Psychology, 65,* 315–341.

Rothbart, M. K., Ahadi, S. A., & Evans, D. E. (2000). Temperament and personality: Origins and outcomes. *Journal of Personality and Social Psychology, 78,* 122–135.

Rothbart, M. K., Ahadi, S. A., & Hershey, K. L. (1994). Temperament and social behavior in childhood. *Merrill-Palmer Quarterly, 40,* 21–39.

Rothbart, M. K., Ahadi, S. A., Hershey, K. L., & Fisher, P. (2001). Investigations of temperament at three to seven years: The Children's Behavior Questionnaire. *Child Development, 72,* 1394–1408.

Rothbart, M. K., & Derryberry, D. (1981). Development of individual differences in temperament. In M. E. Lamb & A. L. Brown (Eds.), *Advances in developmental psychology* (Vol. 1, pp. 37–86). Hillsdale, NJ: Erlbaum.

Rothbart, M. K., Derryberry, D., & Hershey, K. (2000). Stability of temperament in childhood: Laboratory infant assessment to parent report at seven years. In V. J. Molfese & D. L. Molfese (Eds.), *Temperament and personality development across the life span* (pp. 85–119). Hillsdale, NJ: Erlbaum.

Rothbart, M. K., Ellis, L. K., Rueda, M. R., & Posner, M. I. (2003). Developing mechanisms of conflict resolution. *Journal of Personality, 71,* 1113–1143.

Rueda, M. R., Fan, J., McCandliss, B., Halparin, J. D., Gruber, D. B., Pappert, L., & Posner, M. I. (2004). Development of attentional networks in childhood. *Neuropsychologia, 42,* 1029–1040.

Rueda, M. R., Posner, M. I., & Rothbart, M. K. (2004). Attentional control and self-regulation. In R. F. Baumeister & K. D. Vohs (Eds.), *Handbook of self regulation: Research, theory, and applications* (pp. 283–300). New York: Guilford Press.

Ruff, H. A., & Rothbart, M. K. (1996). *Attention in early development: Themes and variations.* New York: Oxford University Press.

Rumbaugh, D. M., & Washburn, D. A. (1995). Attention and memory in relation to learning: A comparative adaptation perspective. In G. R. Lyon & N. A. Krasengor (Eds.), *Attention, memory and executive function* (pp. 199–219). Baltimore, MD: Brookes.

Swanson, J., Oosterlaan, J., Murias, M., Moyzis, R., Schuck, S., Mann, M., et al. (2000). ADHD children with 7-repeat allele of the DRD4 gene have extreme behavior but normal performance on critical neuropsychological tests of attention. *Proceedings of the National Academy of Sciences of the United States of America, 97,* 4754–4759.

Tipper, S. T., Bourque, T. A., Anderson, S. H., & Brehaut, J. C. (1989). Mechanisms of attention: A developmental study. *Journal of Experimental Child Psychology, 48,* 353–378.

Tucker, D. M. (1993). Spatial sampling of head electrical fields: The geodesic sensor net. *Electroencephalography and clinical neurophysiology: Evoked potentials, 87,* 154–163.

van Veen, V., & Carter, C. S. (2002). The timing of action-monitoring processes in the anterior cingulate cortex. *Journal of Cognitive Neuroscience, 14,* 593–602.

Washburn, D. A. (1998). Stroop-like effects for monkeys and humans: Processing speed or strength of association? *Psychological Science, 5,* 375–379.

Welch, M. C. (2001). The prefrontal function and the development of the executive function in childhood. In A. F. Kalverboer & A. Gramsbergen (Eds.), *Handbook of brain and behavior in human development* (pp. 767–790). Dordrecht, Netherlands: Kluwer Academic.

Whalen, P. J., Bus, G., McNally, R. V., Wilhelen, S., McInerney, S. C., Michael, A., et al. (1998). The emotional counting Stroop paradigm: A functional magnetic resonance imaging probe of the anterior cingulate affective division. *Biological Psychiatry, 44,* 1219–1228.

10

Socioeconomic Influences on Brain Development: A Preliminary Study

Martha J. Farah and Kimberly G. Noble

The emergence of cognitive neuroscience in the final decades of the 20th century resulted from a number of technical and conceptual breakthroughs, and Michael Posner was behind many of them. From his fundamental contributions to the information processing framework in cognitive psychology to his pioneering uses of reaction time methods with neurological patients and his revolutionary adaptation of functional neuroimaging for the study of human cognition, he helped make cognitive neuroscience what it is today.

But that was all last century. In recent years, Posner has embarked on a new scientific quest, to understand individuality and development. Whereas cognitive neuroscience has made considerable progress toward understanding neurocognitive function in the typical adult brain, much less is known about the ways in which normal, healthy individuals differ or about the genetic and environmental factors that lead to these differences. Posner is at work again, this time with babies and school children, linking genes, behavior, and brain activity, and inspiring his colleagues to follow.

This chapter focuses on the relation between one aspect of children's life experiences and the resulting pattern of their individual cognitive strengths and weaknesses. That aspect of life experience is referred to as socioeconomic status. A child's socioeconomic status is generally estimated by measuring parental education and occupational status along with family income. It is a far more complex construct than the composite of these straightforward measures, however, with associated differences in health status, child-rearing practices, family structure (particularly the number of parents in home), and neighborhood characteristics, to name but a few correlated factors. Not surprisingly,

We are indebted to the staff and students of the Jenks, Henry, Harrington, and Longstreth schools, and their families, for their help in carrying out the research reported in this chapter. We also thank Frank Norman and Andrew Leon for advice on data analysis and Bruce McCandliss and Steven Keele for insightful comments on an earlier draft of this chapter. The work reported was supported by National Science Foundation Grant 0226060, National Institutes of Health Grants R21-DA01586 and R01-DA14129, R01-HD043078, and National Institutes of Health graduate fellowship T32-MH17168.

given these factors, socioeconomic status has an effect on children's neurocognitive development.

Socioeconomic Status and Cognitive Development

Although the existence of socioeconomic status effects on development is not surprising, the magnitude of these effects is. For example, in one cohort of low-socioeconomic-status children, screened for a host of prenatal and neonatal complications including gestational cocaine exposure, and judged to be in good physical health in semiannual assessments, the average IQ at age 4 was 81 (Hurt et al., 1998). Beginning as early as preschool, and persisting throughout childhood and beyond, individuals of low socioeconomic status perform below their higher socioeconomic status counterparts on a variety of psychometric tests, including IQ and school achievement test scores (e.g., Bradley & Corwyn, 2002; Brooks-Gunn & Duncan, 1997; McLoyd, 1998). Indeed, socioeconomic status has stronger associations with cognitive performance than with other seemingly more concrete outcomes, such as health and behavior (Duncan, Yeung, Brooks-Gunn, & Smith, 1998). As already noted, these effects are quite large. Furthermore, there is no single cause that fully accounts for the socioeconomic status gap in cognitive performance. In one study, for example, low- and middle-income 5-year-olds, matched on birth weight, gender, ethnicity, mother's education, and number of adults in the home, had IQs that differed by an average of 9 points, or over half a standard deviation (Duncan, Brooks-Gunn, & Kiebanov, 1994). In general, the effect of lowering income by one standard deviation, holding constant the other family and child variables, lowers performance on intelligence and school achievement tests by a third of a standard deviation (Brooks-Gunn, Duncan, & Britto, 1999). Of course, if one is interested in understanding how childhood poverty affects cognitive development, one ought not exclude these family and child variables as they are, in reality, a component of socioeconomic status.

The developmental gap between children of low and middle socioeconomic status has been studied within the disciplinary frameworks of sociology (e.g., Mercy & Steelman, 1982), psychology (e.g., Bradley & Corwyn, 2002), and behavior genetics (e.g., Turkheimer, Haley, Waldron, D'Onofrio, & Gottesman, 2003). The goal of this chapter is to analyze the problem in terms of the framework of cognitive neuroscience. The empirical work reported here is more fully described in an article by Noble, Norman, and Farah (in press).

Socioeconomic Status and the Developing Brain: What Is Affected?

Intelligence tests and school achievement are relatively broad-band measures that could reflect either selective socioeconomic status effects on specific neurocognitive systems or global effects on brain development. Our initial goal was to characterize the effects of childhood poverty in terms of the specific neurocognitive systems affected. To characterize the effect of low versus middle socioeconomic status on children's neurocognitive development in greater detail, and in terms that can be related to current cognitive neuroscience conceptions of mind and brain, we used a battery of behavioral tests to assess the neurocognitive profile of two groups of kindergarteners, differing in socioeconomic status.

One hypothesis is that socioeconomic status affects all neurocognitive systems equally, across the board. Alternative hypotheses are that socioeconomic status affects certain systems more than others. There is already reason to believe that the development of the left perisylvian language system is influenced by socioeconomic status, as a number of relatively pure tests of language development have revealed a robust socioeconomic status gap (Whitehurst, 1997). What other systems undergo prolonged postnatal development and would they also show specific sensitivity to socioeconomic status? Prefrontal cortex is a brain region that continues to mature throughout childhood, with pronounced cellular changes in the preschool and early childhood years (Johnson, 1997). It is also a region on which many of the cognitive achievements of early childhood depend (Case, 1992; Diamond, 1990; Diamond, Prevor, & Callender, & Druin, 1997); Johnson, 1997; Posner & Rothbart, 1998). A disproportionate effect of socioeconomic status on prefrontal function is therefore a hypothesis of particular interest.

Participants

Sixty children were recruited from Philadelphia schools, 30 of whom met criteria for middle socioeconomic status and 30 of whom met criteria for low socioeconomic status. Specifically, the middle group was limited to children whose families had income-to-needs ratios (total family income divided by the official poverty threshold for a family of that size) greater than 1.5. In addition, at least one adult in the household was required to have at least 2 years of college education, and the occupation of at least one adult was required to fall into Hollingshead occupational status categories (Hollingshead, 1975) corresponding 1 to 4, ranging from higher executives to technical or clerical occupations. The low-socioeconomic-status group was limited to children whose family income-to-needs ratio was less than 1.2, with no college-educated adults in the household and occupations rated from 4 to 7, in other words from technical or clerical occupations to unskilled. Exclusionary criteria for all children included low birth weight (<1500 grams); maternal alcohol or drug use reported during pregnancy; history of head injury, attention-deficit/hyperactivity disorder (ADHD), learning disability, developmental delay, or other neurological or psychiatric problems. Twenty-six low-socioeconomic-status and 24 middle-socioeconomic-status parents provided consent to contact their pediatrician's office; of pediatricians who were contacted, we received responses from 90% from the consenting middle sample and 49% from the consenting low sample, which in every case confirmed the information provided by parents (birth weights inaccurate by no more than 17 oz and no exclusionary criteria violated). Key predictions were also tested with the data from the subset of children with pediatrician-verified medical histories, as reported below. All participating children in both groups were Black native English speakers. Table 10.1 shows the demographics of the two samples.

Table 10.1. Demographics of Low- and Middle-Socioeconomic-Status Samples

	Low socioeconomic status	Middle socioeconomic status
Mean age	5 years, 10 months	5 years, 10 months
Gender	17 male, 13 female	13 male, 17 female
Mean birth weight	111 oz.; 3 known NICU stays	111 oz.; 2 known NICU stays
Race	Black	Black
Mean income-to-needs ratio	0.77	3.57
Mean parental education	11.4 years	14.8 years
Mean Hollingshead occupation score	6.2	3.1

Note. NICU = neonatal intensive care unit.

Neurocognitive Systems and Tasks Used to Assess Them

We developed a battery of tasks designed to parse cognition into five broad neurocognitive systems: visual cognition, visuospatial processing, memory, language, and executive function. The five systems assessed cover a range of cognitive abilities, grouped into broad categories whose validity is supported both by anatomical and information-processing considerations.

Each neurocognitive system was assessed using two or more tasks that were superficially different, but that predominantly taxed that system. Although a child's entire brain is working while performing a given task, the tasks were relatively selective measures of particular neurocognitive systems in that they taxed one system and placed relatively light demands on the others. The level of functioning of each of the five neurocognitive systems was measured by a composite score derived from that system's tasks.

The battery consisted of paper-and-pencil and computerized tasks, each lasting approximately 5 to 10 minutes, with the complete battery requiring three 30-minute sessions. Children were tested individually in a quiet location at their school. Each session included tasks from multiple systems and the order of sessions was randomized between research participants.

Occipitotemporal–Visual Cognition System

Pattern perception and visualization from memory are functions of occipitotemporal visual association cortex, which are likely to play a role in range of nonverbal cognitive abilities.

SHAPE DETECTION TASK. The Shape Detection Task is a subtest of the Visual Object and Space Perception Battery (VOSP; Warrington & James, 1991) that taxes the perception of global pattern structure. Twenty black and white images of visual noise are presented, half with no coherent pattern and half with a weakly coherent X, and participants must detect the X. Agnosic patients with damage to visual association cortices in the occipital and inferior temporal regions have difficulty with this task (Milner & Goodale, 1995).

COLOR IMAGERY TASK. The Color Imagery Task is a visualization task that tests the ability to retrieve knowledge of the color of objects such as a tomato or a frog. For each item, children were shown a black and white drawing and were asked which of three crayons could be used to color the picture as realistically as possible. Color imagery may be impaired after bilateral or left hemisphere occipitotemporal damage (De Vreese, 1991) and is associated with occipitotemporal cortex in functional neuroimaging studies (Howard et al., 1998).

Parietal–Spatial Cognition System

Spatial cognition is a multifaceted aspect of intelligence, involving the perception and mental manipulation of spatial relations, and plays a role in mathematics and technical subjects as well as artistic endeavors.

LINE ORIENTATION TASK. The Line Orientation Task is a modified version of the classic clinical neuropsychology test (Benton, Varney, & des Hamsher, 1978) in which a participant judges the orientation of pairs of line segments at the top of the page, selecting the corresponding orientations from a response display of 11 numerically labeled, radially arranged lines at the bottom of the page. Because knowledge of the written numerals used to label the lines in the original version could potentially confound any group differences, we modified the task slightly. In our version, all but two of the radially arranged lines at the bottom of the page have been erased, and no numerical labels are used. The participant must decide if the lines at the top of the page are the same as or different from the lines at the bottom of the page. The task consists of five practice items with feedback, and 30 test items without feedback. Line orientation judgment is most impaired by lesions to the parietal cortex in humans (Walsh, 1978).

MENTAL ROTATION TASK. In the Mental Rotation Task, the experimenter used laminated pictures of candy canes to demonstrate how, when the hooks of two candy canes point the same way, they can be superimposed, but when they point different ways, they cannot be superimposed no matter how they are rotated. The child was then told to decide, without touching them, whether the candy canes could be placed perfectly on top of each other. Three practice trials with feedback ensued, followed by 30 test trials without feedback. The candy cane on the right was always rotated 0, 45, or 90 degrees clockwise from the reference candy cane on the left. Candy canes had the same handedness in half the trials. Both patient data (Ratcliff, 1979) and pediatric functional magnetic resonance imaging (fMRI) (Booth et al., 1999) have linked mental rotation to the parietal lobes.

Medial Temporal–Memory System

The ability to form new memories is essential to success in school and most other aspects of life. The memory tasks used here assess incidental memory, that is, memory formed without the benefit of strategic effort to learn. It affords a relatively pure measure of medial temporal memory processing, independent of prefrontally mediated strategy. The critical feature of incidental learning paradigms is that the participant does not know that memory will be tested during presentation of the to-be-remembered stimuli.

INCIDENTAL PICTURE LEARNING TASK. In the Incidental Picture Learning Task, the child is shown 20 pairs of line drawings from the Snodgrass and Vanderwart (1980) corpus (e.g., a book and a clock), and is asked to point to one picture of each pair (e.g., the clock). The test phase follows immediately. During the test phase the child is shown 40 pictures, half of which were the first set of named pictures, and the other half were novel pictures; the child is asked which pictures were seen before. Patients with medial temporal damage are impaired at recognizing stimuli presented in incidental learning tasks (Mayes, Meudell, & Neary, 1978); functional neuroimaging studies support this localization (Squire, 1992).

INCIDENTAL FACE LEARNING TASK. The Incidental Face Learning Task is analogous to the preceding one, except that the stimuli are 25 faces, presented individually, which the child must classify as a boy or girl. During the test phase the child is presented with 50 faces, half of which were seen previously, and is asked to classify each face as being from the earlier set or new. Medial temporal damage impairs incidental learning of faces (Mayes, Meudell, & Neary, 1980), and face learning is known to activate medial temporal regions of normal humans (Haxby & Hoffman, 2002).

Left Perisylvian–Language System

Language acquisition is crucial for many aspects of cognition as well as communication. Socioeconomic status effects have been found in all domains of linguistic competence, but especially in lexical–semantic knowledge and phonological awareness. Three standardized tests offering relatively pure measures of vocabulary, phonological awareness, and syntax were administered.

PEABODY PICTURE VOCABULARY TEST. Peabody Picture Vocabulary Test (PPVT) is a test of lexical–semantic knowledge. On each trial the child hears a word and must select the corresponding picture from among four choices. Certain forms of aphasia (Goodglass & Kaplan, 1982) and semantic memory impairments (McCarthy & Warrington, 1990), both of which involve damage to left perisylvian cortex, produce impairments in this task. Similar word–picture matching tasks used in functional neuroimaging studies also implicate left perisylvian cortex (Thompson-Schill et al., 1998).

TEST OF PHONOLOGICAL AWARENESS–KINDERGARTEN, SUBTESTS 1 AND 2. The Test of Phonological Awareness (TOPA) is a standardized test that assesses phonological awareness, a crucial predictor of reading ability. Subtests 1 and 2 consist of 10 trials each, and test the recognition of phonological similarity and difference, respectively. Phonological processing is often compromised after perisylvian damage (Blumstein, 1994) and has been linked to a left perisylvian network in neuroimaging studies (Pugh et al., 1996).

TEST OF RECEPTION OF GRAMMAR. The Test of Reception of Grammar (TROG) is a test of syntactic knowledge designed by Bishop (1983) for children between 4 and 12 years of age. On each of 80 trials, the child hears a sentence and must choose the picture, from a set of four, which depicts the sentence. The syntactic abilities tested here engage perisylvian frontal and temporal cortex on the basis of patient studies (Rothi, McFarling, & Heilman, 1982) and fMRI (Just, Carpenter, Keller, Eddy, & Thulborn, 1996).

Prefrontal–Executive Function System

Prefrontal function has been characterized in many interrelated ways, which for simplicity's sake will together be termed executive function. Evidence from animal models (Bourgeois, 1994; Diamond, 1990), structural imaging (Giedd et al., 1999; Klingberg et al., 1999), functional imaging (Casey et al., 2000; Chugani, Phelps, & Mazziotta, 1987) and human autopsy (Huttenlocher & Dabholkar, 1997) suggests that prefrontal cortex continues to undergo extensive development, including synaptogenesis (Huttenlocher & Dabholkar, 1997), pruning (Giedd et al., 1999) and myelination (Klingberg et al., 1999) well into childhood. Consistent with this, psychological research demonstrates substantial development of executive systems past the age of the kindergarteners studied here (Casey et al., 2000; Gerstadt, Hong, & Diamond, 1994). The prefrontal–executive composite was based on performance in two tasks from the cognitive neuroscience literature and a measure of false alarm rate across three previously described tasks. Supplementary evidence on prefrontal–executive function was obtained in two other tasks that yield noncontinuous measures not suitable for incorporating into a continuous composite measure.

GO–NO-GO TASK. In the go–no-go task, children are told that they will see pictures of different animals on the computer screen, and that they should press the space bar every time they see an animal, but never when they see the cat. Items are pseudorandomized, and the cat appears on 10 out of 60 trials. This task assesses the child's ability to inhibit a prepotent response, an ability that has been linked to prefrontal cortex (PFC) in both lesion studies (Drewe, 1975) and pediatric and adult fMRI (Casey et al., 1997).

SPATIAL WORKING MEMORY TASK. The Spatial Working Memory Task, adapted from Hughes (1998) involves eight identical opaque bottles, each with a ball placed inside. The bottles are placed in a rectangular container with one compartment for each bottle, arranged in two rows of four. The child is instructed to point to any bottle; when the child points to a bottle, the ball is removed. The entire container (containing all eight bottles) is then covered with a cloth, spun, and returned to its original position relative to the child. The child is then instructed to pick a new bottle that he or she has not already looked in. The game is repeated until all eight balls are found, or until 15 trials are conducted, whichever comes first. Performance is measured by an average of the z-score for the total number of trials, and the negative z-score of the number of correct trials until the first error. Spatial working memory has been linked to prefrontal cortex function, particularly dorsolateral PFC, in both lesion studies (Pigott & Milner, 1994) and functional neuroimaging studies, including fMRI of pediatric populations (Thomas et al., 1999).

FALSE ALARMS. Finally, we included in the executive composite an average of the total number of false alarms observed in the incidental face memory, incidental picture memory, and shape detection tasks, combined. Although overall error rate in these tasks is not a measure of executive function, the pattern of errors at any given level of performance is indicative of prefrontal executive function, with a preponderance of false alarms consistent with dysfunction (Parkin, Bindschaedler, Harsent, & Metzler, 1996; Schacter, Curran, Gulluccio, Milberg, & Bates, 1996).

Additional Measures of Prefrontal–Executive Function

Three additional tasks assessing prefrontal–executive function were administered. They were not included in the composite because of the noncontinuous nature of their dependent measures.

DIMENSIONAL CHANGE CARD SORT TASK. In the Dimensional Change Card Sort Task, developed by Zelazo, Frye, and Rapus (1996), children are shown a set of cards with pictures of a yellow car, a yellow flower, a blue car, and a blue flower. They are then asked to sort the cards by color or by shape (the color game and the shape game, the order of which is randomly assigned). After the first sorting, which is easily accomplished, they must then sort on the other dimension, and number of cards sorted perseveratively on the first dimension is recorded. If the child has continued to sort by the first dimension, the task is administered again, with verbal prompts for each card reminding the child of which game they are playing. This task is based on the Wisconsin Card Sort Test (WCST), a clinical test sensitive to prefrontal damage (Drewe, 1974), which also activates the prefrontal cortex of normal participants in fMRI (Konishi et al., 1999).

THEORY OF MIND. The theory of mind is a cluster of abilities related to the understanding of mental states, including the ability to view the world from a different individual's point of view. All of our tasks were adapted from Frye and colleagues (Frye, Zelazo, & Palfai, 1995). The understanding of appearance as opposed to reality (Flavell, Green, & Flavell, 1990) was tested using the following task: a band-aid box containing crayons is shown and the child is asked what is inside. After eliciting the answer "band-aids," the child is shown the contents of the box and is asked what he originally thought was in the box, and what it looks like is in the box. Understanding of false belief was then tested within this task by then producing a toy horse and asking the child what the horse thinks is in the box. A second false belief task (Wimmer & Perner, 1983) involved an unexpected transfer of a toy from one box to another; the child was asked to report which box the toy horse, who had not "seen" the transfer, thought contained the toy. Theory of mind has been associated with medial PFC in lesion studies (Stone, Baron-Cohen, & Knight, 1998) and using fMRI (Gallagher et al., 2000).

DELAY OF GRATIFICATION. In each of the three testing sessions for delay of gratification, after the first task, the child is shown a variety of stickers. The child is given the choice of having either one sticker immediately or of having more stickers later, specifically two, three, or four stickers at the end of the first, second, and third session, respectively. The ability to delay gratification has been decreased in rats (Newman, Gorenstein, & Kelsey, 1983) with lesions to the orbital PFC and is noted clinically in patients with prefrontal damage (Stuss & Benson, 1984).

Result

Means and standard deviations of the scores for each task and each socio-economic status group are shown in Table 10.2, demonstrating the absence of ceiling or floor effects, in that all means were at least one standard deviation from the maximum possible score and from chance. Scores were converted to z scores relative to the entire distribution of 60 children, thus putting all task performances on a common scale, and a composite score for each neurocognitive system was then constructed by averaging the relevant z scores.

The composite scores from the five neurocognitive systems were submitted to repeated measures MANOVA with factors socioeconomic status and gender. This showed a main effect for socioeconomic status, $F(1, 57) = 13.6, p < 0.0005$, replicating the well-documented socioeconomic status gap in global measures of cognitive performance. There was no main effect of gender, $F(1, 57) = 1.7$, $p = 0.19$), nor did gender interact with neurocognitive system, $F(4, 54) = 1.12$, $p = 0.35$.

The question of whether socioeconomic status equally predicts the variance in performance of all neurocognitive systems or else disproportionately explains the variance in certain systems was answered by testing the socioeconomic status by neurocognitive system interaction. This interaction was significant, $F(4, 54) = 2.77, p < 0.036$.

Five independent t tests were then carried out on the composite scores for each system, comparing the performance of low and middle-socioeconomic-status children. To correct for the effect of multiple tests on the likelihood of a type I error, a significance cutoff of $p < 0.01$ was adopted. The two neurocognitive systems for which differences were predicted showed highly significant effects of socioeconomic status. For the left perisylvian–language system, $t(58) = -4.3$,

Table 10.2. Raw Scores, Effect Sizes, t and p Values for Tasks, and Composite Measures

Task	Mean (*SD*) low socioeconomic status / Mean (*SD*) middle-socioeconomic status	Effect size	t	p
Left perisylvian–language		**1.10**	**−4.3**	**<0.0001**
PPVT (percentile)	28.2 (22.1)/ 52.7 (22.0)	1.11	−4.3	<0.0001
TROG (percentile)	30.3 (24.2)/41.1 (23.9)	0.45	−1.7	0.09
TOPA (percentile)	34.2 (24.8)/ 61.5 (24.8)	1.10	−4.3	<0.0001
Prefrontal–executive		**0.68**	**−2.8**	**0.007**
Go-no-go correct no-gos (10)	7.4 (1.8) / 8.2 (1.2)	0.56	−2.2	0.03
Spatial-working memory	# correct trials (15): 11.1 (2.5)/11.1 (2.8) # trials till 1st error: 4.9 (1.5)/ 6.3 (1.6)	0.31	−1.2	0.23
False alarms	Shape detection: 0.3 (0.6) / 0.2 (0.4) Picture memory: 1.7 (2.1) / 0.9 (0.9) Face memory: 2.9 (4.5) / 1.2 (2.1)	0.58	−3.0	0.004
Occipitotemp–visual		**0.48**	**−1.8**	**0.08**
Color imagery (17)	13.8 (2) / 14.9 (1)	0.70	−2.7	0.01
Shape detection (20)	18.5 (1.5) / 18.6 (1.5)	0.09	−.33	0.74
Parietal–spatial		**0.48**	**−1.9**	**0.07**
Line orientation (30)	21.2 (2.3)/ 21.9 (2.9)	0.27	−1.04	0.30
Mental rotation (30)	26.0 (4)/ 27.8 (3)	0.48	−1.8	0.07
Medial temporal–memory		**0.04**	**−.16**	**0.87**
Picture memory (40)	36.6 (2.8)/36.9 (2.0)	−0.06	−.53	0.60
Face memory (50)	41.5 (6.1)/41.1 (5.3)	0.14	0.25	0.81

Note. Significant differences were observed on language and executive composites, but not visual, visuospatial, or memory composites. PPVT = Peabody Picture Vocabulary Test; TOPA = Test of Phonological Awareness; TROG = Test of Reception of Grammar.

$p < 0.0001$. For the prefrontal–executive system, t (58) = −2.8, $p < 0.007$. In contrast, there were nonsignificant trends in the occipitotemporal–visual cognition system and the parietal–spatial system composites, t (58) = −1.8, $p < 0.08$ and t (58) = −1.9, $p < 0.07$, respectively, and no difference in the medial temporal–memory composite, t (58) = −0.16, $p < 0.87$. The same pattern held among the subset of children for whom a pediatrician verified the parent-reported medical history: large differences were observed across socioeconomic status in performance of tasks comprising the language (t (28) = −3.4; p < 0.002) and executive (t (28) = −3.2; p < 0.003) composites, whereas no differences were seen in the visual (t (28) = −1.7; p < 0.11), visuospatial (t (28) = −1.1; p < 0.32) or memory (t (28) = −1.6; p < 0.13) composites. The lack of socioeconomic status effect on memory performance cannot be attributed to a ceiling effect. However, the retention interval was brief, in that the test was administered immediately following the learning phase, and it would be of interest to assess incidental retention over a longer duration.

The size, as well as the significance level, of socioeconomic status effects on the different neurocognitive system composites suggest disproportionate effects on language and executive function: As shown in Table 10.2, the effect size for the left perisylvian–language system was 1.1 standard deviations between the means of the groups and for the prefrontal–executive system it was 0.68 standard deviations. Both are considered large by conventional effect size criteria, whereas the size of the (nonsignificant) effects of socioeconomic status on the remaining system composites varied from .04 to .48 standard deviations.

With so many tasks, and with unequal numbers of tasks being used to assess different neurocognitive systems, it is important to verify that the disproportionate effect on the language and executive systems is manifest at the individual task level, rather than emerging artifactually from a more thorough sampling of those systems. Table 10.2 summarizes the inferential statistics on socioeconomic status differences for the 13 individual tasks with continuous measures. Of the posterior brain systems, one of the occipitotemporal–visual cognition tasks showed a significant socioeconomic status effect, and one of the parietal–spatial tasks showed a trend, whereas the other tasks used to test those systems, and the two medial temporal–memory tasks, showed no differences. In contrast, within the left perisylvian–language system, two tasks showed highly significant differences and one showed a trend. Norms for the PPVT show that the socioeconomic status effect can be interpreted as depressed performance for the low-socioeconomic-status children rather than enhanced performance for the middle-socioeconomic-status children, in that the mean percentiles of the two groups were 28th and 53rd, respectively.

Among the three continuous measures of prefrontal–executive function, two showed significant differences: go–no-go and the false alarm index. The task that did not show a difference, spatial working memory, was similar to a task found to be insensitive to prefrontal dysfunction in children with early treated phenylketonuria (Diamond, 1990).

Turning next to the noncontinuous measures of prefrontal–executive function, we continue to find trends suggestive of a socioeconomic-status disparity in two of the three tasks. In the dimensional change card sort task, the majority of children scored either five or zero correct on each trial (i.e., either all correct or all incorrect), requiring ordinal regression analysis. In the first rule change block there was a nonsignificant trend for better performance by the middle-socioeconomic-status children (22 of 30 vs. 15 of 30 children with errorless blocks, for middle and low socioeconomic status respectively; pseudo R-squared = 0.051; p < 0.075). In the second rule change block, performed only by children who made errors in the first, three of eight middle-socioeconomic-status children and four of 15 low-socioeconomic-status children had error-free blocks. Combining both blocks, with the assumption that perfect performance on the first would have been followed by perfect performance on the second (required because such children were not given the second block), the difference between groups was near-significant (pseudo R-squared = 0.06; $p < 0.054$).

Performance on the combined set of theory of mind problems, which included appearance–reality and false belief tasks, did not show a significant difference across socioeconomic status overall. However, for false belief alone, ordinal regression analysis showed a borderline difference, such that middle-socioeconomic-status children were more likely to perform more accurately (pseudo R squared = .059; p < 0.056).

In contrast to most of the other prefrontal–executive tasks, the delay of gratification task showed no socioeconomic status effect at all. The two groups were equally inclined to delay their sticker reward to get more stickers (mean delay choices 22.6 for both low and middle-socioeconomic-status children), and this was true even for the most tempting delay problem, of one sticker now or just two later (18 vs. 20 children, out of 30, choosing to delay gratification for low and middle socioeconomic status, respectively, Chi-square = 0.287, $p < 0.59$). Note that this null result, which cannot be attributed to floor or ceiling effects, conflicts with the reported finding of a socioeconomic status difference in this characteristic in adults (Goodman, 1992). Although null results are always ambiguous, this is consistent with the preference for smaller immediate rewards in low socioeconomic status adults emerging as a pragmatic adaptation to the contingencies of their adult lives rather than as a result of childhood socioeconomic status influences on the maturation of prefrontal cortex.

Taken together, the results from the individual continuous and noncontinuous measures generally affirm the conclusions drawn from the composite measures, namely that socioeconomic status differences may be apparent in multiple systems, but that socioeconomic status differences are most pronounced in the functioning of the left perisylvian–language and prefrontal–executive systems. Whether or not socioeconomic status effects might be found in memory tasks with longer delays, and whether or not the trends toward socioeconomic status effects in parietal–spatial and temporo–occipital vision would remain and attain significance in a larger sample are open questions.

An important limitation of behavioral tests as assays for specific neurocognitive systems is that they always engage multiple systems, most commonly language and prefrontal–executive function regardless of the system of interest. Thus, it is possible that the socioeconomic status differences in nonlinguistic and nonexecutive tasks, such as the color imagery task that showed a significant difference between groups in the present study, result from the linguistic and executive demands implicit in the task. It is also possible that socioeconomic status influences many neurocognitive systems. Although the present data do not allow us to conclude that socioeconomic status effects are confined to particular neurocognitive systems, they do demonstrate that socioeconomic status effects are significantly disproportionate for those systems as tested here.

Socioeconomic Status and Neurocognitive Development:
From Correlation to Causality

The research just described shows an association between socioeconomic status and performance on tests of language and executive function. So far we have been referring to the effect of socioeconomic status on these functions, but the data are equally consistent with the reverse direction of causality. Perhaps families with higher innate language and executive abilities tend to acquire and maintain a higher socioeconomic status. Note that the direction of causality is an empirical issue. It should not be confused with the ethical issue of society's obligation to help children of any background become educated, productive citizens.

Direction of Causality

Given that the direction of causality is an empirical issue, are there data that bear on the issue? The methods of behavioral genetics research can, in principle, tell us about the direction of causality in the association between socioeconomic status and the development of specific neurocognitive functions, although these methods have yet to be applied to the question. They have been applied to a related question, however, namely the heritability of IQ and socioeconomic status. Cross-fostering studies of within—and between—socioeconomic status adoption suggest that roughly half the IQ disparity in children is experiential (Capron & Duyme, 1989; Schiff & Lewontin, 1986). If anything, these studies are likely to err in the direction of underestimating the influence of environment because the effects of prenatal and early postnatal environment are included in the estimates of genetic influences. A recent twin study by Turkheimer and colleagues (2003) showed that, within low-socioeconomic-status families, IQ variation is far less genetic than environmental in origin. Additional evidence comes from studies of when, in a child's life, poverty was experienced. Within a given family that experiences a period of poverty, the effects are greater on siblings who were young during that period (Duncan et al., 1994). In sum, multiple sources of evidence indicate that socioeconomic status does indeed have an effect on cognitive development, although its role in the specific types of neurocognitive system development investigated here is not directly known.

Mechanisms of Causation: Somatic

The environments of low and middle-socioeconomic-status children differ in innumerable ways, many of which could affect brain development. Some of these would affect brain development by their direct effects on the body. Three somatic factors have been identified as significant risk factors for low cognitive achievement by the Center for Children and Poverty (1997): Inadequate nutrition, substance abuse (particularly prenatal exposure), and lead exposure.

Malnutrition can effect brain development and brain function, permanently and acutely, prenatally and postnatally. Few people in the United States suffer severe malnutrition. The more common problems are mild-to-moderate protein-energy malnutrition (PEM), which involves shortages of both protein and calories, and iron deficiency. There is disagreement whether mild-to-moderate PEM has a significant effect on children's neurocognitive development (e.g., see Ricciuti, 1993; Sigman, 1995). The issue has been difficult to resolve for two reasons. First, unlike severe malnutrition, which causes easily measurable differences in body size and other clinical and biochemical indices, mild-to-moderate PEM is difficult to detect. Researchers must therefore rely on intrinsically less reliable data from family reports of food intake. Second, nutritional status is strongly correlated with a host of other family and environmental variables likely to affect neurocognitive development, including all of the potential mechanisms of causation to be reviewed. Supplementation programs have the potential to deconfound these variables, but are often coupled with other, nonnutritional forms of enrichment or simply affect children's lives in nonnutritional ways which perpetuate the confound (e.g., children given school breakfast are absent and late less often). A report from the Center on Hunger, Poverty and Nutrition Policy (CHPNP, 1998) concludes that it is possible that mild-to-moderate PEM has little effect on its own. Iron-deficiency anemia afflicts about one quarter of low income children in the United States (CHPNP, 1998) and is known to impair brain development when severe. Numerous correlational studies have shown an association between iron-deficiency anemia and lower cognitive performance, although the confounding between nutrition and other aspects of the environment make it difficult to assess the impact of iron deficiency per se. Supplementation studies have shown that normalizing iron levels increases motor and behavioral development in severely anemic infants. It has been suggested that nutritional effects on cognitive development may be mediated, at least in part, by an indirect mechanism whereby lethargy of parent as well as child results in less interaction, support and stimulation (Valenzuela, 1997). In sum, the consensus regarding the role of nutrition in the cognitive outcomes of poor children has shifted over the past few decades, from primary cause to a factor that contributes indirectly and through synergizies with other environmental disadvantages (CHPNP, 1998).

Lead is a neurotoxin that accumulates in the bodies of low-socioeconomic-status children at far greater levels, on average, than in the middle-socioeconomic-status children (Brody et al., 1994). Lead-containing paint is present in most older homes, and when walls and woodwork are not well maintained the resulting peeling and powdered paint is ingested and inhaled by young children. A meta-analysis of low-level lead exposure on IQ indicates estimated that every 10 ug/dL increase in lead is associated with a 2.6 point decrease in IQ (Schwartz, 1994). As with nutrition, the effect of lead synergizes with other environmental factors and is more pronounced in low-socioeconomic-status children (Bellinger, Leviton, Waternaux, Needleham, & Rabinowitz, 1987). For example, low iron stores render children more susceptible to environmental lead (CHPNP, 1998).

Prenatal substance exposure is a third factor that affects low-socioeconomic-status children disproportionately. Maternal use of alcohol, tobacco and marijuana have all been associated with adverse cognitive outcomes in children (Chasnoff et al., 1998). The sharpest socioeconomic status differences in prenatal substance exposure involve cocaine. Although animal models indicate general effects on fetal well-being because of dopaminergic restriction of blood flow and specific effects on brain development (Mayes, 2002), epidemiological studies have found the effects on cognitive performance to be subtle (Hurt et al., 1998; Mayes, 2002; Vidaeff & Mastrobattista, 2003). For example, the low-socioeconomic-status 4-year-olds of Hurt's cohort, whose average IQ was 81, served as control research participants for a cohort with prenatal cocaine exposure, whose average IQ was a statistically indistinguishable 79. This lack of difference contrasts with the substantial difference between both low socioeconomic-status groups' scores and those of typical middle-socioeconomic-status children.

The set of potentially causative factors just reviewed is far from complete. There are socioeconomic status gradients in a wide variety of physical health measures, many of which could affect children's neurocognitive development through a variety of different mechanisms (Adler et al., 1997). Having briefly reviewed the most frequently discussed factors, we turn now to a consideration of the psychological differences between the experiences of low and middle-socioeconomic-status children that could affect neurocognitive development.

Mechanisms of Causation: Psychological

As with potential physical causes, the set of potential psychological causes for the socioeconomic status gap in cognitive achievement is large, and the causes are likely to exert their effects synergistically. Here we will review research on differences in cognitive stimulation, parenting styles, and stress levels.

One difference between low- and middle-socioeconomic-status families that seems predictable, even in the absence of any other information, is that low-socioeconomic-status children are likely to have fewer toys and books and less exposure to zoos, museums, and other cultural institutions because of the expense of such items and activities. This is indeed the case (Bradley, Corwyn, McAdoo, et al., 2001) and has been identified as a mediator between socioeconomic status and measures of cognitive achievement (Bradley & Corwyn, 1999; Brooks-Gunn & Duncan, 1997; McLoyd, 1998). Such a mediating role is consistent with the results of neuroscience research with animals, showing that complex environments that afford exploration and activity to young animals have a favorable effect on brain development (Greenough, Black, & Wallace, 1987).

Other types of cognitive stimulation are also less common in low-socioeconomic-status homes, for example parental speech designed to engage the child in conversation (Adams, 1998). The average number of hours of one-on-one picture book reading experienced by children before kindergarten entry has been estimated at 25 for low-socioeconomic-status children and between 1000 and 1700 for middle-socioeconomic-status children (Adams, 1990). Thus, in addition to material limitations, differing parental expectations and concerns also contribute to differences in the amount of cognitive stimulation experienced by low and middle-socioeconomic-status children.

There is a huge literature on socioeconomic status differences in parenting attitudes and behavior, with certain findings robust across geographic and ethnic variation (Bradley, Corwyn, Burchinal, et al., 2001). These include a greater middle-socioeconomic-status emphasis on verbal skills, independence, achievement and creativity and a greater low-socioeconomic-status emphasis on obedience and staying out of trouble (Adams, 1990). Physical punishment is more common in low-socioeconomic-status homes, and harsh physical punishment has been associated with lower IQ (Brooks-Gunn, 1999).

The lives of low-socioeconomic-status individuals tend to be more stressful for a variety of reasons, some of which are obvious: concern about providing for basic family needs, dangerous neighborhoods, and little control over one's work life. Recent research in neuroscience with animal models has uncovered mechanisms by which such psychological stress is transduced into neurochemical changes involving cortisol and other stress hormones (McEwen, 2001). High levels of stress in early life, such as prolonged maternal separation, impacts the development of medial temporal and prefrontal brain systems involved in the regulation of the stress response (Meany et al., 1996). Lupien and colleagues (Lupien, King, Meany, & McEwen, 2001) extended the study of stress and neuroendocrine function to children and socioeconomic status by assessing salivary cortisol levels in 6-year-olds and found higher levels in children of lower socioeconomic status.

Conclusion

Children's neurocognitive development is affected by their socioeconomic status. We know that the effects are large and that they have real world importance, insofar as they influence school and job success. We also know some of the ways in which socioeconomic status influences neurocognitive development, although the list of potential factors is long and synergisms among factors are likely to be as important as any individual factor's contribution.

The present study was an attempt to add to our understanding of the effect of socioeconomic status on neurocognitive development by asking: What systems of the developing brain are affected by socioeconomic status? The conclusion of this preliminary study is that the left perisylvian–language system and prefrontal–executive system are most sensitive to childhood socioeconomic status. This conclusion has implications for basic science and for the well-being of low-socioeconomic-status children.

The basic science implications of our research concern the influences of the environment on human brain development. The animal literature on environmental influences on brain development typically contrasts plain laboratory cages with so-called enriched environments, but both types of environment are unnatural for the animals and it is difficult to say whether the contrast is between an impoverished versus normal environment, normal versus enriched, or impoverished versus enriched. The present results concern our species in its normal environment. The less advantaged children here were not raised in isolated orphanages or subjected to socially unacceptable abuse or neglect. They were among the estimated 12 million American children living below the poverty line. Our results show that variation in childhood environment, within the normal range for our society, leads to large and significant effects on the development of at least two brain systems important for language and executive function. Additional studies are under way to address some of the new questions raised by these preliminary findings. For example, prefrontal cortex is a large region with distinct subsystems. How is the development of each of these subsystems influenced by socioeconomic status? Which of the many differences between low and middle-socioeconomic-status children's lives contribute to the differences observed in language and executive function?

At a practical level, our approach to the study of socioeconomic status has the potential to inform a number of real-world issues. As we learn more about the neurocognitive profile of socioeconomic status, we become better equipped to counteract its negative effects through more targeted intervention programs. Knowledge of the specific neurocognitive effects of socioeconomic status also allows a more specific and hence more sensitive search for causal factors which can then be addressed directly. Finally, by framing the socioeconomic status gap in cognitive achievement in terms of brain development, we can see it as a matter public health in addition to economic opportunity.

References

Adams, B. N. (1998). *The family: A sociological interpretation.* New York: Harcourt Brace.

Adams, M. J. (1990). *Beginning to read: Thinking and learning about print.* Urbana-Champaign: University of Illinois, Reading Research and Education Center.

Adler, N. E., & Ostrove, J. M. (1999). Socioeconomic status and health: What we know and what we don't. *Annals of the New York Academy of Science, 896,* 15–206.

Bellinger, D., Leviton, A., Waternaux, C., Needleham, H., & Rabinowitz, C. (1987). Longitudinal analyses of prenatal and postnatal lead exposure and early cognitive development. *New England Journal of Medicine, 316,* 1037–1043.

Benton, A. L., Varney, N. R., & des Hamsher, K. (1978). Visuospatial judgement: A clinical test. *Archives of Neurology, 35,* 364–367.

Bishop, D. V. M. (1983). *The test for reception of grammar.* Manchester, England: University of Manchester, Age and Cognitive Performance Research Centre.

Blumstein, S. E. (1994). Impairments of speech production and speech perception in aphasia. *Philosophical Transactions of the Royal Society of London. Series B Biological Sciences, 346,* 29–36.

Booth, J., MacWhinney, B., Thulborn, K., Sacco, K., Voyvodic, J., & Feldman, H. (1999). Functional organization of activation patterns in children: fMRI during 3 different cognitive tasks. *Progress in Neuro-Psychopharmacology and Biological Psychiatry, 23,* 271–294.

Bourgeois, J. P., Goldman-Rakic, P. S., & Rakic, P. (1994). Synaptogenesis in the prefrontal cortex of rhesus monkeys. *Cerebral Cortex, 4,* 78–96.

Bradley, R. H., & Corwyn, R. F. (1999). Parenting. In C. L. B. Tamis-Lemonda (Ed.), *Child psychology: A handbook of contemporary issues* (pp. 339–362). New York: Psychology Press.

Bradley, R. H., & Corwyn, R. F. (2002). Socioeconomic status and child development. *Annual Review of Psychology, 53,* 371–399.

Bradley, R. H., Corwyn, R. F., McAdoo, H. P., & Garcia Coll, C. (2001). The home environments of children in the United States. Part 1: Variations by age, ethnicity, and poverty–status. *Child Development, 72,* 1844–1867.

Bradley, R. H., Corwyn, R. F., Burchinal, M., McAdoo, H. P., & Garcia Coll, C. (2001). The home environments of children in the United States. Part 2: relations with behavioral development through age 13. *Child Development, 72,* 1868–1886.

Brody, D. J., Pirkle, J. L., Kramer, R. A., Flegal, K. M., Matte, T. D., Gunter, E. W., et al. (1994). Blood lead levels in the U.S. population. *Journal of the American Medical Association, 272,* 277–281.

Brooks-Gunn, J., & Duncan, G. J. (1997). The effects of poverty on children. *The Future of Children, 7,* 55–71.

Brooks-Gunn, J., Duncan, G. J., & Britto, P. R. (1999). Are socioeconomic gradients for children similar to those for adults? In D. P. Keating & C. Hertzman (Eds.), *Developmental health and the wealth of nations* (pp. 94–149). New York: Guilford Press.

Capron, C., & Duyme, M. (1989). Assessment of effects of socio-economic status on IQ in a full cross-fostering study. *Nature, 340,* 552–554.

Case, R. (1992). The role of the frontal lobes in the regulation of cognitive development. *Brain and Cognition, 20,* 51–73.

Casey, B. J., Thomas, K. M., Welsh, T. F., Badgaiyan, R. D., Eccard, C. H., Jennings, J. R., et al. (2000). Dissociation of response conflict, attention selection, and expectancy with functional magnetic resonance imaging. *Proceedings of the National Academy of Sciences of the United States of America, 97,* 8728–8733.

Casey, B. J., Trainor, R. J., Orendi, J. L., Schubert, A. B., Nystrom, L. E., Giedd, J. N., et al. (1997). A developmental functional MRI study of prefrontal activation during performance of a go–no-go task. *Journal of Cognitive Neuroscience, 9,* 835–847.

Center on Hunger, Poverty, and Nutrition Policy. (1997). *Poverty and brain development.* Retrieved April 1997 from http://www.centeronhunger.org

Center on Hunger, Poverty, and Nutrition Policy. (1998). *Statement on the link between nutrition and cognitive development in children.* Retrieved December 2004 from http://www.center onhunger.org

Chasnoff, I. J., Anson, A., Hatcher, R., Stenson, H., Laukea, K., & Randolph, L. A. (1998). Prenatal exposure to cocaine and other drugs. Outcome at four to six years. *Annals of the New York Academy of Sciences, 846,* 314–328.

Chugani, H. T., Phelps, M. E., & Mazziotta, J. C. (1987). Positron emission tomography study of human brain functional development. *Annals of Neurology, 22,* 487–497.

De Vreese, L. P. (1991). Two systems for color naming defects. *Neuropsychologia, 29,* 1–18.

Diamond, A. (1990). The development and neural bases of memory functions as indexed by the A(not)B and delayed response tasks in human infants and infant monkeys. In A. Diamond (Ed.), *The development and neural bases of higher cognitive functions* (pp. 267–317). New York: New York Academy of Science.

Diamond, A., Prevor, M. B., Callender, G., & Druin, D. P. (1997). *Prefrontal cortex cognitive deficits in children treated early and continuously for PKU.* Chicago: University of Chicago Press.

Drewe, E. A. (1974). The effect of type and area of brain lesion on Wisconsin Card Sorting Test performance. *Cortex, 10,* 159–170.

Drewe, E. A. (1975). Go–no-go learning after frontal lobe lesions in humans. *Cortex, 11,* 8–16.

Duncan, G. J., Brooks-Gunn, J., & Kiebanov, P. K. (1994). Economic deprivation and early-childhood development. *Child Development, 65,* 296–318.

Duncan, G. J., Yeung, W. J., Brooks-Gunn, J., & Smith, J. R. (1998). How much does childhood poverty affect the life chances of children? *American Sociological Review, 63,* 416–423.

Flavell, J., Green, F., & Flavell, E. (1990). Developmental change in young children's knowledge about the mind. *Cognitive Development, 5,* 1–27.

Frye, D., Zelazo, P. D., & Palfai, T. (1995). Theory of mind and rule-based reasoning. *Cognitive Development, 10,* 483–527.

Gallagher, H., Happe, F., Brunswick, N., Fletcher, P., Frith, U., & Frith, C. (2000). Reading the mind in cartoons and stories: An fMRI study of "theory of mind." *Neuropsychologia, 38,* 11–21.

Gerstadt, C., Hong, Y., & Diamond, A. (1994). The relationship between cognition and action: Performance of 3 1/2 to 7 year-old children on a Stroop-like day-night test. *Cognition, 53,* 129–153.

Giedd, J. N., Jeffries, N. O., Blumenthal, J., Castellanos, F. X., Vaituzis, A. C., Fernandez, T., et al. (1999). Childhood-onset schizophrenia: Progressive brain changes during adolescence. *Biological Psychiatry, 46,* 892–898.

Goodglass, H., & Kaplan, E. (1982). *The Assessment of Aphasia and Related Disorders* (2nd ed.). Philadelphia: Lea & Febiger.

Goodman, N. (1992). *Introducing sociology.* New York: HarperCollins.

Greenough, W. T., Black, J. E., & Wallace, C. S. (1987). Experience and brain development. *Child Development, 58,* 539–559.

Haxby, J. V., & Hoffman, A. (2002). Human neural systems for face recognition and social communication. *Biological Psychiatry, 51,* 59–67.

Hollingshead, A. B. (1975). *Four factor index of social status.* New Haven, CT: Yale University Department of Sociology.

Howard, R., Fytche, D., Branes, J., McKeefrey, D., Ha, Y., Woodruff, R., et al. (1998). The functional anatomy of imaging and perceiving colour. *NeuroReport, 9,* 1019–1023.

Hughes, C. (1998). Executive function in preschoolers: Links with theory of mind and verbal ability. *British Journal of Developmental Psychology, 16,* 233–253.

Hurt, H., Malmud, E., Braitman, L., Betancourt, L. M., Brodsky, N. M., & Giannetta, J. M. (1998). Inner-city achievers: Who are they? *Archives of Pediatric and Adolescent Medicine, 152,* 993–997.

Huttenlocher, P. R., & Dabholkar, A. S. (1997). Developmental anatomy of prefrontal cortex. In N. A. Krasnegor, G. R. Lyon, & Goldman-Rakic (Eds.), *Development of the prefrontal cortex* (pp. 167–178). Baltimore: Brookes.

Johnson, M. H. (1997). *Developmental cognitive neuroscience.* Cambridge, MA: Blackwell.

Just, M. A., Carpenter, P. A., Keller, T. A., Eddy, W. F., & Thulborn, K. R. (1996). Brain activation modulated by sentence comprehension. *Science, 274,* 114–116.

Klingberg, T., Hedehus, M., Moseley, M. E., Poldrack, R. A., & Gabrieli, J. (1999). Myelination and organization of the frontal white matter in children: A diffusion tensor MRI study. *Neuroreport, 10,* 2817–2821.

Konishi, S., Nakajima, K., Uchida, I., Kikyo, H., Kameyama, M., & Miyashita, Y. (1999). Common inhibitory mechanism in human inferios prefrontal cortex revealed by event-related functional MRI. *Brain, 122,* 981–991.

Lupien, S. J., King, S., Meany, M. J., & McEwen, B. S. (2001). Can poverty get under your skin? Basal cortisol levels and cognitive function in children from low and high socioeconomic status. *Development and Psychopathology, 13,* 653–676.

Mayes, A. R., Meudell, P. R., & Neary, D. (1978). Must amnesia be caused by either encoding or retrieval disorders? In M. M. Grueneberg, E. Morris, & R. N. Sykes (Eds.), *Practical aspects of memory.* London: Academic Press.

Mayes, A. R., Meudell, P. R., & Neary, D. (1980). Do amnesiacs adopt inefficient encoding strategies with faces and random shapes? *Neuropsychologia, 18,* 527–541.

Mayes, L. C. (2002). A behavioral teratogenic model of the impact of prenatal cocaine exposure on arousal regulatory systems. *Neurotoxicology and Teratology, 24,* 385–395.

McCarthy, R. A., & Warrington, E. K. (1990). *Cognitive neuropsychology: A clinical introduction.* New York: Academic Press.

McEwen, B. S. (2001). Plasticity of the hippocampus: Adaptation to chronic stress and allostatic load. *Annals of the New York Academy of Sciences, 933,* 265–277.

McLoyd, V. C. (1998). Socioeconomic disadvantage and child development. *American Psychologist, 53,* 185–204.

Meany, M. J., Diorio, J., Francis, D., Widdowson, J., LaPlante, P., Caldji, C., et al. (1996). Early environmental regulation of forebrain glucocorticoid receptor gene expression: Implications for adrenocortical responses to stress. *Developmental Neuroscience, 18,* 49–92.

Mercy, J. A., & Steelman, L. C. (1982). Familial influence on the intellectual attainment of children. *American Sociological Review, 47,* 532–542.

Milner, A. D., & Goodale, M. A. (Eds.). (1995). *The visual brain in action.* Oxford, England: Oxford Science.

Newman, J., Gorenstein, E., & Kelsey, J. (1983). Failure to delay gratification following septal lesions in rats. *Personality and Individual Differences, 4,* 147–156.

Noble, K. G., Norman, M. F., & Farah, M. J. (in press). Neurocognitive correlates of socioeconomic status in kindergarten age children. *Developmental Science.*

Parkin, A. J., Bindschaedler, C., Harsent, L., & Metzler, C. (1996). Pathological false alarm rates following damage to the left frontal cortex. *Brain and Cognition, 32,* 14–27.

Pigott, S., & Milner, B. (1994). Capacity of visual short-term memory after unilateral frontal or anterior temporal lobe resection. *Neuropsychologia, 32,* 969–981.

Posner, M. I., & Rothbart, M. K. (1998). Attention, self-regulation and consciousness. *Transactions of the Philosophical Society of London, 353,* 1915–1927.

Pugh, K., Shaywitz, B., Constable, R., Schwaywitz, R., Skudlarski, P., Fulbright, R., et al. (1996). Cerebral organization of component processes in reading. *Brain, 119,* 1221–1238.

Ratcliff, G. (1979). Spatial thought, mental rotation and the right cerebral hemisphere. *Neuropsychologia, 17,* 49–54.

Ricciuti, H. N. (1993). Nutrition and mental development. *Current Directions in Psychological Science, 2,* 43–46.

Rothi, L. J., McFarling, D., & Heilman, K. M. (1982). Conduction asphasia, syntactic alexia, and the anatomy of syntactic comprehension. *Archives of Neurology, 39,* 272–275.

Schacter, D. L., Curran, T., Galluccio, L., Milberg, W. P., & Bates, J. F. (1996). False recognition and the right frontal lobe: A case study. *Neuropsychologia, 34,* 793–808.

Schiff, M., & Lewontin, R. (1986). *Education and class: The irrelevance of IQ genetic studies.* Oxford, England: Clarendon Press.

Schwartz, J. (1994). Low-level lead exposure and children's IQ: A meta-analysis and search for a threshold. *Environmental Research, 65,* 42–55.

Sigman, M. (1995). Nutrition and child development. *Current Directions in Psychological Science, 4,* 52–55.

Snodgrass, J. G., & Vanderwart, M. (1980). A standardized set of 260 pictures: Norms for name agreement, image agreement, familiarity, and visual complexity. *Journal of Experimental Psychology: Human Learning and Memory, 6,* 174–215.

Squire, L. (1992). Memory and the hippocampus: A synthesis of findings from rats, monkeys and humans. *Psychological Review, 99,* 195–231.

Stone, V. E., Baron-Cohen, S., & Knight, R. T. (1998). Frontal lobe contributions to theory of mind. *Cognitive Neuroscience, 10,* 640–656.

Stuss, D. T., & Benson, D. F. (1984). Neuropsychological studies of the frontal lobes. *Psychological Bulletin, 95,* 3–28.

Thomas, K. M., King, S. W., Franzen, P. L., Welsh, T. F., Berkowitz, A. L., Noll, D. C., et al. (1999). A developmental functional MRI study of spatial working memory. *NeuroImage, 10,* 327–338.

Thompson-Schill, S. L., Swick, D., Farah, M. J., D'Esposito, M., Kan, I. P., & Knight, R. T. (1998). Verb generation in patients with focal frontal lesions: A neuropsychological test of neuroimaging findings. *Proceedings of the National Academy of Sciences of the United States of America, 95,* 15855–15860.

Turkheimer, E., Haley, A., Waldron, M., D'Onofrio, B., & Gottesman, I. (2003). Socioeconomic status modifies heritability of IQ in young children. *Psychological Science, 14,* 623–628.

Valenzuela, M. (1997). Maternal sensitivity in a developing society: The context of urban poverty and infant chronic undernutrition. *Developmental Psychology, 33,* 845–855.

Vidaeff, A. C., & Mastrobattista, J. M. (2003). In utero cocaine exposure: A thorny mix of science and mythology. *American Journal of Perinatalogy, 20,* 165–172.

Walsh, K. W. (1978). *Neuropsychology: A clinical approach.* New York: Churchill-Livingstone.

Warrington, E. K., & James, M. (1991). *Visual object and space perception battery.* Gaylord, MI: National Rehabilitation Services.

Whitehurst, G. J. (1997). Language process in context: Language learning in children reared in poverty. In L. B. Adamson & M. A. Romski (Eds.), *Research on communication and language disorders: Contribution to theories of language development* (pp. 233–266). Baltimore: Brookes.

Wimmer, H., & Perner, J. (1983). Beliefs about beliefs: Representation and constraining function of wrong beliefs in young children's understanding of deception. *Cognition, 13,* 103–128.

Zelazo, P., Frye, D., & Rapus, T. (1996). An age-related dissociation between knowing rules and using them. *Cognitive Development, 11,* 37–63.

11

Development and Plasticity of Human Cognition

Helen J. Neville

It was a wonderful pleasure and great honor to participate in the exuberant celebration of Michael Posner. We were all reminded of the many monumental contributions that he has made and, indeed, of the paradigm shifts that he has initiated within psychology and in the formation of the field of cognitive neuroscience. Whereas most of us, in the course of our careers, research the phenomenon we study primarily from one perspective and one level of analysis, Posner has radically shifted course about once every 7 years, and each of these changed perspectives has led to significant changes in the nature of our fields. These shifts are beautifully summarized in the opening chapter by Keele and Mayr, as well as in Posner's chapter at the end of the book. As many others have noted, we could have looked at what Posner was doing at any one point in time and predicted the kinds of approaches we would be taking in the next few years. We still could.

One of the questions that has captured Posner's attention lately, and that has occupied the minds of parents, educators, and philosophers for millennia, is at the heart of the research I describe here: the nature of and the interactions between biological constraints and the role of experience (i.e., input from the environment) in human cognitive and neural development. Although this issue has long been central in philosophical and societal debate, it has only been systematically researched over the past 40 years. It began, of course, with the work of Hubel and Weisel and their followers, who reported marked effects of visual experience on the development of visual cortex and related functions (Wiesel & Hubel, 1965). Until recently, most of this research had been performed with nonhuman animals and was concerned with sensory development. With the advent of noninvasive methods for imaging the human brain, we can now more directly seek answers to the following questions about the human mind/brain: to what extent do different brain systems possess intrinsic

I am grateful to my current and former students and postdoctoral fellows whose research is summarized here and to Linda Heidenreich and Ean Huddleston for help in manuscript preparation. This research is supported by National Institutes of Health, DC00128 and DC00481.

constraints that make them capable of processing some but not other types of information? What is the role of inputs from the environment in specifying the functional properties of the brain regions they contact?

These are fundamental questions about who we are and where we come from. On a practical level, answers to these questions can contribute information important to the design of educational and rehabilitative programs in that they will help us identify the functional brain systems that are most modifiable and the time periods when they are most modifiable.

Over the past several years, we have approached these questions in two ways. In the first, we have compared cerebral organization in normally hearing, seeing, monolingual, speaking adults with that observed in individuals who have had altered sensory and/or language experience. This latter group includes deaf and blind adults, bilinguals who learned English at different ages, and those who have learned a visual/manual language. The second approach has been to compare brain organization in children of different ages and stages of cognitive development, as well as before and after various intervention programs. In these studies we have employed both event related potentials (ERPs) and functional magnetic resonance imaging (fMRI) methods. We have studied the development of perceptual/attentional systems, as well as the development of the language systems of the brain.

In this chapter, I first review the structural development of the human brain, relevant literatures on sensory plasticity, as well as our newer studies of sensory plasticity and development. Second, I review literature relevant to the plasticity and development of the language systems, as well as our newer studies along these lines.

Structural Development of the Human Brain

The structural development of the human brain displays a protracted time course of postnatal development that in some regions does not reach maturity until the third decade of life. There is great variability in the rate of maturation of different neural systems and subsystems, as indexed by the extent of dendritic branching, number of dendritic spines, neuronal size and density, number and type of synapses, pharmacological composition, gray-to-white matter ratios, and cortical volumes (Chugani, Phelps, & Mazziotta, 1987; Huttenlocher & Dabholkar, 1997; Neville, 1998). Following this protracted development, the mature human brain is a complex mosaic of systems and subsystems that display considerable specificity in their functional properties. A burgeoning literature in animals has identified several molecular and genetic factors important in specifying aspects of the initial anatomy and physiology of developing brain systems (Kahn & Krubitzer, 2002; Krubitzer & Huffman, 2000; Silver et al., 2001; Taha & Stryker, 2002). The overarching goals of the research summarized in this chapter are to characterize both biological constraints and the degree to which, and the time periods during which, the functional specializations of different neural systems are dependent on and modifiable by experience in human development.

Cortical Plasticity

During the past 30 years, research with animals has documented marked and specific effects of both sensory deprivation and training on the organization of cortical areas that represent a particular sensory system and on the development of remaining sensory modalities (Frost, Boire, Gingras, & Ptito, 2000; Metin & Frost, 1989; Roe, Pallas, Kwon, & Sur, 1992; Sur & Garraghty, 1986; von Melchner, Pallas, & Sur, 2000). These studies have shown that some neural systems and associated behavioral capabilities are affected by such experience only during specific time periods (sensitive periods) and that different systems have different sensitive periods. For example, within the visual system, the development of acuity, orientation preferences, ocular dominance columns, stereopsis, and photoptic and scotopic vision display different sensitive periods (Harwerth, Smith, Duncan, Crawford, & von Noorden, 1986; Horton & Hocking, 1997; Hubel & Wiesel, 1977; Mitchell, 1990). This variability in the timing of experience-dependent modifiability likely arises in part from subsystem differences in rate of maturation, extent and timing of redundant connectivity, and presence of chemicals and receptors known to be important in plasticity. By contrast, some neural systems appear not to be constrained by sensitive periods. For example, remapping of the representation of the visual fields following retinal lesions can occur throughout life (Kaas et al., 1990), as can remapping of the primary cortical representation of the digits following amputation or training (Merzenich & Jenkins, 1993).

Recent studies support the view that in humans, as in other animals, there is considerable variability in experience-dependent plasticity. For example, if cataracts are not removed by 5 months of age, visual acuity never reaches normal values, and if convergent input to the two eyes is not achieved by 11 months of age, stereopsis is not acquired (Maurer, Lewis, Brent, & Levin, 1999; Tychsen, 2001). In addition, lack of patterned visual input during the first 2 to 6 months of age results in permanent deficits in configural but not featural aspects of face processing (Le Grand, Mondloch, Maurer, & Brent, 2001), and visual deprivation occurring as late as 6 years of age leads to deficits in the ability to orient to peripheral visual information (Kovacs, Polat, Pennefather, Chandna, & Norcia, 2000). In contrast, other systems appear not to show sensitive period effects in humans: for example, amputation in adults results in reorganization of cortical areas that formerly represented the lost limb (Elbert et al., 1994; Ramachandran, Rogers-Ramachandran, & Stewart, 1992).

Plasticity Within the Visual System
After Auditory Deprivation

Motion and Color

Anatomical, physiological, and psychophysical evidence from several lines of investigation has defined the distinction between the dorsal visual pathway, projecting from V1 to parietal cortex, that includes structures important for the processing of spatial location and motion, and the ventral visual pathway, projecting from V1 to anterior inferior temporal cortices, that includes systems important for processing color and form information (Tootell et al., 1995; Ungerleider & Mishkin, 1982). Additional evidence confirmed that the central visual field is largely represented along the ventral pathway while the peripheral visual fields are largely represented along the dorsal pathway (Baizer, Ungerleider, & Desimone, 1991). Consistent with this, in several early studies we observed that sensory and attentional processing of visual information presented to the central and peripheral visual fields elicits activity in different neural systems in normally hearing adults. Furthermore, we observed that congenital auditory deprivation—but not the acquisition of American Sign Language (ASL)—results in enhanced detection of motion and enhanced ERPs in the peripheral (but not the central) visual fields (Neville, 1995; Neville & Lawson, 1987a, 1987b, 1987c; Neville, Schmidt, & Kutas, 1983). These results suggested the hypothesis that the dorsal visual pathway might be more modified following auditory deprivation than the ventral pathway. To test this, we employed stimuli designed to selectively activate either the parvocellular neurons that project strongly (but not solely, see Sawatari & Callaway, 1996; Stoner & Albright, 1993) to the ventral pathway or the magnocellular system that projects strongly to the dorsal pathway. The parvo system is highly responsive to color information and to stimuli of high spatial frequency, while the magno system is responsive to motion and to stimuli of low spatial frequency and low contrast (Livingstone & Hubel, 1988; Merigan & Maunsell, 1993).

We tested normal hearing and congenitally deaf participants. Peripheral stimuli were presented 8° from the central (foveal) stimulus in the upper and lower left and right visual fields. The parvo stimuli were isoluminant blue and green high spatial frequency gratings (adjusted for the cortical magnification factor) continuously visible at all locations. The eliciting stimulus was a color change: randomly at one location, the blue bars changed to red for 100 ms. The magno stimuli consisted of low spatial frequency gratings of light and dark gray bars with a low luminance contrast. The eliciting stimulus consisted of the bars at one location (random) moving transversely to the right for 100 ms. Research participants fixated centrally and monitored all locations for the rare occurrence of a black square (Armstrong, Hillyard, Neville, & Mitchell, 2002).

In normal hearing adults, the color and motion stimuli elicited ERPs that differed in their componentry, latencies, and distributions and were consistent with the hypothesis that these stimuli activated distinct neural systems (see Figure 11.1). An early positivity (100 ms) focal to medial occipital regions was largest in response to motion, and a later, lateral (130 ms) positivity was larger in response to color changes. In addition, the latency of the negativity around 170 ms (N170) was faster to motion stimuli. The earliest responses (P100, P130) were similar in deaf and hearing participants, suggesting that processing within early visual cortical areas may be unaffected by auditory deprivation. The N170 component was similar in response to color changes in deaf and hearing participants, but in response to motion it was significantly larger and was distributed more anteriorly in deaf than hearing participants. These results were more pronounced for peripheral than central motion. These results are consistent with the hypothesis that early auditory deprivation has more

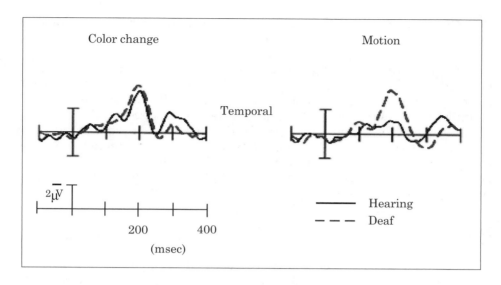

Figure 11.1. ERPs to color and motion in normally hearing and congenitally deaf adults.

pronounced effects on the functions of the dorsal than the ventral visual pathway.

Motion Processing

To more precisely identify the visual areas that might underlie the enhanced behavioral and ERP responses to motion in deaf participants, we employed the fMRI technique (details in Bavelier et al., 2000). In particular, we tested the hypothesis that area MT/MST, shown in previous studies to be responsive to motion and attention to motion, displays enhanced activation in deaf as compared to hearing individuals. Participants included hearing and congenitally, genetically deaf individuals who viewed alternating blocks of static dots and flow fields of moving dots. Motion flow fields strongly recruit the motion pathway, including the motion-selective area MT/MST (O'Craven, Rosen, Kwong, Triesman, & Savoy, 1997; Tootell & Taylor, 1995). On separate runs, participants attended the center or the periphery (6° to 8pdg) of the display to detect luminance changes.

MT/MST was identified individually for each participant, and the data were analyzed for each participant by computing the temporal correlation between the magnetic resonance signal and a reference function for each voxel. Analyses of the extent of activation in MT/MST revealed that whereas MT/MST recruitment was comparable across populations when the center of the visual field was monitored, deaf individuals displayed greater MT/MST activation than hearing participants when the peripheral visual field was monitored. This finding indicates a specific modulation of attention to peripheral moving stimuli in the deaf and suggests that changes in MT may have contributed to the behavioral and ERP effects described in our previous research (Neville & Lawson, 1987b).

To further characterize the altered MT activation in the deaf, we used structural equation modeling to estimate the strength of cortical connections between early visual areas (V1/V2), area MT/MST, and part of the posterior parietal cortex (PPC; Beauchamp & DeYoe, 1996; Buchel & Friston, 1997; McIntosh & Gonzalez-Lima, 1994). During attention to the center the connectivity was comparable across groups but during the attend-periphery condition the effective connectivity between MT/MST and PPC was increased in the deaf as compared with the hearing participants. This finding suggests that the enhanced responsiveness to peripheral motion in deaf individuals may be specifically linked to attention.

Motion Velocity

In another study we further characterized the effects of auditory deprivation on several motion sensitive areas and separated them from the effects of the acquisition of ASL (Bavelier et al., 2001). Congenitally deaf and hearing native signers and normally hearing controls attended either the center or periphery of a moving flow field to detect a transient acceleration of the dots. Cortical areas V1/V2, MT/MST, V3A, PPC, and posterior superior temporal sulcus (pSTS) were delineated separately for each individual on the basis of functional and anatomical criteria. We observed marked and specific differences in the recruitment of motion-related areas as a function of sensory and language experience. Both of the hearing populations displayed better behavioral performance and greater recruitment of MT/MST under central than peripheral attention, whereas the opposite pattern was observed in deaf signers, indicating enhanced peripheral attention following early deafness per se. In addition, deaf signers, but neither of the hearing populations, displayed an overall increase in the activation of the PPC, supporting the view that parietal functions are significantly modified after early auditory deprivation. Finally, only in deaf signers did attention to motion velocity result in enhanced recruitment of the pSTS, establishing for the first time functionally specific compensatory plasticity in this polymodal area following altered sensory experience. These results add support to the proposal that experience-dependent plasticity in humans can be highly specific and is likely constrained both by features of the biological substrates involved and by functionally driven processes.

Plasticity and Vulnerability

We are also conducting studies to assess the hypothesis that the same subsystems that display the greatest plasticity and are enhanced in deaf are more vulnerable in development and will display the greatest deficits in developmental disorders, including dyslexia. A considerable body of research has reported selective deficits among at least some individuals with dyslexia in functions mediated by the magnocellular, but not parvocellular, visual pathway

(Cornelissen, Richardson, Mason, Fowler, & Stein, 1995; Demb, Boynton, Best, & Heeger, 1998; Everatt, Bradshaw, & Hibbard, 1999; Hansen, Stein, Orde, Winter, & Talcott, 2001; Lovegrove, Martin, & Slaghuis, 1986; Sperling, Lu, Manis, & Seidenberg, 2003; Talcott et al., 1998; Talcott, Hansen, Assoku, & Stein, 2000). Individuals with dyslexia also show reduced (Demb et al., 1998) or even nonsignificant (Eden et al., 1996) activations in motion-sensitive areas MT/MST when processing motion stimuli, and evidence from postmortem autopsies reveal abnormalities in the magnocellular, but not parvocelluar, layers of the lateral geniculate nucleus (LGN) of adults with dyslexia (Livingstone, Rosen, Drislane, & Galaburda, 1991).

This pattern of results has been taken to support the hypothesis that the deficits observed in visual M-pathway functions are reflective of a more general deficit in magnocellular pathways throughout the brain, including those in the medial geniculate nucleus that subserve auditory processing (Stein & Talcott, 1999). An impairment in fast-processing streams could result in poor temporal integration of stimuli from the two modalities during reading, which requires both visuo-orthographic and auditory-phonological representations of letters (Breznitz & Maya, 2003). However, previous research on M- versus P-pathway visual deficits has been criticized on the grounds that the tasks used to assess M-pathway function are typically more attentionally and cognitively demanding than those used to assess P-pathway function (Newport, Bavelier, & Neville, 2002). It remains unclear whether the selective M-pathway deficits observed could be explained by attentional differences in individuals with dyslexia. Preliminary data from our laboratory suggests that the visual deficit in adults with dyslexia persists even for simple tasks of M-pathway function. In this study, research participants indicated at which point in the far periphery (~50 degrees) they detected a dot moving along a straight trajectory to the center of vision. Whereas deaf participants detected the moving dots significantly sooner (i.e., at greater eccentricity) than controls, participants with dyslexia detected them significantly later than controls. By contrast, both groups performed within normal limits on a detection task in the center of the visual field (Darves & Neville, 2004). These data together with other lines of evidence (Atkinson et al., 1997; Bellugi, Lichtenberger, Jones, Lai, & George, 2000) support the hypothesis that more modifiable systems may be more vulnerable in developmental disorders.

Development of Visual Pathways

As noted above, many investigators have documented greater vulnerability of the dorsal pathway in developmental disorders including dyslexia (Eden et al., 1996; Galaburda & Livingstone, 1993; Livingstone et al., 1991; Lovegrove, 1993; Lovegrove, Garzia, & Nicholson, 1990) and Williams Syndrome (Atkinson et al., 1997; Bellugi et al., 2000). In recent experiments, we tested the hypothesis that the greater modifiability/vulnerability may arise in part from a longer maturational period of the dorsal system, because the available evidence (largely psychophysical) on this is currently conflicting (Dobkins & Teller, 1996; Hickey, 1977; Hollants-Gilhuijs, Ruijter, & Spekreijse, 1998a, 1998b; Johnson,

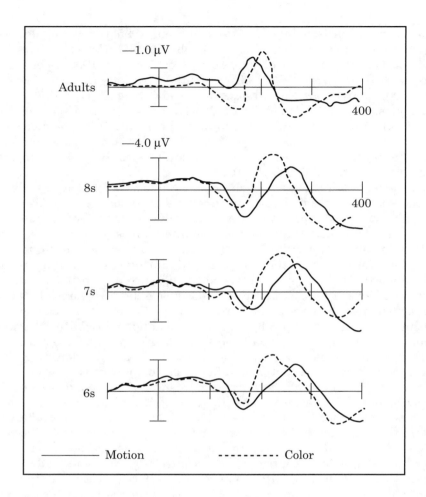

Figure 11.2. ERPs to motion and color in adults and 6-, 7-, and 8-year-old children.

Mareschal, & Csibra, 2001). We recently tested 30 children aged 6 to 10 on the same paradigm that we employed in studies of deaf and hearing adults (Armstrong et al., 2002; Mitchell & Neville, in press). ERPs were recorded to the same stimuli employed in the study of ERPs to color and motion in adults described above and in Armstrong and colleagues (2002). Whereas in adults the latency of the N100 responses to the motion stimuli were significantly earlier than the N100 latencies to the color stimuli (consistent with studies of single neurons in the two pathways), all of the children displayed the opposite pattern: responses to motion were slower than those to color (see Figure 11.2). Moreover, latencies to the color changes were equivalent in the children and adults, but the children's responses to motion were slower than those of adults (see Figure 11.2).

Additional evidence for the relative immaturity of the motion responses was evident in the amplitudes: whereas the color and motion responses were of equivalent amplitude in the adults, in children the ERP amplitudes to motion were considerably smaller than were those to color. Thus these data are consistent with the hypothesis that the greater vulnerability/modifiability of the dorsal stream may be due in part to its more protracted development.

Plasticity Within the Auditory System After Visual Deprivation

To test the generality of the results from our studies of the effects of auditory deprivation, we conducted studies of the effects of visual deprivation on the development of remaining sensory systems. While relatively little is known about the organization of the auditory system, as in the visual system there are larger (magno) cells in the medial geniculate nucleus that conduct faster than the smaller parvo cells, and recent evidence suggests that there may be dorsal and ventral processing streams with different functional specializations (Rauschecker, 1995). Furthermore, animal and human studies of blindness have reported changes in parietal cortex (i.e., dorsal pathway). To determine whether parallel patterns of plasticity occur following auditory and visual deprivation, we developed two auditory paradigms that are parallel to visual paradigms that we had previously employed in studies of the deaf.

In the first paradigm, participants detected infrequent pitch changes in a series of tones that were preceded by different interstimulus intervals (Röder, Rösler, & Neville, 1999). Congenitally blind participants were faster at detecting the targets and displayed ERPs that were less refractory, that is, recovered amplitude faster than normally sighted participants. These results are parallel to those from our study showing faster amplitude recovery of the visual ERP in deaf than hearing participants (Neville et al., 1983) and suggest that rapid auditory and visual processing may show specific enhancements following sensory deprivation.

In a second experiment, we tested the generality of our finding of a specific enhancement of the representation of the visual periphery in deaf participants. We first developed a paradigm to compare attention to central and peripheral auditory space in normal controls (Teder-Salejarvi, Hillyard, Roder, & Neville, 1999). Participants attended selectively to brief noise bursts delivered in free-field via central and peripheral arrays of speakers extending from midline to 90° right of center. In separate runs, participants selectively attended to the center or rightmost speaker to detect infrequent target stimuli occurring at that location. Behavioral detection rates and concurrently recorded ERPs indicated that attentional gradients were steeper for the central than the peripheral array, indicating that attention can be more sharply focused on sound sources directly in front of the listener. In the study of congenitally blind participants, we observed that, when attending central auditory space, blind and sighted participants displayed similar localization abilities and ERP attention effects. By contrast, blind participants were superior to sighted controls at localizing sounds in peripheral auditory space, and ERPs revealed sharper tuning of early spatial attention mechanisms in the blind research participants only when attending to the periphery (Röder, Teder-Sälejärvi, et al., 1999).

Differences in the scalp distribution of brain electrical activity between the two groups suggested a compensatory reorganization of visual areas in the blind that may contribute to the improved spatial resolution for peripheral sound sources.

Development of Sustained Attention

The results showing increased auditory attention in the blind suggest that auditory attention may also be a system displaying a long developmental time course. Behavioral studies have indicated that auditory selective attention skills develop throughout childhood at least until adolescence. Both the abilities to selectively attend to relevant stimuli and to successfully ignore irrelevant stimuli improve progressively with increasing age across childhood (Doyle, 1973; Geffen & Sexton, 1978; Geffen & Wale, 1979; Hiscock & Kinsbourne, 1980; Lane & Pearson, 1982; Maccoby & Konrad, 1966; Sexton & Geffen, 1979; Zukier & Hagen, 1978). The ability to shift attention quickly and effectively also develops across childhood at least until adolescence (Andersson & Hugdahl, 1987; Geffen & Wale, 1979; Hiscock & Kinsbourne, 1980; Pearson & Lane, 1991). Furthermore, there is some evidence that background noise creates greater masking effects for younger children as compared to adolescents or adults (Elliott, 1979).

While behavioral studies offer evidence for the development of selective auditory attention in school-age children, there is little comparable electro-physiological evidence from children in this age range. One published study employed a typical ERP dichotic listening attention paradigm using tones and syllables with young participants (groups with mean age 8 and 14 years; Berman & Friedman, 1995). The expected effect of attention, the difference between the N100 amplitude to the stimuli when attended relative to when unattended (Nd), was observed in all participants, with Nd amplitude increasing with age and more so for syllables than for tones. The primary effect of age appeared to be smaller negative ERPs elicited by stimuli in the unattended channel, which the authors suggested might reflect a narrowing of attentional focus or greater facility in suppressing unattended inputs with age (Berman & Friedman, 1995).

Moreover, in the selective auditory attention paradigm, the expected N100 attention effect was observed in control adolescents aged 12 to 14 (Loiselle, Stamm, Maitinsky, & Whipple, 1980). Other studies have reported similar attention effects in adolescent boys (Lovrich, Stamm, Maitinsky, & Whipple, 1983; Zambelli, Stamm, Maitinsky, & Loiselle, 1977).

Recently we developed a dichotic listening task to characterize the development of sustained auditory attention across the early school age years. Our paradigm was modeled after those that we and many others have employed in adults (Hillyard, Hink, Schwent, & Picton, 1973; Röder, Teder-Sälejärvi et al., 1999; Spezio, Sanders, & Neville, 2000; Teder-Salejarvi, Hillyard et al., 1999; Teder-Salejarvi, Munte, Sperlich, & Hillyard, 1999; Woods, Hillyard, & Hansen, 1984) and was designed to be difficult enough to demand focused selective attention while maintaining the same physical stimuli, arousal levels, and task demands during attended and unattended runs (Coch, Sanders, & Neville, in press; Woods, Coch, Sanders, Skendzel, & Neville, 2002; Woods, Coch, Sanders, Skendzel, Capek, et al., 2002). Two children's stories (one read by a man, one by a woman) were presented concurrently from speakers to the left and right of a central monitor. Participants were asked to attend to one story and ignore the other. Every so often the stories switched sides and a pointing cartoon character on the monitor reminded research participants to follow the attended story to the other side. Superimposed on the stories were linguistic and nonlinguistic "probe" stimuli to which ERPs were recorded: these were a 100 ms token of the syllable "ba" and a 100 ms "buzz" created by scrambling 6 ms segments of the "ba" so that the frequency spectra, and other acoustic characteristics, of the two stimuli were the same. After the experiment, participants were asked questions about the attended and unattended stories.

We first tested 16 adults on this paradigm. ERPs to the attended and unattended probes elicited the classic effects of auditory attention including enhanced negativity to the probes when attention was directed toward as compared to away from them (see Figure 11.3). We then tested 24 6-year-olds, 24 7-year-olds, and 24 8-year-olds. Behaviorally, all groups performed well; however, the percent of correctly answered questions increased with age for the attended story and decreased for the unattended story. The ERPs from each age group showed clear and significant attention effects, however, these were opposite in polarity to those in the adults; that is, when attended, probes elicited greater positivity than when unattended (see Figure 11.3). Whereas the attention effect to the nonlinguistic probes displayed an anterior, bilateral distribution in all groups, the attention effect to the linguistic probes displayed a different distribution in the children and adults. In the adults it was posterior and left-lateralized, while in the children it displayed a bilateral and central distribution. These results indicate that slowly developing, nonidentical neural systems mediate aspects of linguistic and nonlinguistic auditory attention.

Plasticity Within the Language Systems

It is reasonable to propose that the principles and mechanisms that govern the development of sensory systems also guide the development of neural systems important for language processing. In particular, to the extent that different subsystems within language depend on nonidentical neural substrates with different developmental time courses, it is likely that they display different patterns of experience-dependent plasticity. One way this question has been investigated is to compare cerebral organization in adults who learned language at different times in development.

Delayed Second Language Acquisition

Changes in several postnatal maturational processes during neural development have been implicated as potential mechanisms underlying sensitive period phenomena. Lenneberg (1967) hypothesized that maturational processes

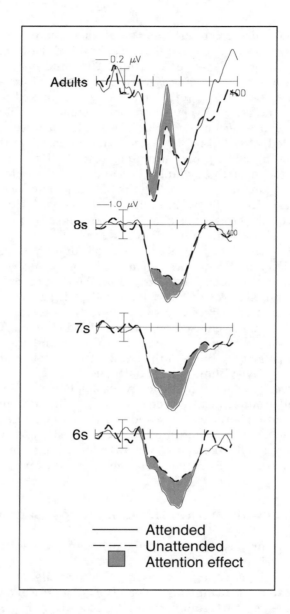

Figure 11.3. Effects of selective auditory attention on ERPs from adults and 6-, 7-, and 8-year-old children.

similar to those that govern sensory and motor development may also constrain capabilities for normal language acquisition. In this study we investigated the hypothesis that maturational constraints may have different effects on the development of the functional specializations of distinct subsystems within language (Weber-Fox & Neville, 1996a). Research participants were Chinese/ English bilinguals who were exposed to English at different points in development. ERPs and behavioral responses were obtained as participants read sentences that included semantic anomalies, three types of syntactic violations (phrase structure, specificity constraint, and subjacency constraint), and their controls. Accuracy in judging the grammaticality of the different types of syntactic sentences and their associated ERPs were affected by delays in second language exposure as short as 4 to 6 years. By comparison, the N400 response and the behavioral accuracy in detecting semantic anomalies were altered only in participants who were exposed to English after 11 to 13 and 16 years of age, respectively. Furthermore, the type of ERP changes concomitant with delays in exposure were qualitatively different for semantic and syntactic processing. All groups displayed a significant N400 effect in response to semantic anomalies, however, the peak latencies of the N400 elicited in bilinguals who were exposed to English between 11 to 13 and greater than 16 years occurred later, suggesting a slight slowing in processing. For syntactic processing, ERP differences associated with delays in exposure to English were observed in the morphology and distribution of components. Our findings are consistent with the view that maturational changes significantly constrain the development of neural systems relevant for language, and in addition, that subsystems specialized for processing different aspects of language display different sensitive periods (Weber-Fox & Neville, 1996b).

In similar groups of monolingual and Chinese/English bilinguals, we compared responses to open-class (nouns, verbs) and closed-class words (articles, conjunctions) embedded in normal, written sentences to further explore the hypothesis that there are different effects of delays in language exposure on the processing of words that carry different amounts of semantic and grammatical information (Weber-Fox & Neville, 1999). Whereas the latencies and distributions of the N350 response to open-class words were similar in all groups of research participants, the peak latency of the N280 response to closed-class words was significantly delayed in all groups exposed to English after 7 years of age. In both of these studies we were able to separately assess the contributions of age of exposure and years of experience. The results clearly show that delays in L2 acquisition have more pronounced effects on grammatical than on lexical-semantic aspects of language processing.

Sentence Processing in American Sign Language

The study of ASL provides a rare opportunity to determine which of the language relevant aspects of cerebral organization are independent of the modality of language production and perception and so therefore may be candidates for biological universals of language. It also provides the opportunity to isolate those modality specific effects that are determined by the nature of language experience. In several studies we have attempted to extend to ASL our findings from studies of English that suggest that different subsystems mediate aspects of grammatical and semantic processing and that subsystems have different sensitive periods. In addition, we investigated different hypotheses that could account for why, in earlier studies (Neville, Mills, & Lawson, 1992), our deaf participants did not display evidence for specialization within the left hemisphere when processing English. It could be, as has been proposed by several investigators, that the left hemisphere is specifically specialized for the auditory encoding of language and for the visual to auditory or phonological decoding that characterizes reading by hearing, but not deaf participants. However, if grammatical recoding is an important variable in the development of left hemisphere specialization for a language (Liberman, 1974), then deaf participants should display left hemisphere specialization when processing ASL. In fact, a sizeable literature has accumulated during the past 100 years that suggests lesions to the left hemisphere impair the use of signed languages in much the same way as is the case for spoken languages (Corina, 2002; Hickok, Bellugi, & Klima, 1996; Poizner, Klima, & Bellugi, 1987). Less is known about the contribution of the right hemisphere to sign language, as fewer right hemisphere damaged deaf patients have been studied systematically, and the results are not consistent. However language comprehension deficits have been reported following right hemisphere damage (Corina, 2002; Poizner & Tallal, 1987).

In one study, ERPs were recorded from deaf and hearing native signers as they viewed ASL signs that formed sentences. The results suggest that there are constraints on the organization of the neural systems that mediate formal languages and that these are independent of the modality through which language is acquired. These include different specializations of anterior and posterior cortical regions for aspects of grammatical and semantic processing and a bias for the left hemisphere to mediate aspects of mnemonic functions in language. In addition, the results suggest that the nature and timing of sensory and language experience significantly impacts the development of the language systems of the brain. Effects of early acquisition of ASL include an increased role for the right hemisphere and parietal cortex that occurs in both hearing and deaf native signers. An increased role of posterior temporal and occipital areas occurs only in deaf native signers and thus may be attributable to auditory deprivation (Neville et al., 1997).

Because our ERP evidence for right hemisphere activation in ASL was unexpected given previous clinical studies, we began a series of fMRI studies to more precisely specify and compare the brain areas active in processing ASL and English. Effects of deafness, age of language acquisition, and bilingualism were assessed by comparing results from (a) normally hearing, monolingual, native speakers of English; (b) congenitally, genetically deaf, native signers of ASL who learned English late and through the visual modality; and (c) normally hearing bilinguals who were native signers of ASL and speakers of English. All groups, hearing and deaf, processing their native language, English or ASL, displayed strong and repeated activation within classical language areas of the left hemisphere. Deaf native signers reading English did not display activation in these regions suggesting that the early acquisition of a natural language is important in the expression of the strong bias for these areas to mediate language, independently of the form of the language. In addition, native signers (hearing and deaf) processing ASL (but not English) displayed extensive activation of homologous areas within the right hemisphere, indicating that the specific processing requirements of the language also in part determine the organization of the language systems of the brain (Bavelier et al., 1998; Neville et al., 1998). Since our publication, other groups have performed related studies and report evidence of left and right temporal lobe activation during ASL processing (Petitto et al., 2000; Soederfeldt et al., 1997).

To assess the possibility that the increased right hemisphere activation to signed as compared to written sentences might be attributable to factors including the presence of prosody in ASL (but not in written sentences), we compared activation for written and signed sentences with that for sentences spoken by a person that was both heard and viewed. Activations for spoken and written sentences were both strongly left-lateralized, in contrast to the activations for ASL sentences, which were bilateral or larger over the right hemisphere (Capek et al., 1998; Capek, Bavelier, Corina, & Neville, 2004).

In a recent study we assessed the hypothesis that for ASL, like other natural languages, there may be a sensitive period beyond which exposure to the language is associated with deficits in acquisition and altered brain organization (Newman, Bavelier, Corina, Jezzard, & Neville, 2002). As described above, when native learners of ASL view ASL sentences, in addition to left hemisphere (LH) activation, they show a unique pattern of extensive right hemisphere (RH) activation. In this study, we demonstrated that one of these RH regions, the angular gyrus, is active when hearing native signers process ASL, but not when late learners, who acquired ASL after puberty, do so. This suggests the existence of a sensitive period, during which, but not after, the acquisition of ASL results in the recruitment of the angular gyrus for language processing. This result has implications both for language acquisition, and more broadly for an understanding of age-related changes in neuroplasticity (Newman et al., 1998; Newman et al., 2002).

Delay in First Language Acquisition

As noted above, many investigations of the critical or sensitive period for language have examined the effects of delays in second language acquisition on proficiency and brain organization for that language. While many effects of such delays have been reported, it has been difficult to determine whether these are the result of changes in cortical maturation that limit the time periods when a language can be optimally acquired or whether they are due to interference from the first language. The deaf population provides a rare and powerful opportunity to address this issue because more than 90% of deaf people are born to hearing parents who try to teach their children to speak and/or lipread. Understandably many fail and thus the acquisition of a first language is delayed until they are exposed to ASL. Behavioral studies of such individuals indicate that with increasing age of acquisition, proficiency decreases (Mayberry, 1993, 2003; Mayberry & Eichen, 1991; Mayberry, Lock, & Kazmi, 2002; Newport, 1990), however there have not been studies of brain organization of delayed first language acquisition. We have recently studied groups of deaf individuals who acquired ASL either from birth, from 2 to 10 years or between 11 and 21 years of age (Capek, 2004; Capek et al., 2003; 2004). We employed the ERPs paradigm described above to separately assess the effects of delayed acquisition of a first language on semantic and syntactic processing. The results clearly show that the N400 index of semantic processing displayed the same amplitude, latency, and cortical distribution in all three groups of participants. However the early anterior negativity thought to index more automatic aspects of syntax was only evident in those who acquired ASL before the age of 10 years. These results strongly indicate that interference effects from a first language are not necessary to observe the effects of delayed language acquisition and supports the hypothesis that there are maturational constraints that determine the optimal time period for the acquisition of a first language.

Language Processing Following Visual Deprivation

Individuals blind since birth provide another important opportunity to assess the effects of altered sensory and language experience on the development of language-relevant brain systems. We employed ERPs to test the hypothesis that auditory language processing occurs more rapidly in blind than sighted adults. We confirmed this hypothesis in two experiments, one of sentence processing and the other of auditory memory. (Röder, Rösler, & Neville, 2000; Röder, Stock, Bien, Neville, & Rösler, 2002). In addition, we hypothesized that, in the absence of visuo-spatial input to the right hemisphere (which in normal development gradually becomes less responsive to auditory language; Neville & Mills, 1997), the right hemisphere may retain the capacity for processing auditory language, resulting in a more bilateral pattern of activation in blind individuals. This hypothesis was strongly confirmed, suggesting that many factors, including age of acquisition, modality of the language acquired, and the presence of other specialized brain systems operate together to determine the mature pattern of hemispheric specialization for language.

We also recently used fMRI to map language-related brain activity in congenitally blind adults (Röder, Stock, Neville, Bien, & Rösler, 2002). Participants listened to sentences, with either an easy or a more difficult syntactic structure, which were either semantically meaningful or meaningless. Results show that blind adults not only activate classical LH perisylvian language areas during speech comprehension, as did a group of sighted adults, but that they additionally display an activation in the homologous RH structures and in extrastriate and striate cortex. Both the perisylvian and occipital activity varied as a function of syntactic difficulty and semantic content. The results demonstrate that the cerebral organization of complex cognitive systems such as the language system is significantly shaped by the input from the environment.

Outlook: Individual Differences in Semantic and Grammatical Processing

Most of what we know about functional and neural plasticity has come from studies of adults who have had different early experiences. This is a valuable approach with clear advantages. An additional, powerful approach to these issues is to compare cognition and cerebral organization in children of different ages and stages of cognitive development and before and after specific interventions. We will likely see more of this type of research in the future as the field of developmental cognitive neuroscience grows. We have employed this approach in a few studies (Mills, Coffey, & Neville, 1993; Mills, Coffey-Corina, & Neville, 1997) and continue to extend it to other paradigms. Recently, in studying the development and role of experience in the differentiation of the semantic and syntactic subsystems described above, we adapted the stimuli we have used in studies of adults for use with children. In the course of validating this new sentence set, we demonstrated that it elicited effects comparable to those we have previously reported in adults and that, in addition, there were considerable individual differences in the data from adult participants (Pakulak et al., 2002; Yamada, Harris, Pakulak, Schachter, & Neville, 2002). In follow-up studies we compared responses to these sentences in normal, monolingual adults who scored high and low on a standardized test of grammatical knowledge—the Test of Adolescent and Adult Language–3 (TOAL-3; Hammil et al., 1994). The results clearly show the typical left-lateralized effects for closed-class words and grammatical anomalies in high-scoring individuals, but significant reductions of these effects in low-scoring individuals. These results were replicated in the visual and auditory modalities (see Figure 11.4).

We have also tested 30 children, aged 32–38 months, on these sentences. Whereas semantic anomalies elicited a clear N400 response with a bilateral posterior distribution similar to adults, the grammatical anomalies elicited an anterior negativity that tended to be larger over the left hemisphere—left anterior negativity (LAN). However, the onset of this effect was 200 ms later than that seen in adults. (Adamson, 2000; Adamson-Harris, Mills, & Neville, 2000; see Figure 11.5).

We observed considerable individual variability in these effects in the children. To assess the hypothesis that differences in language knowledge might account for this variability, we compared responses from children of the same age (35 months) who scored high (84th percentile) on tests of language (Dunn & Dunn, 1997; Semel, Wiig, & Secord, 1995) and those scoring lower (but well within normal limits—approximately 50th percentile). These analyses clearly show that the LAN effect to the grammatical anomalies is present in the high-scoring children but is not reliably present in the lower-scoring children (see Figure 11.6).

In ongoing studies, we are employing this paradigm in larger groups of 3-, 4- and 5-year-old children to determine when these systems are reliably present and distinct. In addition we are exploring the different factors that may determine the large individual differences in language knowledge and rate of maturation of these systems. Considerable behavioral data show that children with more talkative parents have higher language proficiencies than those with less talkative parents (Hart & Risley, 1999; Huttenlocher, Haight, Byrd, Seltzer, & Lyons, 1991; Huttenlocher, Vasilyeva, Cymerman, & Levine, 2002). These results can be (and have been) interpreted either as showing (a) that experience drives neural development (Hart & Risley, 1999) or (b) that genetic factors shared by parents and children determine individual differences in language proficiency and brain organization (Pinker, 2002). The problem of course is that children and parents share both genes and environment.

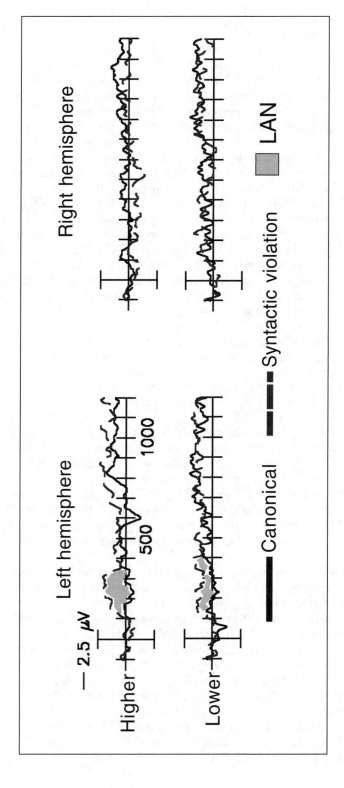

Figure 11.4. Adult native English speakers: Individuals scoring high and low on tests of grammar. ERPs to syntactically canonical and anomalous auditory sentences. LAN = left anterior negativity.

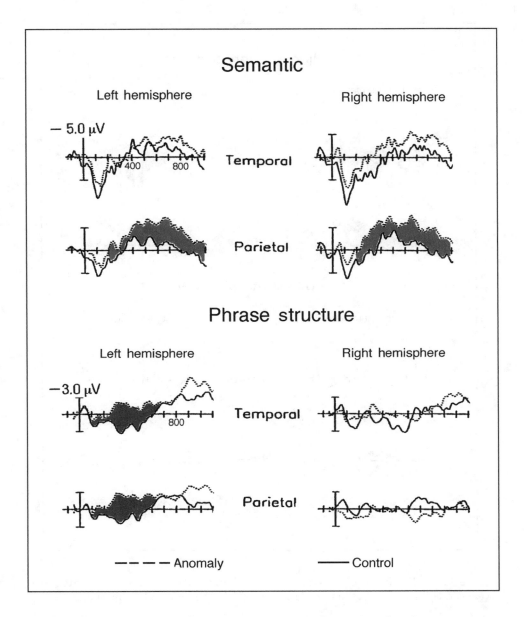

Figure 11.5. ERPs to semantically and grammatically canonical auditory sentences in 3-year-old children.

Conclusion

While it is widely accepted that language acquisition depends in part on innate, intrinsic structures and in part on environmental input, few behavioral studies have separately assessed the contribution of intrinsic and extrinsic variables

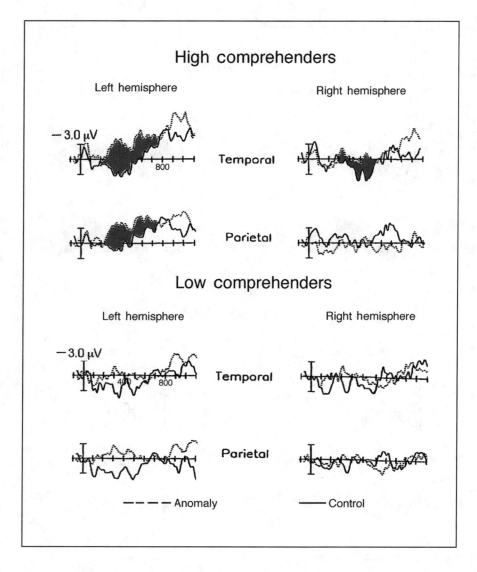

Figure 11.6. ERPs to grammatically canonical and anomalous auditory sentences in 3-year-old children scoring high or low on tests of grammar and comprehension.

to language proficiency, and none have directly assessed the effects of language input on the development of language-relevant neural systems in the developing child. Therefore in ongoing studies, we have been assessing the hypothesis that normal variation in language input from children's teachers and specific interventions drive change in these systems in normal children. This type of research will provide direct evidence on the effects of biological constraints and environmental input on language development and this, in turn, will provide practical information about the design and timing of educational and interventional programs. Furthermore, we are delighted to see that in his current work, Posner is addressing similar issues within the domain of attentional control. We are priviledged to have him as a colleague and friend.

References

Adamson, A. (2000). *Processing semantic and grammatical information in auditory sentences: Electrophysiological evidence from children and adults.* Unpublished doctoral dissertation, University of Oregon, Eugene.

Adamson-Harris, A. M., Mills, D. L., & Neville, H. J. (2000). Children's processing of grammatical and semantic information within sentences: Evidence from event-related potentials [Abstract]. *Cognitive Neuroscience Society, 7,* 58.

Andersson, B., & Hugdahl, K. (1987). Effects of sex, age, and forced attention on dichotic listening in children: A longitudinal study. *Developmental Neuropsychology, 3,* 191–206.

Armstrong, B., Hillyard, S. A., Neville, H. J., & Mitchell, T. V. (2002). Auditory deprivation affects processing of motion, but not color. *Cognitive Brain Research, 14,* 422–434.

Atkinson, J., King, J., Braddick, O., Nokes, L., Anker, S., & Braddick, F. (1997). A specific deficit of dorsal stream function in Williams Syndrome. *NeuroReport, 8,* 1919–1922.

Baizer, J. S., Ungerleider, L. G., & Desimone, R. (1991). Organization of visual inputs to the inferior temporal and posterior parietal cortex in macaques. *Journal of Neuroscience, 11,* 168–190.

Bavelier, D., Brozinsky, C., Tomann, A., Mitchell, T., Neville, H., & Liu, G. (2001). Impact of early deafness and early exposure to sign language on the cerebral organization for motion processing. *Journal of Neuroscience, 21,* 8931–8942.

Bavelier, D., Corina, D., Jezzard, P., Clark, V., Karni, A., Lalwani, A., et al. (1998). Hemispheric specialization for English and ASL: Left invariance-right variability. *NeuroReport, 9,* 1537–1542.

Bavelier, D., Tomann, A., Hutton, C., Mitchell, T., Liu, G., Corina, D., et al. (2000). Visual attention to the periphery is enhanced in congenitally deaf individuals. *Journal of Neuroscience, 20,* 1–6.

Beauchamp, M., & DeYoe, E. (1996). Brain areas for processing motion and their modulation by selective attention. *NeuroImage, 3*(Suppl.), S245.

Bellugi, U., Lichtenberger, L., Jones, W., Lai, Z., & George, M. S. (2000). The neurocognitive profile of Williams Syndrome: A complex pattern of strengths and weaknesses. *Journal of Cognitive Neuroscience, 12*(Suppl. 1), 7–29.

Berman, S., & Friedman, D. (1995). The development of selective auditory attention as reflected by event-related brain potentials. *Journal of Experimental Child Psychology, 59,* 1–31.

Breznitz, Z., & Maya, M. (2003). Speed of processing of the visual-orthographic and auditory-phonological systems in adult dyslexics: The contribution of "asynchrony" to word recognition deficits. *Brain and Language, 85,* 486–502.

Buchel, C., & Friston, K. J. (1997). Modulation of connectivity in visual pathways by attention: Cortical interactions evaluated with structural equation modeling and fMRI. *Cerebral Cortex, 7,* 768–778.

Capek, C. M. (2004). *The cortical organization of spoken and signed sentence processing in adults.* Unpublished doctoral dissertation, University of Oregon, Eugene.

Capek, C. M., Bavelier, D., Corina, D., & Neville, H. J. (2004). The cortical organization for audio-visual sentence processing: A fMRI study at 4 Tesla. *Cognitive Brain Research, 20,* 111–119.

Capek, C. M., Corina, D., Grossi, G., McBurney, S. L., Neville, H. J., Newman, A. J., et al. (2003). American Sign Language sentence processing: ERP evidence from adults with different ages of acquisition [Abstract]. *Cognitive Neuroscience Society, 10,* 105.

Capek, C. M., Corina, D., Grossi, G., McBurney, S. L., Neville, H. J., Newman, A. J., et al. (2004). *American Sign Language sentence processing: ERP evidence from adults with different ages of acquisition.* Manuscript in preparation.

Capek, C. M., Newman, A., Murray, S., Mitchell, T., Corina, D., Bavelier, D., et al. (1998). Cortical organization of auditory sentence comprehension: A functional magnetic resonance imaging (fMRI) study [Abstract]. *Society for Neuroscience Abstracts, 24,* 1174.

Chugani, H. T., Phelps, M. E., & Mazziotta, J. C. (1987). Positron emission tomography study of human brain functional development. *Annals of Neurology, 22,* 487–497.

Coch, D., Sanders, L., & Neville, H. (in press). An ERP study of selective linguistic auditory attention in children and adults. *Journal of Cognitive Neuroscience.*

Corina, D. P. (2002). Sign language aphasia. In S. E. Petersen (Ed.), *Aphasia in atypical populations.* Hillsdale, NJ: Erlbaum.

Cornelissen, P., Richardson, A., Mason, A., Fowler, S., & Stein, J. (1995). Contrast sensitivity and coherent motion detection measured at photopic luminance levels in dyslexics and controls. *Vision Research, 35,* 1483–1494.

Darves, C., & Neville, H. (2004). Two sides of neural plasticity in the dorsal visual pathway: Evidence from deaf, dyslexic and control adults [Abstract]. *Cognitive Neuroscience Society, 11,* 117.

Demb, J. B., Boynton, G. M., Best, M., & Heeger, D. J. (1998). Psychophysical evidence for a magnocellular pathway deficit in dyslexia. *Vision Research, 38,* 1555–1559.

Dobkins, K. R., & Teller, D. Y. (1996). Infant motion: Detection (M-D) ratios for chromatically defined and luminance-defined moving stimuli. *Vision Research, 36,* 3293–3310.

Doyle, A. B. (1973). Listening to distraction: A developmental study of selective attention. *Journal of Experimental Child Psychology, 15,* 100–115.

Dunn, L. M., & Dunn, L. M. (1997). *Peabody picture vocabulary test* (3rd ed.). Circle Pines, MN: American Guidance Services.

Eden, G. F., Van Meter, J. W., Rumsey, J. M., Maisog, J. M., Woods, R. P., & Zeffiro, T. A. (1996). Abnormal processing of visual motion in dyslexia revealed by functional brain imaging. *Nature, 382,* 66–69.

Elbert, T., Flor, H., Birbaumer, N., Knecht, S., Hampson, S., Larbig, W., et al. (1994). Extensive reorganization of the somatosensory cortex in adult humans after nervous system injury. *NeuroReport, 5,* 2593–2597.

Elliott, L. L. (1979). Performance of children aged 9 to 17 years on a test of speech intelligibility in noise using sentence material with controlled word predictability. *Journal of the Acoustical Society of America, 66,* 651–653.

Everatt, J., Bradshaw, M. F., & Hibbard, P. B. (1999). Visual processing and dyslexia. *Perception, 28,* 243–254.

Frost, D. O., Boire, D., Gingras, G., & Ptito, M. (2000). Surgically created neural pathways mediate visual pattern discrimination. *Proceedings of the National Academy of Sciences of the United States of America, 97,* 11068–11073.

Galaburda, A., & Livingstone, M. (1993). Evidence for a magnocellular defect in developmental dyslexia. In P. Tallal, A. M. Galaburda, R. R. Llinas, & C. von Euler (Eds.), *Temporal information processing in the nervous system* (pp. 70–82). New York: New York Academy of Sciences.

Geffen, G., & Sexton, M. A. (1978). The development of auditory strategies of attention. *Developmental Psychology, 14,* 11–17.

Geffen, G., & Wale, J. (1979). Development of selective listening and hemispheric asymmetry. *Developmental Psychology, 15,* 138–146.

Hammil, D. D., Brown, V. L., Larsen, S. A., & Wiederholt, J. L. (1994). *Test of adolescent and adult language* (3rd ed.). Austin, TX: Pro-Ed.

Hansen, P. C., Stein, J. F., Orde, S. R., Winter, J. L., & Talcott, J. B. (2001). Are dyslexics' visual deficits limited to measures of dorsal stream function? *NeuroReport, 12,* 1527–1530.

Hart, B., & Risley, T. R. (1999). *The social world of children: Learning to talk.* Baltimore, MD: Brookes.

Harwerth, R., Smith, E., Duncan, G., Crawford, M., & von Noorden, G. (1986). Multiple sensitive periods in the development of the primate visual system. *Science, 232,* 235–238.

Hickey, T. L. (1977). Postnatal development of the human lateral geniculate nucleus: Relationship to a critical period for the visual system. *Science, 198,* 836–838.

Hickok, G., Bellugi, U., & Klima, E. S. (1996). The neurobiology of sign language and its implications for the neural basis of language. *Nature, 381,* 699–702.

Hillyard, S. A., Hink, R. F., Schwent, V. I., & Picton, T. W. (1973). Electrical signs of selective attention in the human brain. *Science, 182,* 177–179.

Hiscock, M., & Kinsbourne, M. (1980). Asymmetries of selective listening and attention switching in children. *Developmental Psychology, 16,* 70–82.

Hollants-Gilhuijs, M. A. M., Ruijter, J. M., & Spekreijse, H. (1998a). Visual half-field development in children: Detection of colour-contrast-defined forms. *Vision Research, 38,* 645–649.

Hollants-Gilhuijs, M. A. M., Ruijter, J. M., & Spekreijse, H. (1998b). Visual half-field development in children: Detection of motion-defined forms. *Vision Research, 38,* 651–657.

Horton, J. C., & Hocking, D. R. (1997). Timing of the critical period for plasticity of ocular dominance columns in macaque striate cortex. *Journal of Neuroscience, 17,* 3684–3709.

Hubel, D. H., & Wiesel, T. N. (1977). Functional architecture of macaque monkey visual cortex. *Proceedings of the Royal Society of London, 198,* 1–59.

Huttenlocher, J., Haight, W., Byrd, A., Seltzer, M., & Lyons, T. (1991). Early vocabulary growth: Relation to language input and gender. *Developmental Psychology, 27,* 236–248.

Huttenlocher, J., Vasilyeva, M., Cymerman, E., & Levine, S. (2002). Language input and child syntax. *Cognitive Psychology, 45,* 337–374.

Huttenlocher, P. R., & Dabholkar, A. S. (1997). Regional differences in synaptogenesis in human cerebral cortex. *Journal of Comparative Neurology, 387,* 167–178.

Johnson, M. H., Mareschal, D., & Csibra, G. (2001). The functional development and integration of the dorsal and ventral visual pathways: A neurocomputational approach. In C. A. Nelson & M. Luciana (Eds.), *Handbook of developmental cognitive neuroscience.* Cambridge, MA: MIT Press.

Kaas, J., Krubitzer, L., Chino, Y., Langston, A., Polley, E., & Blair, N. (1990). Reorganization of retinotopic cortical maps in adult mammals after lesions of the retina. *Science, 248,* 229–231.

Kahn, D. M., & Krubitzer, L. (2002). Massive cross-modal cortical plasticity and the emergence of a new cortical area in developmentally blind mammals. *Proceedings of the National Academy of Sciences of the United States of America, 99,* 11429–11434.

Kovacs, I., Polat, U., Pennefather, P. M., Chandna, A., & Norcia, A. N. (2000). A new test of contour integration deficits in patients with a history of disrupted binocular experience during visual development. *Vision Research, 40,* 1775–1783.

Krubitzer, L., & Huffman, K. J. (2000). A realization of the neocortex in mammals: Genetic and epigenetic contributions to the phenotype. *Brain, Behavior and Evolution, 55,* 322–335.

Lane, D., & Pearson, D. (1982). The development of selective attention. *Merrill-Palmer Quarterly, 28,* 317–337.

Le Grand, R., Mondloch, C. J., Maurer, D., & Brent, H. P. (2001). Early visual experience and face processing. *Nature, 410,* 890.

Lenneberg, E. (1967). *Biological foundations of language.* New York: Wiley.

Liberman, A. M. (1974). The specialization of the language hemisphere. In F. O. Schmitt & F. G. Worden (Eds.), *The neurosciences third study program* (pp. 43–56). Cambridge, MA: MIT Press.

Livingstone, M., & Hubel, D. (1988). Segregation of form, color, movement and depth: Anatomy, physiology, and perception. *Science, 240,* 740–749.

Livingstone, M., Rosen, G., Drislane, F., & Galaburda, A. (1991). Physiological and anatomical evidence for a magnocellular defect in developmental dyslexia. *Proceedings of the National Academy of Sciences of the United States of America, 88,* 7943–7947.

Loiselle, D. L., Stamm, J. S., Maitinsky, S., & Whipple, S. C. (1980). Evoked potential and behavioral signs of attentive dysfunctions in hyperactive boys. *Psychophysiology, 17,* 193–201.

Lovegrove, W. (1993). Weakness in the transient visual system: A causal factor in dyslexia. In P. Tallal, A. M. Galaburda, R. R. Llinas, & C. von Euler (Eds.), *Temporal information processing in the nervous system* (pp. 57–69). New York: New York Academy of Sciences.

Lovegrove, W., Garzia, R., & Nicholson, S. (1990). Experimental evidence for a transient system deficit in specific reading disability. *Journal of the American Optometric Association, 61,* 137–146.

Lovegrove, W., Martin, F., & Slaghuis, W. (1986). A theoretical and experimental case for a visual deficit in specific reading disability. *Cognitive Neuropsychology, 3,* 225–267.

Lovrich, D. L., Stamm, J. S., Maitinsky, S., & Whipple, S. C. (1983). Event-related potential and behavioral correlates of attention in reading retardation. *Journal of Clinical Neuropsychology, 5,* 13–37.

Maccoby, E., & Konrad, K. (1966). Age trends in selective listening. *Journal of Experimental Child Psychology, 3,* 113–122.

Maurer, D., Lewis, T. L., Brent, H. P., & Levin, A. V. (1999). Rapid improvement in the acuity of infants after visual input. *Science, 286,* 108–110.

Mayberry, R. (1993). First-language acquisition after childhood differs from second-language acquisition: The case of American Sign Language. *Journal of Speech and Hearing Research, 36,* 1258–1270.

Mayberry, R., & Eichen, E. (1991). The long-lasting advantage of learning sign language in childhood: Another look at the critical period for language acquisition. *Journal of Memory and Language, 30,* 486–512.

Mayberry, R. I. (2003). Age constraints on first versus second language acquisition: Evidence for linguistic plasticity and epigenesis. *Brain and Language, 87,* 369–384.

Mayberry, R. I., Lock, E., & Kazmi, H. (2002). Linguistic ability and early language exposure. *Nature, 417,* 38.

McIntosh, A. R., & Gonzalez-Lima, F. (1994). Structural equation modelling and its application to network analysis of functional brain imaging. *Human Brain Mapping, 2,* 2–22.

Merigan, W., & Maunsell, J. (1993). How parallel are the primate visual pathways? *Annual Review of Neuroscience, 16,* 369–402.

Merzenich, M. M., & Jenkins, W. M. (1993). Reorganization of cortical representations of the hand following alterations of skin inputs induced by nerve injury, skin island transfers, and experience. *Journal of Hand Therapy, 6,* 89–104.

Metin, C., & Frost, D. (1989). Visual responses of neurons in somatosensory cortex of hamsters with experimentally induced retinal projections to somatosensory thalamus. *Proceedings of the National Academy of Sciences of the United States of America, 86,* 357–361.

Mills, D. L., Coffey, S. A., & Neville, H. J. (1993). Language acquisition and cerebral specialization in 20-month-old infants. *Journal of Cognitive Neuroscience, 5,* 317–334.

Mills, D. L., Coffey-Corina, S. A., & Neville, H. J. (1997). Language comprehension and cerebral specialization from 13 to 20 months. *Developmental Neuropsychology, 13,* 397–445.

Mitchell, D. E. (1990). Sensitive periods in visual development: Insights gained from studies of recovery of function in cats following early monocular deprivation or cortical lesions. In C. Blakemore (Ed.), *Vision: Coding and efficiency* (pp. 234–246). Cambridge, England: Cambridge University Press.

Mitchell, T. V., & Neville, H. J. (in press). Asynchronies in the development of electrophysiological responses to motion and color. *Journal of Cognitive Neuroscience.*

Neville, H. J. (1995). Developmental specificity in neurocognitive development in humans. In M. Gazzaniga (Ed.), *The cognitive neurosciences* (pp. 219–231). Cambridge, MA: MIT Press.

Neville, H. J. (1998). Human brain development. In M. Posner & L. Ungerleider (Eds.), *Fundamental neuroscience* (pp. 1313–1338). New York: Academic Press.

Neville, H. J., Bavelier, D., Corina, D., Rauschecker, J., Karni, A., Lalwani, A., et al. (1998). Cerebral organization for language in deaf and hearing subjects: Biological constraints and effects of experience. *Proceedings of the National Academy of Sciences of the United States of America, 95,* 922–929.

Neville, H. J., Coffey, S. A., Lawson, D. S., Fischer, A., Emmorey, K., & Bellugi, U. (1997). Neural systems mediating American Sign Language: Effects of sensory experience and age of acquisition. *Brain and Language, 57,* 285–308.

Neville, H. J., & Lawson, D. (1987a). Attention to central and peripheral visual space in a movement detection task: An event-related potential and behavioral study. I. Normal hearing adults. *Brain Research, 405,* 253–267.

Neville, H. J., & Lawson, D. (1987b). Attention to central and peripheral visual space in a movement detection task: An event-related and behavioral study. II. Congenitally deaf adults. *Brain Research, 405,* 268–283.

Neville, H. J., & Lawson, D. (1987c). Attention to central and peripheral visual space in a movement detection task. III. Separate effects of auditory deprivation and acquisition of a visual language. *Brain Research, 405,* 284–294.

Neville, H. J., & Mills, D. (1997). Epigenesis of language. *Mental Retardation and Developmental Disabilities Research Reviews, 3,* 282–292.

Neville, H. J., Mills, D., & Lawson, D. (1992). Fractionating language: Different neural subsystems with different sensitive periods. *Cerebral Cortex, 2,* 244–258.

Neville, H. J., Schmidt, A., & Kutas, M. (1983). Altered visual-evoked potentials in congenitally deaf adults. *Brain Research, 266,* 127–132.

Newman, A. J., Bavelier, D., Corina, D., Jezzard, P., & Neville, H. J. (2002). A critical period for right hemisphere recruitment in American Sign Language processing. *Nature Neuroscience, 5,* 76–80.

Newman, A. J., Corina, D., Tomann, A., Bavelier, D., Braun, A., Clark, V., et al. (1998). Effects of age of acquisition on cortical organization for American Sign Language (ASL): An fMRI study. *NeuroImage, 7,* 5194.

Newport, E. (1990). Maturational constraints on language learning. *Cognitive Science, 14,* 11–28.

Newport, E. L., Bavelier, D., & Neville, H. (2002). Critical thinking about critical periods: Perspectives on a critical period for language acquisition. In E. Dupoux (Ed.), *Language, brain and cognitive development* (pp. 481–502). Cambridge, MA: MIT Press.

O'Craven, K., Rosen, B., Kwong, K., Triesman, A., & Savoy, R. (1997). Voluntary attention modulates fMRI activity in human MT-MST. *Neuron, 18,* 591–598.

Pakulak, E., Harris, A. M., Yamada, Y., Coch, D., Schachter, J., & Neville, H. (2002). Syntactic processing without semantic cues in adult monolinguals of varying proficiency: An ERP study [Abstract]. *Cognitive Neuroscience Society, 9,* 135.

Pearson, D. A., & Lane, D. M. (1991). Auditory attention switching: A developmental study. *Journal of Experimental Child Psychology, 51,* 320–334.

Petitto, L. A., Zatorri, R. J., Gauna, K., Nikelski, E. J., Dostie, D., & Evans, A. C. (2000). Speech-like cerebral activity in profoundly deaf people processing signed language: Implications for the neural basis of human language. *Proceedings of the National Academy of Sciences of the United States of America, 97,* 13961–13966.

Pinker, S. (2002). *The blank slate: The modern denial of human nature.* New York: Viking.

Poizner, H., Klima, E. S., & Bellugi, U. (1987). *What the hands reveal about the brain.* Cambridge, MA: MIT Press.

Poizner, H., & Tallal, P. (1987). Temporal processing in deaf signers. *Brain and Language, 30,* 52–62.

Ramachandran, V. S., Rogers-Ramachandran, D. R., & Stewart, M. (1992). Perceptual correlates of massive cortical reorganization. *Science, 258,* 1159–1160.

Rauschecker, J. (1995). Compensatory plasticity and sensory substitution in the cerebral cortex. *Trends in Neurosciences, 18,* 36–43.

Röder, B., Rösler, F., & Neville, H. J. (1999). Effects of interstimulus interval on auditory event-related potentials in congenitally blind and normally sighted humans. *Neuroscience Letters, 264,* 53–56.

Röder, B., Rösler, F., & Neville, H. J. (2000). Event-related potentials during auditory language processing in congenitally blind and sighted people. *Neuropsychologia, 38,* 1482–1502.

Röder, B., Stock, O., Bien, S., Neville, H., & Rösler, F. (2002). Speech processing activates visual cortex in congenitally blind humans. *European Journal of Neuroscience, 16,* 930–936.

Röder, B., Stock, O., Neville, H., Bien, S., & Rösler, F. (2002). Brain activation modulated by the comprehension of normal and pseudo-word sentences of different processing demands: A functional magnetic resonance imaging study. *NeuroImage, 15,* 1003–1014.

Röder, B., Teder-Sälejärvi, W., Sterr, A., Rösler, F., Hillyard, S. A., & Neville, H. J. (1999). Improved auditory spatial tuning in blind humans. *Nature, 400,* 162–166.

Roe, A. W., Pallas, S. L., Kwon, Y. H., & Sur, M. (1992). Visual projections routed to the auditory pathway in ferrets: Receptive fields of visual neurons in primary auditory cortex. *Journal of Neuroscience, 12,* 3651–3664.

Sawatari, A., & Callaway, E. M. (1996). Convergence of magno- and parvocellular pathways in layer 4B of macaque primary visual cortex. *Nature, 380,* 442–446.

Semel, E., Wiig, E. H., & Secord, W. A. (1995). *Clinical evaluation of language fundamentals* (3rd ed.). San Antonio, TX: Psychological Corporation.

Sexton, M. A., & Geffen, G. (1979). Development of three strategies of attention in dichotic monitoring. *Developmental Psychology, 15,* 299–310.

Silver, M. A., Fagiolini, M., Gillespie, D. C., Howe, C. L., Frank, M. G., Issa, N. P., et al. (2001). Infusion of nerve growth factor (NGF) into kitten visual cortex increases immunoreactivity for NGF, NGF receptors, and choline acetyltransferase in basal forebrain without affecting ocular dominance plasticity or column development. *Neuroscience, 108,* 569–585.

Soederfeldt, B., Ingvar, M., Roennberg, J., Eriksson, L., et al. (1997). Signed and spoken language perception studied by positron emission tomography. *Neurology, 49,* 82–87.

Sperling, A. J., Lu, Z.-l., Manis, F. R., & Seidenberg, M. S. (2003). Selective magnocellular deficits in dyslexia: A "phantom contour" study. *Neuropsychologia, 41,* 1422–1429.

Spezio, M. L., Sanders, L. D., & Neville, H. J. (2000). Covert audiospatial attention using virtual sound sources [Abstract]. *Cognitive Neuroscience Society, 9,* 81.

Stein, J., & Talcott, J. B. (1999). Impaired neuronal timing in developmental dyslexia: The magnocellular deficit hypothesis. *Dyslexia, 5,* 59–77.

Stoner, G. B., & Albright, T. D. (1993). Image segmentation cues in motion processing: Implications for modularity in vision. *Journal of Cognitive Neuroscience, 5,* 129–149.

Sur, M., & Garraghty, P. (1986). Experimentally induced visual responses from auditory thalamus and cortex [Abstract]. *Society for Neuroscience, 12,* 592.

Taha, S., & Stryker, M. P. (2002). Rapid ocular dominance plasticity requires cortical but not geniculate protein synthesis. *Neuron, 34,* 425–436.

Talcott, J. B., Hansen, M. C., Willis-Owen, C., McKinnell, I. W., Richardson, A. J., & Stein, J. F. (1998). Visual magnocellular impairment in adult developmental dyslexics. *Neuro-Ophthamology, 20,* 187–201.

Talcott, J. B., Hansen, P. C., Assoku, E. L., & Stein, J. F. (2000). Visual motion sensitivity in dyslexia: Evidence for temporal and energy integration deficits. *Neuropsychologia, 38,* 935–943.

Teder-Salejarvi, W. A., Hillyard, S., Roder, B., & Neville, H. J. (1999). Spatial attention to central and peripheral auditory stimuli as indexed by event-related potentials (ERPs). *Cognitive Brain Research, 8,* 213–227.

Teder-Salejarvi, W. A., Munte, T. F., Sperlich, F.-J., & Hillyard, S. A. (1999). Intra-modal and cross-modal spatial attention to auditory and visual stimuli. An event-related brain potential (ERP) study. *Cognitive Brain Research, 8,* 327–343.

Tootell, R., & Taylor, J. (1995). Anatomical evidence for MT and additional cortical visual areas in humans. *Cerebral Cortex, 1,* 39–55.

Tootell, R. B., Reppas, J. B., Kwong, K. K., Malach, R., Born, R. T., Brady, T. J., et al. (1995). Functional analysis of human MT and related visual cortical areas using magnetic resonance imaging. *Journal of Neuroscience, 15,* 3215–3230.

Tychsen, L. (2001). Critical period of development of visual acuity, depth perception and eye tracking. In D. B. J. Bailey, J. T. Bruer, F. J. Symons, & J. W. Lichtman (Eds.), *Critical thinking about critical periods: Perspectives from biology, psychology and education* (pp. 67–80). Baltimore: Brookes.

Ungerleider, L. G., & Mishkin, M. (1982). Two cortical visual systems. In D. J. Ingle, M. A. Goodale, & R. J. Mansfield (Eds.), *Analysis of visual behavior* (pp. 549–586). Cambridge, MA: MIT Press.

von Melchner, L., Pallas, S. L., & Sur, M. (2000). Visual behavior mediated by retinal projections directed to the auditory pathway. *Nature, 404,* 871–876.

Weber-Fox, C., & Neville, H. J. (1996a). *Effects of delays in second-language immersion on functional neural subsystems* [Abstract]. Poster presented at the American Academy for the Advancement of Science Symposium: The brain, cognition, and education: Exploring the bridge between research and practice.

Weber-Fox, C., & Neville, H. J. (1996b). Maturational constraints on functional specializations for language processing: ERP and behavioral evidence in bilingual speakers. *Journal of Cognitive Neuroscience, 8,* 231–256.

Weber-Fox, C., & Neville, H. J. (1999). Functional neural subsystems are differentially affected by delays in second-language immersion: ERP and behavioral evidence in bilingual speakers. In D. Birdsong (Ed.), *New perspectives on the critical period for second language acquisition* (pp. 23–38). Hillsdale NJ: Erlbaum.

Wiesel, T., & Hubel, D. (1965). Comparison of the effects of unilateral and bilateral eye closure on cortical unit responses in kittens. *Journal of Neurophysiology, 28,* 1003–1017.

Woods, D., Hillyard, S., & Hansen, J. (1984). Event-related brain potentials reveal similar attentional mechanisms during selective listening and shadowing. *Journal of Experimental Psychology, 10,* 761–777.

Woods, J., Coch, D., Sanders, L., Skendzel, W., Capek, C., & Neville, H. (2002). The development of selective auditory attention to linguistic and non-linguistic sounds [Abstract]. *Cognitive Neuroscience Society, 9,* 122.

Woods, J., Coch, D., Sanders, L., Skendzel, W., & Neville, H. (2002). *The development of selective auditory attention to linguistic and non-linguistic stimuli.* Unpublished master's research, University of Oregon, Eugene.

Yamada, Y., Harris, A. M., Pakulak, E., Schachter, J., & Neville, H. (2002). Language proficiency in monolinguals and bilinguals reflected in ERPs during sentence processing [Abstract]. *Cognitive Neuroscience Society, 9,* 135.

Zambelli, A. J., Stamm, J. S., Maitinsky, S., & Loiselle, D. L. (1977). Auditory evoked potentials and selective auditory attention in formerly hyperactive adolescent boys. *American Journal of Psychiatry, 134,* 742–747.

Zukier, H., & Hagen, J. W. (1978). The development of selective attention under distracting conditions. *Child Development, 49,* 870–873.

12 _____

How I Got Here

Michael I. Posner

One day Ulrich Mayr, who arranged this meeting that resulted in this volume, asked me how we should title the meeting. Although it was to be about my career in psychology the grant required a volume that would point toward future developments. I said with a surprisingly short latency how about "Developing Individuality in the Human Brain." The title arose to mind without any effort or thought as though it had been primed, and in this chapter I try to explain to myself as well as to readers how that could be.

Nothing in my graduate training would have predicted that I would be interested in individual differences, brain mechanisms, or development. My graduate years were spent running adults in studies of reaction time to understand how people performed high-level skills, particularly those that might be said to involve thought. My doctoral dissertation's title, "An Informational Approach to Thinking," captured this theme.

Life is about choice and encounters. My choices arose to a large degree from experimental results, but perhaps even more important were the encounters with various people, many of whom are represented in this book.

The Human Brain

It takes about .08 seconds longer to determine that two letters differing in case (e.g., "Aa") are the same letter than for letters of the same case (e.g., "AA" or "aa"; Posner & Mitchell, 1967). This finding had a profound effect on my thinking. After all, my research participants had a lifetime of learning that "A" and "a" were the same letter, but reaction time (RT) measures were sensitive enough to distinguish between the identical information involved in the same case match and the more abstract level needed to match across cases. I believed at the time the difference between same and cross-case matches reflected the time to reach a phonological from a visual code, but later it appeared that there were visual areas that dealt with identical letters and other visual areas for more abstract case neutral information (Boles & Eveland, 1983; McCandliss, Cohen, & Dehaene, 2003). Nonetheless, RT appeared to be a way to study information flow in the brain. It led me to want to explore methods for the study of brain mechanisms that might underlie cognitive performance.

It seemed to me that the study of attention was a particularly appropriate topic for psychologists interested in aspects of cognition that might relate to brain mechanisms. After all, Wundt had defined psychology as distinct from physiology as "the study of consciousness." Later Titchener had called attention the center of psychology. If we were to form links between cognitive psychology and brain science, attention seemed to be the right level. For this goal I chose to study a simple aspect of attention. The task was to see whether it would be possible to give priority to a visual stimulus by an act of attention, which could not be attributed to any other system such as eye movements or getting ready to press the key. Of course, we knew this was possible when the visual field was cluttered. If you know where the target is going to be in a complex field, you can see it without any search based on knowing what to look at. A study by Engle (1971) demonstrated that attention could extend the area of priority to peripheral events while not replacing the unique properties of the fovea. However, when the field was an empty one, there was a considerable dispute about whether knowledge in advance could improve performance.

Starting in 1978, we began to use a cue in an otherwise empty visual field as a way of moving attention to a target. We used electrodes to monitor eye movements, and because only one response was required there was no way to prepare the response differently depending on the cue. The results seemed to me to be spectacular. We (Posner, 1980; Posner, Davidson, & Snyder, 1980; Shulman, Remington, & McLean, 1979) found that covert shifts could enhance the speed of responding to the onset on a stimulus in a nearly empty field. Within half a second, one could shift attention to a visual event and, when it indicated a likely target at another location, move attention to enhance processing at the new location. We had trapped a covert attention shift and observed its movement. In fact, three students (Shulman, Remington, & McLean, 1979) showed that response times to probes at intermediate locations were enhanced at intermediate times as though attention actually moved through the space. Whether attention moves through the intermediate space is still a disputed matter (LaBerge, 1995), suggesting the limitation of a purely behavioral study. At the time, it was also hard to conceive how a movement of attention could possibly be executed by neurons. Subsequently it was shown that the population vector of a set of neurons in the motor system of a monkey could carry out what would appear behaviorally, as a mental rotation (Georgopoulos, Lurito, Petrides, Schwartz, & Massey, 1989). After that finding, a covert shift of attention did not seem too far-fetched.

About this time I became aware of a number of papers using intracellular recording to study the properties of cells in the posterior parietal lobe of the monkey (Mountcastle, 1978; Wurtz, Goldberg, & Robinson, 1980). These papers suggested the possibility of attention cells in the parietal cortex that might be critically involved in orienting attention toward visual events. At a Tuesday night meeting of our research group, which had been assigned to read these papers, I asked if we were measuring with reaction time behavior that results from such attention cells. I thought if the covert shifts of attention in humans could be connected with the monkey work, it might contribute to linking cognitive psychology to brain mechanisms. I do not think there was much enthusiasm for this idea at the time. After all, cognition was about software and what did it have to do with the parts of the brain in which cells were found in the monkey?

In 1979, I met Oscar Marin, an outstanding behavioral neurologist. He was about to move to Portland, Oregon, to set up a service and research effort at Good Samaritan Hospital and he invited me to set up a neuropsychology laboratory in conjunction with the hospital. It was a perfect time for me because I had spent 6 months of 1979 in New York working with Michael Gazzaniga, whose career in psychology is probably familiar to most readers, and my brother Jerry Posner, who is a world-leading neurologist. I tested patients who mostly had lesions of the parietal lobe. Gazzaniga had reported that such patients could make same–different judgments concerning objects that they were unable to report consciously (Volpe, LeDoux, & Gazzaniga, 1979). That seemed like something that could be followed up in more analytic cognitive studies. What did a right parietal lesion do that made access to material on the left side difficult or impossible for consciousness and yet still left the information available for other judgments?

This is the question I pursued in the new laboratory in Portland. In the end, I commuted from Eugene to Portland once a week for 7 years. It was such a pleasure to work with Marin that the long drive was worthwhile. Among those who worked with us over those years were Bob Rafal, Avishai Henik, Fran Friedrich, Steve Keele, Alan Wing, Albrecht Inhoff, Richard Ivry, and many others.

The results were a revelation for me. Patients with different lesion locations in the parietal lobe, the pulvinar, and the colliculus tended to show neglect of the side of space opposite the lesion. But in a detailed cognitive analysis, it was clear that they differed in showing deficits in specific mental operations involved in shifting attention (Posner, 1988). As I saw it at the time, we had found a new form of brain localization. Different brain areas executed individual mental operations or computations such as disengaging from the current focus of attention (parietal lobe), moving or changing the index of attention (colliculus), and engaging the subsequent target (pulvinar). No wonder Lashley thought the whole brain was involved in mental tasks. It was not the whole brain, but a widely dispersed network of quite localized neural areas. Even looking back from the perspective of 20 years, I can again feel the excitement I had surrounding this idea at the time.

I read an article in *Scientific American* (Lassen, Ingvar, & Skinhoj, 1978) indicating changes in cerebral blood flow in the brain when reading silently. In cognitive psychology, reading had been studied quite a lot and we knew something about the orthographic, phonological, and semantic operations that must have taken place while reading, but they would be combined in the overall blood flow. Even more compelling for the possible anatomy of mental operations was a paper appearing in 1985 by Per Roland (Roland & Friberg, 1985) indicating that different parts of the brain were active during way finding, mental arithmetic, and verbal tasks. However, even in this paper there was no effort to uncover the specific operations that might be performed by the brain areas involved.

About this time the Washington University School of Medicine started a national search for a psychologist who might work in conjunction with the developing positron emission tomography (PET) center led by Marc Raichle. It might be surprising to people how reluctant psychologists at that time were to take a chance on brain imaging. For me this was the opportunity to test the idea that arose from the neurological studies that individual mental operations would be localized in separate brain tissue. Raichle and his colleagues at Washington University recognized the importance of being able to use PET to illuminate questions of higher brain function. I worked to create a neuropsychology laboratory in St. Louis with the help of Eric Sieroff, Steve Petersen, and Patti Reuter-Lorenz, and later Gordon Shulman and Maurizio Corbetta. The laboratory examined many patient types and with the leadership of Raichle and the help of Petersen, who was recruited from National Institutes of Health (NIH), developed research using PET.

The story of this work is presented in Raichle's and in Tom Carr's chapters (chaps. 6 and 2, this volume). I have also provided a perspective in a recent paper reviewing work in this field (Posner, 2004). For the most part, early work has held up and it represented an important methodological and substantive development.

The St. Louis studies did quite a lot for the development of neuroimaging and in the main, supported the idea that widely scattered brain areas were involved when any task was studied. Some people have thought that these areas were specific for domains of function such as language or face stimuli, and so on. I have maintained the importance of mental operations, without denying that domain specificity may also play a role in understanding localization (Posner, 2004). In the area of face processing, there has been a lot of dispute over whether there is a specific face area because experts in other domains activate the same area when thinking about their domain of expertise. However, if one thinks about localization of mental operations, it seems clear that faces and other objects, where we come to recognize individuals, via fine distinctions, share operations in common. A similar argument has recently been applied to the visual word form area (McCandliss, Cohen, & Dehaene, 2003).

I had gone to St. Louis in the hopes of pursuing work on attention. When I talked to neurologists about covert shifts of attention (without eye movements) and then proposed to break the invisible shift into component operations such as disengaging and moving, I saw eyes glaze and interest wane. Language studies have the advantage that the operations were more concrete and that neurosurgeons valued knowledge about the localization of language areas to aid them in avoiding such areas during surgery. Fortunately, the imaging group was able to recruit Corbetta and Shulman who have carried out attention studies, better designed than I ever could have done. My reading of their fascinating review paper (Corbetta & Shulman, 2002) suggests that there is localization of quite separate mental operations within two areas of the parietal lobe that form a portion of a larger network whose functions are to align attention with the target. Although my initial speculation of which operations were important may not have been correct, the beautiful localized brain areas support the overall localization hypothesis.

Development

The other phrases in the title of this book come from my joint work with Mary K. Rothbart over the past quarter century. The idea of studying development began with a request to write a paper for the *Nebraska Symposium on Motivation,* which was having a meeting devoted to attention. I did not want to write on the usual attentional topics as carried out by cognitive psychologists, but instead I wanted to address the criticism of the cognitive enterprise that Ulric Neisser (1976) had made in his latest book. Neisser had complained that cognitive psychology lacked ecological validity by not being applicable outside a narrow laboratory environment. Rothbart was interested in temperamental differences in infancy; there could hardly be any topic with greater ecological validity as any parent of more than one child can attest. When the book was reviewed by James Deese (Deese, 1982) he wrote:

> I was delighted and stimulated by the chapter on "The Development of Attentional Mechanisms" by Posner and Rothbart.
> They enter the real world. . . . If there is to be a real experimental science of cognition, it must make contact with . . . disciplines rooted in physical theory and physical measurement. Posner and Rothbart begin to point in this direction. (p. 279)

Judging from Deese's reaction, we had been, at least, a little successful in attempting to answer the Neisser challenges. I also wonder how Deese, who has since passed away, would respond to the measurement of blood flow used in the imaging results described earlier.

Rothbart and I spent many intense hours trying to meld together the different perspectives of developmental and cognitive psychology. For example, I had shown that orienting of attention to sensory events could take place in the absence of eye movement, but in infant development, eye movements were the key to the study of the child's interest. More important, nearly all adult attention experiments provide the research participant with instructions about what is to be attended, but in developmental psychology attention is more in the domain of self or internal regulation. The hours we spent discussing these issues were well worth it, not only because we produced the chapter, but in addition, our discussion set the occasion for the many experiments and papers we were to do together in the coming years.

When I returned to Eugene from St. Louis in 1989, it was with the goal of forwarding research in two directions. It was my conviction that the findings we made in St. Louis on processing visual and auditory words would lead to evidence for many networks of brain areas involved in mental activity. Although I did not dream that the work would grow to the magnitude that actually took place, particularly following the use of functional magnetic resonance imaging (fMRI), the general shape of what has happened seemed clear right from the start. I also realized that the skills needed to improve localization and understand the anatomy of cognition were far removed from what I could do best. Instead I concentrated on measuring the operation of these networks in real time.

Even before leaving St. Louis, I teamed with Avi Snyder and Raichle, to carry out studies of the time course of processing visual words and nonsense material using the 16-channel electroencephalogram (EEG) system available there (Snyder, Abdullaev, Posner, & Raichle, 1995). However, in Eugene, Don Tucker was developing a new way of taking EEGs from the skull, which would allow many electrodes to be put into place at once. Together we set up a laboratory in Straub Hall and began to compare his 32-channel Electrical Geodesics Inc. (EGI) system with a 32-channel electro-cap using the Grass amplifiers from older studies. The results convinced me that there was no great loss from the relatively high impedances used in the EGI system. We were able to support many students at this point as a result of a generous grant to support centers in cognitive neuroscience from the James S. McDonnell Foundation. Our studies of visual word processing using high-density EEG together with Yalchin Abdullaev, Paul Compton, Peter Grossenbacher, and Rajendra Badgaiyan convinced me that we could see signatures on the scalp of brain areas corresponding to the major generators found in the previous PET and later fMRI studies. It was exciting to see the visual word form area and anterior cingulate in real time, as the network computed aspects of the tasks we used (Posner, Abdullaev, McCandliss, & Sereno, 1999; Posner & McCandliss, 1999). At about the same time the EEG studies were taking place, Rothbart and I began to carry out studies on the development of brain networks related to attention. It seemed to me then as it does now, that once brain networks can be localized and shown to be activated in real time in adults, the next major issue is plasticity. Of course, learning and brain damage can be used to study plasticity in adults, but the most interesting challenge would be to see how networks are put together in childhood. We chose to use marker tasks involving careful measurement of eye movement, and it was some time before we also began to use event related potentials (ERP) measures, although Ghislaine and Stan Dehaene working in the Straub Hall laboratory showed clearly how this could be done.

With the leadership of Rothbart, an outstanding team of researchers including Mark Johnson, Cathy Harmon, and Anne Clohessy explored the role of orienting in infants during the first year of life. Infants, particularly at 4 months, are little looking machines. We traced the development of preference for locations and objects and showed them to be independent at 6 months and demonstrated how orienting to input temporarily reduced distress. By 1991, when Gazzaniga offered to make a special issue of the *Journal of Cognitive Neuroscience* available to the centers supported by the McDonnell Foundation, the Oregon studies were able to fill the issue. The cover, an infant with one eye patched, illustrated a study by Clohessy showing the role of the colliculus in inhibition of return (Clohessy, Posner, Rothbart, & Vecera, 1991; also see Klein, chap. 3, this volume for an update).

According to theories developed by Rothbart, a control system develops in late infancy or early childhood that involves attention and can also be measured through parental reports as a higher-order variable called effortful control. Because the executive attention system involves the anterior cingulate, which is well activated by conflict, we developed a series of conflict tasks that could be executed by children. One of these tasks involved conflict between location and identity and Gina Gerardi-Caulton found that it showed a strong development between 2.5 and 4 years of age. Another was a flanker task, which required key presses, and Charo Rueda found development from 4 to 7 years (Rueda, Posner, & Rothbart, 2004).

During the late 1990s, as the result of a donation by the Mortimer Sackler family, I had the unique opportunity to set up an Institute for Developmental Psychobiology in New York City. The clear need for students trained to understand the developing human brain and the presence of scanning and other facilities in New York was attractive. During my stay in New York it was possible to recruit B. J. Casey, Bruce McCandliss, Kathleen Thomas, and Michael Worden to the Sackler Institute faculty, and they have given it a leadership role in pediatric neuroimaging and in the new area of brain and education. It was also possible, with Rothbart's help, to coordinate some of the research in Eugene and New York. For example, Jin Fan working as a postdoctoral fellow in New York found in using fMRI that the conflict task developed by Gerardi-Caulton along with other such tasks activated similar areas of the anterior cingulate gyrus (Fan, Flombaum, McCandliss, Thomas, & Posner, 2003). Amir Raz, another postdoctoral fellow at the Sackler Institute, showed that a posthypnotic suggestion to view a word as meaningless given to highly hypnotizable research participants eliminated the Stroop effect (Raz, Shapiro, Fan, & Posner, 2002) and also the conflict-related activation in the anterior cingulate.

Meanwhile in Eugene, Gerardi-Caulton (2000) found that individual differences in RT between congruent and incongruent stimuli in her conflict task was correlated with effortful control as measured by the Children's Behavior Questionnaire. In addition, Rothbart and her team (Rothbart, Ellis, Rueda, & Posner, 2003), found that at 3 years of age, performance on the spatial conflict task correlated with performance on an ambiguous eye movement task. We seemed to have methods to trace the origins of effortful control in infancy and early childhood and thus to understand the roots of how self-regulation develops (Rueda, Posner, & Rothbart, 2004). One of the most intriguing findings by Rueda was that executive attention reaches adult levels at about age 7. If this turns out to be true, beyond the limited domain in which we have tested it, we may gain better ideas of how to proceed with the programming of educational experiences.

Individuality

I never expected to study individual differences. Cognitive psychology was about mental processes in common among humans, and I thought one of the most important results of the early neuroimaging studies was evidence that the data of people could be averaged to provide a common anatomy even for higher mental tasks where one might have suspected a lot of individuality. Of course, the early PET data had a large area of activity because of averaging. So despite evidence for commonality, there was also opportunity for individuality. The development of fMRI has allowed enough data to be collected on an individual that activity can be plotted in relation to the anatomy of the individual brain, thus opening the way for more detailed analysis of individuality in brain activation.

Two things tipped me in the direction of wanting to study individual differences. First was the influence of Rothbart's elegant theory of the role of effortful control in child socialization. The data showed that during childhood there were correlations between component operations in cognitive tasks and parental reported effortful control (Gerardi-Caulton, 2000). This seemed remarkable evidence that individual differences in laboratory experiments were important enough to relate to the diverse behaviors of everyday life that would be obvious to parents.

The second reason was owed to meeting John Fossella and Tobias Sommer at the Sackler Institute in New York. They both had been trained in molecular biology and were eager to explain to me some of the new opportunities opened up by the human genome program. We were later joined at the Institute by Jim Swanson who had developed evidence that a particular gene was involved in attention deficit disorder (Swanson et al., 2000).

With the support of Rothbart and her team in Eugene, we set out to measure adult individual differences both by questionnaire and experimental test and to determine how they might be influenced by genetics. John Fossella took cheek swabs from 200 New York adults and using the magic of polymerase chain reaction (PCR) was able to genotype them for dopamine genes. We found that individual differences in the attentional network that related to effortful control were influenced by dopamine genes (Fossella et al., 2002), and an fMRI study showed that the genetic differences influenced the degree of brain activation in the anterior cingulate (Fan, Fossella, Sommer, & Posner, 2003). The questionnaire and experimental data were also useful for us in the study of personality disorders (Posner et al., 2002). The potential importance of these links between individual differences in attention and temperament, genetic polymorphisms and brain activity seems obvious for the future of how brain networks differ among individuals. Approaching genetic influences on developing brain networks through the study of individual variation may seem rather indirect. However, the genes that are related to individual differences are also likely to be involved in the main effects of building brain networks appropriate to the common aspects of human thought and activity.

Sometimes the effort to relate genes to brain networks and complex behavior is taken as evidence that everything is hard wired and that experiences are unimportant. This of course is not at all true. Rothbart and I are working with a team of researchers including Rueda to implement a form of attention training for 4-year-olds. Although we do not know as yet whether our methods will work, we remain confident that networks can be influenced during development by appropriate training regimes. It may also be true that some day individual differences within the genome will give us valuable clues about which individuals would most likely benefit from a given form of experience. The evidence of lifelong brain plasticity and the importance of genes for the development of brain networks, as well as for individual variability, are important findings that will have to guide future efforts.

Conclusion

It is a somewhat typical mystery of the human brain that a complex story of a lifetime odyssey could suggest a specific title to the conscious mind within just a few seconds. Certainly I was not aware of all the events discussed in this chapter when I provided the title of this volume to Mayr. Somehow the dense array of connection must intrude themselves on consciousness, not directly but rather through a conscious product, which in this case is this volume's title. After reading Dehaene's chapter (chap. 4, this volume), I feel confident that studies relating brain activity to conscious report will provide some answers to this mystery within the lifetime of some of the younger readers.

In the meantime, perhaps the effort to determine how I came up with the title for this book may have given the reader some perspective into what has been for me an exciting quest, full of wonderful allies and moments both of frustration and of insight. Together these chapters provide support for the view that the past 30 years have seen impressive and cumulative progress (Posner, 1982) on many topics at the heart of psychology.

References

Boles, D. B., & Eveland, D. C. (1983). Visual and phonetic codes and the process of generation in letter matching. *Journal of Experimental Psychology: Human Perception and Performance, 9,* 657–674.

Clohessy, A. B., Posner, M. I., Rothbart, M. K., & Vecera, S. P. (1991). The development of inhibition of return in early infancy. *Journal of Cognitive Neuroscience, 3,* 345–350.

Corbetta, M., & Shulman, G. L. (2002). Control of goal-directed and stimulus-driven attention in the brain. *Nature Neuroscience Reviews, 3,* 201–215.

Deese, J. (1982). The year of cognitive motivation. *Contemporary Psychology, 24,* 279.

Engle, F. L. (1971). Visual conspicuity, directed attention and retinal locus. *Vision Research, 11,* 563–576.

Fan, J., Flombaum, J. I., McCandliss, B. D., & Thomas, K. M., & Posner, M. I. (2003). Cognitive and brain consequences of conflict. *NeuroImage, 18,* 42–57.

Fan, J., Fossella, J. A., Sommer, T., & Posner, M. I. (2003). Mapping the genetic variation of executive attention onto brain activity. *Proceeding of the National Academy of Sciences of the United States of America, 100,* 7406–7411.

Fossella, J., Sommer, T., Fan, J., Wu, Y., Swanson, J. M., Pfaff, D. W., et al. (2002). Assessing the molecular genetics of attention networks. *BMC Neuroscience, 3,* 14.

Georgopoulos, A. P., Lurito, J. T., Petrides, M., Schwartz, A. B., & Massey, J. T. (1989). Mental rotation of the neuronal population vector. *Science, 243,* 234–236.

Gerardi-Caulton, G. (2000). Sensitivity to spatial conflict and the development of self-regulation in children 24–36 months of age. *Developmental Science, 3,* 397–404.

LaBerge, D. (1995). *Attentional processing.* Cambridge, MA: Harvard University Press.

Lassen, N. A., Ingvar, D. H., & Skinhoj, E. (1978). Brain function and blood flow. *Scientific American, 238,* 62–71.

McCandliss, B. D., Cohen, L., & Dehaene, S. (2003). The visual word form area: Expertise for reading in the fusiform gyrus. *Trends in Cognitive Science, 7,* 293–299.

Mountcastle, V. M. (1978). The world around us: Neural command functions for selective attention. *Neuroscience Research Progress Bulletin, 14*(Suppl.), 1–47.

Neisser, U. (1976). *Cognition and reality.* San Francisco: Freeman.

Posner, M. I. (1980). Orienting of attention. The 7th Sir F. C. Bartlett lecture. *Quarterly Journal of Experimental Psychology, 32,* 3–25.

Posner, M. I. (1982). Cumulative development of attentional theory. *American Psychologist, 32,* 53–64.

Posner, M. I. (1988). Structures and functions of selective attention. In T. Boll & B. Bryant (Eds.), *Master lectures in clinical neuropsychology and brain function: Research, measurement, and practice* (pp. 171–202). Washington, DC: American Psychological Association.

Posner, M. I. (2004). The achievements of brain imaging: Past and present. In N. Kanwisher & J. Duncan (Eds.), *Attention and performance* (pp. 505–528). Oxford, England: Oxford University Press.

Posner, M. I., Abdullaev, Y., McCandliss, B. D., & Sereno, S. E. (1999). Neuroanatomy, circuitry and plasticity of word reading. *NeuroReport, 10,* R12–R23.

Posner, M. I., Davidson, B. J., & Snyder, C. R. R. (1980). Attention and the detection of signals. *Journal of Experimental Psychology: General, 109,* 160–174.

Posner, M. I., & McCandliss, B. D. (1999). Brain circuitry during reading. In R. Klein & P. McMullen (Eds.), *Converging methods for understanding reading and dyslexia* (pp. 305–337). Cambridge, MA: MIT Press.

Posner, M. I., & Mitchell, R. F. (1967). Chronometric analysis of classification. *Psychological Review, 74,* 392–409.

Posner, M. I., Rothbart, M. K., Vizueta, N., Levy, K., Thomas, K. M., & Clarkin, J. (2002). Attentional mechanisms of borderline personality disorder. *Proceeding of the National Academy of Sciences of the United States of America, 99,* 16366–16370.

Raz, A., Shapiro, T., Fan, J., & Posner, M. I. (2002). Hypnotic suggestion and the modulation of Stroop interference. *Archives of General Psychiatry, 59,* 1155–1161.

Roland, P. E., & Friberg, L. (1985). Localization of cortical areas activation by thinking. *Journal of Neurophysiology, 53,* 1219–1243.

Rothbart, M. K., Ellis, L., Rueda, M. R., & Posner, M. I. (2003). Developing mechanisms of temperamental self regulation. *Journal of Personality, 71,* 1113–1143.

Rueda, M. R., Posner, M. I., & Rothbart, M. K. (2004). Attentional control and self regulation. In R. F. Baumeister & K. D. Vohs (Eds.), *Handbook of self regulation* (pp. 283–300). New York: Guilford Press.

Shulman, G. L., Remington, R., & McLean, J. P. (1979). Moving attention through visual space. *Journal of Experimental Psychology: Human Perception and Performance, 5,* 522–526.

Snyder, A. Z., Abdullaev, Y., Posner, M. I., & Raichle, M. E. (1995). Scalp electrical potentials reflect regional cerebral blood flow responses during processing of written words. *Proceeding of the National Academy of Sciences of the United States of America, 92,* 1689–1693.

Swanson, J., Oosterlaan, J., Murias, M., Moyzis, R., Schuck, S., Mann, M., et al. (2000). ADHD children with 7-repeat allele of the DRD4 gene have extreme behavior but normal performance on critical neuropsychological tests of attention. *Proceeding of the National Academy of Sciences of the United States of America, 97,* 4754–4759.

Volpe, B. T., LeDoux, J. E., & Gazzaniga, M. S. (1979). Information processing of visual stimuli in an extinguished visual field. *Nature, 282,* 1947–1952.

Wurtz, R. H., Goldberg, E., & Robinson, D. L. (1980). Behavioral modulation of visual responses in monkey: Stimulus selection for attention and movement. In *Progress in psychobiology and physiological psychology* (Vol. 9, pp. 43–83). New York: Academic Press.

Author Index

Numbers in italics refer to listings in reference sections.

Subject Index

Absence seizures, 116
Abstract letter identities, 34, 68
Abstract word form area, 34
"Acid-bath" theory of short-term memory, 5
Activations, 115, 116
Active firing, 77, 81–82
ACT* model, 92
Adenosine triphosphate (ATP), 112
Adrenaline, 157
Advanced Research Projects Agency, 5
Affective disorders, 142
Aggression, 170
Agnosia, 193
Alcohol use, 202
Alerting signal, 6–7
Alexia, 32, 33
Alphabetic writing systems, 23
Alpha power, 117
American Sign Language (ASL), 212, 221–224
Amygdala, 116, 125, 170, 171
Anagrams, 69–70
Anesthesia-induced loss of consciousness, 116
Anger, 170
Angular gyrus, 35, 38, 223
Animal studies
    brain development, 210, 211, 217
    delay of gratification, 197
    neuronal workspace, 79
    prefrontal function, 195
    prenatal substance exposure, 203
    psychological stress effects, 204
    See also Monkey studies
A-not-B tasks, 142, 173
Anterior cingulate cortex, 117, 138
    attentional network, 10, 244
    cognitive control disorders, 143, 152, 155
    effortful control, 170–172, 176–177, 180,
        181, 184, 242
    neuronal workspace, 66, 78–80, 83
    prefrontal task modeling, 94–96
    word processing, 242
Anterior cingulate gyrus, 243
Anterior inferior temporal cortices, 212
Anterior insula, 94, 95
Anxiety disorders, 144
Apes, 79
Aphasia, 194
Artificial intelligence programs, 88, 92–93
Attention
    componential analysis, 3–11

as controlling mental operations, 18–20
development of executive attention. *See* Effortful control
as focus of research, 45, 238–242, 244
gaze perception as triggering, 132–136
orienting of. *See* Inhibition of return
selective attention, 176
without consciousness, 79–80
Attentional bias, 141. *See also* Cognitive control
Attentional blink, 81–82
Attentional control setting theory, 56–57
Attention-deficit/hyperactivity disorder
    (ADHD), 12, 13, 142–144, 146, 147,
        149–151, 154–160, 180, 181, 183, 244
Attention Network Test (ANT), 180, 182
Auditory cortex, 115
    auditory deprivation, and visual system
        development, 211–214
    auditory system development, 217–219
Auditory language processing, 224
Autism, 60, 137, 142, 143, 147
Automaticity, 19–20
Automatic processing, 141. *See also* Cognitive control
Autopsy evidence, 195, 215
Axon terminals, 110

Basal forebrain, 78
Basal ganglia, 55
    cognitive control disorders, 10, 143–147,
        151, 154–156, 159–160
Behaviorist theory, 45
Behavior studies, 148–150
Benefits and costs of orienting, 47
Beta power, 117
Bilingual speakers, 210, 220–222
Biological preparation, 20–21
Birkbeck College, 125n
Blindness, and brain plasticity. *See* Structural
    brain development
Blink, 74, 81–82
Blood oxygen level dependent (BOLD)
    activity, 117
Bottom-up processes, 57, 79, 81–82
Brain blood flow and metabolism, 110–111,
    239, 241
    cognitive control disorders, 143
    energy budget, 9, 111–114
    substance abuse effects, 203

265

About the Editors

Ulrich Mayr, PhD, received his diploma in psychology from the Free University Berlin in 1987 and his doctoral degree in philosophy in 1992 while working at the Max Planck Institute for Human Development in Berlin, Germany. After a postdoctoral year at the University of Oregon, he worked as a research scientist at the University of Potsdam, Germany, until 2000. Since then he has been associate professor at the University of Oregon, Eugene. His current research focuses on executive control of thought and action as well as on issues in cognitive aging.

Edward Awh, PhD, received his bachelor's degree in psychology in 1989 from Northwestern University, Chicago. He received his doctoral degree in cognitive neuroscience from the University of Michigan in 1996. He received postdoctoral training at the University of California, San Diego, from 1997 to 1998. Since 1999 he has been a faculty member of the psychology department of the University of Oregon, Eugene. His current research focuses on behavioral and neuro-imaging studies of attentional control.

Steve W. Keele, PhD, received his doctoral degree from the University of Wisconsin in 1966. Afterward he spent two years on a postdoctoral fellowship with Michael I. Posner at the University of Oregon, Eugene, where he became assistant professor. In 1996, he retired from the University of Oregon, becoming professor emeritus. His areas of research have been in motor control and attention and more recently in cognitive neuroscience. His most recent work has emphasized common functions and the supporting brain areas that underlie both motor control and cognitive processes.